MAKING SENSE OF MASS ATROCITY

"Who done it?" is not the first question that comes to mind when seeking to make sense of mass atrocity. So brazen are the leader–culprits in their apologetics for the harms, so wrenching the human destruction clearly wrought and meticulously documented by many credible sources. Yet in legal terms, mass atrocity remains disconcertingly elusive. The perversity of its perpetrators is polymorphic, impeding criminal courts from tracing true lines of responsibility in ways intelligible through law's pre-existing categories, designed with simpler stuff in mind.

Genocide, crimes against humanity, and the worst war crimes are possible only when the state or other organizations mobilize and coordinate the efforts of many people. Responsibility for mass atrocity is always widely shared, often by thousands. Yet criminal law, with its liberal underpinnings, prefers to blame particular individuals for isolated acts. Is such law, therefore, constitutionally unable to make any sense of the most catastrophic conflagrations of our time? Drawing on the experience of several recent prosecutions (national and international), this book both trenchantly diagnoses law's limits at such times and offers a spirited defense of its moral and intellectual resources for meeting the vexing challenge of holding anyone criminally accountable for mass atrocity. Just as today's war criminals develop new methods of eluding law's historic grasp, so criminal law flexibly devises novel responses to their stratagems. Mark Osiel examines several such recent legal innovations in international jurisprudence and proposes still others.

Mark Osiel's writings seek to show how legal responses to mass atrocity can be improved by understanding its organizational dynamics, as revealed through comparative historical analysis. His writings have inspired several conferences and are assigned at many leading universities in North America and Western Europe in a number of fields. He lives in The Hague, where he is director of public international law programs at the T.M.C. Asser Institute, a think tank associated with the University of Amsterdam.

His books include *Mass Atrocity, Collective Memory, and the Law* (1997); *Obeying Orders: Atrocity, Military Discipline, and the Law of War* (1999); *Mass Atrocity, Ordinary Evil, and Hannah Arendt: Criminal Consciousness in Argentina's Dirty War* (2002); and *The End of Reciprocity: Terror, Torture, and the Law of War* (2009).

Osiel regularly advises international organizations and governments in post-conflict societies on issues of transitional justice. He has been a visiting Fellow at Cambridge University, Harvard's Kennedy School of Government, and the London School of Economics, as well as universities in Argentina, Brazil, France, the Netherlands, and India (as a Fulbright lecturer).

Making Sense of Mass Atrocity

MARK OSIEL
College of Law,
University of Iowa
Director of International Criminal and Humanitarian Law,
T.M.C. Asser Institute, The Hague

CAMBRIDGE UNIVERSITY PRESS
Cambridge, New York, Melbourne, Madrid, Cape Town,
Singapore, São Paulo, Delhi, Tokyo, Mexico City

Cambridge University Press
32 Avenue of the Americas, New York, NY 10013-2473, USA

www.cambridge.org
Information on this title: www.cambridge.org/9781107403185

First published 2009
Reprinted 2010
First paperback edition 2011

A catalog record for this publication is available from the British Library

Library of Congress Cataloging in Publication data
Osiel, Mark.
Making sense of mass atrocity / Mark J. Osiel.
p.   cm.
Includes bibliographical references and index.
ISBN 978-0-521-86185-4 (hardback)
1. Crimes against humanity.   2. Criminal liability.   1. Title.
K5301.O833   2009
345'.0235–dc22   2008047965

ISBN 978-0-521-86185-4 Hardback
ISBN 978-1-107-40318-5 Paperback

Contents

The Nazi crimes, it seems to me, explode the limits of the law; and that is precisely what constitutes their monstrousness.

Hannah Arendt (1946)

The logic of law can never make sense of the illogic of extermination.

Lawrence L. Langer (1995)

Preface

Pinpointing responsibility for mass atrocities on particular individuals – as the criminal law demands – is an elusive and perilous enterprise.[1] Genocide, war crimes, and crimes against humanity occur in the havoc of civil strife, in teeming prison camps, and in the muck and messiness of heated combat. The victims are either dead or, if willing to testify, "unlikely to have been taking contemporaneous notes."[2] There are the anonymity of mass graves, the gaps and uncertainties in forensic evidence, the complexity of long testimony covering several places and periods, years ago. There is also the fluidity of influence by leaders over followers and of equals in rank over one another, as well as the uncertain measure of freedom from others – both superiors and peers – enjoyed by all. The central questions become:

How does mass atrocity happen?

How should criminal law respond?

The two queries are generally asked in isolation: the first by social scientists and historians, the second by courts and lawyers. Properly understood, the questions are inseparable, this book shows, for the law stands to learn much from careful attention to atrocity's actual dynamics. The law itself permits the trial of hundreds or even thousands, each for any number of serious

[1] The author thanks the editors of the *Columbia Law Review* and the *Cornell International Law Journal* for allowing republication here of portions from Mark Osiel, "The Banality of Good: Aligning Incentives Against Mass Atrocity," 105 Colum. L. Rev. 1751 (2005), and Osiel, "Modes of Participation in Mass Atrocity," 38 Cornell Int'l L. J. 793 (2005). In developing those articles into a book, the comments of several Harvard Law School students in the 2005 International Law Workshop, taught by William Alford and Ryan Goodman, were especially helpful. The sustained support of the T.M.C. Asser Institute in The Hague and the College of Law, University of Iowa, have also been indispensable. Valuable research assistance was provided by Louis Ebinger, Jeffrey Elkins, Bojan Lazic, David Osipovich, and Duvel Pierre, Christopher Shaw, Benjamin To, and Helen Yu.

[2] David Luban, "Modes of Participation," unpublished manuscript, 2005.

offenses (as is often the case). Prosecutors hence confess that they enjoy great discretion over how to proceed.[3] This freedom should surely be exercised in light of the best understandings of how and why mass atrocity occurred.[4]

Historians and social scientists offer considerable counsel to this end, perhaps especially in identifying the particular persons bearing greatest responsibility for the most grievous wrongs. In a comparative survey of recent rebel movements, for instance, one leading scholar finds that when people are lured to insurgencies by immediate prospects for material gain – whether natural resources available at home or external funding from a foreign patron – they often commit mass atrocities because their survival and success do not greatly depend on the local communities they occupy.[5]

By contrast, when insurgent movements recruit and inspire their members on the basis of long-term grievances shared with such environing communities, atrocities against civilians are quite rare. Mass atrocity by rebel movements results, in other words, when leaders do not require much support from the noncombatant population to initiate and continue their struggle against the state. If infractions of the organization's formal "code of honor" do occur,[6] the discipline of members – especially for mistreatment

---

[3] Hassan B. Jallow, "Prosecutorial Discretion and International Criminal Justice," 3 J. Int'l Crim. Justice 145 (2005). The author, at the time, was Chief Prosecutor at the ICTR.

[4] It is tempting to say as well that the more accurately law can reflect the real distribution of responsibility for such large-scale horrors, the more likely its conclusions will be accepted, rather than rejected as scapegoating or mythmaking. If law can find a way to get the facts right – in all their admitted complexity – its conclusions cannot be so readily dismissed, one hopes, by the often skeptical communities whose leaders are thereby impugned. This claim proves more difficult to sustain and may well reflect no more than wishful thinking. Perhaps mythmaking has a legitimate role to play, to be sure, in the societal reconstruction following mass atrocity. Mark Osiel, *Mass Atrocity, Collective Memory, and the Law* 200–92 (1997). But this goal, when it guides the telling of a new "official story," often threatens to run afoul of inconvenient historical facts. The tension between the aims of historical accuracy and national reconciliation cannot readily be resolved by legal doctrine standing alone. Identifying the possible trade-offs that are likely involved and how they might best be managed has been the focus of considerable recent thinking. Id. *passim*; Leora Bilsky, *Transformative Justice: Israeli Identity on Trial* (2004); Ruti Teitel, *Transitional Justice* (2000); Lawrence Douglas, *The Memory of Judgment: Making Law and History in the Trials of the Holocaust* (2001); Marouf Hasian Jr, *Rhetorical Vectors of Memory in National and International Holocaust Trials* (2006); Nehal Bhuta, "Between Liberal Legal Didactics and Political Manichaenism: The Politics and Law of the Iraqi Special Tribunal," 6 Melbourne J. Int'l L. 245 (2005).

[5] Jeremy Weinstein, *Inside Rebellion: The Politics of Insurgent Violence* 327–41 (2007). This study concentrates on several rebel organizations in Peru, Mozambique, and Uganda, but looks further afield to many other such movements.

[6] Id. at 127.

of civilians – has been consistently more effective within the second type of insurgent organization than the first. Authority is also less centralized in this second variety of rebel group.[7]

Empirical regularities of this sort will prove pertinent to how the law of "superior responsibility" – by which leaders are held responsible for their followers' crimes – should apply in a given case. At the very least, such regularities will bear on the credibility of evidence, about where control actually resided and what purposes it sought, offered by prosecution and defense in particular trials. The factual patterns uncovered by this social science, however, are complex and their legal implications are by no means transparent. For instance, "although many opportunistic groups" – the first, atrocity-generative variety of an insurgent organization – "exhibit a high degree of centralization in military command, much of the violence for which they are responsible is committed in a decentralized fashion as a result of a culture of indiscipline – one that goes unpunished by local, rather than national, commanders."[8] Also, each incident of mass atrocity displays certain features unique to it, often relevant to the assessment of those implicated at various levels of the organization responsible.

The most fundamental question such morally relevant complexities present is whether law can comprehend and conceptualize mass atrocity with enough clarity and precision. This issue arises even before political constraints impose themselves, constraints often preventing the legal system from acting on any such comprehension. Revering precedent, we lawyers are tempted to follow well-trod pathways, developed in redress of more garden-variety criminality. This way of thinking has led many nonlawyers to wonder whether the peculiar contours of mass atrocity may throw up novel challenges that criminal law is incapable of meeting. In response to that skepticism, this book shows how legal responses to mass atrocity are benefiting from closer attention to the organizational patterns and causal processes by which it occurs.

There is surely no more noble aspiration than ridding the world of genocide, of violent persecution, of the slaughter of innocents in war – horrors that repeatedly plagued the twentieth century and conspicuously continue into the twenty-first. To this end, many people across the globe today place great hope in international criminal law. Courts now elaborate and refine its rules, while idealistic young people flock to its study. It provides the common vocabulary of any serious search for moral consensus across national

[7] Id. at 38–44, 145–59, 349–50.
[8] Id. at 350.

borders today. Unity in opposition to the conduct it proscribes virtually defines the meaning of "the international community," insofar as one really exists.

Yet beneath the surface enthusiasm for this burgeoning enterprise, there pervades a deep undercurrent of doubt. Dictators may no longer necessarily die happily in office or in luxurious exile on the French Riviera. But their complicated trials prove interminable, allowing them to elude conviction. Victims of mass atrocity regularly resign themselves in apparent ease to reconciliation with their tormenters,[9] moreover, if only because criminal punishment is rarely a high priority for anyone during the social and economic collapse that often accompanies regime breakdown and civil war.[10]

Current skepticism about law's promise focuses on the failure of so many countries seriously to implement the ideal of transitional justice: that past crimes of former despots be addressed systematically and fairly. In the 1990s, transitional justice quickly became a norm to which postconflict states had formally to subscribe to be seen as committed to the rule of law, and therefore safe for foreign aid or investment. But follow-through by domestic legal institutions often proved incomplete, even disingenuous. Transitional justice even became a rhetorical banner under which new rulers often sought to repress legitimate political opponents.[11] International criminal law thereby came to be hijacked for purposes alien to its ideals.

Yet this tension between the ideal and reality of transitional justice should not lead us to minimize the very real tensions within the ideal itself. Mass atrocity proves to present more fundamental challenges that are threatening to elude law's understanding and evaluation. Law's critics insistently point to a series of seeming contradictions: Criminal law sees a world of separate persons, whereas mass atrocity entails collective behavior. Both victims and perpetrators act less as individuals than as members of social groups. The state normally punishes torture and homicide; here, it instead rewards these crimes, performed for official ends. A murderer usually deviates from social norms, yet conforms to them in these cases. Extreme violence, generally

[9] Helena Cobban, *Amnesty after Atrocity: Healing Nations after Genocide and War Crimes* 128–35 (2007); Rama Mani, *Beyond Retribution: Seeking Justice in the Shadows of War* 118, 125 (2002).

[10] *My Neighbor, My Enemy: Justice and Community in the Aftermath of Mass Atrocity* 325 (Eric Stover & Harvey Weinstein, eds., 2004) (reporting from survey results that their "informants told us that jobs, food, adequate and secure housing, good schooling for their children, and peace and security were their major priorities").

[11] A compelling account of this development is offered by Jelena Subotić, "Decoupling International Norms: Domestic Politics of Transitional Justice Norm Diffusion," International Studies Association Convention paper, March 2006.

rare, becomes commonplace. Criminal law usually highlights the defendant's deeds, treating sociopolitical context as irrelevant. The accused's contribution to mass atrocity, however, is unintelligible in isolation from many others' actions, often distant in place and time. The law generally asks what harm the accused has caused. Yet here lines of causation are multiple and muddied, agency is dispersed, labor divided. Responsibility for mass atrocity is widely shared. But its far-reaching scope often lies beyond anyone's complete control or contemplation.

The moral world that the law assumes is thus rendered topsy-turvy, its familiar furniture rearranged. The criminal law developed its conceptual repertoire to redress conventional deviance, to which individualistic notions readily apply – notions of responsibility, causal agency, intention.[12] These ideas sit uneasily, however, with the defining features of modern mass atrocity: officially endorsed, bureaucratically enforced, perpetrated by and against groups, often motivated as much by vocational obligation as personal inclination. Such atrocities must also often be addressed by international law, applied in international courts. These courts are often unresponsive to national nuances of the societies whose members they presume to judge, particularly to the widespread desire within such societies for reconciliation among former antagonists in civil war or other internal strife.

Most lawyers do not even perceive these problems, it is claimed, because doing so would admit the limits of our learning, disabling us from dominating a society's response to such pivotal events. Many observers, however, find criminal law inherently incapable of coping with these persistent perplexities.

This book argues the contrary. It shows the law's considerable resourcefulness and resilience in conceptualizing mass atrocity's myriad forms. Critics blame law's failings on its commitment to liberalism, often denigrated as "liberal legalism,"[13] although the term is something of a caricature in that

---

[12] Articulating this view without endorsing it, Christopher Kutz writes, "Because individuals are the ultimate loci of normative motivation and deliberation, only forms of accountability aimed at and sensitive to what individuals do can succeed in controlling the emergence of collective harms." *Complicity: Ethics and Law for a Collective Age* 7 (2000).

[13] This is a common term of derision in "law and society" circles, denoting the view that Western law enshrines an individualism – methodological and normative – disabling it from adequately understanding or evaluating the social conduct it presumes to judge. Stuart Scheingold, "'The Dog That Didn't Bark': A Sociolegal Tale of Law, Democracy, and Elections," in *The Blackwell Companion to Law and Society* 523, 525–32 (Austin Sarat, ed. 2004). But the liberal tradition has actually long been much more attentive than this view suggests to the social causation of personal misconduct and the desirability of its redress by means of social policy other than individual punishment. This strand of

actual liberal thinkers are rarely cited nor their claims refuted.[14] A generation ago, such a critique could only have sounded from the political left.
Today, it emerges instead simply from the honest, face-to-face encounter
(of one author, for instance, Mark Drumbl) with the many thousands of
plebeian *genocidaires* rotting for years, awaiting trial, in Rwanda's jails.[15] For
another, George Fletcher, the new critique of law's liberalism emerges in a
more rarefied way, from a former arch-Kantian, passionately converted –
seemingly overnight and mid-life – to a steamy brew of nineteenth-century
European, collectivist-Romantic social thought (the political valence of
which often historically inclined to the political right).[16]

In rejoinder to both brands of criticism, the criminal law must offer a
defense of liberalism's flexibility and continuing appeal in the face of the

---

social liberalism, as it is sometimes called, runs from such Victorians as Hobhouse to
contemporary self-declared liberals like Paul Starr. Leonard Hobhouse, *Liberalism* (1911);
Paul Starr, *Freedom's Power: The True Force of Liberalism* (2007). See also Stefan Collini,
Liberalism and Sociology: L. T. Hobhouse and Political Argument in England, 1880–1914
(1979). The prevalent methodological individualism of Anglo-American moral philosophy
manifests itself not in any reluctance to judge and blame individual persons for their role in
criminality that others might consider essentially collective, but rather in doubts about the
defensibility of blaming collectivities as such for the wrongs of their individual members.
See, e.g., Philip Pettit, "Groups with Minds of Their Own," in *Socializing Metaphysics*,
F. Schmitt, ed. 167 (2003); David Copp, "On the Agency of Certain Collective Entities,"
30 Midwest Studies in Phil. 194 (2006).

[14] See, e.g., Mark Drumbl, *Atrocity, Punishment and International Law* 5, 35–41, 127–8 (2007)
(attributing criminal law's limitations in confronting mass atrocity to the presuppositions
of something called "liberal legality," but referencing only other critics of this enigmatic
and apparently elusive intellectual adversary). Admittedly, criminal law presupposes "that
each individual should be treated as responsible for his or her own behaviour" and that
"individuals in general have the capacity and sufficient free will to make meaningful
choices." Andrew Ashworth, *Principles of Criminal Law* 28 (4th ed. 2003). Liberals have
no monopoly over such claims, however. What distinguishes the liberal view of criminal
law is its normative commitment to "the principle of autonomy," which "assigns great
importance to liberty and individual rights in any discussion of what the state ought to
do in a given situation." Id. at 29. Thus, a liberal "theory of criminal responsibility ought
at least to be consistent with the principle that we should respect, promote and protect
autonomy." Victor Tadros, *Criminal Responsibility* 45 (2005).

[15] Mark Drumbl, "Rule of Law Amid Lawlessness: Counselling the Accused in Rwanda's
Domestic Genocide Trials," 29 Colum. Human Rights L. Rev. 545 (1998); Drumbl, "Punishment, Postgenocide: From Guilt to Shame to Civis in Rwanda," 75 N.Y.U. L. Rev. 1221
(2000); Drumbl, "Law and Atrocity: Settling Accounts in Rwanda," 31 Ohio N.U. L. Rev.
41 (2005).

[16] "I am very much drawn to the idea that the guilt of the German nation as a whole should
mitigate the guilt of particular criminals like Eichmann, who is guilty to be sure, but
guilty like so many others of a collective crime." George Fletcher, "The Storrs Lectures:
Liberals and Romantics at War: The Problem of Collective Guilt," 111 Yale L. J. 1499, 1539
(2002).

collective conflagrations here at issue.[17] Liberalism must rise to the challenge of mass atrocity, for although these events are so clearly at odds with liberal morality, they are also emblematic of our era. If liberal thought could not make much sense of them, it would indeed stand denuded of its claim of offering meaningful redress. Yet although social scientists and historians condemn the "inherent limits" of something they call "legal logic,"[18] the law itself finds ways to adapt – albeit never effortlessly, not without fresh thinking. In its fundamental theoretical ideas no less than in its practical implementation, international criminal law is very much a work in progress. I do not at all wish to suggest that anyone has yet neatly or satisfactorily resolved the key question here assayed. Although I will defend particular answers to it, my chief aim is rather to convey to nonlawyers (and lawyers specialized in other matters) a vivid sense of the refined professional debate and of the field's advancement through close engagement with some unconventional ideas about how law affects conduct through incentives and about how to understand the philosophical puzzle of shared responsibility. My aim is to deepen analysis and understanding of the problems, on their own terms, as much as to advance the details of any particular solutions to them.[19]

In postconflict societies, there often will be good reason, to be sure, not to rely primarily on criminal law in redressing large-scale wrong. These are mostly reasons of political prudence, however, not limitations on law's inherent capacity to comprehend and evaluate the relevant events. We should thus never reject criminal prosecution on the basis of internal inadequacies – however they are characterized.

The law's limits lie not within but beyond it, in other words – most prominently in the enduring power of potential defendants, whose threats of future violence generate demands for social peace. Such power eventually wanes, however, often well before its holders' deaths, prompting renewed public demands for prosecution even decades after the events, as prominently occurred in Chile and Argentina, for instance. As in those two

---

[17] Others, especially in western Europe, are similarly committed to this objective. See, e.g., Katrina Gustafson "The Requirement of an 'Express Agreement' for Joint Criminal Enterprise Liability: A Critique of *Brdanin*," 5 J. Int'l Crim. J. 134, 157 (2007) ("It is not necessary to deviate from basic criminal law principles of individual responsibility in order to attribute the appropriate degree of responsibility to these individuals").

[18] The author has heard such terms casually bandied about, for instance, at a conference on transitional justice in May 2008, at L'École de Hautes Études en Science Sociales, Paris.

[19] In support of this stance, see Austin Sarat & Susan Silbey, "The Pull of the Policy Audience," 10 L. & Policy 97 (1988) (contending that legal sociology should retain considerable intellectual independence, in its explanatory concerns, from efforts to influence immediately the content of law and public policy).

countries, earlier amnesties may then be overturned on legally acceptable grounds.[20]

Postconflict societies may frequently favor alternatives to criminal trials, of course. Truth commissions, victim reparations, and vetting of perpetrators from public office can prove valuable, but serve other purposes and reveal themselves, on close inspection, as no panaceas.[21] The heavy focus on such institutional innovations in current thinking about transitional justice should not diminish our appreciation of criminal law's practical availability, moral defensibility, and analytical coherence in analyzing and grappling with these events. To this end, we should become more fully aware of its enduring potential and practical dexterity as an intellectual resource at such times.

The argument herein for collective sanctioning of military officers, for instance, arises from widespread frustrations with the two reigning legal alternatives of civil liability for entire states and criminal liability for individual persons.[22] International law's efforts to prevent and punish mass

---

[20] In Chile, judges have been investigating twenty-five hundred cases, issued five hundred indictments, and convicted more than two hundred and fifty persons for crimes arising from human rights abuse during military rule. Fundación de Ayuda Social de las Iglesias Cristianas, Estadísticas, July 2008. In Argentina, where far more people were "disappeared" at the juntas' hands, more than thirty people have been sentenced for such offenses and dozens more prosecutions are pending. Centro de Estudios Legales y Sociales, "Juicios: más de mil imputados por crímenes de lesa humanidad," July 25, 2008. "União assume a defesa de acusados de tortura na ditadura," oglobo.globo.com/pais/mat/2008/10/21/uniao_assume_defesa_de_acusados_de_tortura_na_ditadura-586060736.asp; "Chile: Pinochet Official Sentenced," www.nytimes.com/2008/07/01/world/americas/01briefs-PINOCHETOFFI_BRF.html?_r=1&scp=1&sq=Chile%20 Pinochet&st=cse; "Chile: Pinochet Security Forces Arrested," query.nytimes.com/gst/fullpage.html?res=9901EED91E38F93BA15756C0A96E9C8B63&scp=3&sq=Chile%20 Pinochet%202008&st=cse; "Governo aprova indenização para ex-ministro Nilmário Miranda," http://www1.folha.uol.com.br/folha/brasil/ult96u487098.shtml; "Comissão de Anistia quer pesquisar ligações entre empresas e ditadura," http://www1.folha.uol.com.br/folha/brasil/ult96u470074.shtml; "Parlamentares pedem para Procuradoria investigar ex-tenente do Exército por tortura," http://www1.folha.uol.com.br/folha/brasil/ult96u474710.shtml; "Diputados oficialistas piden reabrir juicio por crimen de Víctor Jara," http://www.emol.com/noticias/nacional/detalle/detallenoticias.asp?idnoticia=304856.

[21] On some of the dangers of truth commissions, see Mark Freeman, *Truth Commissions and Procedural Fairness* (2006); of personnel vetting, see Adam Michnik, "Waiting for Freedom, Messing It Up," N.Y. Times, March 25, 2007, at A13 (criticizing the perceived excesses of Polish lustration). On the moral complexities and political complications involved in victim reparations programs throughout the world, see *The Handbook of Reparations* (Pablo de Greiff, ed., 2006).

[22] The strengths and weakness of these alternatives are assessed by Thomas Franck, "State Responsibility in the Era of Individual Culpability," unpublished paper; Eric Posner & Alan Sykes, "An Economic Analysis of State and Individual Responsibility under International Law," 9 Amer. L. & Econ. Rev. 72 (2007).

atrocity have shifted decisively in recent years from the first of these remedies to the second. Among the several good reasons for this reorientation
is that responsibility for mass atrocity is never equally shared among all
citizens of the offending state. Yet sanctioning the state as a collective entity
lets the moral and pecuniary burden fall equally on them all. The threat
of such collective liability also fails to induce state leaders to prevent and
punish mass atrocity when its perpetrators themselves control the state. The
burden of future liability then falls only on their successors.

Yet the switch to individual criminal liability gives rise to difficulties
of its own. Responsibility for mass atrocity, although not *equally* shared
among all citizens, is nonetheless very *widely* shared, in ways that make
it difficult to identify, with satisfactory precision, the nature and extent
of any individual defendant's culpability and contribution, distinguishable
from other participants, including many who will avoid prosecution. That
problem is the central focus of this study, which contends that collective
sanctions directed against responsible groups – intermediate between the
state and the individual – offer a workable middle way.[23]

A NOTE ON AUTHORIAL VOICE

Writing about mass atrocity, even the legal response to it, inevitably requires
an author to establish a suitable measure of distance – moral and emotional –
from the "raw material," which often proves very raw indeed. One's first
impulse may be to dive into the wreck, striving to feel and reproduce the
victims' agony and righteous indignation, and perhaps too the perpetrators'
zealous fury. How else to convey the human experience of mounting distress
amidst approaching disaster, the vertiginous awfulness, the sheer terror of
such times?

This strategy poses twin risks, however. It may merely titillate the reader
with the vicarious effervescence of a theme-park ride.[24] One sells more
books this way, but only by descending to the prurience of a Hollywood
disaster flick. We live in an age, after all, where glimpses of a revolution's
greatest savagery become ready grist for coffee-table best sellers. In the U.S.
Holocaust Memorial Museum, by welcome contrast, the graphic depiction
of mass death by gas chamber skirts sensationalism, being rendered only in
dioramic miniature; the victims – arms raised in gasping delirium – stand

[23] Such sanctions would be combined with criminal trials of persons most blameworthy. See
Chapters 9 and 10.
[24] This and ensuing paragraphs are inspired by Martin Jay, "Diving into the Wreck: Aesthetic
Spectatorship at the Turn of the Millennium," in his *Refractions of Violence* (2003).

scarcely two inches tall. How deeply are most readers, in any event, really prepared to accompany an author into the belly of such a beast?[25]

Diving into the wreck also risks evoking a simple sympathy for the victims of mass atrocity and a corresponding wrath for perpetrators that paints too reassuring a portrait of "good guys" and "bad guys." The resulting picture sits uneasily with any serious effort at understanding the relevant complexities – moral and explanatory – that come to the fore in all but the most superficial discussions. Stray too close to the fire, then, and one is quickly immersed in the wrenching passions of the calamity itself. Effacing the line between spectacle and spectator, this approach easily ends as low entertainment, high melodrama, or both.

Stray very far from the horror, however, and one soon finds oneself gazing down on its frail human participants from too high above the battle, at a contemplative remove. No hint remains of the messy, sanguinary sources of it all: the torn flesh and tears, the loathing and pity. There is comfort in the safety of spectatorial distance, to be sure, and the prospect for ethical judgment it may afford. But we surely recoil from any tranquil taxonomizing of mass atrocity, an academic exercise more suitable to a collection of sea shells.

Most legal scholarship on the subject is written just so, in a sanitizing spirit, with seeming indifference to the world's true nuttiness. This standpoint lets us tell a heartening story about the ever-widening scope of humanitarian sensibility, a Whig history of moral progress through the international rule of law. In fact, we jurists secretly almost welcome every new conflagration as a chance to advance our legal schemes for humankind's improvement. We forgive ourselves with the reminder that a crisis is a terrible thing to waste.

But such high-minded aloofness from our distasteful, even grisly subject matter only ensures that we are read exclusively by fellow specialists in this already arcane subfield of international law, itself a most precious, insular enclave.[26] The dry land on which such writers purport to stand is ultimately an illusion, in any event, for as they write about the most recently completed

---

[25] One of my earlier efforts seeks to take the reader far into the perpetrators' worldview. Mark Osiel, *Mass Atrocity, Ordinary Evil, and Hannah Arendt: Criminal Consciousness in Argentina's Dirty War* 25–61, 104–30 (2001).

[26] Within the enormous scholarship on the law of armed conflict, for instance, one finds almost no serious effort to grapple with relevant details of the military technologies, operational issues, or tactical challenges essential to applying such law intelligently and realistically. For a rare exception, see Richard J. Butler, "Modern War, Modern Law, and Army Doctrine: Are We in Step for the 21st Century," *Parameters: U.S. Army War College Quarterly* (Spring 2002); cf. Mark Osiel, *Obeying Orders: Atrocity, Military Discipline, and the Law of War* (1999).

catastrophe, their minds race ahead to the next, incipiently under way –
Darfur, the Congo, Chechnya, Georgia – and the implications their legal
arguments may have for its redress. (This is gently reinforced by delusions of
grandeur, of course.) The likely inaction of "the international community"
to which they prominently belong distinguishes them from truly innocent
bystanders. Any hope of impartial authority, of the magisterial repose or
scientific detachment it might bestow, eludes them. Like the shipwrecked
passengers themselves, they too are adrift on high seas.

At what measure of distance or proximity, then, should one stand when
speaking and writing of such events? How to strike an authorial posture
that is scholarly, yet humane; "disinterested," yet not disengaged? How to
represent the victims' suffering, for instance, in a way that is neither luridly
salacious nor unduly solicitous and sycophantic? For the victims sometimes
turn out to be perpetrators as well. How to render the perpetrators' self-
understanding at once as supremely malevolent yet humanly intelligible?
How to depict the zealotry of international prosecutors in both its sincere
humanitarianism and its professional self-aggrandizement?

Whether I have succeeded in meeting this challenge any better than
others is for the reader to say. But it is this aspiration, at least, that impels
and informs my continuing efforts (over the course of five volumes) to
educate the law's response to mass atrocity with greater understanding of
how such events occur and how alternative legal responses to them implicate
the interests of relevant groups,[27] including military officers and the lawyers
who both advise and prosecute them. Lawyers, in particular, turn out not
to be the disinterested instrument through which the idea of human rights
realizes itself in history, as some studies of "advocacy networks" imply.[28]
Humanitarianism's lofty aims gain a purchase on political reality, this book
shows, only through the earthier claims and counterclaims of legal and
military professionals.

The raging disagreements within humanitarian law today do not simply reflect diverging ideals of international order or competing normative
visions of a better world, in other words. They also disclose a new and
shifting vocational field – international criminal law – within which various professionals struggle to establish and defend their expertise and, in so
doing, secure a commodious place for themselves at the big table. My main

---

[27] The present volume is the fifth in a series: *Mass Atrocity, Collective Memory,* op.cit., *Obeying
Orders,* op. cit.; *Ordinary Evil,* op. cit; *The End of Reciprocity: Terror, Torture, and The Law
of War (2009).*

[28] Nicolas Guilhot, *The Democracy Makers: Human Rights and International Order* 166–87
(2005).

point here, however, is not to reduce the genuine concern of humanity's defenders to a fig leaf over raw material interests, but rather to begin to appreciate disinterestedness as itself a type of what Max Weber called "ideal interest" (that is, in valorizing ethical universals over local attachments),[29] and to investigate the social conditions of its advent and apparent ascendance within world politics today.[30]

---

[29] Id. at 26.

[30] This approach draws inspiration from Pierre Bourdieu, *Méditations Pascaliennes* 148 (1997) and especially Max Weber, "The Social Psychology of World Religions," in *From Max Weber* 267, 280–1 (H. H. Gerth and C. Wright Mills, eds. & trans.) 1948.

Introduction

From Dachau to Darfur, it is often surprisingly hard to say precisely who is really responsible for what horrors, for which share of a long and tangled episode of mass atrocity. Historians and social scientists generally pride themselves on explaining such a large event entirely in collective terms, irreducible to the acts or intentions of any participant. These scholars are content to speak of Serbs and Bosnians, armies and terrorist networks, of the political dynamics and social forces at play.[1]

But for lawyers – those who must prosecute such wrongs (and defend the accused) – the devil necessarily lies in the proverbial details of who did which terrible thing to whom, in what manner, at a given time and place, with what purpose in mind. Our approach is thus unabashedly "reductionist," in the sense of reducing all large abstractions to the most concrete particulars.

Yet can this lawyerly reductionism offer a coherent and defensible account of and response to massive genocide?[2] After all, even the most powerful heads

---

[1] In recent years, to be sure, some of the best social science has shifted toward an insistence on the so-called micro-foundations of violent collective behavior in the incentives of individual participants. See, e.g., Stathis N. Kalyvas, *The Logic of Violence in Civil War* 10, 390 (2006).

[2] This study will use the word *genocide* in two different senses: first, as a legal term of art, defining the international crime of this name, and second, in the lay sense, as employed by journalists, historians, and social scientists. The legal offense differs from the lay meaning in its insistence that perpetrators display a specific intent to destroy the protected group, rather than simply an understanding that such destruction will likely result from a more proximate intention – forcible deportation (or "ethnic cleansing"), in many cases. The criminal offense further differs from the lay meaning in its indifference to the number of people actually harmed. Indictments before the ICTY, for instance, often accused defendants of seeking the destruction of small numbers of people. It is enough for the law that such victims were "part" of a protected group whose destruction was intended. The present book generally employs the term *genocide* in the more common, lay sense, except where the discussion turns clearly to more technical questions of legal doctrine.

of states need not fully control all those around and below them, especially high-level comrades or death squads beyond their formal authority, often with agendas of their own. Almost never are the worst wrongs readily traceable to direct orders from above, descending through an orderly chain of command to regular army troops.[3] And rarely does a head of state have any advance knowledge of the factual specifics that courts would normally require to convict anyone of such grievous wrongs.

It seems beyond doubt that dictators like Augusto Pinochet, Slobodan Milošević, and Saddam Hussein must be "responsible for" widespread barbarities that clearly furthered their political agendas while they held high office, committed by kindred spirits under their influence or inspiration. Yet the law's conventional resources for linking such "big fish" to more immediate wrongdoers are disconcertingly crude and clumsy, developed historically to deal with simpler crimes. This is true when seeking to tie a head of state to the acts of both powerful rivals within a military junta[4] and of "small fry" among informal militias who often commit the worst violence.[5]

With its focus on discrete deeds and isolated intentions, legal analysis risks missing the collaborative character of genocidal massacre, the vast extent of unintended consequences, and the ways in which "the whole" conflagration is often quite different from the sum of its parts. Some allege that the law, in its relentless individualism, fails at such times to apprehend the paradox of collective responsibility: how large-scale wrongdoing is at once divided into many small pieces, yet still widely shared. With these limitations, criminal law must surely fail to do justice to the implicated parties, in resolving whom to blame for which harms and how much to punish any given participant.[6]

---

[3] There are notable exceptions, however, to this empirical regularity. The single worst massacre in Bosnia, at Srebrenica in 1995, was committed in a well-organized manner by regular forces, not by paramilitary hooligans on a spontaneous rampage.

[4] The members of Argentina's military juntas, for instance, were ultimately held liable only for crimes committed by those within their formal chain of command (i.e., particular branch of service – army, navy, air force), even though the regime functioned integrally, with the junta as its governing institution, according to scholars. Nothing of wider political significance could occur within any service without the approval of those governing the other branches, and policy concerning the "dirty war" was centrally made in key respects at the junta level.

[5] By "small fry," I refer to those at the lowest echelons of a military or paramilitary organization. This term is not intended to minimize the enormous human suffering such individuals are often capable of causing during the violent conflagrations here examined.

[6] That sentencing in international criminal tribunals is therefore incoherent and indefensible is contended by Mirko Bagaric & John Morss, "International Sentencing Law: In Search of Justification and Coherent Framework," 6 Int'l Crim. L. Rev. 191 (2006); see also Olaoluwa Olusanya, "Sentencing War Crimes and Crimes against Humanity under the International

When it narrows its lens to the person in the dock, the law risks underestimating the significance of his or her deeds, for their gravity is comprehensible only when seen in relation to those of many others, above and below the accused within a chain of command. Responding to this concern, international criminal offenses are now often defined to widen the narrative frame, encompassing a broader picture.[7] A crime against humanity, for instance, must be part of a "widespread or systematic attack" on civilians. Prosecutors need to show that the defendant's actions took place within such a context and that he or she was aware of it.

Yet here the law almost immediately succumbs to the opposite danger: blaming the defendant for wrongs beyond his or her control or contemplation. Criminal law seems to find itself impaled on the horns of this dilemma. It is widely claimed that these frailties derive ultimately from law's "liberalism,"[8] which insists on viewing social collectivities as no more than "infinite combinations of the number one."[9] This moral and political creed thus stands condemned as well, along with the legal rules enshrining it. That is the challenge, at any rate, to which this book responds.[10]

It is a natural challenge for a social theorist of law like the author, because sociology has been virtually defined since its inception, as notes Bruno Latour,[11] by efforts to resolve the question of "whether the actor is 'in' a system or if the system is made up 'of' interacting actors." In other words, to what extent must we understand the institutional properties of such a system to assess the conduct of those within it? Large-scale atrocity, sponsored by the political system, poses this perennial question in particularly vivid and perplexing form.

The key hurdle that criminal justice confronts in coping with mass atrocity reduces, in a sense, to a single dilemma. Law and evidence permit liability

---

Criminal Tribunal for the Former Yugoslavia," 5 J. Int'l Crim. J. 1221 (2007); Robert Sloane, "Sentencing for the 'Crime of Crimes': The Evolving 'Common Law' of Sentencing of the International Criminal Tribunal for Rwanda," 5 J. of Int'l Criml. Just. 713 (2007).

[7] Antonio Cassese, *International Law* 270 (2001) (observing that formal elements of the offense, such as crimes against humanity, often require courts to consider "the historical or social context of the crime").

[8] For a recent argument to this effect, see Paul Kahn, *Out of Eden: Adam and Eve and the Problem of Evil* 56 (2006).

[9] Arjun Appadurai, *Fear of Small Numbers: An Essay on the Geography of Anger* 60 (2006).

[10] It responds, more particularly, to those aspects of this challenge concerning the difficulty of attributing the acts of dispersed followers at the lowest levels to leaders at the upper echelons.

[11] Bruno Latour, *Reassembling the Social* 169 (2005). As he characterizes the conundrum, it cannot easily be dismissed as posing a false dichotomy. "Actors [are] simultaneously held by the context and holding it in place, while the context [is] at once what makes actors behave and what is being made in turn." Id.

far beyond the few individuals who can practically be prosecuted; yet even these few can be convicted only through theories of indirect liability that blame them for wrongs beyond their control or contemplation. Since so few can actually be tried, the impulse to blame those prosecuted for wrongs beyond their culpability becomes overwhelming.[12]

Responses to this dilemma differ at the national and international levels. International prosecutors in The Hague have sought to empower their emergent professional field of international criminal law by maximizing convictions through resort to the doctrine of "participation in a joint criminal enterprise." National prosecutors in transitional democracies, by contrast, must placate executives wishing to limit prosecution in the interests of social reconciliation. Other legal doctrines, such as "superior responsibility," serve this end. National and international courts are thus employing different legal methods to characterize offenders similarly situated, reaching disparate results and imperilling international law's coherence.

This fact troubles some people profoundly, striking them as "inherently unfair."[13] Other observers – equally knowledgeable – are wholly unconcerned, not merely in practice but also on principle. They think it essential, on the contrary, that "international criminal law . . . be adapted to local legal culture, the contours of communal experience, and local moral sensibilities."[14] Thus, the raging question of how much coherence

---

[12] This is a particularly extreme expression of the general human propensity to ascribe greater control to people than they actually enjoy and to blame them accordingly. Psychological experiments confirm the frequency of this cognitive distortion. Richard Nisbett & Lee Ross, *Human Inference: Strategies and Shortcomings of Social Judgment* (1980).

[13] Ciara Damgaard, *Individual Criminal Responsibility for Core International Crimes* 257 (2008) ("it . . . seems inherently unfair that an accused could not be held accountable for a particular act [i.e., core international crime] before a domestic court [in a state that had ratified the ICC Statute], but that he could be held accountable for that same act before the ICC."). On the other hand, a rather different "problem" would arise if national courts resolved to apply the new, international law approaches to modes of liability. Those prosecuted in such courts for international offenses (conducted jointly with others) would then be held to different – probably more demanding – standards than those tried for even the most serious offenses of domestic origin. This prospect troubles still others. Elies van Sliedregt, "Complicity to Commit Genocide," unpublished manuscript, 26 (2009); Harmen van der Wilt, "Equal Standards? On the Dialectics Between National Jurisdictions and the International Criminal Court," 8 Int'l Crim. L. Rev. 229, 231–32 (2008).

[14] Mirjan Damaška, "What is the Point of International Criminal Justice?" 83 Chi.-Kent L. Rev. 329, 349 (2008). He continues, however, "But realization of this ideal would entail fragmentation of international criminal law: the multiplicity of its variations would be difficult to order in ways capable of preserving the system's coherence." The queries then arise: what it might mean, and would it be possible, to "harmonize" national variations in the domestic incorporation of international criminal law on the basis of general principles,

international law really requires – or, alternatively, how much fragmentation it rightly permits – becomes important to the present inquiry. The matter is particularly pressing as states, having adopted the Statute of the International Criminal Court (ICC), increasingly apply such law within their domestic courts.

This book proposes an integral "economic" response to these challenges by endorsing an interpretation of superior responsibility that reduces this doctrine's high risks of acquittal, thereby weakening incentives for international prosecutors to rely excessively on enterprise participation and permitting convictions consistent with defendants' culpability. It further argues that enterprise participation should be employed to impose collective monetary sanctions on the officer corps, who can readily monitor prospective wrongdoers and redistribute costs to individual members who are actually culpable. In abjuring appeal to humanitarian or other disinterested motives, this study argues that the behavior necessary to avert and redress mass atrocity may spring from motivations that are surprisingly banal. This approach brings the law into closer harmony with what historians and social scientists now conclude about how atrocity actually occurs.

COLLECTIVE CRIMINALITY

Even as the Holocaust still raged, lawyers were quick to realize that an adequate response would require creation of new offenses such as genocide and crimes against humanity. With these offenses, international law soon began to take on board the idea that the victim of crime could be understood as a group, independent of the attendant suffering by particular members. The laws of genocide and of persecution as a crime against humanity recognize this idea by making the defendant's discriminatory animus against the protected group integral to the definition of the offense. The mental state

---

rather than seeking perfect uniformity across all societies, jot for jot, in the details of statutory provisions and judicial interpretation. Such harmonization efforts have often been quite effective in other areas of international law. Mireille Delmas-Marty, *Global Law: A Triple Challenge*, Naomi Norberg trans. 74–96 (1998). These other areas, however, generally involve frequent and deep cross-border interaction, as with regulation of products in foreign trade. There, the imperative and incentives to cooperate with other states are generally greater than in many aspects of international criminal law. Cooperation among national police agencies already works relatively well, on most accounts, despite enduring differences between the criminal codes of many states. Ethan Nadelmann & Peter Andreas, *Policing the Globe: Criminalization and Crime Control in International Relations* 96–104, 224–28 (2006); Ethan Nadelmann, *Cops Across Borders: the Internationalization of U.S. Criminal Law Enforcement* (1993).

for genocide is thus the "intent to destroy, in whole or in part" a protected group, whereas persecution entails deprivation of rights "by reason of the identity of the group or collectivity."[15]

International law has been much slower, however, to grapple seriously with the notion that crime's *perpetrators* might also be groups – or, at least, individuals acting through groups. Only in 1998 was the offense of crimes against humanity revised to acknowledge the perpetrator's group character. The ICC Statute thus specifies that the prohibited attack must have been "in furtherance of a state or organizational policy."[16] As the International Criminal Tribunal for the former Yugoslavia (ICTY) announced in its first case, "Most of the time the crimes [before us] do not result from the criminal propensity of single individuals but constitute manifestations of collective criminality: the crimes are often carried out by groups of individuals acting in pursuance of a common criminal design."[17] In rising to this challenge, the ICTY has found that apprehending the group character of the perpetrator requires new conceptions of criminal association and of how offenses may be committed.[18]

Yet the law has nonetheless been largely content to rely on fictions remote from the empirical reality of mass atrocity discerned by historians and social scientists. The fictions are invoked to understand large numbers of disparately motivated people – performing very different actions, only partly coordinated – as engaged in a single criminal endeavor and to distinguish those in the dock from those who bear substantial responsibility for major wrong but will escape prosecution, in the interests of political prudence, social stability, and resource limitations. Transitional justice demands such legal fictions for much the same reason as the politics of transitional justice demands "noble lies." The fictions and political dissimulations are, in fact, largely the same, in that both seek to draw lines of accountability departing in significant ways from the social realities and moral complexities apparent in any close examination of how mass atrocity occurs.

---

[15] Rome Statute of the International Criminal Court, July 17, 1998, arts. 6, 7(2)(g), 2187 U.N.T.S. 90, 93–4.
[16] Id. art. 7(2)(a). As early as 1945, however, A. N. Trainin observed that "[a]s distinct from common crimes, international crimes are almost always committed not by one person but by several or many persons – a group, a band, a clique." *Hitlerite Responsibility under Criminal Law* 79 (A. Y. Vishinski, ed., 1945).
[17] *Prosecutor v. Tadić,* Case No. IT-94–1, Judgment, ¶ 191 (July 15, 1999).
[18] At Nuremberg, to be sure, the International Military Tribunal (IMT) employed the novel doctrine of "membership in a criminal organization." But the doctrine of that name has since been almost universally repudiated within international law. Stanislaw Pomorski, "Conspiracy and Criminal Organization," in *The Nuremberg Trial and International Law* 213, 229 (George Ginsburg & V. N. Kudriavtsev, eds., 1990).

This book suggests several ways in which historiography and social science can help criminal law conceptualize central aspects of mass atrocity more consistently with what is known about how and why such events take place. In particular, scholarly accounts of atrocity's organizational forms and interactional dynamics prove helpful in refining and choosing among legal renderings of how and by whom it has been "committed."

Mass atrocity could not transpire without the organized cooperation of many, often numbering in the several thousands. There may have been more than two-hundred thousand immediate participants in the Rwandan genocide, for instance.[19] Regular and irregular military forces, which did most of the killing, numbered about ten thousand. In the Third Reich, more than one-hundred thousand Germans participated in mass slaughters.[20] In the former Yugoslavia, killers and rapists numbered at least ten thousand.[21] These numbers include both soldiers of various rank and sympathetic civilians in government and private life.

Their cooperation takes innumerable forms, and a satisfactory method for ascribing particular harms to specific defendants is not always readily at hand.[22] This is particularly true of those not physically present at the "crime scene," such as high-ranking civilian leaders located many miles away.[23] Criminal law in the common law world – unlike civil law – has insisted on shoehorning all these modes of commission into a handful of categories, preferring simplicity to nuance. Recent additions and revisions

[19] Scott Straus, "How Many Perpetrators Were There in the Rwandan Genocide? An Estimate," 6 J. Genocide Res. 85, 93 (2004). This figure does not include those who identified Tutsi neighbors to militias or were present in mobs whose other members committed murderous acts.

[20] Daniel Jonah Goldhagen, *Hitler's Willing Executioners* 164, 167 (1996). This is probably a conservative estimate, given that the Gestapo numbered nearly fifty thousand and the number of Waffen-SS in combat divisions alone reached more than four-hundred thousand. Int'l Military Tribunal, 4 *Trial of the Major War Criminals before the International Military Tribunal: Nuremberg* 14 Nov. 1945–Oct. 1946, at 195–6, 241–2 (1947).

[21] Michael Mann, *The Dark Side of Democracy: Explaining Ethnic Cleansing* 418, 424 (2005). Estimates for twentieth-century victims of mass killings (including genocides), as distinguished from war deaths (other than through war crimes), range between 60 million and 150 million. Benjamin Valentino, *Final Solutions: Mass Killing and Genocide in the Twentieth Century* 1, 255 (2004).

[22] David Cohen, "Bureaucracy, Justice, and Collective Responsibility in the World War II War Crimes Trials," 18 Rechtshistorisches J. 313, 324 (1999) (suggesting "the inadequacy of existing analytical tools" in criminal law for "apprehending the collective, organizational, and systematic dimensions of Nazi war crimes").

[23] An Argentine legal scholar thus dryly observes that "the rules on telling perpetrators from accessories were not written with the crime of genocide in mind." Edgardo Alberto Donna, *El Concepto de Autoría y la Teoría de los Aparatos de Poder de Roxin* 295, 315 (Carlos Julio Lascano, ed., 2001).

8 *Making Sense of Mass Atrocity*

to this short list seek to acknowledge the subtleties of shared responsibility in mass atrocity, but present vexing problems of their own.

A recurring set of questions arises in mass atrocity prosecutions: How should the law allocate responsibility between those with different roles in the division of labor? What is the relative importance of their respective contributions, and how may the answer to this question best be rendered into legal form? Which such renderings most risk exaggerating a defendant's culpability? Or does a preoccupation with individual culpability simply prevent proper recognition of the collective nature of mass atrocity, thereby foreclosing the collective sanctions that may offer an efficient response?

Moreover, if international criminal law is to be truly cosmopolitan in nature, as all admit it should, then it cannot simply extend Western doctrine onto the transnational plane without considering the implications for societies not sharing similar underlying assumptions. For example, many non-Western societies simply do not insist that penal sanction presupposes and requires clear proof of personal culpability,[24] at least not with such punctiliousness as do we Westerners.[25] If international law is to be made by different types of courts – national, international, or hybrid – then how might these courts be made to work in sync, for instance, to harmonize their interpretations of a given doctrine?

An episode of mass atrocity will likely display, through its forms and processes, features resonating with this or that "mode of commission" – the alternative doctrines for linking the big fish to one another and to the small fry.[26] Does close assessment of these features lead us to endorse serious punishment of only the big fish? If so, then how may prosecutions

[24] Daryl J. Levinson, "Collective Sanctions," 56 Stan. L. Rev. 345, 352–7 (2003) (evidencing the frequent use of legal sanctions against groups, including inculpable members, by many non-Western societies, from contemporary Japan and Africa to medieval Iceland); Michael Barkun, *Law without Sanctions* 20 (1968) ("Primitive law has long been known to be weak in concepts of individual responsibility. A law-breaking individual transforms his group into a law-breaking group, for in his dealings with others he never stands alone."); Saul Levmore, "Rethinking Group Responsibility and Strategic Threats in Biblical Texts and Modern Law," 71 Chi.-Kent L. Rev. 85, 91–101 (1995) (demonstrating, from Old Testament sources, the frequent reliance on threat and/or use of collective sanctions, especially in international relations and the law governing them).

[25] In fact, American criminal law does not always condition criminal liability on a clear showing of personal culpability, as demonstrated by the rules on felony murder, *Pinkerton* conspiracies, and liability under the Racketeer Influenced and Corrupt Organizations Act (RICO). These doctrines remain controversial, however, precisely to the extent of their apparent departure from that principle.

[26] This admittedly colloquial terminology was widely employed by ICTY prosecutors. Chris Stephen, *Judgement Day: The Trial of Slobodan Milošević* 147 (1st Am., ed. 2004) (describing prosecutors' reference to Milošević as "the Big Fish"). It is also widely used in professional discussion of their cases. The law itself has made much finer distinctions, as between "Class

persuasively and practically be limited to these defendants, considering the gravity of wrongs committed by lower echelons? Or if the small fry deserve penal sanction, then – given their numbers – what punishment other than lengthy incarceration might they properly receive? Which combination of sanctions – incarceration and compensation, formal and informal – is most effective in preventing mass atrocity *ex ante* and redressing it *ex post*? If criminal law sometimes seems so inadequate in grappling with mass atrocity, is this because the law rests on assumptions that are simply inapplicable and irrelevant to such events?[27] Does prosecution of these wrongs therefore require a theory of punishment utterly distinct from that on which we rely for garden-variety wrongs,[28] especially when prosecution shifts from national to international courts?[29]

A striking feature of debate about all such questions is that very different answers tend to be reached at the domestic plane than at the international. No one who attends transitional justice conferences in postconflict societies can long fail to notice the near-total disconnect between the discourse of local participants, often focused on historically specific grievances about who did what horrible thing to whom, and of us more "cosmopolitan," peripatetic academic consultants, touting larger lessons drawn from other countries recently facing predicaments we consider "similar."

One conspicuous feature of this discursive divide is that, in contemplating prosecution of former rulers and their subordinates, international prosecutors tend to favor legal approaches that broaden the reach of criminal law far

One" and other classes of war criminals in the Nuremberg and Tokyo trials after World War II, as well as in Rwandan national prosecutions.

[27] This argument has long been made concerning the legal treatment of defendants at the lower echelons. Hannah Arendt, *Eichmann in Jerusalem: A Report on the Banality of Evil* 251–4 (1963); Mark J. Osiel, *Mass Atrocity, Ordinary Evil, and Hannah Arendt: Criminal Consciousness in Argentina's Dirty War* 150–5 (2001); Mark A. Drumbl, "Collective Violence and Individual Punishment: The Criminality of Mass Atrocity," 99 Nw. U. L. Rev. 539, 539–48 (2005). The present book, by contrast, assesses limitations in the law's treatment of defendants at the highest echelons.

[28] This question has not been squarely posed, even by leading criminologists writing about mass atrocity and possible international legal responses, such as Stanley Cohen, *States of Denial: Knowing about Atrocities and Suffering* (2001) or John Hagan & Scott Greer, "Making War Criminal," 40 Criminology 231 (2002).

[29] These questions are the focus of recent work by Mark Drumbl. See Drumbl, "Collective Violence," op. cit., at 548–51. Drumbl questions whether the implicit criminology and normative theory informing national legal practice may be transplanted, without reconsideration, to the transnational plane. He casts his argument as one about irrational path dependency in legal evolution. See also Danilo Zolo, "Peace through Criminal Law?" 2 J. Int'l Crim. Just. 727, 728 (2004) ("The normative structure of international criminal justice remains quite uncertain and confused when compared to domestic law. This is especially so from the point of view of the philosophy of punishment.").

beyond what national prosecutors – beholden to domestic power holders, who themselves are often implicated in comparable criminality – can afford to endorse. The greater receptivity of international prosecutors to more capacious conceptions of legal accountability for mass atrocity bolsters the growing proclivity of atrocity's victims throughout the world, dissatisfied with the seeming unresponsiveness of national prosecutors, to seek redress in regional and other international legal forums.[30]

Any strategy of legal reform that seeks to align incentives will only succeed if actors can be expected to behave rationally, in the sense of maximizing their personal utility.[31] At first, mass atrocity seems a type of human conduct especially uncongenial to such analysis. During these episodes, passions prevail over interests[32] – or at least so it first appears. These passions prominently include intergroup hatred and the later desire for vengeance against perpetrators. On both sides, emotions are always fierce and often explosive.

Such times arouse nearly the full spectrum of human sentiment, often within the same people in short succession: collective malice, spontaneous sympathy, nationalist frenzy, disinterested kindness, rage and loathing, mercy, mindless cruelty, courageous self-sacrifice, sheer horror, and blood lust. Notably absent from this list, however, is the prudent, individual calculation of material interest.[33] And if law's challenge is to confront the irreducibly collective nature of mass atrocity, then it may first seem quite counterintuitive to seek guidance from so atomistic a worldview as that of economics. Moreover, international efforts to bring perpetrators to justice are inspired by sincere humanitarian sentiment and by remorse at not having done more to prevent the wrong, not by naked self-interest.

Where interests matter at all, they appear utterly irreconcilable, especially in postconflict redress: Prosecutors and victims want punishment,

---

[30] On this development, see Kathryn Sikkink, "The Complementarity of Domestic and International Legal Opportunity Structures and the Judicialization of the Politics of Human Rights in Latin America," unpublished paper, 27 (Mar. 8, 2004).

[31] Economics assumes people generally behave in this fashion. Bruno S. Frey, *Dealing with Terrorism – Stick or Carrot?* 55 (2004) ("Most of the time, and in most circumstances, rational behaviour in the sense of systematic reactions to changes in incentives prevails. Behavioural anomalies should merely be considered as minor deviations."); James G. March, *A Primer on Decision Making* 128 (1994) ("The most obvious strategy for building effective partnerships . . . involves . . . aligning the incentives pursued by rational actors.").

[32] On how modern political theory has viewed the relation of passions to self-interest, see Albert O. Hirschman, *The Passions and the Interests* (1977).

[33] Only when the dust has fully settled, perhaps, do such quotidian calculations reappear – as in, for instance, a Serbian prime minister's decision whether to extradite Milošević to The Hague in exchange for $100 million in U.S. aid. Steven Erlanger, "U.S. Makes Arrest of Milosevic a Condition of Aid to Belgrade," N.Y. Times, Mar. 10, 2001, at A1.

whereas perpetrators seek amnesty.[34] What one calls retributive justice, the other considers vengeance. What the second labels as restorative justice, the first decries as impunity. This is often at least as much a clash *among* high principles as one of principles *versus* peace and pragmatism.[35] That individual interests could be brought into even moderate alignment seems nearly preposterous.

Many believe that the principal choice that society faces at such times is between collective memory and collective amnesia. Individual persons – their specific contribution to large-scale events, their particularized fate thereafter – should not become the focus of public policy, on this view. Preoccupation with their material incentives is still more bizarre, if not morally obtuse. In circumstances of transitional justice, people must relearn to live together and compromise private interest in the service of public reconciliation.[36] Restoring social peace may require forgiveness,[37] which demands self-renunciation, the antithesis of self-interest.

This study takes a decidedly different tack. It seeks not to create or simulate a market exactly. (In what, one wonders. Genocide?[38] Genocide prevention?) Rather, it explores whether an economic vantage point and cast of mind might shed some light on improving the law's response to such horrific events. Specifically, it asks whether the rules on modes of criminal

[34] Indeed, they often also seek moral vindication and ceremonial veneration in official commemoration. Hence, for instance, General Augusto Pinochet's insistence that "the Chilean Army certainly sees no reason to seek pardon for having taken part in a patriotic labor" of helping win the Cold War. "Respuestas de las Fuerzas Armadas y de Orden al Informe de la Comisión Nacional de Verdad y Reconciliación," 41 Estudios Públicos 449, 469 (1991).

[35] The effort to find acceptable terms of trade-off between these competing objectives produced a massive, decade-long debate among social scientists, legal scholars, political activists, and journalists. See, e.g., *Human Rights in Political Transitions; Truth v. Justice* (Robert I. Rotberg & Dennis Thompson, eds., 2000).

[36] Reconciliation is a highly contested concept in this context. Its advocates are often studiously opaque about exactly "who is to reconcile with whom, and on what grounds." Michel Feher, "Terms of Reconciliation," in *Human Rights in Political Transitions*, op. cit., at 325, 327–9.

[37] Much has been written in the last decade extolling this theme, often inspired by the experience of the South African Truth and Reconciliation Commission. See, e.g., Jean Bethke Elshtain, "Politics and Forgiveness," in *Burying the Past: Making Peace and Doing Justice after Civil Conflict* 45, 50–4 (Nigel Biggar, ed., 2003).

[38] Economic considerations may have played some role here, to be sure. There is evidence, for instance, that the incidence of genocide increased once slavery was effectively outlawed, because conquered peoples could no longer be reduced to forced labor and hence lost their potential value to conquerors. Kurt Jonassohn with Karin Solveig Björnson, *Genocide and Gross Human Rights Violations in Comparative Perspective* 123–4 (1998). In this respect at least, one might say that demand for genocide responds to legal incentives.

commission might be slightly revised to align more closely the incentives of parties at both national and international levels facing the perpetration and prosecution of mass atrocity.

The present analysis commits itself to no particular brand of economic theory. It seeks only to employ the market mechanism's essential logic by asking whether relevant rules might produce better results when designed to track the parties' interests, rather than appealing to their moral sentiments and capacity for benevolence.[39] Such an approach does not imply that the interests of pertinent parties can be harmoniously reconciled in some happy equilibrium, after which all further interaction is mutually beneficial.[40] When urging an economic perspective of this sort, the line between playful provocation and outright perversity can be fine. The present approach might at first strike some as counterintuitive – maybe frivolous or flippant. It may first appear lacking, at the very least, in the *gravitas* or sobriety the subject demands. Most scholarship on legal response to mass atrocity veritably drips with righteous fervor, to be sure.[41]

What enables economics to offer fresh insight is precisely its disinclination to moralize, even in the face of great wrong. Often accused of bloodlessness, this very vice proves its virtue in devising a legal response to colossal blood-baths. Its "can-do" attitude is also infectious, especially contrasted to the deterministic world-weariness of sociology and political science, the disciplines so far offering the deepest insights into mass atrocity.[42] Of course, a

---

[39] "Better" rather than maximal or optimal, since this proposal does not pretend to prevent or punish all atrocities.

[40] It promises equilibrium of sorts, but only in a very soft, nontechnical sense: It lets transitional societies achieve political stability by reducing fratricidal conflict to an extent consistent with doing maximum feasible justice. To observe that a state of affairs is in equilibrium is not, in any event, to say that it is normatively desirable nor to deny that other focal points of equilibrium are equally possible. Thomas C. Schelling, *Micromotives and Macrobehavior* 26–7 (1978).

[41] This is understandably so. See, e.g., Naomi Roht-Arriaza, *The Pinochet Effect* (2005); Diane Orentlicher, "Whose Justice? Reconciling Universal Jurisdiction with Democratic Principles," 92 Geo. L.J. 1057, 1133 (2004) (decrying "the ravages of mass atrocity" and "the abyss of lawless violence"). A rare exception is Larry May, *Crimes against Humanity: A Normative Account* 175–6 (2005), which is as sensitive to the limits of the defendants' true culpability as to the claims of victims of human rights abuse.

[42] See, e.g., Zygmunt Bauman, *Modernity and the Holocaust* 13–18 (1989) (arguing that organizational features of modern Western society greatly facilitated the Holocaust); Helen Fein, *Accounting for Genocide* 64–75, 90–120 (1979) (showing how features of several western European societies influenced their differing degrees of cooperation with Nazi occupiers); Mann, op. cit., at 4 (contending that democratization in unstable societies is conducive to mass atrocity); Jacques Semelin, *Purify and Destory: The Political Uses of Massacre and*

common concern with such "imperialistic" extensions of economics into nonmarket domains is that, through ensuing commodification, their adoption as the basis of law and policy will drive or crowd out the more altruistic behavior that is already there and worthy of sustenance.[43]

With mass atrocity, however, this danger is surely much less of a concern than in social policy.[44] After all, altruism is not a prominent feature of human behavior during genocide or of the retributive animosity arising in its wake. It is not difficult to imagine the genocidal mass murderer as a "bad man" – Holmesian or otherwise – asking only what he can get away with.[45] So it is not implausible that the law should treat him as such. This treatment actually offers grounds for hope. "Genocide is preventable because it is usually a rational act: that is, the perpetrators calculate the likelihood of success, given their values and objectives,"[46] writes a leading scholar. At the top echelons, reminds Luis Moreno-Ocampo, Chief ICC Prosecutor, "These are not passion crimes. These people think in costs."[47]

This study suggests that national and international tribunals currently employ the central doctrines of enterprise participation and superior responsibility[48] without providing any clear criteria – logically coherent or morally sound – by which to know when one or the other will apply to a

Genocide (2007); John Hagan & Wenoma Rymond-Richmond, *Darfur and the Crime of Genocide* (2008), Benjamin Valentino, *Final Solutions: Mass Killing and Genocide in the Twentieth Century* (2004); Jeremy Weinstein, *Inside Rebellion: the Politics of Insurgent Violence* 339–49 (2007); Kalyvas, op. cit.

[43] Steven Lukes, "Invasions of the Market," in *From Liberal Values to Democratic Transition* 57, 63–5 (Ronald Dworkin, ed., 2004). This objection is further addressed in Chapter 10.

[44] Robert Pinker, "From Gift Relationships to Quasi-Markets: An Odyssey along the Policy Paths of Altruism and Egoism," 40 Soc. Pol'y & Admin. 10 (2006) (assessing the current state of debate over Richard Titmuss's influential findings that commercializing the motivations for contributing blood reduces the quality of the blood supply).

[45] Oliver Wendell Holmes, "The Path of the Law," 10 Harv. L. Rev. 457, 459–61 (1897).

[46] Helen Fein, "Patrons, Prevention, and Punishment of Genocide," in *The Prevention of Genocide: Rwanda and Yugoslavia Reconsidered* 5 (Helen Fein, ed., 1994).

[47] Quoted in Elizabeth Rubin, "If Not Peace, Then Justice," N.Y. Times, April 2, 2006.

[48] The older term is "command responsibility," which was first codified in Protocol Additional to the Geneva Conventions of 12 August 1949, and Relating to the Protection of Victims of International Armed Conflicts, arts. 86–7, adopted June 8, 1977, 1125 U.N.T.S. 3 (entered into force Dec. 7, 1978). The term is still in wide use. But the doctrine now clearly encompasses civilians with duties and powers comparable to those of military commanders. See, e.g., *Prosecutor v. Nahimana et al.*, Case No. ICTR-99-52-T, Summary, ¶¶ 5–7 (Dec. 3, 2003). Employing this broader reading, international tribunals have convicted prominent officials in civilian governments and even in the private sector. This study therefore uses the term "superior responsibility" except when referring exclusively to military commanders.

given case,[49] despite their quite disparate results. The analysis employs some simple economic reasoning to account for the behavior of prosecutors, perpetrators, and bystanders capable of preventing the wrongs, in recognition that a satisfactory legal response to mass atrocity requires simultaneously understanding the interests of all three groups. The book then offers the beginnings of a unified approach encompassing these respective incentives and interactions.[50]

It does not evaluate all aspects of the two principal liability doctrines, but focuses instead on those features concerning the organizational structure and group dynamics of mass atrocity.[51] Most analysis is in the way of diagnosis, but some definite suggestions are offered about how any ensuing "surgery" should be conducted, so that international criminal law may better address the problems here identified. To be workable, any solution to the doctrinal dilemmas should seek to harness the incentives of all parties – prosecutors, perpetrators, and powerful bystanders – rather than insisting that they all transcend their interests in the service of nobler, disinterested aspirations.

Chapter 1 examines how the organizational dynamics and economics of mass atrocity influence our assessments of responsibility in such episodes; it also articulates the normative and practical challenges the law faces in seeking to punish perpetrators. The next four chapters then describe and dissect the primary approaches to liability from which prosecutors choose in seeking to punish mass atrocity. Chapter 2 examines the law of "superior responsibility," whereas Chapters 3 and 4 discuss the doctrine of "participation in a joint criminal enterprise." Chapter 5 assesses the recent law on perpetration "through an organizational apparatus." Chapter 6 responds to the criticism, levied against all three of these novel methods of linking big fish to small fry, that they violate first principles of liberal legality by

[49] Elies van Sliedregt, *The Criminal Responsibility of Individuals for Violations of International Humanitarian Law* 195 (2003) ("The trial chambers in *Krstić* and *Krnojelac* do not make clear why they chose one ground of responsibility over the other.").
[50] Absent from this list are the victims of mass atrocity. The present emphasis follows simply from concern with understanding legal and political results over which victims generally exercise less influence than other groups. Victims have thus far played their most conspicuous role in democratic transitions via testimony before national truth commissions. In many countries, victims' groups nonetheless play an increasingly important role in pressing for enforcement of international criminal law. Roht-Arriaza, op. cit., at 204–7 (describing the central, assertive role that victims have played in Chilean cases).
[51] Scholars of group dynamics seek to counter the notion that "groups can be adequately understood as collections of independently acting individuals," because individual behavior is influenced by patterns of interaction with others. Holly Arrow et al., *Small Groups as Complex Systems* 3 (2000).

punishing people who are not morally culpable. Chapters 7 and 8 step back from the law to analyze the differing incentives of prosecutors in national and international courts grappling with the aftereffects of mass atrocity and how these incentives affect their preferred legal strategies. These chapters describe how international prosecutors have turned repeatedly to enterprise participation and national prosecutors to much narrower approaches, leading to disparate treatment of similar misconduct.

The next two chapters propose solutions to this disparity. Chapters 9 and 10 then show how the law of enterprise participation might be used to impose collective monetary sanctions against the officer corps, as a means of enhancing the law's deterrent effect. Finally, Chapter 11 assesses how economic reasoning might inform the concession of amnesty to accomplices of departing dictators and criminal commanders, with a view to minimizing the moral compromise such amnesties entail.

1

The Challenge of Prosecuting Mass Atrocity

When prosecuting those at the highest echelons – a Slobodan Milošević, Saddam Hussein, or Charles Taylor – a foremost question often becomes: On what basis may the acts of the lowliest subordinate be fairly ascribed to the most elevated superior, from whom they are so distant in space and time?

Prosecutors today generally lack direct evidence that atrocities were expressly ordered from above. Since the Nuremberg trials at least, high-level perpetrators of mass atrocity have, with rare exceptions,[1] been careful not to leave any record of such orders. For instance, testimony before the International Criminal Tribunal for the former Yugoslavia (ICTY) confirmed that Serbs "erased records and cleaned out archives."[2] When Argentina's military juntas gathered to plot the dirty war, their minutes expressly registered their concern to avoid "another Nuremberg."[3]

Even oral orders are generally couched in insinuation and innuendo, through euphemistic terms of art, which prosecutors must convincingly decode.[4] It would not be obvious to outsiders, for instance, that satellite intercepts from field commanders referring to "Belgrade" always really meant "Milošević." Little evidence of criminal commands was available to

---

[1] Judy Dempsey, "East German Shoot-to-Kill Order Is Found," N.Y. Times, Aug. 13, 2007, at A5.

[2] Marlise Simons, "Tribunal in Hague Finds Bosnia Serb Guilty of Genocide," N.Y. Times, Aug. 3, 2001, at A1.

[3] Luis Moreno-Ocampo, "The Nuremberg Parallel in Argentina," 11 N.Y.L. Sch. J. Int'l & Comp. L. 357, 357 (1990).

[4] John Hagan, *Justice in the Balkans: Prosecuting War Crimes in The Hague Tribunal* 233–4 (2003); see generally Marguerite Feitlowitz, *A Lexicon of Terror: Argentina and the Legacies of Torture* 50 (1998) (describing the Argentine army manual and listing its appropriate euphemisms).

prosecutors at the ICTY, in fact.[5] The court concluded it could infer their existence from circumstantial facts only if no other reasonable inference were possible.[6] The prosecutorial burden here proved quite onerous in most cases. The law, in this respect, simply has not yet fully recognized and redressed how mass atrocity evolves in evasive response to the law's own demands on those seeking to prove it.

Several national and international courts – including most prominently the ICTY – have had occasion to consider the question of how to tie the big fish to the smaller fry.[7] The most common choice in these cases, as defined by the ICTY, has been between the doctrines of "superior responsibility"[8] and "participation in a joint criminal enterprise."[9] Both were employed against Milošević[10] and Hussein.[11] And both will be invoked against the Khmer Rouge leaders currently on trial in Cambodia.[12]

---

[5] A rare conviction based partly on direct ordering is *Prosecutor v. Blaškić*, Case No. IT-95-14-T, Judgment, ¶¶ 433–41, 519–31, 641–61 (Mar. 3, 2000). The defendant was also convicted on some counts under superior responsibility. Id. at 721.

[6] For instance, *Prosecutor v. Galić*, Case No. IT-98-29-T, Judgment, ¶ 171 (Dec. 5, 2003).

[7] For such judgments in the ICTY, see, e.g., *Prosecutor v. Krstić*, Case No. IT-98-33-A, Judgment, 145–51 (Apr. 19, 2004); *Prosecutor v. Delalić et al.*, Case No. IT-96-21-A, Judgment, 248–68 (Feb. 20, 2001); *Prosecutor v. Tadić*, Case No. IT-94-1-A, Judgment 172–237 (July 15, 1999); *Prosecutor v. Stakić*, Case No. IT-97-24-T, Judgment, 468–98 (July 31, 2003); *Blaškić* Trial ¶¶ 429–95, 513–31, 560–2, 580–92, 635–61, 717–43.

[8] The textual basis for this doctrine is Art. 7(3) of the ICTY Statute, which provides, in pertinent part: "The fact that any of the [prohibited] acts was committed by a subordinate does not relieve his superior of criminal responsibility if he knew or had reason to know that the subordinate was about to commit such acts or had done so and the superior failed to take the necessary and reasonable measures to prevent such acts or to punish the perpetrators thereof." Statute of the International Criminal Tribunal for the Former Yugoslavia art. 7(3), May 25, 1993, 32 I.L.M. 1192, 1194.

[9] Whenever this study refers to "enterprise participation," the reader should understand the term as shorthand for the more cumbersome "participation in a joint criminal enterprise." The first ICTY cases referred to the doctrine as "common purpose" and "common plan" liability. See, e.g., *Tadić* Appeal, ¶¶ 185–229.

[10] The indictments against Slobodan Milošević for atrocities in Bosnia, Croatia, and Kosovo employed the joint criminal enterprise and superior responsibility approaches. Amended Indictment 5–31, *Prosecutor v. Milošević*, Case No. IT-02-54-T (Nov. 22, 2002); Second Amended Indictment 5–33, *Prosecutor v. Milošević*, Case No. IT-02-54-T (Oct. 23, 2002); Second Amended Indictment 16–28, *Prosecutor v. Milošević*, Case No. IT-99-37-PT (Oct. 16, 2001).

[11] Statute of the Iraqi Special Tribunal, Art. 15, Dec. 10, 2003, 43 I.L.M. 231, 242; Michael Newton & Michael Scharf, *Enemy of the State: The Trial and Execution of Saddam Hussein* 178–79 (2008).

[12] Anne-Laure Poree & Chheang Bopha, "Five Khmer Rouge to Go Before Judges," Int'l Just. Tribune, July 23, 2007.

This study examines the strengths and weaknesses of each approach by focusing primarily on their use by the ICTY[13] and on each doctrine's capacity to grapple analytically with the collective, organized, and bureaucratic character of mass atrocity. Both doctrines have been expressly adopted by the Rome Statute of the International Criminal Court (ICC),[14] prosecutors in hybrid courts regularly employ them, and they have been incorporated into U.S. regulations governing the military commissions established to prosecute Guantánamo detainees.[15] Official investigations of the Abu Ghraib controversy, as well as reports about it by leading human rights groups,[16] expressly invoke the law of superior responsibility in evaluating officers whose alleged misconduct may have contributed to abusive treatment of detainees there.[17] The Chief Prosecutor of the ICC has said he will use this same legal doctrine, many others, in the effort to hold Sudanese authorities responsible for atrocities in Darfur.

INDIVIDUAL CULPABILITY AND COLLECTIVE RESPONSIBILITY

As early as Nuremberg, the tribunal there emphasized that its conclusions must be reached "in accordance with well-settled legal principles, one of the most important of which is that criminal guilt is personal, and that mass punishments should be avoided."[18] Reliance on vicarious liability for serious criminal offenses is highly controversial.[19] Vicarious liability arises

---

[13] The ICTR has employed superior responsibility, but has also relied on conspiracy and instigation/incitement. *Prosecutor v. Nahimana* et al., Case No. ICTR-96-52-T, 973, 1033–9, 1055; *Prosecutor v. Niyitegeka*, Case No. ICTR-96-14-T, Judgment, ¶¶ 422–37, 470–8 (May 16, 2003).

[14] Rome Statute, op. cit., Arts. 25, 28. The Rome Statute also, at least implicitly, requires ratifying states to incorporate its terms into their domestic legislation. Jann K. Kleffner, "The Impact of Complementarity on National Implementation of Substantive International Criminal Law," 1 J. Int'l Crim. Just. 86, 91–4 (2001).

[15] 32 C.F.R. § 11.6(c)(3)–(4) (2004) (applying command/superior responsibility); id. § 11.6(c)(6) (where accused has "joined an enterprise of persons who shared a common criminal purpose"); Associated Press, "Pentagon Drafts Rules for Detainee Trials," N.Y. Times, Jan. 18, 2007 ('The new manual includes the death penalty for people convicted of spying or taking part in a "conspiracy or joint enterprise" that kills someone.').

[16] Human Rights Watch, *Getting Away with Torture? Command Responsibility for the U.S. Abuse of Detainees*, 88–92 (2005); Human Rights First Report, *Command's Responsibility: Detainee Deaths in U.S. Custody in Iraq and Afghanistan* (Feb. 2006); see also Philippe Sands, *Torture Team: Rumsfeld's Memo and the Betrayal of American Values* (2008).

[17] *The Abu Ghraib Investigations* 15–19, 40–5 (Steven Strasser, ed., 2004).

[18] 1 Int'l Military Tribunal; Nuremberg 14 Nov. 1945–1 Oct. 1946, at 256 (1947).

[19] George P. Fletcher, *Basic Concepts of Criminal Law* 191–3 (1998) (contending that although vicarious liability serves legitimate public purposes in tort and contract law, it is morally indefensible in criminal law).

when the defendant, although engaged in no wrongful act (or omission), is held accountable for the wrongs of another, to whom he is related in a specified manner, usually as an employer.[20]

Enterprise participation involves vicarious liability, since a defendant's act of contribution to the enterprise, sufficient to make him a participant therein, may not amount to much actual "fault" for the foreseeable but unintended contributions of other participants, for which he too may be punished. The *ad hoc* international tribunals have evinced some concern about the problem.[21] It poses obstacles both for practical institution-building and for the normative theory on which such institutions will rest.

The predicament may be defined by twin facts that, although logically compatible, sit uneasily together and cause discomfiture in many minds. First, in the aftermath of mass atrocity, it is widely understood that culpability for the country's catastrophe extends far beyond the few individuals who can practically be prosecuted.[22] Conviction of even these persons, however, can be won only through conceptions of responsibility that may unduly extend the wrongful acts performed by others that are fairly attributable to these defendants.

The rationale for holding top chieftains responsible for wrongs beyond their complete control or exact contemplation is simply that, as George Fletcher writes, "those who generate a climate of moral degeneracy bear some of the guilt for the criminal actions that are thereby endorsed."[23] But terms like "climate" and "moral degeneracy" – even "endorse" for that matter – occupy no place in the lexicon of criminal liability. The ICTY's first trial, of Dusan Tadić, did not merely concern "what occurred between the accused and the victims of these crimes," stressed his prosecutor. It was "about the tragic destruction of that once proud and beautiful country, Yugoslavia." In this regard, Adolf Eichmann's final words, shortly before his execution, ring uncomfortably close to the truth: "I have the most profound conviction

---

[20] Wayne R. LaFave, *Criminal Law* § 3.9, at 265 (3d ed., 2000).

[21] This is particularly apparent in an important recent judgment of the ICTY Appeals Chamber, *Prosecutor v. Blaškić*, Case No. IT-95-14-A, Judgment 54–7 (July 29, 2004) (holding military superiors liable for criminal acts of subordinates only if having actual, subjective knowledge of facts and giving notice of need to intercede); see also *Krstić* Appeal, ¶¶ 237–9 (holding that defendant who knew of genocidal acts of others could be found guilty of aiding and abetting but not as a direct participant in genocide unless specific intent to commit genocide is shown).

[22] This study uses the terms "culpability" and "blameworthiness" interchangeably, referring to the moral defensibility of ascribing a specific wrong to a particular person.

[23] George P. Fletcher, "The Storrs Lectures: Liberals and Romantics at War: The Problem of Collective Guilt," 111 Yale L.J. 1499, 1541–2 (2002).

that I am being made to pay here for the glass that others have broken."[24] Observing his trial, Hannah Arendt concurred, writing that the "case was built upon what the Jews had suffered, not what Eichmann had done."[25]

Even as many culpable parties must escape prosecution entirely, those prosecuted may sometimes be convicted only in a way that exaggerates the true extent of their blameworthiness. The law's reach is thus at once too timid and too ambitious, both overinclusive and underinclusive vis-à-vis the actual distribution of responsibility. This creates the "inescapable aura of arbitrariness"[26] hovering over so many trials for mass atrocity.[27] The problem is exacerbated by a disconnection between political dynamics at the national and international levels: International prosecutors have an incentive to overcharge,[28] and national prosecutors to undercharge.[29]

Before descending into doctrinal details, we should first ask, in the broadest terms: To what should the law aspire in the aftermath of mass atrocity? On the one hand, we seek fidelity to a longstanding ideal of individual responsibility. Most of Western legality – including the features most normatively compelling about it – is so deeply committed to this ideal that its abandonment would surely set off wide shock waves. On the other hand, we recognize that modern mass atrocity displays peculiar features that are morally relevant to punishing its participants.[30]

Specifically, a bureaucratic state can organize such crimes with unprecedented efficacy – employing advanced technologies, lasting several years,

---

[24] Enrique Gimbernat Ordeig, *Autor y Cómplice en Derecho Penal* 187 (1966).

[25] Hannah Arendt, *Eichmann in Jerusalem* 6 (1962).

[26] Allison Marston Danner & Jenny S. Martinez, "Guilty Associations: Joint Criminal Enterprise, Command Responsibility, and the Development of International Criminal Law," 93 Cal. L. Rev. 75, 97 (2005).

[27] There are several other sources of doubt about the legitimacy of these trials, to be sure, such as concerns about the fairness of their procedural protections for defendants, harmonization of civil law and common law approaches, and the selectivity and criteria with which defendants are chosen.

[28] The propensity to overcharge may be exacerbated by the advent of, and increasing resort to, plea bargaining at the *ad hoc* tribunals. This practice can encourage overcharging because prosecutors know they will not often be called on to prove before a court every charge initially alleged.

[29] There are exceptions to the rule, as in the Rwandan indictments against thousands of lower-echelon *genocidaires*. But few of these defendants actually saw the inside of any real courtroom.

[30] The Chief Nuremberg Prosecutor acknowledged the "novel and experimental" nature of those proceedings in his Opening Statement. 2 Nuremberg Trials, op. cit., at 99. But see Eric A. Posner & Adrian Vermeule, "Transitional Justice as Ordinary Justice," 117 Harv. L. Rev. 761 *passim* (2004) (contending that little is entirely new to the legal issues presented by transitional justice). The phenomena of corporate crime and mafia-type organized crime, for instance, present many of the issues examined in this book.

covering an entire country, being perpetrated by many thousands, victimiz-
ing equal numbers – and harness the legal system to these ends. Such wrongs
seem radically different from the garden-variety crime in response to which
standard legal doctrines were developed. These differences rise to a level
that may not be merely numerical, but categorical, requiring reassessment
of the individualistic categories in which criminal law customarily thinks
and judges. Can such reconsideration be given cognizable legal shape in
ways that do not unduly depart from the culpability principle? Ideally, the
law could both honestly acknowledge the empirical specificity of modern
mass atrocity and keep faith with its moral core, with the principle "that
defendants be convicted for their own conduct and not merely for the
violent trauma experienced by entire nations."[31]

The tension between these two goals comes to the fore because influential
opinion-makers outside the legal-professional universe generally prefer a
mode of explanation and condemnation that finds no place in the lawyer's
more modest vocabulary and worldview.[32] This alternative discourse is more
readily amenable than law to conceptualizing events and actors in avowedly
collective terms. It does not hesitate, for instance, to speak of such collective
entities as "the Serbs," "the Germans," or "the Hutus" – concepts from
which the liberal legal mind recoils.

There are clearly many ways to understand and conceive relationships
among the people who are parties to mass atrocity. A mistake in this regard
might simply mean that a given defendant is convicted under one theory
rather than another. The mistake also may produce, however, a longer or
shorter sentence than would a correct characterization. In certain situations,
the error may even make the difference between guilt and acquittal. As we
shall see, superior responsibility in particular is so narrowly construed by the
ICTY today that it becomes difficult to convict even a Milošević, whereas
the advent of enterprise participation makes his conviction much easier.
The latter doctrine has thus become the "dominant strategy"[33] of ICTY
prosecutors because it outperforms all others, regardless of defendants' trial
strategies.

What if Milošević had been acquitted instead of dying just before the
trial's completion? Some might have been content to applaud a procedural
scrupulousness that could yield such a result, despite so much pressure from

---

[31] Danner & Martinez, op. cit., at 100.

[32] Mark Osiel, *Mass Atrocity, Collective Memory, and the Law* 142 (1997) (examining conflicts
between legal and historiographic accounts of mass atrocity).

[33] Avinash K. Dixit & Barry J. Nalebuff, *Thinking Strategically* 58–9 (1991) (defining the quoted
term and its place within game theory).

world opinion to convict him. But most of the world would have dismissed the entire project of international criminal law as an enormous waste of time and money – at best, a noble experiment that had failed.[34] What worth and necessity could there be in an institution that could not secure the conviction of someone everyone "knew" to be guilty, guilty, guilty, they would surely say.

Hence this is no mere shell game or idle exercise in analytical acrobatics; each way of conceptualizing the link between big fish and small fry has differing repercussions for how particular defendants will be treated by the courts.[35] Each way of describing the relation among parties to mass atrocity also has implications for the story the trial will tell and the history to which it will contribute.[36] Because such trials are often closely observed by many and contribute to collective memory, it is important for the law to convey the proper significance of the events it judges and the relative weight of each defendant's contribution.[37]

THE ORGANIZATIONAL DYNAMICS OF MASS ATROCITY

Behind the choice between doctrinal devices resides a more fundamental problem. As a leading Holocaust historian writes,

[34] That it has failed is a conclusion already reached by many committed to its purposes. See, e.g., Ralph Zacklin, "The Failings of *Ad Hoc* International Tribunals," 2 J. Int'l Crim. Just. 541, 545 (2004) (arguing, as UN Assistant Secretary-General for Legal Affairs, that "the verdict is now largely in. The *ad hoc* Tribunals have been too costly, too inefficient and too ineffective. As mechanisms for dealing with justice in post-conflict societies, they exemplify an approach that is no longer politically or financially viable.").

[35] On the practical difficulties investigators face in factually establishing such linkage, see Morten Bergsmo & William Wiley, "Human Rights Professionals and the Criminal Investigation and Prosecution of Core International Crimes," in *Manual on Human Rights Monitoring* (Siri Skåre, Ingvild Burkey & Hege Mørk, eds., Norwegian Centre for Human Rights, Univ. of Oslo 2008).

[36] The way a legal case is constructed can influence historical and collective memory in several ways, and prosecutors and courts often seek to influence such memory. Osiel, *Collective Memory*, op. cit., at 229–39.

[37] But see Mirjan Damaška, "The Henry Morris Lecture: What is the Point of International Criminal Justice?" 83 Chi.-Kent L. Rev. 329, 343–63 (2008) (rejecting these purposes as excessively ambitious and often inconsistent with the more standard goals of criminal law). Damaška takes the present author to task for arguing that international criminal trials should serve didactic purposes. Id. at 347, 353. However, I made no such argument, explicitly confining my proposal to domestic prosecutions and faulting efforts by international prosecutors since Nuremberg to evoke a global "collective conscience" that often simply does not exist, i.e., in any depth or specificity. Osiel, *Collective Memory*, op. cit., at 2, 26, 29, 31, 35–6, 62–6, 91, 96–7, 103, 122, 134, 157–8, 192, 205–8, 225–6, 238, 245, 288. In fact, others have criticized me precisely for declining to extend my argument to such international proceedings. Larry May, *Aggression and Crimes Against Peace* 68 (2008).

The entrepreneurs of genocide are like the organizers of Adam Smith's pin factory who have discovered the division of labor. Ideologues conjure up a monstrous conspiracy. Ambitious administrators define target categories and compete for jurisdiction; different officials pass sentences or create administrative authorities; others arrest, some load onto trains, others unload, some guard, others herd people to the killing ground or into the gas chambers; still others shake cyanide crystals into the vents.[38]

Contrasted with conventional crimes conducted by a single person or a small cabal, state atrocities are instead often

the product of collective, systematic, bureaucratic activity, made possible only by the collaboration of massive and complex organizations in the execution of criminal policies initiated at the highest levels of government. How, then, is individual responsibility to be located, limited, and defined within the vast bureaucratic apparatuses that make possible the pulling of a trigger or the dropping of a gas canister in some far-flung place?[39]

If all this were not complicated enough, there is also the fact that mass atrocity – like most large-scale organizational behavior – does not often respect bureaucratic formalities; subordinates often turn out to exercise autonomy they were not intended to have, in pursuit of purposes all their own. Typical in this regard was the Cambodian experience, in which, writes a leading scholar

Not all of the killings during the Khmer Rouge regime were directly ordered by the central leadership. Authority to kill certain categories of individuals was delegated to local administrations, and they used this power liberally. Once the central directives to exterminate certain categories of "enemies" had been disseminated, and the bureaucratic apparatus became fully engaged with the task, local officials sometimes misinterpreted the leadership directives as requiring even greater scope of killing. Others used the authority they had been granted to pursue personal agendas, taking revenge for slights felt in local disputes.[40]

The law's tentative efforts at formulating a response to the resulting conundrums raise many questions, to which no fully satisfactory answers have been offered. This study examines some of the more complex incarnations of the problem. But the problem itself arises from the very simple fact that it is sometimes possible for each element of a given offense to be

---

[38] Charles S. Maier, *The Unmasterable Past* 69–70 (1988).
[39] David Cohen, "Beyond Nuremberg: Individual Responsibility for War Crimes," in *Human Rights in Political Transitions* 53 (Carla Hesse & Robert Post, eds., 1999).
[40] Craig Etcheson, *After the Killing Fields: Lessons from the Cambodian Genocide* 84 (2005).

committed by a different person, so that no single participant realizes all of the constituent elements. Thus, "if every group member has to answer only for the harm that wouldn't have occurred without him, there will be a lot of harm unanswered for."[41] The division of labor might even be deliberately arranged so that this result ensues. To ensure against this scenario, the law seeks a defensible way to link up the requisite elements of the offense to contributions by multiple participants, so that all may be held responsible for the resulting wrong. This task proves devilishly difficult and has only been solved in ways that present quandaries no less troubling.

The intellectual resources of international criminal law for grappling with the organized division of labor in episodes of mass atrocity are still quite rudimentary, surprisingly crude, despite the regular recurrence of such events over the last half-century. We need a conceptual repertoire that enables us to make conviction of high-level criminals neither too easy, as currently with enterprise participation law, nor too difficult, as with the doctrine of superior responsibility. It should remain close to the ground of mass atrocity, to its factual contours, rather than contenting itself with implausible fictions that are empirically dubious and conceptually contrived.

Developing this conceptual repertoire requires careful attention to research into the nature and origins of mass atrocity. Each of the two legal doctrines here examined takes a particular view of how, and perhaps why, such events occur. This is not to say that either legal doctrine perfectly corresponds, jot for jot, to any widely accepted theory of how mass atrocity occurs. But in choosing one or the other of these approaches in their indictments and judgments, prosecutors and courts are tacitly, often haphazardly, taking a stand on such large questions. Debate among international lawyers over the respective merits of the two doctrines nonetheless takes no account of the considerable scholarship on these issues, which are wrongly considered extralegal. In fact, prosecutors frequently make decisions about which doctrine to employ with greater attention to how the choice affects their professional prospects.

They may be forgiven for displaying little curiosity about the sociological assumptions implicit in their legal approaches. Legal academicians, however, enjoy the luxury to dig beneath the surface of demanding caseloads and so should perhaps not be so readily forgiven here. Most striking to any novice reader of academic international criminal law, in fact, is surely the way it operates according to its own self-referential practices and autopoeitic

---

[41] Leo Katz, *Bad Acts and Guilty Minds* 254 (1987).

logics, rather than in dialogue with serious scholarly models of the larger world it yearns to govern. Surely, an open mind would begin not by asking what legal doctrines offer precedents to cope quickly with this new challenge. Rather, it would ask these questions: What kind of influence do participants in such collective criminality actually exercise over one another, through what organizational devices and interactional dynamics? What have scholars, devoted to plumbing the origins and nature of mass atrocity, learned in answer to these questions, answers from which we, the law's guardians, might learn?

Among U.S. legal scholars, only Fletcher and Drumbl have thus far gingerly entertained the possibility that the first principle of domestic criminal law – personal culpability – may have to be modified or abandoned if international law is ever to successfully "adapt the paradigm of individual guilt to the cauldron of collective violence" epitomized by mass atrocity.[42] They and others also acknowledge the improbability of deterring criminal elites who monopolize state power[43] and that the retributive rationale for punishment makes little sense when perpetrators adhere to prevailing socio-ethical norms, rather than breach them.[44]

In ascribing liability, the law of superior responsibility looks at relationships vertically, whereas enterprise participation views them more horizontally and nonhierarchically. There is, of course, both a vertical and lateral dimension to the social dynamics between those involved in state-sponsored mass atrocity.[45] On the one hand, instructions are generally given from top

---

[42] Mark A. Drumbl, "Pluralizing International Criminal Justice," 103 Mich. L. Rev. 1295, 1309 (2005) ("Recourse to generous – and at times somewhat vicarious – liability theories becomes eminently understandable insofar as these theories permit the [*ad hoc* international] tribunals to ascribe individual guilt in cases where violence has several, and often murky, organic sources"); see also George P. Fletcher, "Collective Guilt and Collective Punishment," 5 Theoretical Inquiries L. 163, 168–9, 173–4 (2004) (suggesting that collective guilt is a "plausible and sometimes healthy response to collective wrongdoing"). Others observe that mass atrocity "may have its origins in strategy and planning by a select group of individuals but ultimately relies on the force of group power to achieve its ends. Trials [have] limitations with respect to addressing the social and collective forces that lead to the violence." Laurel E. Fletcher & Harvey M. Weinstein, "Violence and Social Repair: Rethinking the Contribution of Justice to Reconciliation," 24 Hum. Rts. Q. 573, 636 (2002).

[43] See, e.g., Frédéric Mégret, "The Politics of International Criminal Justice," 13 Eur. J. Int'l L. 1261, 1282 (2002).

[44] See, e.g., Mark A. Drumbl, "Sclerosis: Retributive Justice and the Rwandan Genocide," 2 Punishment & Soc'y 287, 296–8 (2000).

[45] It would be wrong to infer that the difference between the legal doctrines lies in the fact that co-participation is characterized by the voluntariness of the connection among members of the criminal enterprise, whereas superior responsibility is defined by its coerciveness. Individuals may voluntarily submit themselves to the control of another, after all, agreeing

to bottom and information conveyed from bottom to top. On the other hand, those at the same level in the hierarchy – and beyond its formal boundaries – often have to cooperate to implement such instructions.

Still more important, those involved often display considerable initiative in implementing criminal policies beyond the terms of superiors' directives.[46] Interaction among interested parties is thus simultaneously organized and spontaneous, vertical and horizontal. Influence and information circulate in both directions. Criminal conduct by non-elites often both is directed from above and springs spontaneously from below.[47] In outbursts of collective enthusiasm, for instance, military subordinates often exceed the terms of their criminal orders.[48]

Mass atrocity organized by a state and effected on a large scale always involves a great deal of planning by people with much power, employing it to dominate and oppress. But the causes and consequences of mass atrocity prove diffuse and elusive, largely escaping the intentions of any small group of perpetrators, no matter how elevated in rank. "It is difficult to accept that often there is no person and no group that planned or caused it all," writes an influential Holocaust scholar.[49] Yet if we can be sure of anything about such enigmatic episodes, it is precisely this fragmentation of responsibility.

When conceptualizing the relationships among perpetrators of mass atrocities, on what basis should the law give primacy to the vertical or horizontal dimensions? This is not a question of legal doctrine, strictly speaking, so perhaps it is not surprising that the ICTY has never articulated it explicitly. But it lies just beneath that tribunal's judgments, and it

---

to do whatever the other directs them to do. Control, not coercion, is what superior responsibility requires prosecutors to show.

[46] See, e.g., Christopher R. Browning, *Fateful Months: Essays on the Emergence of the Final Solution* 7, 66–7 (1985); Raul Hilberg, *Perpetrators, Victims, Bystanders* 25–6 (1992).

[47] This second aspect of mass atrocity is emphasized by so-called functionalist scholars who dispute the "intentionalist" conviction that top leadership was responsible for most wrongdoing. Robert Gellately & Ben Kiernan, "The Study of Mass Murder and Genocide," in *The Specter of Genocide: Mass Murder in Historical Perspective* 3, 10–11 (Robert Gellately & Ben Kiernan, eds., 2003) (identifying differences between these two schools of thought); see also Robert Gellately, *Backing Hitler: Consent and Coercion in Nazi Germany* 199–203 (2001) (emphasizing how mutually reinforcing interaction between ordinary Germans and Nazi leadership made repression more effective).

[48] See, e.g., Mark Osiel, *Mass Atrocity, Ordinary Evil, and Hannah Arendt* 36–9 (discussing conduct of German and Argentine soldiers during the Holocaust and the Argentine Dirty War); Benjamin Valentino, *Final Solutions: Mass Killing and Genocide in the Twentieth Century* 47–8, 53–6 (2004) (noting Holocaust perpetrators often exceeded their orders or complied with violent orders without supervision).

[49] John Lachs, *Responsibility and the Individual in Modern Society* 58 (1981).

periodically rises to the surface. The failure to confront directly this question partly explains the ICTY's vacillation and internal struggles in this area.

Each such approach to classification makes certain assumptions about the nature of the relationships among those involved in mass atrocity. In assessing the two approaches, we must also consider whether these relationships should be understood objectively, from a social scientific perspective perhaps, or instead subjectively, as the participants themselves experienced them.

Superior responsibility places a decided emphasis on the chain of command and how power passes through it, from top to bottom. The emphasis is both substantive and rhetorical. This doctrine stresses the formal, hierarchical structure of military organizations and the consequent reasons why a high-ranking superior can reasonably expect his orders to be obeyed, including standing orders to honor the Geneva Conventions. The doctrine accentuates the weighty, nondelegable duties of high office – duties knowingly assumed by anyone agreeing to occupy it. This emphasis is especially clear in how it allows the requisite mental state to drop beneath intentional misconduct.[50] Certain features of mass atrocity, in some instantiations, clearly comport with superior responsibility, as where criminal policymaking and control over events concentrate at the top of a bureaucratic hierarchy.

Enterprise participation, in contrast, is more consonant with differing dimensions of mass atrocity, in which malevolent influence travels through informal and widely dispersed networks. Insofar as much cross-border criminal activity – from drug smuggling to Islamist terror – increasingly operates through networks,[51] its prosecutors will increasingly gravitate toward the law of enterprise participation. Organizational flexibility must be met by doctrinal elasticity so that indictments can mirror the factual contours of defendants' wrongs. Because the network molds itself to best achieve its aims as circumstances shift, the criminal law needs methods to track the resulting configuration. The law of enterprise participation, as we shall see,

---

[50] The treaty creating the International Criminal Court, for instance, explicitly adopts a "should have known" standard. Rome Statute, Art. 28. This is problematic as applied to crimes, like genocide and persecution (as a crime against humanity), which require specific intent.

[51] Even before Al Qaeda's 9/11 attacks, social scientists made bold claims that networks will "be the next major form of organization – long after tribes, hierarchies, and markets – to come into its own to redefine societies, and in so doing, the nature of conflict and cooperation." David Ronfeldt & John Arquilla, "What Next for Networks and Netwars?" in *Networks and Netwars: The Future of Terror, Crime, and Militancy* (David Ronfeldt & John Arquilla, eds., 2001), at 311.

lets prosecutors map and match defendants' organizational ingenuity with a corresponding flexibility of their own.

The ICTY clearly acknowledges the legal significance of interpersonal power dynamics among parties to crime and how these extend beyond bureaucratic boundaries and the borders of nations. But it and other such courts would do well to become more self-conscious and explicit both about models for conceptualizing these more fluid dynamics and empirical methods for evidencing them.[52] Thus, for instance, when several South American military regimes cooperate in killing off one another's dissident refugees,[53] prosecutors today seek to define the enterprise accordingly, encompassing ranking officers across national borders.[54] The law of superior responsibility does not permit this conceptualization.

Similarly, when "rogue" elements in Pakistan's intelligence services clandestinely assist the Lashkar-e-Taiba terrorists who attack Mumbai hotels,[55] no formal chain of command unites these disparate parties as superiors and subordinates. Yet all may plausibly be categorized as participants in the informal enterprise that perpetrated such attacks. The same problem arises – and the same solution presents itself – where U.S. interrogators from the C.I.A., private contractors, and military police collaborate in mistreating detainees.[56]

Criminal law can ignore all such empirical variation only by taking refuge in contrived presumptions and legal fictions that, as abstract generalities, miss many morally weighty nuances in the facts of particular cases.

---

[52] The sociometric block modeling of networks, when joined to telecom data mining, will prove useful to these respective ends. On block modeling, see generally, *Exploratory Social Network Analysis with Pajek* (Wouter de Nooy et al., eds., 2005); Patrick Radden Keefe, "Can Network Theory Thwart Terrorists?" N.Y. Times, March 12, 2006.

[53] In the 1970s, military intelligence services in Chile, Argentina, Uruguay, Paraguay, Brazil, and Bolivia collaborated to this end, to stanch the continent-wide spread of revolutionary groups inspired by the Cuban revolution. J. Patrice McSherry, *Predatory States: Operation Condor and Covert War in Latin America* xvii, 1–33 (2005).

[54] Several such countries have recently initiated criminal investigations into the organizers of Plan Condor. Darío Montero, "Hunting the Condor, 28 Years On," Inter-Press News Agency, at http://ipsnews.net/print.asp?idnews=23836 ("New political winds on both sides of the Río de la Plata . . . have breathed new life into legal investigations of the murders of two Uruguayan legislators in Argentina, which had been frozen for 28 years.").

[55] Eric Schmitt, Mark Mazzetti & Jane Perlez, "Pakistan's Spies Aided Group Tied to Mumbai Siege," N.Y. Times, Dec. 8, 2008, at A1.

[56] Associated Press, "Officer is Acquitted of Charges over Abu Ghraib," N.Y. Times, Aug. 28, 2007, at A1 (describing partial acquittal of Lt. Col. Steven Jordan on the grounds that, according to his defense counsel, Jordan "was outside the chain of command and therefore not responsible for the military intelligence soldiers who interrogated detainees and the military police who guarded them").

These nuances are important to defining accurately the role of particular perpetrators and so determining their proper legal treatment. To be sure, real cases rarely fit either ideal-type because most organizations turn out to be network-hierarchy hybrids. This is particularly true of criminal organizations.[57] And states themselves are never quite precisely honed, top-down instruments of diabolical domination nor, for that matter, effortless facilitators of egalitarian, networked cooperation.

When fictions proliferate in an area of law, there is reason to suspect its concepts have fallen out of touch with the world they aim to govern. Fictions here prominently include the notion that, in the law of enterprise participation, those sharing a criminal purpose form an enterprise of which they can be considered members. This idea is fictive insofar as they might be ignorant of one another's contributions to the enterprise and of their own role within its functioning, which may be entirely dispensable. The notion that such participants subscribe to a common purpose is itself often just as fictional, in that parties to it would likely define it differently in scope – temporally and spatially, in the reach of its aims or ambitions.

If the law's conceptual maneuvers here cannot formally be called fictions, it is only because a legal fiction is partly defined by a consciousness of its falsity.[58] Such fictions are defensible only insofar as there is reason for confidence that defendants corralled together by them share a pernicious "community of interest," as it is sometimes vaguely called.[59] But the existence and nature of that community, in many prosecutions, are precisely the matters in dispute.

By examining what the ICTY has done on questions of shared responsibility, we can uncover the trade-offs it believed it faced, the pros and cons of each answer to the problem. As we shall see, that tribunal has made it too hard to find defendants liable under superior responsibility, but too easy to convict them as participants in a joint criminal enterprise. The latter approach increasingly lures international law to a point at which liability threatens to exceed the scope of moral culpability. It has found such favor in The Hague because the former approach of superior responsibility was previously leading the law to a point where the extent of moral culpability

---

[57] See, e.g., Michael Kenney, "From Pablo to Osama: Counter-terrorism Lessons from the War on Drugs," *Survival* 187, 203 (Autumn 2003) (suggesting that counterterrorism measures should match terrorists' own network-hierarchy hybrids); Phil Williams, "Transnational Criminal Networks," in *Networks and Netwars*, op. cit., at 61, 69 (describing structure of cocaine trade in Colombia and heroin trade in Southeast Asia).

[58] Lon L. Fuller, *Legal Fictions* 6–7 (1967).

[59] Wayne R. LaFave, *Criminal Law* 597 (3d, ed. 2000).

too greatly exceeded that of liability. The challenge, then, is to steer the law
safely between these twin perils.

If the ICTY and other criminal tribunals could find a way to relax requirements for classifying a defendant as an irresponsible commander, they
would not have to rely so heavily on the notion of enterprise participation,
a notion that is dangerously illiberal[60] and trusts too much to prosecutorial self-restraint. Thus, the task is to reduce requirements for conviction
by superior responsibility while adhering to the requirement of individual
culpability.[61]

---

[60] Danner & Martinez, op. cit., at 79 (observing "potential [of doctrine] to lapse into forms
of guilt by association").

[61] This principle, again, requires "that defendants [be] convicted for their own conduct
and not merely for the violent trauma experienced by entire nations." Id. at 100. But see
Drumbl, "Collective Violence," op. cit., at 573 (commending *ad hoc* tribunals for "availing
themselves of theories of liability that contemplate group dynamics").

PART I

LEGAL RULES AND THEIR PROBLEMS

2

The Responsibility of Superiors

In legal terms, "superior responsibility" is a form of culpable omission by superiors – usually military commanders – that leads subordinates to violate international criminal and humanitarian law. Military commanders have a duty to ensure that their subordinates observe such law, a duty enshrined in international treaties,[1] most national military codes, and army training manuals.

Prosecutors should look to superior responsibility when an effective chain of command exists but elites have been too careful to have issued (or left evidence of issuing) criminal orders. Imagine a situation, for instance, in which subordinate interrogators are given to understand that detainees likely have valuable information about future terrorist plots, information not offered voluntarily. Interrogators are told that the Geneva Conventions must be honored, but also that detainees may not actually be covered by these treaties. Supervision of the interrogators is then made very occasional, though superiors may plausibly justify this spottiness on the basis of staffing shortages not of their own creation.

Interrogators seek to resolve ambiguities and inconsistencies in their instructions concerning permissible methods of interrogation. They learn that their questions to immediate superiors will be referred up the chain of command and answered in due course. Yet no answers follow. In the interim,

---

[1] See, e.g., Geneva Convention Relative to the Treatment of Prisoners of War art. 127, Aug. 12, 1949, 6 U.S.T. 3316, 75 U.N.T.S. 135; Geneva Convention for the Amelioration of the Condition of Wounded, Sick, and Shipwrecked Members of Armed Forces at Sea art. 48, Aug. 12, 1949, 6 U.S.T. 3217, 75 U.N.T.S. 85. Helpful recent discussions of the doctrine include Chantal Meloni, "Command Responsibility: Mode of Liability for the Crimes of Subordinates or Separate Offences of the Superior?" 5 J. Int'l Crim. J. 619 (2007); Volker Nerlich, "Superior Responsibility under Article 28 ICC Statute: For What Exactly Is the Superior Held Responsible?" 5 J. Int'l Crim. J. 665 (2007); Beatrice Bonafé, "Finding a Proper Role for Command Responsibility," 5 J. Int'l Crim. J. 599 (2007).

the interrogators continue to employ methods that, they are informed, pose no threat of mortal harm, but that prove in fact to cause the deaths of some detainees.[2] On these facts, superior responsibility offers the most credible legal method by which to hold the upper echelons liable for these deaths.

To prove that a commander breached his responsibilities in this regard, prosecutors must show three elements: the requisite mental state, a "superior–subordinate relationship," and the superior's failure to prevent or punish the subordinates' wrongs.

THE SUPERIOR'S "EFFECTIVE CONTROL" OVER AND CAPACITY
TO PREVENT SUBORDINATES' WRONGS

Virtually all discussion focuses on the defendant's requisite mental state.[3] This emphasis reflects a perennial preoccupation throughout the Western world. It betrays an intellectual orientation more curious about the mind's inner workings than about causal mechanisms in the external world, such as those on which the doctrine's other two requirements concentrate.

For a superior–subordinate relationship to exist, the former must have exercised effective control over the latter.[4] This control is what enables the superior to punish the subordinate or prevent him from criminal conduct. The doctrine's first and third elements are thus inextricable. They are very demanding, and the ICTY Prosecutor's Office has regularly failed to meet them.[5] They raise evidentiary hurdles that have "generated difficulty in application," but scholars have tended to believe that they are otherwise "not conceptually controversial."[6] In fact, however, these evidentiary problems

---

[2] This hypothetical scenario bears some resemblance to events reported at the U.S. detention center in Bagram, Afghanistan. Tim Golden, "Abuse Cases Open Command Issues at Prison," N.Y. Times, Aug. 8, 2005, at A1.

[3] See, e.g., Mirjan Damaška, "The Shadow Side of Command Responsibility," 49 Am. J. Comp. L. 455, 463–4 (2001).

[4] *Čelebići Appeal*, ¶ 197. There is considerable literature on the history and current contours of the doctrine. See generally Timothy Wu & Yong-Sung (Jonathan) Kang, "Criminal Liability for the Actions of Subordinates – The Doctrine of Command Responsibility and its Analogues in United States Law," 38 Harv. Int'l L.J. 272 (1997); Harmen van der Wilt, "Halilović on Appeal: The Intricate Concept of 'Effective Control,'" 2 Hague Justice J. 5 (2007).

[5] See *Blaškić Appeal* 407–8, 421 (holding that the defendant did not have effective control over brigades committing the pertinent criminal acts); see also *Čelebići* Appeal 268, 293, 313–14 (affirming acquittals of defendants Zejnil Delalić and Hazim Delić on the same basis).

[6] Allison Marston Danner & Jenny S. Martinez, "Guilty Associations: Joint Criminal Enterprise, Command Responsibility, and the Development of International Criminal Law," 93 Cal. L. Rev. 75, 130 (2005).

themselves present some difficult conceptual questions – most prominently, What kind of control – over whom and in what respects – is morally relevant?

The control requirement might mean many things. It might mean, for instance, that the superior decides which subordinate or subordinates will perform the criminal actions; he would then, of course, have to know their names in advance of the wrongful acts. Or the requirement might mean that the superior determines which offenses – torture, murder, rape – the subordinates will commit and perhaps also the conditions under which they might be committed. The control requirement might even be understood to entail that the superior chooses the particular persons whom the subordinate will victimize in these ways. Or it could mean that he merely identifies the type of person to be subjected to such treatment, such as Bosnians or Shiites.

At various times in different forums, judges and juries have thought it necessary for prosecutors to prove one or all of these aspects of control. For example, jurors in an Alien Tort Claims Act (ATCA) and Torture Victim Protection Act (TVPA) suit against two Salvadoran generals interrupted their deliberations to ask the court, "Shouldn't it be absolutely necessary for the torturers to be identified or at least prove to be subordinates of the defendant commanders? It seems a lot is missing."[7]

And the ICTY acquitted Bosnian Serb reconnaissance commander Dragoljub Kunarac of command responsibility for rape, despite finding that for several months he had often chosen Muslim women at a detention center and escorted them to suites where they were repeatedly raped by militia members.[8] But since members of Kunarac's unit were picked for particular missions on an *ad hoc* basis, the tribunal held that there was no clear superior–subordinate relationship between the defendant and the specific inferiors at the rapes' time and place.

As the control requirement becomes more specific in the kind of information it demands, it becomes increasingly difficult to meet. Which of the various types of control just mentioned should be adopted by the law as most suitable to its purposes is thus a crucial and largely unexamined question. The more demanding interpretations of the control requirement do not follow from its purpose. Within large organizations, many tasks are necessarily delegated, with the result that those at the highest echelons are virtually never involved in deciding them.

[7] Transcript of Jury Questions at 2515, *Arce v. Garcia*, No. 99-8364-Civ-Hurley (S.D. Fla. July 19, 2002).
[8] *Prosecutor v. Kunarac et al.*, Case Nos. IT-96-23-T & IT-96-23/1-T, Judgment, 583, 626–9 (Feb. 22, 2001).

From the CEO's vantage point, such tasks are rightly considered minutiae. Although it would be possible for him or her to resolve some of them, the organization's effective functioning does not require or even permit such micro-management on a regular basis.[9] It is unreasonable to expect strategic decision makers at top levels of large organizations to exert control over their myriad operational details. This does not mean, however, that their failure to know and decide the details of the company's activities at lower levels should exempt them from legal responsibility for criminal conduct by subordinates.

It is not defendants' position within an official chain of command that creates the superior–subordinate relationship between them and the immediate perpetrator. Formal authority over criminal juniors is enough only if the defendants do not challenge the inference that they actually exercised effective control over them. Defendants almost always challenge this inference, however. They claim that their *de facto* power was significantly less than, or simply different from, their *de jure* authority.[10]

The relationship of superior to subordinate may also exist *de facto*, without legal basis.[11] *De facto* power is often based on personal or "charismatic" authority, in Weber's sense.[12] But charisma is notoriously elusive, often ephemeral[13] – and so difficult to establish factually in a criminal court. Milošević lacked *de jure* authority over Bosnian Serb forces during the massacre at Srebrenica, but may have exercised a more personalistic, *de facto* control over them.[14] Proving this beyond a reasonable doubt, however, was very difficult, and many observers expected the ICTY Prosecutor to fail. The most detailed assessment of the question, by an historian who served as an expert witness for the prosecution, concludes that the prosecution did not make its case in this regard for the relevant time period:

> The prosecutor ... did his best to show that Milošević exerted influence over Karadžić and Mladić. However, almost all the testimony related to the

---

[9] Charles Perrow, *Complex Organizations* 145–76 (1972).
[10] *Čelebići* Appeal, ¶ 197.
[11] Id. ¶ 193.
[12] Max Weber, *Theory of Social and Economic Organization* 358–62 (A. R. Anderson & Talcott Parsons, trans., 1947).
[13] Charles Lindholm, *Charisma* 30–31 (1990).
[14] Tim Judah, *Milosevic on Trial, Survival* 157, 162, 164, Summer 2002. Still, there is some doubt about whether Milošević could have exercised this control in sufficient time to prevent the massacre. Louis Sell, *Slobodan Milosevic and the Destruction of Yugoslavia* 233–4 (2002); cf. Gary Jonathan Bass, *Stay the Hand of Vengeance* 227 (2000) ("Relations between Milošević's regime in Belgrade and the Bosnian Serb leaders in Pale were always fractious and often poisonous.").

periods up to early 1993 or from August till December 1995. Either wittingly or unwittingly, the fact was overlooked that the power relations between Milošević and the Bosnian Serb leaders fluctuated, and that Milošević exerted no influence on the latter at the time of the mass murders following the fall of Srebrenica in July 1995.[15]

Or consider another illustration of *de facto* power without *de jure* authority: the case of a Serbian investigating judge, appointed to inquire into a recent massacre, who arrived on the scene to find some victims still alive. She reportedly gave instructions, in the presence of thirty members of the Special Anti-Terrorist Units accompanying her, to kill them.[16] She lacked any formal legal authority over these forces.

One way to approach this issue – *de facto* power, absent *de jure* authority – would be to reverse the presumptions and require defendants to prove that their actual power was less than their formal authority would suggest. Once prosecutors establish defendants' *de jure* authority over criminal juniors, the burden of production on the issue of effective control would then shift to the defendants. U.S. courts have sometimes employed this approach in civil suits seeking damages from state torturers under the ATCA and TVPA.[17] But presuming criminal guilt – as opposed to civil liability (even when accompanied by punitive damages)[18] – from the formality of one's bureaucratic position rightly evokes greater skepticism. International prosecutors retain the burden of production even after demonstrating the formal chain of command linking defendants to perpetrators on the scene.

Since rulers who orchestrate mass atrocity have often seized power by armed force, their entire regime will generally be unconstitutional and their authority thus fairly characterized as *de facto*, in its entirety. It follows, on some accounts, that all governmental actions taken pursuant to their authority are equally *de facto*. Some legal recognition of their actual control over subordinates is hence indispensable to holding them and their subordinates accountable for ensuing atrocities.

Whether effective control exists is resolved when determining liability. Liability does not admit degrees – a defendant either did or did not have the

[15] Bob de Graff, "The Difference between Legal Proof and Historical Evidence: The Trial of Slobodan Milošević and The Case of Srebrenica," 114 Europ. Rev. 499, 505 (2006).
[16] "Dealing with the Past: Concerns about Milosevic Defence Witness," HLC Newsl. No. 10 (Humanitarian Law Ctr., Belgrade, Serbia and Montenegro), Apr. 15, 2005, at 1.
[17] See, e.g., *Ford ex rel. Estate of Ford v. Garcia*, 289 F.3d 1283, 1290–3 (11th Cir. 2002).
[18] One U.S. civil jury has awarded punitive damages of $2 million against two Salvadoran military officers for human rights abuses suffered by four victims. http://www.cja.org/cases/Carranza%20Docs/VerdictRelease.htm.

requisite control.[19] This binary distinction forces the law into a dilemma: If it is very difficult to find effective control, then serious risk arises of acquitting many whose contributions were considerable – even if they did not completely dominate the behavior of other participants. If the law makes it easy to show sufficient control, however, then it risks classifying too many as superiors, when their contributions were little different from those of many around them, including those of inferior rank. Often the nominal commander greatly influences the behavior of others without completely controlling it, and the law should reflect as much. This is especially true when the superior offers them positive incentives rather than threatening punishment, as by tacitly authorizing – but not ordering – looting and pillage.[20]

The first of these twin dangers is reflected in a failed lawsuit against two Salvadoran generals. The officers were accused of permitting subordinates to torture and murder four foreign churchwomen during that country's civil war.[21] But in finding the officers not liable, the jury was unconvinced that the officers had "effective command" over the subordinates who killed the victims. In the judge's words, the jurors were not ultimately satisfied that the officers had been shown to have "the practical ability to exert control" over the troops.

Control over subordinates can be highly fluid. It may ebb and flow over time, between one location and another, depending on many factors, such as the degree to which combat with adversaries disrupts lines of authority and communication. Japanese General Tomoburni Yamashita made this claim when prosecuted for war crimes by the International Military Tribunal for the Far East.[22] U.S Supreme Court Justices Murphy and Rutledge were persuaded and so dissented from the U.S. Supreme Court's decision confirming his execution.[23] Historians today generally agree that

---

[19] Some contend that this either/or character of liability is unnecessary: All serious offenses might be statutorily "graded" (i.e., graduated in a more elaborate way than the simple differentiation between felony and misdemeanour). Paul H. Robinson & John M. Darley, *Justice, Liability, and Blame* 197–8 (1995). This would allow formal distinctions in the degree of wrongfulness to be made at the liability stage of the proceeding.

[20] On such incentives, see Mark J. Osiel, *Obeying Orders: Atrocity, Military Discipline, and the Law of War* 155–6, 234–5 (1999).

[21] Ford, op. cit., at 1286–7, 1296; see also Susan Benesch, *Salvadoran Generals on Trial: Command Responsibility in a Florida Courtroom* (Crimes of War Project, Washington, D.C.), Aug. 29, 2002 (quoting the jury foreman on the grounds for the jury's decision to acquit). This suit was brought under the Torture Victims Protection Act.

[22] *Yamashita v. Styer*, 327 U.S. 1, 32–3 (1946).

[23] Id. at 35 (Murphy dissenting), 50–1 (Rutledge dissenting).

communication lines were indeed disrupted and that Yamashita, therefore, was, in fact, innocent.[24]

If the law insists that the power of such men be continuously very great over the entire period of subordinate criminal activity, it becomes extremely difficult to supply the necessary evidence. Such evidentiary burdens largely explain why superior responsibility has fallen into such disfavor at the ICTY.[25] Moreover, if power entails the ability to induce others to do something they would not otherwise do, as leading political scientists long argued,[26] then it could not be said that Serbian leaders in Belgrade, for instance, exercised power over local militias and criminal gangs: In many cases, they would have gladly looted and tormented their neighbors of differing ethnicity without any commands from above. Because effective control resides within a particular person – the defendant as superior – the law here adopts a conception of power at odds with postmodern theories, which locate power not in persons but in the professional discourses and "actuarial" practices they are authorized to deploy. Postmodern views of power are therefore irrelevant to the legal assessment of superior-subordinate relations within a military. They offer answers to an entirely different set of questions.

If such theories were relevant here, their implications would be exculpatory for the superior, or at least highly mitigating. Invoking Foucault, a sophisticated defense counsel like Jacques Vergès (attorney for several leading war criminals) would seek to minimize his client's effective control over criminal subordinates compared to more diffuse sources of power over

---

[24] Geoffrey Robertson, "Keynote Address at Cornell Int'l Law Journal Symposium: Milosevic and Hussein on Trial" (Feb. 25, 2005).

[25] E. van Sliedregt, *The Criminal Responsibility of Individuals for Violations of International Humanitarian Law* 364 (2003) (noting that "the role superior responsibility used to play" has been partially supplanted by enterprise participation, which "has become the concept *par excellence* on which to base the criminal responsibility of senior military and political figures"). Also significant here, to be sure, has been the ICTY's increasingly stringent view of *mens rea* requirements, demanding that prosecutors show the defendant received information putting him on actual notice of a developing problem concerning his subordinates' adherence to humanitarian law. *Blaškić* Appeal ¶ 407. But this change occurred only in May 2004, long after the tribunal had begun decreasing its reliance on superior responsibility.

[26] See, e.g., Robert A. Dahl, "The Concept of Power," in *Political Power: A Reader in Theory and Research* 79, 80 (Roderick Bell et al., eds., 1969). Of course, Serbian leaders did possess the pertinent power, on only a slightly different conception of it, insofar as they could have prevented such militias and hooligans from committing these offenses had they made clear that such conduct would be punished. Still, proving the unexercised power to prevent wrong is not easy. "Power is generally demonstrated by its use: proving the existence of unused power is like measuring an electrical current without plugging anything into it." Benesch, op. cit.

them, especially the stringent discipline and intrusive supervision under-
gone in boot camp and barracks. For Foucault, these quotidian practices of
surveillance and self-monitoring are what make effective the other sources
of control over modern soldiers, such as formal commands from sovereign
superiors.[27]

Chains of command often prove more complex than the organizational
chart depicts them because a subordinate may answer to one superior
on certain matters and to another on different issues. The jurisdiction of
two agencies may also overlap – perhaps deliberately so, to encourage their
competition for approval and resources from above. This complexity means,
however, that each superior will be able to point to another in a different
agency who exercised similar responsibility over the criminal subordinate,
but who may not be criminally charged. Defendants routinely call such
ambiguities to the court's attention.[28]

Tracing lines of authority, even in *de jure* terms, has hence proven no easy
matter at the ICTY, as when General Radislav Krstić argued that General
Ratko Mladić had created a separate chain of command that went around
him.[29] In the *Kvočka* trial, the tribunal acquitted the deputy commander
and a shift leader of police guards at the infamous Omarska camp because
there proved to be multiple lines of authority in the camp, and interro-
gations involving torture and murder were not performed by police who
reported to the defendants.[30] Moreover, the crimes committed by those
answering to them were so spontaneous, disorganized, and chaotic that
these guards seemed to have "acted without accountability."[31] Similarly,
the Appeal Chamber acquitted General Tihomir Blaškić of murders and
other crimes in the village of Ahmići on the grounds that, although he did
sometimes issue orders to the police and paramilitary units in question, at
the time of the massacre their members were under the command of Rajic
Kordić and did not recognize Blaškić's authority.[32]

---

[27] Michel Foucault, *Discipline and Punish* 162–70 (Alan Sheridan trans., 1979).

[28] Several major Japanese defendants employed such arguments in trials after World
War II. David Cohen, "The Legacy of Nuremberg: Models of Command Responsibility" 6–9 (2003) (manuscript). Several prominent German defendants did so as well.

[29] John Hagan, *Justice in the Balkans: Prosecuting War Crimes in The Hague Tribunal* 156, 168
(2003).

[30] *Prosecutor v. Kvočka et al.*, Case No. IT-98-30/1-T, Judgment, ¶¶ 410–12 (Nov. 2, 2001).

[31] Id. ¶ 411. The character of the violence suggested, in other words, that such guards were
not a disciplined force acknowledging Kvočka as commander over them. There was no
evidence, however, that the defendants had tried thereafter to punish the crimes of those
reporting to them. Id. *passim*.

[32] *Blaškić* Appeal, ¶¶ 382–400.

The concept of control may be misleading here in that it ultimately involves a normative question, not a mechanical one, about how much power it is reasonable to expect seniors to exercise over juniors in a given circumstance. The concept should be approached in light of the fact that influence between the two flows in both directions. If a commander's orders are to be obeyed, he must necessarily consider his troops' morale and matériel when determining the degree of hardship these commands may impose. The danger that a difficult order cannot or will not be obeyed, with all the implications such failure may have for future obedience, is omnipresent in the mind of every competent commander, who must therefore make a host of subtle determinations before issuing it. Such subtleties are essential to legal judgment about whether a given commander had sufficient control at a particular moment to prevent his subordinates' wrongdoing.

EFFECTIVE CONTROL AND CAUSATION

The law remains unclear on whether the superior's culpable omission must have caused the inferiors' acts or even significantly contributed to them in order to hold him or her liable. "Dereliction of duty," in failing to supervise subordinates in a responsible manner, and failing to report (a subordinate's) wrongs are both criminal offenses in most national military codes. Neither of these allegations implies that the superior's misconduct caused the inferior's wrongdoing. Neither offense is nearly so grievous, however, as those currently within the jurisdiction of international criminal courts – chiefly, genocide, crimes against humanity, and war crimes.

The ICC Statute provision on superior responsibility does appear to demand proof of causation in requiring that the crime occur "as a result of [the defendant's] failure to exercise control properly over such forces."[33] Such a requirement would mean that prosecutors must show that, but for

---

[33] Rome Statute, Art. 28(a). The ICTY Trial Chamber, however, has been less than pellucid about whether causation must be shown. This is not to say that, conceptually, the principle of causality is without application to the doctrine of superior responsibility insofar as it relates to the responsibility of superiors for their failure to prevent the crimes of their subordinates. In fact, a recognition of a necessary causal nexus may be considered to be inherent in the requirement of crimes committed by subordinates and the superior's failure to take the measures within his powers to prevent them. In this situation, the superior may be considered to be causally linked to the offences, in that, but for his failure to fulfill his duty to act, the acts of his subordinates would not have been committed. *Prosecutor v. Delalić et al.*, Case No. IT-96-21-T, Judgment, ¶ 399 (Nov. 16, 1998); see also *Čelebići* Appeal ¶¶ 732–42. U.S. federal courts have rejected a causation requirement. *Ford ex rel. Estate of Ford v. Garcia*, 289 F.3d 1283, 1298–9 (11th Cir. 2002) (Barkett, J., concurring); *Hilao v. Estate of Marcos*, 103 F.3d 767, 776–9 (9th Cir. 1996). Nonetheless, most international precedent

the superior's misconduct, the subordinates would not have committed their criminal acts.

Proving that B would not have acted wrongly had A acted rightly is sometimes easy, albeit circumstantially, even in proverbial the "fog of war." Prosecutors of Argentina's military juntas, for instance, had no difficulty establishing that the country's "mysterious" disappearances stopped on a dime – exactly when the junta itself publicly declared victory in its "dirty war" against subversion.[34] Because the military's underground mischief never ran operationally afoul of its above-ground police operations and investigations, it was fair to infer that the two were well coordinated, suggesting centralized control.[35] That Gen. William Tecumseh Sherman could prevent virtually all rape and murder of civilians by his troops, while they nonetheless inflicted enormous property damage across Georgia, strongly indicates his great influence over them – and inculpates him in their crimes. For if he had enough power over his men to stop them from committing certain crimes, he could have prevented them from committing the others. Applying such inferential reasoning, one could easily adduce further examples from throughout military history.

Often, however, it is considerably harder to show the relevant variety of centralized control. Sometimes this is because of the fungibility of operatives in a large organization, even at very high levels.[36] If *this* superior officer had not misbehaved, very often someone else would have done so in his place or simply farther down the chain of command, producing the same criminal conduct from inferiors.[37] Eichmann's defense counsel employed this very argument, with considerable persuasiveness to many.[38]

and scholarly literature on the matter endorses such a requirement. Guénaël Mettraux, *International Crimes and the ad hoc Tribunals* 309–10 (2005) (reaching this conclusion by analyzing multiple authorities).

[34] For discussion, see Héctor Olásolo & Ana Pérez Cepeda, "The Notion of Control of the Crime and its Application by the ICTY in the Stakić Case," 4 Int'l Crim. L. Rev. 475, 495 (2004) (discussing the relevant Argentine jurisprudence).

[35] Id. at 496.

[36] Jon Elster, *Closing the Books: Transitional Justice in Historical Perspective* 143–5 (2004).

[37] Joachim Vogel, "How to Determine Individual Criminal Responsibility in Systemic Contexts: Twelve Models," Remarks at the Proceedings of the XIVth International Congress on Social Defence: Social Defence and Criminal Law for the Protection of Coming Generations, in View of the New Risks. 151 (May 17–19, 2002), reprinted in *Cahiers de Défense Sociale*, Société Internationale de Défense Sociale pour une Politique Criminelle Humaniste (observing that it is "hardly compatible with the causality concept of 'condicio *sine qua non*'" to hold someone liable when he would "have [been] probably or even certainly replaced by another person willing and capable to commit the offence").

[38] Matilde Bruera, "Autoría y Dominio de la Voluntad a Través de los Aparatos Organizados de Poder," in *Nuevas Formulaciones en las Ciencias Penales* 259, 261 (Carlos Julio Lascano, ed., 2001).

Some authoritarian regimes, particularly military juntas in South America, have been so fully institutionalized that even the head of state was merely *primus inter pares*.[39] In Argentina, for instance, junta members were appointed and retired in a routine, predictable way over several years. There, the notional leader was in no more position to call off "his" forces than Osama bin Laden could have called an end to Islamist terror.[40] He could credibly claim that, had he sought to do more, little would have turned out differently.[41] Sometimes an entire group of top leaders can make this same contention, in situations in which intermediate ranks below them exercised great influence in interpreting and implementing central policy. This has apparently occurred during certain revolutions, such as the Cambodian.[42]

The intermediaries then predictably respond – often credibly – that they neither initiated nor committed the violent acts and could not have prevented their occurrence. This was argued, for instance, by Ernst von Weizsäcker, second in command at the German Foreign Ministry.[43] General Herman Hoth, who commanded Panzer Group 3, similarly defended himself on the grounds that, although he had received the notorious "Commissar Order," he simply passed it on to units under his command without comment or endorsement.[44]

In such cases, one might seek to finesse the question of causation, shifting instead to statistical risk assessment.[45] This would require gauging how

[39] Such regimes have often been described as "bureaucratic authoritarian," in contrast with so-called personalist or sultanist authoritarianism. Guillermo O'Donnell, *Bureaucratic Authoritarianism: Argentina, 1966–1973, in Comparative Perspective*, 31–3, 194 (James McGuire and Rae Flory trans., 1988).

[40] On the doctrine of leaderless resistance within religious terrorist organizations, see Jessica Stern, *Terror in the Name of God* 150–1 (2003).

[41] These cases must be distinguished from those in which a single ruler monopolizes power, such that little of political significance can occur without his consent. Four of the twentieth century's largest mass killings, in particular, probably would not have occurred (or been nearly so extensive) but for the wishes of a single man: Hitler's Germany, Stalin's Russia, Mao's China, and (more debatably) Pol Pot's Cambodia. Benjamin Valentino, *Final Solutions: Mass Killing and Genocide in the Twentieth Century* 61–2, 234 (2004).

[42] Serge Thion, "The Cambodian Idea of Revolution," in *Revolution and its Aftermath in Kampuchea* 10, 28 (David P. Chandler & Ben Kiernan, eds., 1983) (contending that power was concentrated at a regional rather than central level of government). But see Anthony Barnett, "Democratic Kampuchea: A Highly Centralized Dictatorship," in *Revolution and its Aftermath in Kampuchea*, id. at 212, 216 (maintaining the contrary).

[43] David Cohen, "Bureaucracy, Justice, and Collective Responsibility in the World War II War Crimes Trials," 18 Rechtshistorisches J. 313, 329 (1999).

[44] David Cohen, "Beyond Nuremberg: Individual Responsibility for War Crimes," in *Human Rights in Political Transitions*, 53, 81–2 (Robert Post & Carla Hesse, eds., 1999).

[45] The ICTR has sometimes done this, as when writing that a commander "must have contributed to, or have had an effect on, the commission of the crime." *Prosecutor v. Kayishema & Ruzindana*, Case No. ICTR-95-1-T, Judgment, ¶ 199 (May 21, 1999).

much the superior's malfeasance increased the probability of wrongdoing by his subordinates.[46] But this approach does not help much, for the degree of risk created may still be no greater than that generated by anyone else who would have occupied the defendant's position.

Proving causation is further complicated by the need to do so by omission.[47] Doing so is difficult enough in any context, as it requires both a duty to act and the unexercised capacity to do so in a way that would have prevented the harm. The second of these requirements can be particularly difficult to fulfill in the military context because of the uncertainties of cause and effect on the battlefield during war.

The only plausibly satisfactory solution to the causation conundrum is that reached most recently by the ICC[48]: that the presence of the defendant himself, as an individual, need not have been essential, given how the crime was carried out, only his function or role, e.g., serving as lookout, hitman, or intellectual architect. There may be some doubt about just how the defendant's function should be understood and its scope precisely defined. But these are quibbles at the margins, on the disputed facts of particular cases. The fact that certain other people may have been able to fill his shoes poses no significant obstacle to his conviction. In fact, the fungibility of subordinates, at least, will often contribute to the case against their superior, as is seen in Chapter 5. In any event, no one has suggested that this doctrinal resolution is inconsistent with liberal principles of individual responsibility on which criminal law rests.

THE LIMITS OF SUPERIOR RESPONSIBILITY:
NETWORKS OF INFORMAL ALLIANCE

Mass atrocity often occurs through organizational forms that escape the conceptual clutches of superior responsibility as currently conceived. The

---

[46] On this view, it should be enough for liability that the superior knows his order will create a high probability of wrongdoing by subordinates and that their intervening voluntary acts will thereby cause great harm.

[47] George P. Fletcher, *Rethinking Criminal Law* 582, 611–34 (1978). It is by no means clear that, as a more general matter, international law accepts the possibility of criminal guilt through "commission by omission." Michale Duttwiler, "Liability for Omission in International Law," 6 Int'l Crim. L. Rev. 1 (2006).

[48] *Prosecutor v. Thomas Lubanga Dyilo*, ICC-01/04-01/06, Pre-Trial Chamber I, Decision on the Confirmation of Charges, ¶¶ 332 (January 29, 2007), at http://www.icc-cpi.int/library/cases/ICC-01-04-01-06-803-tEN_English.pdf; *Prosecutor v. Germain Katanga and Mathieu Ngudjolo Chui*, ICC-01/04-01/07, Pre-Trial Chamber I, Decision on the Confirmation of Charges, September 30, 2008, ¶¶ 485, at http://www.icc-cpi.int/library/cases/ICC-01-04-01-07-717-ENG.pdf.

doctrine is simply defeated by the absence of thorough subordination, despite intimate collaboration and deep mutual reliance among parties to atrocity. Even when one organization effectively controls another, the fact or extent of such control can often easily be concealed in ways that make superior responsibility unavailable.

One way to conceal control is to structure the relevant relationship as what economists call a quasi-firm or interfirm network. This is a relationship, common in certain industries, whereby companies contract with one another so regularly and on such consistent terms that their formally separate status becomes functionally irrelevant.[49] They interact neither through an arm's-length exchange in a competitive market nor by formal subordination to a single bureaucratic center.

Organizations that cooperate in mass atrocity, like other quasi-firms, might similarly preserve their legal separation precisely to limit the vicarious liability of each for harm they anticipate will be legally ascribed to a related party. In particular, a mainstream organization seeking major social and legal change might publicly offer inspiration – through its Web site, promotional literature, open meetings, and litigation efforts – to others embracing a more radical interpretation of the same general program.

Sometimes both groups take the shape of formal, lawful organizations, but only the moderate wing might be legally incorporated and possess any publicly visible presence, such as rented offices and mailing lists. The mainstream and the underground group may originate in a single social movement. The visible organization may be the avowedly political expression of this movement, whereas its clandestine cousin may describe itself as the military wing. The former disavows any responsibility for the latter's violent actions. This was the official relationship for many years between Sinn Féin and the Irish Republican Army (IRA), for instance.[50]

In a different configuration, the movement's public branch may contrast its confessedly radical nature to the merely charitable, educational, or religious character of its opposite number. With this characterization, the latter body can often enjoy favorable tax treatment. The entity describing itself as political draws away public opprobrium, whereas its more dignified partner enjoys the public accolades generally accorded educational and religious

---

[49] Mark Ebers, "Explaining Inter-Organizational Network Formation," in *The Formation of Inter-Organizational Networks* 3, 5–15 (Mark Ebers, ed., 1997). Another advantage, to be sure, is that the resulting informality impedes legal characterization of any given unit as effectively controlled by another.

[50] Brian Feeney, *Sinn Féin* 14, 197, 203–8 (2002).

entities. In fact, the educational institution may clandestinely preach violence as part of its pedagogy, rendering it functionally equivalent to its more
radical partner.

This is reportedly the arrangement between certain Islamist mullahs and
mosques in the Arab world and the educational foundations they establish to teach the Koran through instruction within madrassas.[51] In such
cases, however, the educational and professedly nonpolitical entity does not
remain underground, for it does not publicly admit to advocating violence.
In practice, nonetheless, the two organizations may often be inextricable,
with one fully controlling the other.[52]

In these several situations, the two organizations do a dissimulative dance,
ensuring that evidence of control entirely escapes all possibility of prosecutorial demonstration. The practical effect of such opaqueness – which both
groups struggle mightily to maintain – is to preclude the use of superior
responsibility against those who may effectively control the policymaking
and planning of mass atrocity. Formal separation, secrecy about actual
cooperation, and a public posture of dissociation from unlawful methods
employed by the more radical partner combine to make it impossible, as a
practical matter, to hold responsible parties liable as superiors. It takes little
by way of maneuver in managerial behavior, or machination in organizational design, to accomplish this result.

Superior responsibility becomes even less useful when the extent of real
control actually is diminished, such as when the relationship becomes one
of mutual, though still asymmetrical, influence – some of which may be
deliberate and some unintended. Such nuances in power relations elude
the doctrine's conceptual crudities, which insist on classifying all parties as
either fully controlling or controlled. Influence admits of subtle patterns
and permutations, however, evading so blunt an intellectual instrument.
As the ICTY Appeals Chamber concludes, "Substantial influence as a means
of control in any sense which falls short of possession of effective control
over subordinates" does not support liability under this approach.[53] Hence

---

[51] Rick Bragg, "Shaping Young Islamic Hearts and Hatreds," N.Y. Times, Oct. 14, 2001, at
A1. Bookstores and university student societies also form part of such networks. Amy
Waldman, "Seething Unease Shaped British Bombers' Newfound Zeal," N.Y. Times, July
31, 2005, at A1.

[52] For instance, the Communist Party of the United States of America controlled many front
organizations for several decades. *The Soviet World of American Communism* 109–10, 141–2
(Harvey Klehr et al., eds., 1998).

[53] *Čelebići* Appeal, ¶ 266; Mettraux, op. cit., at 300.

there is the real danger that, without some doctrinal alternative, high-level perpetrators might easily slip between the law's conceptual cracks.

The response to this danger, however, has been to take a novel tack that readily succumbs to the opposite danger: extending liability to anyone remotely associated with the "purposes" of responsible parties.

3

Participating in a Criminal Enterprise

The preceding chapter uncovered several major problems with employing the law of superior responsibility, in the aftermath of mass atrocity, to ascribe the acts of the lowest echelons to leaders like Milošević, Pinochet, and Saddam Hussein. As of 2008, only one ICTY defendant, Pavle Strugar, had been convicted solely on the basis of superior responsibility, and he was sentenced to only eight years' imprisonment.[1]

Confronted with such obstacles, international prosecutors began to show great affinity for indicting defendants instead as "participants in a joint criminal enterprise." This approach has been favored even when the accused clearly exercised a formal position of command. Of the indictments entered since judicial acceptance of this doctrine in 2001, nearly 65 percent rely on it.[2] In fact, after 2004, the ICTY no longer proceeded at all with an analysis

---

[1] *Prosecutor v. Strugar*, Case No. IT-01-42-T, Decision on Defence Motion Requesting Judgment of Acquittal Pursuant to Rule 98bis, ¶ 481 (Jan. 31, 2005).

[2] Allison Marston Danner & Jenny S. Martinez, "Guilty Associations: Joint Criminal Enterprise, Command Responsibility, and the Development of International Criminal Law," 93 Cal. L. Rev. 75, 107 (2005) (describing this doctrine as "the method of choice for targeting senior military and political leaders"). It also has been widely used against the lower echelons, however, as in the *Kvočka* Trial. Helpful recent discussions of joint criminal enterprise include Jens David Ohlin, "Three Conceptual Problems with the Doctrine of Joint Criminal Enterprise," 5 J. Int'l Crim. J. 69 (2007); Harmen van der Wilt, "Joint Criminal Enterprise: Possibilities and Limitations," J. Int'l Crim. J. 92 (2007); Antonio Cassese, "The Proper Limits of Individual Responsibility under the Doctrine of Joint Criminal Enterprise," 5 J. Int'l Crim. J. 109 (2007); Katrina Gustafson "The Requirement of an 'Express Agreement' for Joint Criminal Enterprise Liability: A Critique of Brdanin," 5 J. Int'l Crim. J. 134 (2007); Kai Ambos, "Joint Criminal Enterprise and Command Responsibility," 5 J. Int'l Crim. J. 159 (2007); Elies van Sliedregt, "Joint Criminal Enterprise as a Pathway to Convicting Individuals for Genocide," 5 J. Int'l Crim. J. 184 (2007); Kai Hamdorf, "The Concept of a Joint Criminal Enterprise and Domestic Modes of Liability for Parties to a Crime: A Comparison of British and English Law," 5 J. Int'l Crim. J. 208 (2007);

of superior responsibility once it found the defendant liable under at least one form of "commission," such as enterprise participation.

This shift has been attributed to the simple fact that the term "joint criminal enterprise" sounds "more serious" than the alternatives[3] and hence more seriously stigmatizes its perpetrators than does simply labeling them irresponsible superiors. It thereby advances the didactic aims of transitional justice, embraced by their democratic successors, it is said. But the political pressures of transitional justice cannot ultimately explain the shift in legal approach to linking big fish to small fry.

To be sure, transitional leadership will prefer a prosecutorial strategy mirroring its own view of how the wrongs of prior despots should be described and circumscribed. But such leaders do not have any influence on how prosecutors in The Hague couch their indictments. International prosecutors face incentives quite distinct from national counterparts in this regard, which lead their legal arguments in different directions. A more parsimonious explanation of the doctrinal shift would be that prosecutors simply discovered a colossal obstacle – proving "effective control" – to convicting almost anyone on the basis of culpable omission in the exercise of command.[4] This failure left them "desperate," they reported,[5] and joint criminal enterprise thereafter became their "darling," in the words of one former prosecutor.[6]

In endorsing this alternative approach, the ICTY has found that a joint criminal enterprise consists of "an understanding or arrangement amounting to an agreement between two or more persons that they will commit a crime."[7] The essential idea is simple enough. As ICTY Judge Mohamed Shabuddeen wrote in one case:

Mohamed E. Badar, "'Just Convict Everyone!" – Joint Perpetration: From *Tadić* to *Stakić* and Back Again,' 6 Int'l Crim. L. Rev. 293 (2006).

[3] Danner & Martinez, op. cit., at 145 (arguing that the enterprise approach "allows the prosecution and judges to capture the seriousness of a leader's responsibility for the violent course of events").

[4] The most recent, significant prosecutorial failure in this regard at the ICTY is *Prosecutor v. Naser Orić*, Case No. IT-03-68-A, Judgment, ¶¶ 24, 60–1, 700–07 (July 3, 2008) (acquitting defendant due to lack of control over events at Srebrenica and lack of evidence that the accused had knowledge or reason to know these subordinates had engaged in crime or were about to do so).

[5] July 2005 Interview.

[6] Andrew Cayley, barrister Q.C., former Senior Prosecuting Counsel at the ICTY and ICC, currently defense counsel to several defendants before international criminal tribunals. Conference presentation at International Criminal Justice and the Military, Norwegian Red Cross, Oslo, Sept. 2008.

[7] *Prosecutor v. Krnojelac*, IT-97-25-T, Judgment, ¶ 80 (Mar. 15, 2002).

One party to such an enterprise is not acting as the agent of another – at least not in the ordinary sense. All the parties are acting together to achieve an agreed result. In acting together, they are really acting as one. On this basis, the acts of each are the acts of all.[8]

This basic notion is indeed simple, but deceptively so, as we will see.

The ICC Rome Statute refines the definition somewhat to encompass the defendant who

> in any . . . way contributes to the commission . . . of . . . a crime by a group of persons acting with a common purpose. Such contribution shall be intentional and shall either: (i) Be made with the aim of furthering the criminal activity or criminal purpose of the group . . . or (ii) Be made in the knowledge of the intention of the group to commit the crime.[9]

The common purpose need not be criminal in itself, according to the Special Court for Sierra Leone, as long as the agreed-on means to that end are so. "Taking over the country" is not an inherently criminal purpose, for instance. But if participants understand (or foresee) that the methods adopted for so doing will include war crimes and crimes against humanity, then a joint criminal enterprise would exist, the Special Court found.[10]

One becomes liable for the criminal acts of other participants, in other words, through the link established by the enterprise. Leading European legal thinkers have seen this as tantamount to the civil law doctrine of co-participation.[11] Some take comfort in this approximation of a still-controversial and arguably novel doctrine to long-settled principles of European law. Yet an early ICC decision casts serious doubt on this stance, holding that, to be characterized as a co-perpetrator (accountable for the acts of all other perpetrators), a person must have assumed an "essential" part of the common plan, such that the plan would fail if he or she withheld participation.[12]

---

[8] *Prosecutor v. Vasiljević*, Case No. IT-98-32-A, Appeals Chamber, ¶ 31 (Feb. 25, 2004) (dissenting opinion of Judge Shabuddeen, but not dissenting on this point).

[9] Rome Statute of the International Criminal Court, Art. 25(3)(d).

[10] *Prosecutor v. Alex Tamba Brima, Brima Bazzy Kamara, Santigie Borbor Kanu*, Case No. SCSL-2004-16-A, Judgment, ¶ 79 (Feb. 22, 2008).

[11] Ambos, op. cit, at 160.

[12] Decision on Confirmation of Charges, *Prosecutor v. Thomas Lubanga Dyilo*, PTC I, (ICC 01/04–01/06), ¶¶ 332, 342, 347 (Jan. 29, 2007). This view, that the accused's contribution must have been indispensable for him to be treated as a co-perpetrator, is by no means universally shared in the tradition of German legal thought on which the ICC Pre-Trial Chamber here relies. Thomas Weigent, "Intent, Mistake of Law, and Co-Perpetration in the *Lubango* Decision on Confirmation of Charges," 6 J. Int'l Crim. Justice 471, 479–80 (2008) (reviewing contrary answers to this question offered by several leading German sources).

Participation in a joint criminal enterprise may take three forms. The first involves shared intent to bring about a certain offense, manifested in an agreement with others and reflected in a common design.[13] This form of enterprise closely resembles the common law of conspiracy, except that it is not a separate offense but rather a method by which offenses are committed.[14]

The second form of enterprise, which some see as really a subset of the first, concerns "organized systems of repression and ill treatment" – specifically, death or detention camps. As with the ICTY cases, in the postwar German convictions (analyzed in the *Tadić* Appeal) of very low-level accessories, "all of the defendants were present or in the immediate vicinity of the murders, and none of the defendants was charged with participation in some larger plan outside of the unlawful treatment of the prisoners involved."[15] American Stephen Rapp, Chief Prosecutor of the Special Court for Sierra Leone, has gone so far as to venture that the U.S. detainee camp at Guantánamo might meet the legal criteria for such a criminal "system of . . . ill-treatment."[16]

In truly repressive societies, however, the "organized system" in question could plausibly be defined in much broader terms. It might be defined functionally, for instance, rather than spatially and geographically. Hence, all concentration camps – throughout the entire area under Serbian control – might be said to have constituted "the system," just as prosecutors in postwar trials so classified all German hospitals employed in Nazi medical experimentation.[17] So, too, the German national judiciary was treated in one major postwar prosecution as "a nation wide government-organized system of cruelty and injustice, . . . perpetrated . . . by the authority of the Ministry of Justice, and through the instrumentality of the courts."[18]

With each broader definition of "the system" in question, the scope of a defendant's crimes would enlarge. Defining the scope of the relevant system thus has momentous consequences for any defendant who can be found to

---

[13] *Tadić* Appeal, ¶ 196.

[14] *Prosecutor v. Milutinović et al.*, Case No. IT-99-37-AR72, Decision on Dragoljub Ojdanić's Motion Challenging Jurisdiction – Joint Criminal Enterprise, ¶ 23 (May 21, 2003). The ICTY Statute adopts conspiracy only in connection with genocide, not war crimes or crimes against humanity. ICTY Statute, art. 4(3)(b).

[15] *Tadić* Appeal, ¶ 202. Danner & Martinez, op. cit., at 111.

[16] Stephen Rapp, Chief Prosecutor, Special Court for Sierra Leone, talk to students and faculty, College of Law, Univ. of Iowa, April 2008.

[17] Paul Julian Weindling, *Nazi Medicine and the Nuremberg Trials: From Medical War Crimes to Informed Consent* 66, 299 (2004).

[18] 3 Trials of War Criminals Before the Nuremberg Military Tribunals Under Control Council Law No. 10, at 985 (1951).

have participated in it. Apart from reasons of (Nuremberg) precedent, the ICTY has offered no particular reason, however, for defining the pertinent system as it has. The question is especially puzzling in light of the fact that prosecutors need not establish that there was regular, face-to-face interaction among all members of a putative system. And those working within a given encampment generally understand it to be part of a larger system, coordinated with other such camps, administered by a common authority. The law thus currently offers no coherent account of why the scale of the repressive "system" should be defined broadly or narrowly.

The final type of participation involves criminal acts beyond the common design, but "a natural and foreseeable consequence of effecting it."[19] This form resembles U.S. rules on *Pinkerton* conspiracies[20] and felony murder[21] and is therefore the most controversial expression of the doctrine.[22] But it is also the only ready means to reach certain forms of mass atrocity. It is surely the easiest way to reach, for instance, the abduction (and ensuing adoption) of infants from victims of Argentina's death squads. The junta defendants acquiescing in the abduction of the parents did not order (nor initially authorize) the unlawful adoption by junior officers of the victims' young children. But the defendants' reasonable reflection on their criminal plan would surely have led them to anticipate this possibility.[23]

The rationale for extending criminal liability this far is that, when one joins a group committed to criminal ends, one knows in advance that one will not be able fully to control the conduct of all other members

---

[19] *Tadić* Appeal, ¶¶ 204, 206.

[20] *Pinkerton v. United States*, 328 U.S. 640, 647–8 (1946).

[21] The felony murder rule makes any participant in a dangerous felony liable for murder caused by another. Richard J. Bonnie et al., *Criminal Law* 855–95 (2d, ed. 2004).

[22] Some have charged that this form of enterprise participation effectively lowers the requisite mental state for certain offenses from intent or knowledge to mere negligence. But the ICTY Appeals Chamber has clarified, in the *Brdanin* case, that foreseeability pertains only to the defendant's "mode of liability." The prosecution must also establish the *mens rea* for the given offense itself – specific intent, for instance, in the case of genocide. Hence, no one may negligently commit genocide, even though acting through a type-three enterprise.

The U.S. Model Penal Code rejects the *Pinkerton* doctrine of liability for the reasonably foreseeable crimes of co-conspirators. See Model Penal Code § 210.2 (1962). So do other countries. See, e.g., Marco Sassòli & Laura M. Olson, "The Judgment of the ICTY Appeals Chamber on the Merits in the Tadić Case," 82 Int'l Rev. Red Cross 733, 749 (2000) (documenting that Holland, Switzerland, Germany, and other countries exclude *Pinkerton*-type liability from their criminal law); Edward M. Wise, "RICO and its Analogues: Some Comparative Considerations," 27 Syracuse J. Int'l L. & Com. 303, 312 (2000) (noting that no civil law country employs *Pinkerton*-type liability).

[23] Marcelo A. Sancinetti & Marcelo Ferrante, *El Derecho Penal en la Protección de los Derechos Humanos* 165–6 (José Luis Depalma, ed., 1999).

at all times and that their conduct may not remain entirely within the bounds of the purposes to which other members have agreed. In joining such a group, one recognizes that other members will have agendas of their own and that such agendas are likely to be pursued, especially insofar as they are not incompatible with the group's own. One knows all this because of the number of people involved and because of the measure of autonomy that members will necessarily be able to exercise at certain points in the realization of the group's "common purpose." All this entails a complex web of mutual awareness among individuals, encompassing the knowledge that some but not all of their purposes will be shared and a measure of indulgence that individual members may simultaneously pursue nongroup purposes insofar as these actions do not obstruct those of the group as a whole. Most simply put, the accused was aware of and accepted the risk that other members would commit criminal acts beyond the scope of the particular purpose shared with them.[24] In this way, the "criminal enterprise" may be defined in terms somewhat broader than the "common purpose" to which its members all subscribe.

To admit the conceptual possibility of this scenario requires no recourse to organicist notions of "group mind," such as "that crowds obliterate individuality and develop minds of their own."[25] Neither does it entail, at the other extreme, a hyper-individualization of mental states; there need be no infinite regress of the sort, "I believe that you believe that I believe that you believe that I believe . . ." we share a purpose of, say, ethnic cleansing. Rather, the doctrine implicitly accepts an intermediate view, suggested by John Searle in another context:

> Individual agents can have in their individual heads intentionality of the form "we intend," "we hope," and so on. . . . The requirement that all intentionality be in the heads of individual agents, a requirement that is sometimes called "methodological individualism," does not require that all intentionality be expressed in the first-person singular.[26]

Consider an example from one case before the ICTY Appeals Chamber. The judges defined the relevant enterprise in terms of "a common, shared

---

[24] In the civil law tradition, this mental state is described as *dolus eventualis*. In the common law world, it is usually characterized as "recklessness." There is some disagreement over how high the likelihood must be that a particular risk (which materialized) would do so. Weigent, op. cit. at 483–4 (2008) (assessing several contending answers to this question).

[25] Charles Tilly, *The Politics of Collective Violence* 18 (2003). Tilly rejects the view here quoted.

[26] John Searle, *Mind, Language, and Society: Doing Philosophy in the Real World* 119–20 (1999); see also Margaret Gilbert, *On Social Facts* 75 (1989).

intention on the part of a group to forcibly remove members of one ethnicity from their town, village or region . . . with the consequence that, in the course of doing so, one or more of the victims is shot and killed."[27] The tribunal then added that "while murder may not have been explicitly acknowledged to be part of the common design, it was nevertheless foreseeable that the forcible removal of civilians at gunpoint might well result in the deaths of one or more of those civilians." This approach to establishing the big fish-small fry link has since been adopted in several ICTY judgments.

THE ATTRACTION OF ENTERPRISE PARTICIPATION

Enterprise participation appeals to international prosecutors because of its reach beyond the formal military hierarchy to civilian bosses, such as Radovan Karadžić,[28] and paramilitaries over whom no formal command is exercised.[29] The doctrine is also valuable in reaching the many new private armies to which states increasingly subcontract military work, including combat itself.[30] The amplitude and elasticity of enterprise participation let indictments transcend the confines of an official bureaucracy to reach the informal networks connecting it to outsiders, who often exercise greater power than many within. The doctrine's appeal thus lies in its "unique ability to describe criminal arrangements too complex to fit within traditional theories of criminal liability."[31]

The person with the most power in a social network is often a broker between organizations whose members wish to have little direct contact with one another.[32] Brokers mediate between them, in a way that gives them vital information neither party could obtain about the other's activities. Such brokers sometimes occupy no formal position within either organization – unlike liaison officers, whom they superficially resemble. Brokers' ties to each organization may be quite weak. This feature contributes to their

---

[27] *Tadić* Appeal, ¶ 204.

[28] On the importance of his role, see James Gow, *The Serbian Project and Its Adversaries: A Strategy of War Crimes* 11 (2003).

[29] See, generally, Liesbeth Zegveld, *Accountability of Armed Opposition Groups in International Law* 1 (2002).

[30] On the increasing use of privately contracted soldiers, see P. W. Singer, *Corporate Warriors: The Rise of the Privatized Military Industry* 40–70 (2003).

[31] Allen O'Rourke, "Joint Criminal Enterprise and *Brdanin*: Misguided Over-Correction," 47 Harv. Int'l L.J. 307 (2006).

[32] Ronald S. Burt, *Structural Holes: The Social Structure of Competition* 30–49 (1992) (describing power available to anyone occupying such a "structural hole" within social network).

political strength, however,[33] for both entities recognize that it is the brokers' mediation that permits their advantageous interaction.[34] Where personal bonds are tight, by contrast, disagreement among group members tends to be more disruptive; so sociologists have found in studies of neighborhood groups and corporate teams.[35]

Brokers often are central to mass atrocity.[36] They provide the essential nodal point linking regular army units and the irregular militias who perpetrate the worst violence.[37] Because it permits operation through informal networks, this link enables regime rulers to deny responsibility for resulting atrocities with some plausibility, often enough to create reasonable doubt at least. An example is the central role of Arkan, a Serbian gangster, in placing at Milošević's service the "Tiger" hooligans, a group otherwise surely wishing no contact with law enforcement authorities.

The Yugoslav Army could then secure the perimeters of a Croat or Bosnian town while these irregulars terrorized its denizens – a mutually convenient division of labor. Arkan's rise to wealth and prominence followed from occupying the key node in a network unifying the formal and informal instruments of genocidal power. According to his secretary's testimony in The Hague, he was always paid in cash, and his headquarters were moved from Serbia to Croatia. Both steps aimed to create the appearance of social distance from Milošević. Still, Arkan never deployed his forces without express orders from Belgrade.[38]

Enterprise participation is further useful for prosecuting officers in staff – rather than line – positions[39] (e.g., the Main Staff of the Bosnian Serb

---

[33] Mark Granovetter, "The Strength of Weak Ties: A Network Theory Revisited," 1 Soc. Theory 201, 220–8 (1983).

[34] Evidence of such mediating ties is increasingly available to prosecutors through novel data-mining technologies. See, e.g., Douglas Jehl, "4 in 9/11 Plot are Called Tied to Qaeda in '00," N.Y. Times, Aug. 9, 2005, at A1 ("A computer analysis seeking to establish patterns in links between the four men had found that 'the software put them all together in Brooklyn.'").

[35] For an informal summary of such research, see Benedict Carey, "Close Doesn't Always Count in Winning Games," N.Y. Times, March 7, 2005, at A1.

[36] See, e.g., Marc Sageman, *Understanding Terror Networks* 168–71 (2004) (describing the role of brokers in linking friendship cliques to broader jihadist organizations).

[37] This was true, for instance, in Rwanda, where the Interahamwe and Impuzamugambi militias perpetrated a substantial share of the genocidal killing.

[38] Paul Wood, "Gangster's Life of Serb Warlord," BBC News, Jan. 15, 2000. "Arkan" was the nickname of Željko Raznatović. Other such criminal groups identified in the Milošević indictments include "Seselj's men," "Martic's Police," and the "White Eagles."

[39] Allied tribunals differed in the late 1940s over how to treat members of the German General Staff. David Cohen, "Bureaucracy, Justice, and Collective Responsibility in the World War II War Crimes Trials," 18 Rechtshistorisches J. 313, 324 (1999).

Army,[40] who provided advisory expertise and intelligence, but lacked command authority). Staff officers may powerfully influence events, as in devising a strategic plan, but typically do not have authority to issue orders.[41]

The law of enterprise participation also tells a darker story about organizational superiors than does the law of superior responsibility, for it depicts them not as simply asleep at the wheel, but as driving purposively toward disaster. In this regard, it more closely tracks the available evidence on most mass atrocities. As one expert writes of Rwanda, "You would have to look far and wide to find a person in command who did not intend to commit genocide, but who should have known it was being committed and did not take appropriate steps to prevent or punish it."[42] At such times, although the requirements of superior responsibility may technically be satisfied, that doctrine misconstrues the significance of the facts before it. It thereby tells the story in a manner quite askew, almost beside the point.

Enterprise participation also allows prosecutors to view those engaged in criminal conduct, jointly and voluntarily, as evidencing a variety of relationships that are more multifarious, although no less pernicious, than that of domination-subordination. In fact, this last sort of relationship becomes completely irrelevant to liability. Mass atrocity is often the result of a mutual connivance, in which no perpetrator thoroughly controls any other.[43] The law of enterprise participation dexterously captures this fact. After all, participants in an enterprise – lawful or otherwise – can contribute to one another's actions and advance a common purpose in many ways.

The law of superior responsibility also compelled consideration of how its original application to military officers would require reconsideration when extended to civilian leaders, like those of the Bosnian Serbs.[44] With

---

[40] See generally *Blaškić* Appeal (discussing the prosecution of an officer of the Main Staff of the Bosnian Serb Army on enterprise participation and other charges).

[41] On the role of U.S. staff officers in the abuse of detainees at Abu Ghraib, see *The Abu Ghraib Investigations* 45–6 (Steven Strasser, ed., 2004).

[42] William Schabas, Dir., Irish Ctr. for Human Rights, Nat'l Univ. of Ir., correspondence with author (July 2005).

[43] Mark Osiel, *Obeying Orders: Atrocity, Military Discipline and The Law of War* 187–93 (1999).

[44] For extensions of the doctrine to such civilians by international courts, see, e.g., *Čelebići* Appeal, ¶¶ 195–6; *Prosecutor v. Aleksovski*, Case No. IT-95-14/1-A, Judgment, ¶ 76 (Mar. 24, 2000); *Prosecutor v. Musema*, Case No. ICTR-96-13-A, Judgment and Sentence, ¶ 148 (Jan. 27, 2000). On this issue, see generally Greg R. Vetter, "Command Responsibility of Non-Military Superiors in the International Criminal Court (ICC)," 25 Yale J. Int'l L. 89 (2000). Domestic law in certain countries, including the U.S., has long extended civil and criminal liability to civilians who fail to honor their supervisory responsibilities, thereby permitting crime by subordinates. Such "responsible corporate officer" liability reaches employees within the federal government. *United States v. Park*, 421 U.S. 658, 672 (1975);

enterprise participation, however, civilians are treated no differently from military officers in that identical criteria are employed in defining each as participants. There is no conceptual obstacle to treating civilians and officers as part of the same criminal enterprise, and the ICTY Prosecutor did so in several indictments, including those against Milošević.[45]

The enterprise approach captures still other features of mass atrocity that the law of superior responsibility does not. In any effective enterprise, there is generally a climate of shared commitment to its purposes, as well as a sensation of spontaneity in serving them. This climate effaces the distinction between leaders and the led. There is an élan, a sense of "all for one and one for all." Successful leaders thus speak of striving to coordinate, not to dominate or even control. Still distinguishable, of course, are those with greater and lesser degrees of influence over events and fellow participants. But one can now draw such distinctions at the punishment stage of the proceeding, after the defendant's guilt has been established.

Because these distinctions no longer determine liability, the court does not face a question that must be answered with a yes or no. Participation admits of degrees. In fact, there is not a single continuum, but several, because each aspect of participation – duration, extent, and depth of involvement in policy formulation, transmission, and execution – could be said to establish a separate spectrum, along which individual participants might be arrayed. Making such distinctions on a rational basis is now possible because the tribunal has developed a set of factors directed to this end. These include the length of time defendants were involved, their proximity to policymaking, the indispensability of their contributions, the heinousness of their motives, and their degree of knowledge about the larger enterprise to which their actions contributed.[46] In constructing this multifactor test, the tribunal relied heavily on immediate postwar prosecutions of ordinary German soldiers, death camp guards, and employees who operated the gas chambers. The ICTY employed these cases to gauge the state of pertinent customary international law.

William Knepper & Dan Bailey, *Liability of Corporate Officers and Directors* 255 (1998); John Monroe, "Applying the Responsible Corporate Officer and Conscious Avoidance Doctrines in the Context of the Abu Ghraib Prison Scandal," 91 Iowa L. Rev. 1367, 1389 (2006).

[45] See, e.g., Bosnia Amended Milošević Indictment, ¶¶ 6–26.

[46] The facts of these cases do not always support the tribunal's application of participation doctrine, however, to situations where the criminal act was foreseeable but not within the scope of the common objective or design. Steven Powles, "Joint Criminal Enterprise: Criminal Liability by Prosecutorial Ingenuity and Judicial Creativity?," 2 J. Int'l Crim. Just. 606, 615–17 (2004).

Instead of a binary opposition – a choice between acquittal and conviction – the law thus now has a range of possibilities, permitting a more
subtle and fine-grained assessment of the relative importance of different
contributors to the harm. The distinction between perpetrators and accessories remains, and that distinction is still binary. But before using it to
classify a defendant as one or the other, a court must consider a wide range
of morally pertinent factors that the law now identifies. These factors are
legally relevant both to deciding the nature of liability – as perpetrator
versus accessory – and to deciding the proper measure of punishment.

A further appeal of enterprise participation is that fact-finders no longer
have to try to imagine what subordinates would have done differently had
their superior behaved properly. With enterprise participation, courts look
simply at what each participant actually did, rather than what he or she
did not do, but hypothetically might have done, and what difference that
might have made. Still another advantage over superior responsibility is
that enterprise participation makes it no longer essential to ascribe each
culpable contributor to a particular position with delimited responsibilities
in an organizational hierarchy.

It is also attractive to prosecutors that enterprise participation does not
demand very much in the way of any actual, working "relationship" among
members, as ordinary language understands the term. In contrast, American
courts have regularly held that, for a single conspiracy to exist, there must
have been a continuing relationship among its members, at least when their
respective crimes were disparate in nature and method, occurred at different
times and places, and were not dependent for their success on the crimes of
other members.[47]

Enterprise participation, by contrast, resembles a discredited version of
racketeering (RICO) conspiracy, according to which prosecutors did not
have to connect putative members to one another by evidence of a single
wheel or chain, because these concepts were thought to have been replaced
by that of the criminal enterprise.[48] Enterprise participation does not require
prosecutors to delineate specifically even such simple structures as wheels
and chains, much less the more complex social networks through which

[47] Model Penal Code § 5.03(3) (2002); William LaFave, *Criminal Law* § 6.5(d)(2), at 595–7 (2000).
[48] *United States v. Elliott*, 571 F.2d 880, 898 (5th Cir. 1978), cert. denied, 439 U.S. 953 (1978). This view enjoyed brief popularity in two circuits, but was ultimately rejected by all circuits. James F. Holderman, "Reconciling RICO's Conspiracy and 'Group' Enterprise Concepts with Traditional Conspiracy Doctrine," 52 U. Cin. L. Rev. 385, 402–3 (1983).

mass atrocity generally occurs. The weaker the ties necessary to link one person's contribution to another's, the easier it becomes to define both as participants in each other's endeavors.

By contrast, as the ICTY has confirmed,[49] complicity requires that the accessorial contribution of A to B's actions – as instigator or aider and abettor – has been substantial to hold A accountable for them.[50] What should count as substantial can be uncertain, to be sure, and subject to disagreement. For instance, a few U.S. jurisdictions allow that "encouragement," viewed expansively, may be sufficient to pass this test.[51] But at least the substantiality requirement bespoke an awareness of the danger that liability could potentially be stretched too far, beyond the proper scope of an individual's true culpability.[52] Enterprise participation, as developed by the ICTY, contains no such clear threshold for corralling a person into the status of participant in others' crimes.[53] It is enough that he or she participated in the putative enterprise, itself a construction of the prosecution's legal theory.

The breadth of this rule's reach permits even the most minor participant in an enterprise to be liable for the gravest offenses, offenses that necessarily heap opprobrium on anyone convicted of them. Hence it is unsatisfactory to defer issues about the degree of actual wrongdoing until after the defendant has been judged guilty of those offenses. This suggests that much of importance may be at stake in the temporal switch from analysis at the point of liability to analysis at the point of punishment. It can make little sense for prosecutors to be able essentially to tell the accused, "We will sort out the details of how seriously involved you really were after you are found guilty (of genocide, etc . . .), when we get around to choosing your punishment."

---

[49] *Blaškić* Appeal, ¶¶ 45–8.

[50] As this study later suggests, the law of complicity displays several inadequacies in prosecuting regime rulers, which explain prosecutors' preference for other legal methods.

[51] LaFave, op. cit., § 6.7(c), at 625–6.

[52] The ICTY has nonetheless held that mere presence at the crime scene can constitute aiding and abetting where it had "a significant encouraging effect on the principal offender." *Prosecutor v. Vasiljević*, Case No. IT-98-32-T, Judgment, ¶ 70 (Nov. 29, 2002); *Kvočka* Trial, ¶ 257. For criticism of the ICTY's failure to respect the limits of culpability in its few convictions for aiding and abetting, see Drumbl, *Pluralizing*, op. cit., at 1308 ("Notwithstanding its circumspection, the ICTY continues to convict [defendants] based on collective-liability theories that . . . tinker with traditional understandings of individual criminal culpability in order to suit this culpability to the special context of mass atrocity.").

[53] Danner & Martinez, op. cit., at 105–06. Two Trial Chambers, however, have required that the defendant's contributions have been "significant." *Prosecutor v. Simić et al.*, Case No. IT-95-9-T, ¶ 159 (Oct. 17, 2003); *Kvočka* Trial, op. cit., ¶¶ 309, 311.

ENTERPRISE PARTICIPATION AS *SUB ROSA* CONSPIRACY

Defense counsel at the ICTY assert that the court's creation of enterprise participation amounts to embracing Anglo-American conspiracy doctrine,[54]
even liability for "membership in a criminal organization." These two doctrines represent Nuremberg's most controversial legacy for international
law today. There, conspiracy was used *molto con brio*, eliciting "the largest
and most persistent legal controversy of the trial," notes one historian.[55] In
fact, the IMT ultimately rejected most of the conspiracy charges, confining
them to Hitler's top associates, in connection only with waging aggressive
war.[56] These convictions, moreover, played little role in sentencing. And
only eight of the twenty-two major war criminals charged with conspiracy
were convicted of this offense.[57]

Like conspiracy, liability for membership in a criminal organization was
widely condemned, even at the time, and eventually construed very narrowly
by the IMT.[58] It held that, for liability to attach to the acts of others, group
members must have recognized their contribution to a criminal purpose,
which was known to be shared by these other members. The group itself
must also have taken a form that could be described as clearly discernible
and well defined. Group membership must further have been voluntary. In
short, the fact of formal membership as such did not ultimately lead anyone
to be held liable at Nuremberg for acts by other members. As a result,
today most international lawyers believe virtually nothing of the criminal
organization charge remains good law.

Like the abandoned writs of medieval common law, however, that doctrine may rule us surreptitiously from the grave through its unacknowledged

[54] Interview with ICTY Defense Counsel, in The Hague, Neth. (Oct. 2003). In its Pinochet
rulings, the House of Lords similarly invoked conspiracy law as the basis by which the
general might be blamed for his subordinates' wrongs. *R v. Bow St. Metro. Stipendiary
Magistrate, ex parte Pinochet* (No. 3), [2000] 1 A.C. 147, 190, 235–6 (H.L. 1999) (appeal
taken from Q.B. Div'l Ct.) (U.K.). Unlike most "civil law" countries, Chile maintains this
doctrine within its criminal law. Código Penal, tit. I, art. 8 (Chile).
[55] Stanislaw Pomorski, "Conspiracy and Criminal Organization," in *The Nuremberg Trial
and International Law* 213, 229 (George Ginsburgs & V. N. Kudriavtsev, eds., 1990); see
also Richard Overy, "The Nuremberg Trials: International Law in the Making," in *From
Nuremberg to The Hague* 1, 14–22 (Philippe Sands, ed., 2003).
[56] Pomorski, op. cit., at 235.
[57] Id. The charges of conspiring to wage aggressive war and to engage in certain war crimes
were at least equally questionable with respect to several Japanese defendants before the
International Military Tribunal for the Far East. Timothy Brook, "The Tokyo Judgment
and the Rape of Nanking," 60 J. of Asian Stud. 673, 682–90 (2001).
[58] 1 Nuremberg Trials, op. cit., at 255–6.

influence on enterprise participation.[59] At Nuremberg, a criminal organization had to possess a degree of formality that the ICTY does not require of a criminal enterprise.[60] For the IMT, for instance, the names of all members might be expected to appear on a list of personnel that could be introduced into evidence.[61]

Although originating at Nuremberg, the contemporary notion of an "enterprise" gone criminally astray also has been filtered through the later U.S. jurisprudence of racketeering, which employs this term expressly.[62] The U.S. racketeering statute, known as RICO, criminalizes a defendant's contribution to any "enterprise" engaged in "a pattern of racketeering activity," as well as his or her participation in a conspiracy to so contribute.[63] Several U.S. prosecutors at the ICTY had considerable prior RICO experience, which influenced how they conceptualized their arguments in The Hague.

Leading Italian and Swiss prosecutors and investigators there, notably Chief Prosecutor Carla del Ponte,[64] were similarly experienced in Mafia prosecutions employing domestic doctrines of comparable breadth. RICO itself significantly influenced such prosecutions. Even in RICO, however, one finds nothing so demanding as Nuremberg's insistence that the enterprise display formally defined boundaries that clearly distinguish members from others, such as those who may have endorsed its goals or even assisted it occasionally in minor ways. American courts, however, have established limits on how broadly prosecutors may seek to define the enterprise. They have

---

[59] For a rare acknowledgment of the resemblance, see *Prosecutor v. Milutinović et al.*, Case No. IT-99-37-AR72, Separate Opinion of Judge David Hunt on Challenge by Ojdanić to Jurisdiction – Joint Criminal Enterprise, ¶ 30 (May 21, 2003). There also is a resemblance to the offense of "criminal association" in the domestic criminal codes of many civil law countries. Alexander D. Tripp, "Comment, Margins of the Mob: A Comparison of *Reves v. Ernst & Young* with Criminal Association Laws in Italy and France," 20 Fordham Int'l L.J. 263, 265–6, 297–302 (1996) (discussing Italy's crimes of *associazione di tipo mafioso* and *associazione per delinquere*, the former used in many mass Mafia trials of the last half-century). Germany has a similar provision, in StGB § 129, prohibiting "criminal association," but its requirements are very demanding and prosecutors hence seldom employ it. Jacqueline E. Ross, "Dilemmas of Undercover Policing in Germany: The Troubled Quest for Legitimacy" 44–5 & n.85 (Mar. 11, 2005) (unpublished manuscript).

[60] Danner & Martinez, op. cit., at 118–19.

[61] Id. at 113–14.

[62] Morgan Cloud, "Organized Crime, RICO, and the European Union," 27 Syracuse J. Int'l L. & Com. 243, 245–6 (2000) (describing the influence of RICO on European Union efforts to propagate uniform laws against criminal organization).

[63] 18 U.S.C. §§ 1961–1962 (2000).

[64] Del Ponte recounts her professional biography as an international prosecutor in *Madame Prosecutor: Confrontations with Humanity's Worst Criminals and the Culture of Impunity* (2009).

done so by requiring "evidence of an ongoing organization, formal or informal," that its "various associates function as a continuing unit," and that it exists "separate and apart from the pattern of activity in which it engages."[65]

The ICTY's failure even to mention IMT precedents on conspiracy and criminal organizations is at first puzzling, given Nuremberg's revered status as the bedrock of customary international law in this area. In fact, this silence speaks volumes about the ICTY's apparent desire to dissociate itself from widely questioned aspects of those proceedings, even if the IMT's actual verdicts were far more cautious than its charter or the prosecutor's indictments and courtroom arguments. The Nuremberg verdicts, in fact, display a sensitivity to restricting criminal liability within bounds of moral culpability that the ICTY would have done well to observe more closely. Properly understood, then, the Nuremberg legacy on these issues offers some sage counsel for the direction of international criminal law.[66]

The ICTY has often used participation liability in ways that closely resemble the common law of conspiracy, sometimes in its most questionable form.[67] In *Tadić*, for instance, it found the defendant liable for war crimes and crimes against humanity on the basis of his participation in a "common criminal purpose to rid the Prijedor region of the non-Serb population."[68] The court held that, although others sharing this purpose had directly committed the actual violence, Tadić himself had not agreed to these actions.[69] Yet, since Tadić had willingly joined the common plan of ethnic cleansing, he should have foreseen the risk that non-Serbs would be killed in the process.[70] He was acquitted of these charges at trial because the common purpose of forcible deportation does not entail murder.[71] Tadić nonetheless was convicted of them on appeal.[72] He could not have been prosecuted for aiding and abetting, because that would have required some specific act of encouragement or assistance on his part, substantially contributing to the success of others' wrongs.

---

[65] *United States v. Bledsoe*, 674 F.2d 647, 663–4 (8th Cir. 1982); see also *United States v. Turkette*, 452 U.S. 576, 583 (1981).

[66] Richard P. Barrett & Laura E. Little, "Lessons of Yugoslav Rape Trials: A Role for Conspiracy Law in International Tribunals," 88 Minn. L. Rev. 30, 56–8 (2003).

[67] For a notable recent application of American conspiracy doctrine to a mass atrocity, see *United States v. Moussaoui*, 282 F. Supp. 2d 480, 485 (E.D. Va. 2003) partly rev'd and vacated on other grounds, 365 F.3d 292 (4th Cir. 2004).

[68] *Tadić* Appeal, ¶ 231.

[69] Id. ¶¶ 178–80.

[70] Id. ¶¶ 231–2.

[71] Id. ¶ 233.

[72] Id. ICTY procedure departs from common law practice in permitting appellate courts to reverse trial judgments of acquittal. ICTY Statute, Art. 25(2). Such reversals are widely permitted in the "civil law" world.

One concern about conspiracy and its surreptitious cognates is that, although the ICTY seeks to develop international law on terms acceptable to all nations, this doctrine has not existed in the criminal codes of most civil law states – hence in most of the world.[73] In Latin America, for instance, conspiracy is often criminalized only in connection with a small number of the gravest offenses, such as genocide, treason, torture, and terrorism.[74] ICTY prosecutors trained in the civil law tradition expressed concern about this form of conceptual hegemony.[75] Although a common lawyer by origin, Canadian William Fenrick led the only ICTY prosecution team that harbored fears of excessive reliance on enterprise participation. When he retired in 2003, the restraint he had long exercised on others in the Office of the Prosecutor vanished, and its members began to employ the doctrine more and more aggressively before the tribunal.

There are good reasons why the civil law has had virtually no truck with conspiracy; these explain why its adoption by the ICTY has been internally contested and publicly unacknowledged. It is often a pure fiction to contend that a far-flung array of people, engaged in highly disparate activities, ever really reached an agreement shared by all. By allowing the agreement to be tacit,[76] the problem is aggravated. It is commonplace in the social sciences that members of a modern organization often do not uniformly share its avowed objectives, but rather employ it to their own ends – frequently at odds with official ones.[77] To view their sundry activities – their assorted comings and goings – as reflecting a single, shared purpose, plan, or agreement is to miss all that is tragic and comic in the social life of organizations, a considerable portion.

Some ICTY judgments speak of "agreements" among participants, but others have been content instead to find a "common purpose."[78] This presumably requires less of prosecutors, since individuals may independently choose to subscribe to a single purpose without entering into even a tacit

[73] Even in the common law world there subsist continuing doubts about the moral defensibility of conspiracy law. *Krulewitch v. United States*, 336 U.S. 440, 446 (1949) (Jackson, J. concurring) (contending that the "modern crime of conspiracy is so vague that it almost defies definition . . ."); Wayne R. LaFave, *Criminal Law* 616 (4th ed. 2003) (arguing that "the vagueness stems from . . . the uncertainty over what is sufficient to constitute the agreement and what attendant mental state must be shown").

[74] See, e.g., Código Penal, arts. 338, 149 (Peru).

[75] Oct. 2003 Prosecutor Interview.

[76] Such agreements "need not be express, but may be inferred from all the circumstances." *Stakić* Trial, ¶ 435.

[77] Richard Cyert & James March, *A Behavioral Theory of the Firm* 31–5 (2d ed. 1992).

[78] Barrett & Little, op. cit., at 42. But because participation, unlike conspiracy, is only a mode of taking part in offenses, not also an offense in its own right, the tribunal requires that the defendant have taken action in furtherance of the agreement or purpose.

agreement with others. To form an agreement, participants must be aware, at least, that others exist who share its terms. One may share a purpose with others, by contrast, while being completely ignorant of their existence.

In addition to agreements and purposes, the ICTY has sometimes spoken of a "common plan." This language suggests greater programmatic specificity than "purpose," as when one plans an aggressive war, or even a family vacation, concretizing the details of where one will reside on given nights. Unlike plans, common purposes – like tacit agreements[79] – can readily form without the need for any direct interaction among participants. People may unite in highly mediated ways, as by accessing a single Web site advocating a political agenda they share and then physically "swarming" a location where a public demonstration has been announced to occur. In its first years, the ICTY employed the three terms almost interchangeably.

This observation is intended less as a criticism than as an observation of the elusiveness of the social phenomena at issue. Even the term "division of labor," used at times in the present study, oversimplifies in significant ways. It implies a deliberate and self-conscious decision, at a particular time, by a specific individual or individuals, about how to divvy up a list of determinate tasks among a predetermined and relatively stable set of participants.[80] This exaggerates the degree of detailed planning and centralized, self-conscious coordination evident in most episodes of mass atrocity.[81] It ignores, for instance, how authoritarian rulers often deliberately foster interagency rivalries through overlapping jurisdictions.[82] Such organizational structures initially appear completely irrational, from a Weberian

---

[79] Conspiracy law has sometimes finessed the distinction between a tacit agreement and a mere concurrence of wills. LaFave, op. cit., § 6.4(d), at 575–6. On the importance of this distinction, see John Gardner, "Reasons for Teamwork," 8 Legal. Theory 495, 499–502 (2002).

[80] Similar criticism might fairly be made of such terms as "affiliate," "branch," or "wing."

[81] A similar problem today arises in holding corporations criminally liable for their agents' wrongful actions. Early legal theories developed to this end assumed a more centralized concentration of control within such organizations than today prevails in many corporate relationships, especially between parents and subsidiaries. Jonathan Clough, "Bridging the Theoretical Gap: The Search for a Realist Model of Corporate Criminal Liability," 18 Crim. L. Forum 267, 267 (2007); Brent Fisse & John Braithwaite, "The Allocation of Responsibility for Corporate Crime: Individualism, Collectivism, and Accountability," 11 Sydney L. Rev. 468, 483 (1988); James Gobert & Maurice Punch, *Rethinking Corporate Crime* (2003).

[82] See generally Michael Mann, *The Dark Side of Democracy: Explaining Ethnic Cleansing* 24 (2005) (describing "competitive outbidding" among nationalist elites, fostering ethnic cleansing); Ronald Wintrobe, *The Political Economy of Dictatorship* 316–29 (1998) (contending that dictators often deliberately stimulate entrepreneurship among rival agencies and individual officeholders to foster such creativity and initiative).

bureaucratic perspective. But they often prove highly efficient in eliciting proactive problem solving, by middle and lower echelons, in the service of criminal state policies.

For instance, during military rule in the 1970s, Brazilian security organizations engaged in "murderous interagency competition," whereby each "had to justify its existence and protect its achievements vis-à-vis the others" by showing military rulers that it had "most successfully and quickly sought, captured, and extracted information from, and eliminated, political subversives."[83] In the Cambodian terror, "one of the reasons purges and paranoia were so rampant" is that the Khmer Rouge encouraged Cambodians "to compete for honor" to "elevate one's position in the . . . hierarchy."[84] And during the Holocaust, "every individual involved in the program" to kill Jews "knew very well . . . that this was not only the route to higher rank and decorations but the best chance of exemption from conscription . . . and from far more dangerous duty at the front if he was in uniform."[85]

To speak of a single, coherent division of labor in such circumstances minimizes the degree to which many individuals may independently define their contribution to the common purpose without precise instruction or direction from anyone. At their own initiative, they simply join the bandwagon, in whatever manner they see fit, feeling emboldened by an ephemerally frenzied environment to, say, torch the dwelling of a Jewish or Bosnian neighbor or rape his daughter.

---

[83] See Martha Huggins, *Political Policing: The United States and Latin America* 177 (1998).
[84] Alexander Hinton, "Why Did You Kill?: The Cambodian Genocide and the Dark Side of Face and Honor," 57 J. Asian Stud. 93, 115–16 (1998).
[85] Gerhard Weinberg, "The Allies and the Holocaust," in *The Holocaust and History* 480, 488–9 (Michael Berenbaum & Andrew Peck, eds., 1998).

4

Defining the Criminal Enterprise

The last chapter suggested the key problem with enterprise participation: the concept's "elasticity," as ICTY prosecutors euphemistically describe it.[1] How should we determine the scope of the agreement to which members could be said to adhere? Defining the scope of the criminal enterprise is especially difficult when many of its apparent activities are entirely lawful or become unlawful only by virtue of transfers to them of revenues from its criminal endeavors – transfers criminalized by anti-money-laundering statutes. How do the enterprise's terms and limiting conditions – virtually never written down – come to be defined?

With genocide in particular, establishing the specific intent is very demanding,[2] in a way that sits uneasily with the shifting amalgam of motivations – some quite broad, others very narrow – among apparent parties to it. Without specific genocidal intent, an agreement to loot one's Muslim neighbors' homes, for example, does not amount to an intention to destroy a protected group, as required by genocide's legal definition. Hence, a defendant's knowledge of the Srebrenica executions and use of personnel and resources under his command to assist therein were held insufficient to warrant an inference of genocidal intent.[3]

---

[1] July 2005 interview; see also Guénaël Mettraux, *International Crimes and the ad hoc Tribunals* 293 (2005).

[2] The requisite mental state is one of specific intent. The defendant must have acted "with intent to destroy, in whole or in part, a national, ethnical, racial or religious group, as such." Rome Statute of the International Criminal Court, Art. 6.

[3] See, e.g., *Prosecutors v. Krstić*, Case No. IT-98-33A, ¶¶ 129, 134 (April 19, 2004). One might argue that in such persons the desire to dispossess a victim of property is better described as their "motive" than as their intention. Behind the intent to commit a criminal act, there often are a variety of possible motives, after all. Here, the specific intent to destroy simply originates from the motive to dispossess, it is contended. This view is inconsistent, however, with prevailing law and understanding of the relation between motivation and intention.

To be sure, Belgrade's rulers sought to harness local animosities to larger, countrywide goals for an exclusively Serbian society to cover most of the former Yugoslavia.[4] It strains credulity, however, to imagine that most members of local militias, who performed the worst violence, specifically intended anything as ambitious as a geopolitical master plan on this panoramic scale. It would likely be inaccurate, and unfair to the small fry, to classify them all simply as co-participants in some single genocidal enterprise, whether defined by common purpose, plan, or agreement.

Among subordinates, mixed motives are likely, in a way that the mental state for genocide does not readily accommodate.[5] It beggars belief that the intentions of every Serbian militiaman were entirely in sync with those of Radovan Karadžić or Milošević. One Serbian militiaman, for instance, casually invoked three motives – ethnic supremacy, greed, and vengeance – in virtually the same breath: "I am a Serbian patriot. I fought for the Serbian cause. And also for the sake of money. Money was the main thing. . . . Back then, revenge felt very good. Especially when we killed the KLA [Kosovo Liberation Army]."[6] It is doubtful whether such men display the mental state for genocide, according to most views of applicable law, insofar as group destruction did not figure centrally among their motivations, which were admittedly myriad, shifting, and often confused. This is a recurrent empirical fact about mass atrocity.

For instance, in Rwanda, to most low-level perpetrators, the larger "political aims pursued by the masters of this dark carnival were quite beyond their scope," writes one scholar.[7] Below the highest echelons, adds another, "the mixture [of motives] was . . . mundane. Fear of Tutsis generated righteous rage, reinforced by ambition, greed, failure of moral nerve . . . a desire to be 'a man' or receive approval from one's peers, patriotism, and loyalty to one's kinfolk."[8] Not "letting down the others" who had already done their assigned "dirty work" was a particularly salient motive among German police battalions during the Holocaust.[9]

---

[4] Christos Mylonas, "review of Tom Gallagher's *Balkans after the Cold War* and James Gow's *The Serbian Project and its Adversaries: A Strategy of War Crimes*," Survival, 185, 185–6 (Autumn 2004) (noting "effectiveness with which individual violent proclivities were so successfully mobilized in pursuance of" objectives established by regime elites).

[5] International courts and scholarly commentators have differed over how prominent the genocidal purpose must be among a defendant's several simultaneous aims. Diane Amann, "Group Mentality, Expressivism, and Genocide," 2 Int'l Crim. L. Rev. 93, 93–5 (2002).

[6] Tim Judah, *Kosovo* 246–7 (2000).

[7] Gérard Prunier, *The Rwanda Crisis: History of a Genocide* 232 (1995).

[8] Michael Mann, *The Dark Side of Democracy: Explaining Ethnic Cleansing* 472 (2005).

[9] Christopher Browning, *Ordinary Men: Reserve Battalion 101 and the Final Solution in Poland* (1998).

To these motivations may be added sadism, in many cases: "Real psy-chopaths were rampaging across the countryside indulging in cruel, bizarre and sadistic killing," observes a leading reporter of the Balkan wars.[10] Before the genocide, such men "occupied themselves with violence directed against other members of their own ethnic or social groups" and "seemed driven more by an undifferentiated urge to hurt others than by a well-developed hatred"[11] of the ethnic group whose members they later victimized. Such nonideological motives may predominate, given the origins of many Serbian and other paramilitaries in prison populations and criminal gangs. At times, Serbian soldiers and militia members simply seized the opportunity to settle private scores with Bosnian and Croat neighbors. Ethnic cleansing, authorized from above, provided a convenient pretext for indulging violent proclivities toward personal vendetta, as well as greed for neighbors' property and simple sadism. Sadism was clearly a major motive of Dusko Tadić, for instance.[12]

The impulse to "take them down a peg," vis-à-vis the targeted group, may translate into an intention to reduce its members' power, wealth, and social status, without rising to an intention to "destroy" them, even in part. Prosecutors, therefore, are moved to define the common purpose as ethnic cleansing because this is the only middle ground on which rulers' broader genocidal goals and volunteers' narrower personalistic aims might plausibly be said to meet and partly overlap.

The same tangled mélange of motivations is evident in many episodes of mass atrocity. It is difficult to conclude that small fry share the terms of any implicit genocidal agreement with the big fish who initiated the process as the law of enterprise participation may require. The prosecution's argument might be that, although junior participants in the enterprise were motivated by nongenocidal objectives, these goals nonetheless led them to develop an intention to destroy a protected group as a means to these ends.

This notion of a gradually evolving mental state may find some support in the fact that genocide (and other mass killing) often occurs only after other means of obtaining policy goals have failed. "Murderous cleansing

[10] Tim Judah, *The Serbs* 233 (1997).
[11] Benjamin Valentino, *Final Solutions: Mass Killing and Genocide in the Twentieth Century* 41 (2004).
[12] Larry May, *Crimes against Humanity: A Normative Account* 163 (2005). Other Serbian soldiers evidenced it as well. Chris Stephen, *Judgment Day: The Trial of Slobodan Milošević* 152–3, 209 (2004). On its role in motivating some of Argentina's dirty warriors, see Mark J. Osiel, "Constructing Subversion in Argentina's Dirty War," 75 Representations 119, 140 (2001).

is rarely initially intended by the perpetrators. They feel themselves forced into what is in effect a Plan C by the frustration of earlier Plans A and B," notes Michael Mann.[13] Another scholar adds, "National crises, especially major wars, can also create situations that force even moderate leaders to consider the most brutal options available to them."[14]

In China, for instance, both the Cultural Revolution and Great Leap Forward apparently "started out as the unintended consequences of policies designed to produce radical change in Chinese society, but ended up as the welcome punishment of those groups that were perceived as being less than fully cooperative."[15] Comparing Rwanda with Yugoslavia, Richard Wilson similarly concludes that "genocide emerges as the last ditch effort of a collapsing regime, where the elite is losing its grip on power and is facing either the ethno-nationalist break-up of the State (as in Yugoslavia) or, as in Rwanda, power-sharing with the enemy after a long period of ethnically justified theft and corruption."[16] But it remains unclear whether such undoubted escalations in the perniciousness of intention over time extend much below a regime's top leadership.

Even so, it would surely be wrong to describe seemingly wanton local grudge fests as irrelevant to the rulers' aims, when rulers know that these very animosities will be unleashed and that their expression can be directed in ways that advance larger regime goals. Here, we may have neither a bureaucracy nor a network united by common purpose exactly, but something more like "anomie,"[17] almost "crowd behavior."[18] The latter is a concept that – because of its implications of irrationality – sociologists sympathetic to mass movements have spent a century trying to flee.[19] In the archetypal crowd, Durkheim wrote, "each one is borne along by the rest"[20] into an impassioned, trance-like state of ecstasy, bordering on automatism.

[13] Mann, op. cit., at 503–4.

[14] Valentino, op. cit., at 25–6.

[15] Kurt Jonassohn with Karin Solveig Björnson, *Genocide and Gross Human Rights Violations in Comparative Perspective* 231 (1998).

[16] Richard A. Wilson, "Race, Ethnicity and Genocide at the International Criminal Tribunal for Rwanda," unpublished manuscript, July 2007.

[17] Emile Durkheim, *Suicide* 247–53 (George Simpson, ed., John A. Spaulding & George Simpson trans., 1951).

[18] The classic, early formulation is Gustave Le Bon, *The Crowd: A Study of the Popular Mind* (1920).

[19] But see Serge Moscovici, *The Age of the Crowd: A Historical Treatise on Mass Psychology* 381–5 (J. C. Whitehouse trans., 1985) (defending mass psychology's explanatory utility); Stanley Tambiah, *Leveling Crowds: Ethnonationalist Conflicts and Collective Violence in South Asia* 267–329 (1996) (describing aspects of ethnic riots in Sri Lanka in terms of crowd behavior).

[20] Emile Durkheim, *The Rules of Sociological Method*, W. D. Halls, trans. 56 (1982).

Solidarity is perfectly "mechanical," in Durkheim's sense, so no organized division of labor among perpetrators may be discerned or demonstrated.[21] In the midsts of such "collective effervescence," the possibility of defining and delimiting personal accountability in any legally defensible way threatens to evaporate entirely. If individual culpability continues to exist, it is clear only at the early point when one first allows oneself to succumb to the crowd's contagious exaltation, when one consciously submits to the risk of a later, unconscious suggestibility.

We are speaking here, it should be stressed, only in conceptual terms, in the theoretical world of ideal-types. In reality, this conception of the relevant behavior, as crowd-induced automatism, goes much too far in stripping genocide from its social and administrative roots. Even in Rwanda, for instance, where riotous crowds appeared prominent, violence was not random or truly spontaneous, but well organized and directed primarily against members of one ethnic group by those of another. The resulting genocide thus cannot be ascribed to the immediate experience of "the crowd" itself, in liberating normal restraints on destructive passions. Moreover, despite some journalistic reporting of orgiastic frenzy,[22] more thorough accounts have stressed the organized and routinized nature of most work done by Hutu killing teams.[23] If there was nonetheless a wild-eyed or carnivalesque aspect to the perpetrators' personal experience, it may be largely due to their plentiful consumption of alcohol throughout the process.

In any event, where such spontaneity from below is actively encouraged by state authorities from above, but exceeds their control, it is hard to say whether superior responsibility or enterprise participation is the better model. Neither ideal-type fits the facts very closely here. Such perplexities involve not only the spatial scope of the enterprise but also its temporal boundaries. It is often hard to say precisely when the enterprise came into being and when it was supposed to end.[24] Was there one enterprise or several;

---

[21] Charles Lindholm, *Charisma* 33 (1990) (parsing Durkheim's notion of the crowd as embodying "the visceral experience of essential unity and similarity that stimulates collective effervescence").

[22] Helena Cobban, "The Legacies of Collective Violence: The Rwandan Genocide and the Limits of the Law," Boston Rev., Apr.-May 2002 (describing the genocide as "the blood orgy of those terrifyingly irrational weeks").

[23] Jean Hatzfeld, *Machete Season: The Killers in Rwanda Speak* (2005). See also Lars Waldorff, "Mass Justice for Mass Atrocity: Rethinking Local Justice as Transitional Justice," 79 Temple. L. Rev. 1, 131 (2006) (offering considerable evidence to this effect).

[24] U.S. courts have long struggled to find means of limiting the configurations of the conspiracy that prosecutors may allege. See, e.g., *Kotteakos v. United States*, 328 U.S. 750, 771–2 (1946).

that is, a number of linked enterprises, perhaps closely related?[25] The answer makes an enormous difference to the number of criminal acts for which any given member can be held responsible, for the third variant of the doctrine holds every participant in the enterprise liable for the foreseeable criminal acts of all others.

The worst problems that these ambiguities present have not fully materialized because the ICTY Chief Prosecutor has usually shown restraint.[26] There is nothing in the law or theory of enterprise participation, however, ensuring such limitation. In fact, some ICTY prosecutors would like to define the enterprises they pursue to encompass people whose contribution was entirely financial, because "to finance military and paramilitary groups . . . responsible for serious crimes," it was common to use profits gained from "trafficking of drugs, cigarettes, weapons, and stolen cars."[27]

Ordinary commercial activity does indeed often contribute to mass atrocity in innumerable ways, albeit indirectly. That the contribution is circuitous, often deliberately so, does not vitiate its knowing and substantial character. These are the only requirements for accessorial liability, which explains the concern of multinational business executives with the prospect of prosecution by the ICC.[28] Their companies often supply technologies – including information technologies – that, they know, may readily be used by undemocratic rulers to repress their people.

GUILT BY ASSOCIATION

Critics of joint criminal enterprise often accuse it of trading in "guilt by association." This latter notion evokes the prospect of liability attaching

---

[25] Mettraux, op. cit., at 292 (observing that the enterprise "depicted by the Prosecution . . . may in fact consist of several joint criminal enterprises with different alleged objects, membership, and geographical scope"). Conspiracy law often presents essentially the same question: whether there is one agreement with several objectives – that is, encompassing several offenses – or whether each objective is better understood as the basis of a separate agreement. William LaFave, *Criminal Law* § 6.5(d)(1), at 594–5 (3rd ed. 2000).

[26] Antonio Cassese, "The Proper Limits of Individual Responsibility under the Doctrine of Joint Criminal Enterprise," 5 J. Int'l Crim. J. 109, 133 (2007) ("By and large, all the dangers of abuse . . . of the doctrine by international courts, feared by a number of commentators, have not materialized.").

[27] Nicola Piacente, "Importance of the Joint Criminal Enterprise Doctrine for the ICTY Prosecutorial Policy," 2 J. Int'l Crim. Just. 446, 453 (2004). The same conduct could be reached through complicity, insofar as the defendant's contribution need only have been knowing. William A. Schabas, "Enforcing International Humanitarian Law: Catching the Accomplices," 83 Int'l Rev. Red Cross 439, 450–1 (2001).

[28] Schabas, id. at 439, 442–54; Maurice Nyberg, "At Risk from Complicity with Crime," Fin. Times, July 28, 1998, at 15.

to someone who merely happens upon a culpable person in, say, a bar and strikes up a conversation about matters unrelated to criminality in any way. Association of this sort, however, is not rendered criminal by joint enterprise doctrine, as the ICTY Appeals Chamber has stressed.[29] The association with which international law is concerned must take place with a criminal purpose in the minds of both such people, or at least a purpose that they contemplate attaining by criminal means. Still, the doctrine's reach is very broad.

One wonders, for instance, how the doctrine of enterprise participation would apply to a loosely knit, diffuse, informal network spread over many countries, such as Al Qaeda.[30] There is nothing in the law as it currently stands that would preclude a court from finding anyone detained in Al Qaeda's Afghanistan training camps to have been a member of the criminal enterprise responsible for the 9/11 attacks, and so to prosecute him for those acts. In fact, liability may extend to the acts of other groups more loosely associated with Al Qaeda.[31]

Inasmuch as present law permits such results, it is surely in need of some retrenchment. It is unlikely, after all, that members of a single Al Qaeda cell will know of the existence, much less the particular activities, of any other cell; that is the very point of organizing a movement into a clandestine, spoke-like network of cells. Yet it is also fair to say that all such cells and all their members share a common purpose. That purpose might be defined – broadly but credibly – as the use of unlawful violence to kill Jews and Christians, particularly those involved in spreading Western financial and military influence throughout the Muslim world. Whatever intuitive appeal this approach initially displays, however, it may draw as much on ancient notions of taint and pollution as on more modern theories of personal culpability.[32]

Much ordinary crime today clearly displays a profusion of global linkages amenable to analysis as enterprise participation. The global nature of

---

[29] Judgment, *Brdanin*, op. cit., ¶ 428 (rejecting the criticism that joint enterprise doctrine entails "guilt by association").

[30] For a discussion of the organizational structure of Al Qaeda as it has morphed from "group" to "movement" and of its continuing lack of discernible command and control, see Daniel Benjamin & Steve Simon, *The Age of Sacred Terror: Radical Islam's War against America* 167–70 (2003).

[31] Raymond Bonner & Don Van Natta, Jr., "Regional Terrorist Groups Pose Growing Threat," Experts Warn, N.Y. Times, Feb. 8, 2004, at A1 (identifying "militant groups with roots in Southeast Asia, Central Asia, and the Caucasus to North Africa . . . believed to be loosely affiliated with Al Qaeda").

[32] On taint and pollution in early criminal law, see George Fletcher, *Rethinking Criminal Law*, 343–9 (1978).

criminal activity makes it entirely possible, without risk of exaggeration or *reductio ad absurdum*, to tie the drug dealer on a Washington, D.C., street with the cartel potentate in Medellín, and vice versa. The law of enterprise participation allows this linkage with relative ease, held in check only by prosecutorial compunction. In fact, one need only acknowledge "the growing and dangerous links between terrorist groups, drug traffickers and their paramilitary gangs" that have resulted "in all types of violence"[33] across several continents, often cleverly employing the Internet, to sew all these into a single, seamless enterprise of worldwide wrongdoing. This leads a major social thinker to write, only somewhat hyperbolically, that "complex financial schemes and international trade networks link up criminal economy to the formal economy.... The flexible connection constitutes an essential feature of the new global economy."[34]

RELIANCE ON PROSECUTORIAL DISCRETION

Enterprise participation, as the ICTY has used it, is so broad a notion that it requires enormous self-restraint by prosecutors ever to be defensible in practice. The doctrine requires the court to place huge trust in prosecutors' good judgment, gambling that their discretion will be used wisely. Such trust is widely considered unwarranted, however.[35]

Even acting in perfectly good conscience, prosecutors do not currently have any clear criteria for defining the enterprise and its membership. Non-U.S. lawyers at the ICTY, particularly those from civil law countries, find this measure of prosecutorial discretion profoundly vexing.[36] The problem is especially acute as we move beyond the simplest case of those working together in a particular detention camp, perhaps interacting regularly face

---

[33] Emmanouela Mylonaki, "The Manipulation of Organised Crime by Terrorists: Legal and Factual Perspectives," 2 Int'l Crim. L. Rev. 213, 230 (2002).

[34] Manuel Castells, *End of Millennium* 170 (1998).

[35] In the United States, prosecutorial discretion is subject to judicial review under certain circumstances, such as when there is a suspected breach of equal protection. Andrew B. Loewenstein, "Judicial Review and the Limits of Prosecutorial Discretion," 38 Am. Crim. L. Rev. 351, 369–70 (2001). The civil law tradition is even more strongly committed to minimizing prosecutorial discretion. This is reflected in its traditional opposition to plea bargaining, which nonetheless exists in practice, but is by all accounts more limited than in the United States. Marco Fabri, "Theory versus Practice of Italian Criminal Justice Reform," 77 Judicature 211, 213–14 (1994).

[36] Author's interviews, 2003. See also William Stuntz, "Reply: Criminal Law's Pathology," 101 Mich. L. Rev. 828, 830–1 (2002) ("Other countries' prosecutors do not appear to exercise the kind of broad policymaking power their American counterparts wield."). See, generally, Luc Côté, "Reflections on the Exercise of Prosecutorial Discretion in International Criminal Law," 3 J. of Int'l Crim. Just. 162 (2005).

to face. The problem becomes perhaps most acute when prosecution moves to those involved at the very highest levels of policymaking, working in the nation's capital, at great distance from subordinates in the hinterlands, with whom they never directly communicate. Here, the spatial and temporal scope of the enterprise, including the identity of its personnel, might be defined in a virtually infinite number of ways.

Consider Slobodon Milošević or Saddam Hussein: A chief of state may be indicted along with several others – a selected subset of national or regional leaders, civilian and/or military. Other participants in Milošević's enterprises are identified in the indictments simply as his "primary agents" who "acted without dissension to execute [his] policies."[37] This approach may well be convenient as an administrative matter. But it is unclear on what basis, conceptually and morally, the prosecutor determines the scope of the criminal enterprise.[38] There is no way to know, because the ICTY does not require prosecutors to explain and justify their answers to this question. To speak of "elasticity" at this point is a dangerous understatement. Where the broadening interpretation has no textual support in the Statute whatsoever,[39] the ground on which courts tread is even weaker. This is the case with enterprise participation, which finds no explicit basis in the ICTY Statute.[40]

Nonlawyers will have no difficulty perceiving the passionate intensity with which these concerns are today mooted, as in the following, by a

---

[37] Bosnia Amended Milošević Indictment, ¶ 28; Croatia Second Amended Milošević Indictment, ¶ 30. The allusion here to the law of agency goes unremarked and unexamined in the opinion or secondary literature. Agency law assumes that the relevant relationships are highly hierarchical.

[38] Allison Marston Danner & Jenny S. Martinez, "Guilty Associations: Joint Criminal Enterprise, Command Responsibility, and the Development of International Criminal Law," 93 Cal. L. Rev. 75, 108, 134–5 (2005) (doubting "whether there are any limits on the prosecution's discretion to define the scope of the enterprise" and noting "the limited jurisprudence on the relationship between an individual's potential criminal liability and the scope of the relevant enterprise"). Moreover, defendants under sealed indictment could not be named in the public indictments of co-participants without alerting the former that they were likely sought for prosecution. This meant that prosecutors' indictments (sealed vs. public) were often inconsistent from one to another in how they defined the scope and identity of a single criminal enterprise.

[39] The ICTY purports to deduce the doctrine from the interstices of art. 7(1) of its statute, which provides only that "a person who planned, instigated, ordered, committed or otherwise aided and abetted in the planning, preparation or execution of a crime . . . shall be individually responsible for the crime." ICTY Statute, art. 7(1).

[40] Danner & Martinez, op. cit., at 103 ("Ironically, the most complex and conceptually challenging liability theory in international criminal law is the only one not mentioned explicitly in the statutes of the ICTY or ICTR.").

young Swedish human rights lawyer: "The *mens rea* level of recklessness is far too low for the context of armed conflict. Where people are in a daily fight to save their lives, they will be reckless,"[41] in the sense of adverting to certain risks the materialization of which they cannot fairly be expected to prevent. The doctrine of criminal enterprise therefore "combines an uncertain degree of participation" (i.e., a weak *actus reus* requirement, demanding little objective contribution to harm) "with the lowest possible form of *mens rea*."[42] Thus, "just about anyone in the wrong place, at the wrong time, belonging to the wrong ethnic group, doing what is natural for such a person, can be liable for genocide, regardless that the person had no control of the situation whatsoever."[43]

To solve that problem, guidelines for prosecutors might be expected to emerge over time, case by case, from the cumulating judgments of international tribunals themselves. Such a "common law" approach to the matter would be uncontroversial in civil disputes, but is indefensible in the criminal context in which due process requires potential defendants to have clear prior warning about which conduct falls within a statutory prohibition. It is an axiom of statutory interpretation that criminal statutes be construed strictly.[44] It is, therefore, considerably more difficult to extend the scope of a criminal statute by judicial decision.

THE VAGUENESS PROBLEM

It might be said that the criminal enterprise operates as a kind of legal fiction, for none of its supposed members would have defined themselves in this particular manner. In fact, the same period of events, people, and facts are grouped differently (i.e., into differently defined enterprises) from one indictment to the next. As one close observer points out, "There appears to have been little thought about how the same interconnected events should be charged in different cases."[45] Whether the specific dots thus connected in a given case are too few or too many is a function – one is almost tempted to say figment – of the prosecutorial imagination.

Fictions assuredly play an important role in the law – a legitimate role, when acknowledged as such – and are justified insofar as they enable law

---

[41] Linda Engvall, "Extended Joint Criminal Enterprise in International Criminal Law," Master's thesis, Faculty of Law, Univ. of Lund, June 2005, at 60.
[42] Id.
[43] Id.
[44] See, e.g., Rome Statute, op. cit., Art. 22(2).
[45] Mettraux, op. cit., at 292.

to advance justice by comparing a novel phenomenon with a more familiar one that is already well understood.[46] The idea of "the international community" may be just such a fiction, insofar as it is generally invoked – despite its lack of sociological substance, in a dense web of social ties – to advance the claims of justice by analogy to those that any genuine, nonfictional community might make on its members. Implicitly, the speaker is saying the following: if most of humankind truly felt itself to be members of a single community, as perhaps it should and eventually it may, then surely they would endorse – well, whatever it is the advocate is advocating. This is a role that fiction often plays in legal argument.

Maybe such a fictional device is defensible in this situation. But it is unclear why we are prepared to rely so heavily on fiction here, in regard to a criminal enterprise, while not at all in regard to superior responsibility. There, after all, we might just as readily presume effective control to exist – call it constructive control, if one likes – wherever *de jure* authority exists or simply wherever such a fiction produces a result that, on the facts, comports with our moral intuitions. But "comports with our moral intuitions" might simply be a highfalutin' way of saying "just sort of feels right." Such ominous vagueness gives pause.

Only so vague a formulation could explain the particular composition of those categorized alongside Milošević, for instance, as fellow participants in the same criminal enterprises.[47] Prosecutors admitted that they had no intention of indicting many of the individuals so named and that "it is really rather haphazard who gets tossed into the pot" of a given enterprise.[48] They reported that their preferred method was first to identify a particular defendant as the target for prosecution and then assemble a list of co-participants (i.e., those who associated with him most closely in ways pertinent to actionable wrongs "within the scope of his culpability," the term of art such prosecutors frequently employed). To avoid blithely stigmatizing such alleged participants for genocide, however, prosecutors could surely benefit from clearer doctrinal guidelines on how to define the putative enterprise. These guidelines are necessary to overcome "the continuous jurisprudential morphing of the concept" noted by the tribunal's close observers, including its former judicial clerks.[49]

With enterprise participation, after all, the law no longer ascribes responsibility primarily on the basis of an organizational hierarchy – the

---

[46] Lon Fuller, *Legal Fictions* 49–92 (1967). Fictions may therefore be simply a form of reasoning by analogy and, to that extent, can be uncontroversial – at least in the common law world.

[47] Kosovo Second Amended Milošević Indictment, ¶¶ 5–23.

[48] Author's interview, July 2005.

[49] Mettraux, op. cit., at 292.

bureaucratic formalities of which determine who is responsible for preventing what sort of misconduct by whom. But the danger lies in the breadth with which the common purpose of the criminal enterprise has often been couched. By defining that enterprise as the expulsion of non-Serbs from a given region of the former Yugoslavia, a very substantial portion of the Serbian population in that region could credibly be considered participants and prosecuted as such, as members of at least one ICTY prosecution team privately acknowledged.[50]

On first introduction to the two doctrines, superior responsibility clearly seems the more formalistic, whereas enterprise participation appears the more sociologically realistic. After all, superior responsibility dwells on *de jure* competencies and official job descriptions within bureaucratic hierarchies, whereas enterprise participation claims to mold itself to the actual contours of criminal activity – however informal its configuration. The opposite may be closer to the truth, however. *De facto* power – in all its sociological messiness – quickly asserts itself as central to the contemporary application of superior responsibility in international courts, whereas prosecutors there are free to define the criminal enterprise in ways tied only very loosely to any observable patterns of influence and interaction among putative participants.

It is also true, as one Trial Chamber has speculated, that the prosecution deliberately injects a studied vagueness into the indictment's delineation of the enterprise, in order "to mould its case in a substantial way during the trial, according to how its evidence actually turns out."[51] In this way, the configuration of the enterprise shifts back and forth over the course of the trial, expanding and contracting as later witnesses confirm or discredit earlier ones and as evidence about crimes in one region of the country proves more or less convincing than in another. Defense counsel receive no fair notice of the case they must refute, for it is not really until closing argument that they can have any clear idea of the target at which they must aim. Until then, it bobs and weaves with every slight shift in the weight of emerging evidence.

---

[50] Author's interview, July 2005, The Hague.

[51] *Prosecutor v. Brđanin & Talić*, Case No. IT-99-36-PT, Decision on Form of Further Amended Indictment and Prosecution Application to Amend, ¶ 11 (June 26, 2001). Even at a trial's completion, there have sometimes remained intolerable uncertainties regarding the scope of the criminal enterprise that the court claims to have discovered. In one recent case, for instance, the ICTY Appeals Chamber faulted the lower Chamber for failing to specify the geographical or temporal scope of the enterprise and "whether all or only some of the local politicians, militaries, police commanders and paramilitary leaders were rank and file JCE members." *Prosecutor v. Momčilo Krajišnik*, IT-00-39-A ¶ 157 (March 17, 2009).

Is there any way to define the scope of a joint criminal enterprise that is logically coherent and morally consistent and that can cabin prosecutorial discretion within such bounds?[52] There may be an incentive, to be sure, for prosecutors to limit the scope of an alleged enterprise, since (as one ICTY chamber has suggested) the broader the enterprise's purpose and membership, the less that any single defendant's contribution to it can credibly be judged legally significant.[53] On the other hand, it is also true that the broader the enterprise, the more likely it is that a defendant can be found to have made some contribution to it, and so the greater the prosecution's chances, to this extent, of convicting him.

The law of superior responsibility may give excessive weight to control, conditioning the superior's liability on it in an all-or-nothing fashion. There is surely no gainsaying the moral import of power relations, however, in implementing a policy of mass atrocity. For with enterprise participation, the opposite problem arises: an utter indifference to power when determining liability. The doctrine's elasticity impels courts, willy-nilly, to reintroduce a sensitivity to the participants' relative power, albeit at the point of punishment. For only in this way may they set defensible limits on who may ultimately be held responsible for what, despite the shared commitment of all to (what the law now chooses to conceive as) a single endeavor. Close attention to power dynamics is thus inescapable, as long as international criminal law is not content to rest on formalistic fictions and insists instead on some "realistic" apprehension of the workings of the world it purports to govern.

Courts will find it difficult to define the precise purpose and membership of the criminal enterprise as it evolves over time and space. The ICTY offered little early guidance in this regard; the enterprise at issue thus remained entirely the interpretative construction of prosecutors. If the law of superior responsibility draws the line too narrowly in such cases, exempting many culpable parties from prosecution, then enterprise participation surely risks doing so too broadly. National courts in transitional societies will soon be called on to confront such perplexities.

---

[52] It is true that some prosecutions depict the enterprise in more carefully delimited ways. See, e.g., *Prosecutor v. Deronjić*, Case No. IT-02-61-PT, Second Amended Indictment, ¶ 3 (Sept. 29, 2003); *Vasiljević* Trial, ¶ 167. The indictment of Colonel Ljubisa Beara precisely describes the common purpose of the criminal enterprise as "to forcibly transfer the women and children from the Srebrenica enclave to Kladanj . . . and to capture, detain, . . . summarily execute by firing squad, bury, and rebury thousands of Bosnian Muslim men and boys aged 16 to 60 from the Srebrenica enclave." *Prosecutor v. Beara*, Case No. IT-02-58-PT, Amended Indictment, ¶ 17 (March 30, 2005).

[53] *Prosecutor v. Kvočka* et al., Case No. IT-98-30/1-T, Judgment, ¶ 311 (Nov. 2, 2001).

JUSTICE AND THE MODES OF CRIMINAL PARTICIPATION

Because the law aspires to be just, it is natural to ask which of the two legal doctrines here examined is most likely to advance that goal. To this question, one might seek to apply theories of justice. From behind a Rawlsian veil of ignorance, for instance, one might ask: which rule would one choose to govern law's response to mass atrocity if one did not know whether one would find oneself as victim or perpetrator?

At first blush, this seems an impossible question because its premise – that one would not already know one's status as aggressor or aggrieved – is so improbable. If one expected to commit war crimes, one would prefer prosecution as a commander, in that this rule imposes harder burdens for prosecutors to meet and does not necessarily impose any greater punishment than the alternative. Conversely, as the victim, one would favor enterprise participation, insofar as it casts a wider net for defendants, permits their greater punishment, and thus may ultimately have greater deterrent effect on a larger number of potential perpetrators. Not knowing *a priori* whether one would later prove accuser or accused prevents one from choosing either of the two rules *ex ante*. The Rawlsian method thus fails to enlighten us, because we simply cannot really imagine anyone ever agreeing to step behind the veil of ignorance in the first place.

More might be said, however. Let us acknowledge that one might both contemplate suffering war crimes and also committing them. The second scenario might ensue simply from finding oneself in an unfortunate circumstance where such conduct, although not actively desired, became virtually inexorable.[54] This is not as unrealistic an assumption as might first appear. In many episodes of mass atrocity, victims also often become victimizers.

In Guatemala, for instance, although the state was responsible for most victims of the country's long civil war, guerrilla groups murdered some six thousand people in thirty-two separate massacres.[55] Moral complexities of this sort are a frequent theme in sophisticated analyses of many such episodes, from Austria to South Africa.[56] Thus, it is not preposterous at

---

[54] Mark J. Osiel, *Obeying Orders: Atrocity, Military Discipline, and the Law of War* 132–3 (1999).

[55] Commission for Historical Clarification: Guatemala, Memory of Silence ¶¶ 128, 134; see also Susanne Jonas, *Of Centaurs and Doves: Guatemala's Peace Process* 154 (2000).

[56] See, e.g., Hella Pick, *Guilty Victim: Austria From the Holocaust to Haider*, passim (2000) (examining moral ambiguities in Austria's recent history, arising from its status as both party to and victim of German aggression); Tristan Anne Borer, "A Taxonomy of Victims and Perpetrators: Human Rights and Reconciliation in South Africa," 25 Human Rights Q. 1088, 1098–9 (2003) (examining South African "perpetrators who became victims" and "heroes who became perpetrators," such as Winnie Mandela); Leora Bilsky, *Transformative Justice: Israeli Identity on Trial* 19–84 (2004) (describing Israeli prosecutions of Jews who

once to imagine prosecution for one's own wrongs and also suffering from others'. Described in this way, the hypothetical world one inhabits "behind the veil" is not impossible to contemplate.

Rawls defines people in this position as highly risk averse,[57] in that they must imagine themselves ending up "worst off" and choose legal rules or institutions accordingly. If we accept this view of rationality, then they would surely seek, above all else, to prevent their own violent deaths. It would matter far less to be able to harm others wrongfully, unless such acts reduced their own risks of death, as war crime generally does not. They would, therefore, clearly choose the law of enterprise participation because of its wider compass of liability and consequently greater deterrent effect.

Suppose, however, that we alter their hazard propensity, giving them more "appetite for risk."[58] Their choice may then change. They may now be perfectly prepared to suffer somewhat greater risk of wrongful victimization at their enemy's hands in order to gain the military advantage – sometimes significant, alas – afforded by committing war crimes. As with so much in philosophy, where we land at the end of the argument thus depends on where we begin; that is, on the first premises we adopt.

The need to choose between incompatible premises, like alternative assumptions about a taste for risk, presents issues largely beyond the scope of moral philosophy itself. Such appetites, after all, vary widely along lines

---

collaborated in administering Nazi concentration camps and ghetto "councils" within occupied Europe).

[57] John Rawls, *A Theory of Justice* 23, 137, 162, 323 (1972).

[58] There is some empirical evidence to suggest that this is a more accurate account of risk propensity, at least in contemporary American society, exemplified by the popularity of "thrill" sports. In such activities, the risk to life and limb is a source of appeal and attraction, not aversion. Jonathan Simon, "Taking Risks: Extreme Sports and the Embrace of Risk in Advanced Liberal Societies," in *Embracing Risk* 177, 179–81 (Tom Baker & Jonathan Simon, eds., 2002). For an influential utilitarian/welfare-maximizing moral theory developed from a critique of Rawls's premise of high-risk aversion, see John Harsanyi, "Cardinal Utility in Welfare Economics and in the Theory of Risk-Taking," 61 J. Pol. Econ. 434, 434–5 (1953). Harsanyi argues that in the "original position," rational individuals would not be preoccupied with averting the worst-case scenario and so would not insist on maximizing their minimum outcome; rather, they would aim to maximize their expected utility and, to that end, assess the probabilities of various outcomes, using them in turn to weigh the corresponding utilities. Only if the original position presented one with a zero-sum game, such that the other's gain entails one's loss, and only if nature itself is somehow an adversary conspiring against one, would rational individuals choose Rawls' maximin strategy over alternatives offering greater overall welfare. See also Louis Kaplow & Steven Shavell, "Any Non-Welfarist Method of Policy Assessment Violates the Pareto Principle," 109 J. Pol. Econ. 281 (2001).

of culture, history, geography, and socioeconomic status, to such an extent that it is pointless to bracket them out for purposes of writing legal rules. As in many areas of public policy, then, moral philosophy here delivers less than it first seems to promise.[59] First principles of "what justice requires" may be similarly silent about whom to punish and for which offenses. In such decisions, competing policies are at stake,[60] and they are best balanced by elected leadership, responsive to democratic opinion.[61]

THE LAW OF COMPLICITY AND ITS LIMITS

A third possibility for linking the big fish to the small fry is the law of complicity, which is distinct from that of superior responsibility and enterprise participation. One is complicit and deemed an accessory in another's criminal act if one knowingly contributes to it significantly, as by instigating or aiding and abetting it. The prosecution need not show that the wrong would never have occurred but for the accessory's contribution; causation is not required. The contribution must have been substantial, however.[62] Incitement to commit genocide is a form of complicity especially relevant to prosecuting the bigger fish; complicity, unlike conspiracy, is not a free-standing offense in most jurisdictions, however.[63] Hence, it is punishable only if the harm to which it lends support actually occurs.

Complicity casts the net of potential liability very broadly. Once prosecutors start talking about complicity in mass atrocity, it is difficult to know where or how to stop, in the sense that so many people are often complicit in such events, according to its legal definition. The law of complicity reaches even further in this respect than participation in a joint criminal enterprise, and it presents the same problems for prosecutors seeking to limit the scope

---

[59] Richard Posner, "The Problems of Moral and Legal Theory," 111 Harv. L. Rev. 1637, 1694–8 (1998).

[60] "Policy" may here be contrasted to "principle," as Dworkin employs the terms. Ronald Dworkin, *Taking Rights Seriously* 22–8, 90–100 (1977).

[61] Miriam J. Aukerman, "Extraordinary Evil, Ordinary Crime: A Framework for Understanding Transitional Justice," 15 Harv. Hum. Rts. J. 39 (2002) (arguing that we should first identify the goals of transitional justice and then determine which paradigm – retribution, restorative justice, nonprosecutorial alternatives – will best meet those goals); Christin Bell, *Peace Agreements and Human Rights* 288 (2000) (arguing that "transitional criminal justice is not partial merely because full justice is logistically or politically difficult. It is partial because this best serves the transition.").

[62] All of the key terms in this short description are subject to some dispute at the margins, to be sure.

[63] George Fletcher, "Hamdan Confronts the Military Commissions Act of 2006," 45 Colum. J. Transnational L. 427, 444 (2007).

of actual trials in a postconflict society. During Saddam Hussein's prosecution, former Baath Party members were "watching the trial carefully to see whether the legal theories used against [him] sweep in all those complicit in the regime," as Eric Posner observed.[64]

Today, "claims of complicitous participation in wrong" are "socially pervasive," Christopher Kutz observes.[65] Multinational corporations are regularly accused, for instance, of aiding and abetting in human rights abuse, even crimes against humanity, in many of the poor countries in which they invest. States, in turn, are often reproached for complicity in the crimes of foreign private parties, operating within their territories, over which they might have exercised greater control. One may be complicit in another's wrong by failing to take all reasonable measures to prevent it; that is, when one has a legal duty to do so.

The repercussions of the law of complicity are far reaching. For instance, the Genocide Convention requires states "to undertake to prevent and to punish" that crime's occurrence. Virtually all states have ratified this treaty. Thus, the world at large is arguably complicit in genocide wherever it occurs, insofar as we do less than we reasonably could to halt and penalize this wrong. Because of its potential influence over Bosnian Serb commanders, in particular, Serbia was finally found liable in 2007 of failing to prevent genocide at Srebrenica, albeit not by way of complicity.[66] But although states have a treaty-duty to prevent genocide, it is much less clear whether individual statesmen (like Milošević) do.

In a global economy, parties to foreign trade may often "contribute significantly" to one another's wrongful activities in ways that will appear to have been "knowing," given the ready availability of inculpatory information from reliable human rights organizations, whose reports major corporations can be expected to monitor.[67] If one views multinational exchange as an important means of increasing human prosperity, then there is reason for concern over the potentially excessive reach of complicity liability in international criminal law.

---

[64] Eric Posner, "Justice within Limits," N.Y. Times, Op.- Ed., Sept. 26, 2005.

[65] Christopher Kutz, *Complicity: Ethics and Law for a Collective Age* 5 (2000).

[66] The World Court concluded that Serbia had violated its duties under the 1948 Genocide Convention, which requires states to take steps to "prevent and punish genocide," because its geographical proximity and the strength of its links to Bosnian Serb commanders would have enabled it, by its intercession, to have prevented the Srebrenica massacre. *Case Concerning the Application of the Convention on the Prevention and Punishment of the Crime of Genocide, Bosnia and Herzegovina v. Serbia and Montenegro,* ¶¶ 430–8 (Feb. 26, 2007).

[67] The U.S. State Department itself provides annual summaries of the human rights situation in many countries. These reports are sometimes quite damning.

Such fears can be somewhat allayed by construing the defendant's required "knowledge" in ways that prosecutors cannot easily prove. This is a convincing move when the offense, like genocide or persecution as a crime against humanity, demands a showing that the defendant specifically intended the ensuing harm.[68] Establishing evidence of so blameworthy a mental state can be extremely difficult. Consider, for instance, a case in which the defendant supplied the chemicals ultimately used for chemical warfare.[69] On these facts, a Dutch court found the defendant, Dutch manufacturer Frans van Anraat, not guilty of complicity in genocide for selling such chemicals to Saddam Hussein.[70]

And Bosnian Serb commander Vidoje Blagojević was ultimately acquitted of complicity in genocide on similar grounds; although he knew about the forthcoming attack on Srebrenica and the likely ensuing displacement of civilians, he was unaware that the attack would involve mass killings, the ICTY Appeals Chamber concluded.[71] He was, therefore, unaware of the specific intent of the immediate perpetrators to commit genocide. The World Court similarly acquitted Serbia itself of complicity in genocide for the Srebrenica massacre, because despite Milošević's considerable aid to its Bosnian Serb perpetrators, there remained reasonable doubt that Serbian authorities in Belgrade "at the time were clearly aware that genocide was about to take place or was under way."[72]

Even when the offense does not require specific intent, the prosecutor's task is rarely easy. Liability demands more than a showing that the accused "should have" known others' criminal ends, to convict him of complicity in their wrongs. He must have had actual knowledge of such ends and of how his acts would meaningfully contribute to them. Actual knowledge has

[68] Harmen G. van der Wilt, "Genocide, Complicity in Genocide and International v. Domestic Jurisdiction," 4 J. Int'l Crim. Justice 239 (2006); Alexander K.A. Greenawalt, "Rethinking Genocidal Intent: The Case for a Knowledge-Based Interpretation," 99 Colum. L. Rev. 2259 (1999) (showing the difficulties of prosecutorial efforts at "squeezing ambiguous fact patterns into the specific intent paradigm"); Claus Kress, "The Darfur Report and Genocidal Intent," 3 J. Int'l Crim. Justice 575 (2005).
[69] Van der Wilt, op. cit., at 240.
[70] LJN: BA4676, Court of Appeal The Hague, 2200050906 – 2, May 2007, http://zoeken .rechtspraak.nl/resultpage.aspx?snelzoeken=true&searchtype=ljn&ljn=BA6734.
[71] Blagojević was convicted, however, of complicity in crimes against humanity. *Prosecutor v. Vidoje Blagojević & Dragan Jokic*, No. IT-02-60-A, ICTY Appeal (May 9, 2007) available at, http://www.un.org/icty/indictment/english/blajok-jud070509.pdf.
[72] *Bosnia and Herzegovina v. Serbia and Montenegro*, op. cit., ¶ 422. The court neglected to request key documentation, however, that would likely have established the requisite knowledge on the part of Belgrade's authorities. Marlise Simons, "Genocide Court Ruled for Serbia without Seeing Full War Archive," N.Y. Times, April 9, 2007.

sometimes been interpreted, in fact, to mean his awareness "to a substantial certainty,"[73] so that he is not liable where his consciousness at the relevant time falls short of this, even if genocide (in the ordinary, nontechnical sense of the term) ultimately does ensue. It is not enough that he appreciates that his actions may contribute to that end.

Whether these arcane legal subtleties could much assuage the fears of those doing transactions with morally dubious regimes is another matter. Perhaps we should not be too quick to dispel such fears, in any event. If we today have reason to fear the law's possible over-breadth, it is well to remember that under-breadth has surely been the greater problem, for until quite recently international liability for human rights abuse barely existed. But the law of complicity is often unsuitable to the prosecution of mass atrocity for other reasons, as we now see.

In the civil law world, complicity does much of the work done by conspiracy and racketeering law in the United States.[74] It has been occasionally employed by both of the *ad hoc* international tribunals, notably by the ICTY Appeals Chamber in the *Krstić* case.[75] But it has been unappealing to international prosecutors when pursuing heads of state and other high-ranking initiators of mass atrocity. Once viewed as instigators – through incitement to genocide, for instance – such defendants must be classed as accessories, according to most legal systems from which international courts derive their sources.

The classification of head honchos as accessories much understates their contribution to the criminal result, for accessories do not cause harm, but merely assist or otherwise contribute to that caused by others. The stigmatizing effect of conviction as an accessory is much less than as a perpetrator, prosecutors stress.[76] Accessories also receive shorter sentences, *ceteris paribus*.[77] The domestic law of many countries even mandates lesser punishment for accessories than for perpetrators.

In this respect, the goals of international prosecutors coincide with those of new rulers in transitional societies seeking to distance themselves from their predecessors. The political aims of transitional justice require

[73] Id. at 243.

[74] Germany, for instance, recognizes several different degrees of complicity, as well as a separate offense of criminal instigation.

[75] *Krstić* Appeal, op. cit., ¶ 78 (Apr. 19, 2004); see generally Alex Obote-Odora, "Complicity in Genocide as Understood through the ICTR Experience," 22 Int'l Crim. L. Rev. 375 (2002) and Chile Eboe-Osuji, "'Complicity in Genocide' versus 'Aiding and Abetting Genocide,'" 3 J. Int'l Crim. Justice 56 (2005).

[76] Author's interviews, July 2003, The Hague.

[77] *Krstić* Appeal, ¶ 268 ("Aiding and abetting is a form of responsibility which generally warrants a lower sentence than is appropriate to responsibility as a co-perpetrator.").

accentuating the contribution of former dictators, which is inconsistent with their classification as mere accessories to the crimes of subordinates. Conceiving their contribution merely as assistance, implicitly subsidiary to more heinous wrongdoing by others, minimizes their stigma and so sends the wrong signal to pertinent publics.

Closely related, the acts of distant accessories are typically – almost always, in fact – less wrongful than those of perpetrators on the scene. One of the hallmarks of state-sponsored mass atrocity, however, is that this assumption proves entirely inapplicable and unwarranted. The accessories among top chieftains are considerably more blameworthy, their conduct more wrongful, than on-the-scene perpetrators, in most cases. Our customary legal categories thus get the moral valences entirely wrong – almost backward, in fact.[78] To invoke the doctrine of complicity is to employ a deceptive device (although not a "legal fiction," strictly speaking) insofar as it both understates the top leaders' true role and, in focusing on their mere "knowing contribution" to subordinates' wrongs, does not clearly distinguish this role from that of many others who will escape prosecution. Both such failures have sometimes threatened to undermine the prosecution's legitimacy in many minds, as we see later.

One may be complicit in genocide if one merely knows of the specific intent harbored by the actual perpetrator, without sharing it. But here again, the law anticipates a situation that is often the very opposite of what historical experience offers up. In most actual genocides, it is the person behind the scenes – the national leadership, many miles away – who displays the specific intent to destroy a protected group, whereas those on the scene seek only to loot and pillage or repay a personal grudge.

Patterns of violence in civil wars, particularly, reveal that national leaders use local actors to advance large ideological and public-geopolitical purposes while the locals "use" the resources and opportunities afforded by national-level allies to settle their own private scores and inter-kin conflicts.[79] Hence, if leaders and followers must all equally share the "specific intent to destroy" a victimized group, then few cases of genocide will

---

[78] This has been a prominent theme in European and Latin American legal debate. Claus Roxin, *Autoria y Dominio del Hecho en Derecho Penal* 276–7 (Joaquín Cuello Contreras trans. 2000).

[79] Stathis Kalyvas, *The Logic of Violence in Civil War* 14, 103 (2006). "For the many people who are not naturally bloodthirsty and abhor direct involvement in violence, civil war offers irresistible opportunities to harm everyday enemies. It is this banality of violence . . . that gives civil wars a great deal of their appalling connotations." Id. at 389. See also Kalyvas, 'The Ontology of "Political Violence": Action and Identity in Civil Wars,' 1 Perspectives on Politics 475 (2003).

even be proven before criminal courts. Courts have not interpreted the law of genocide, however, to demand such a showing.

In fact, the ICTY has not required that the principal physical participants in a crime of genocide (or against humanity, of war, etc.) be considered members of the joint criminal enterprise to which such wrongs are attributed. The small fry who performs the violent *actus reus* need not even be aware that such an enterprise exists or that his actions advance its ends.[80] Only one named member of the enterprise, moreover, need have had any direct contact with a physical perpetrator of this act; the identity of that lower-echelon person need not be known to other members of the enterprise.[81] These several doctrinal developments have the effect of somewhat weakening the link that prosecutors must establish between the big fish and the small fry.[82] In all these ways, the criminal law has again proven refreshingly flexible, perspicaciously agile. And when the subordinate's motives are banal – self-interested, rather than zealously ideological, as is so often the case – then the law may also realistically rely on material incentives (in the manner proposed by Chapters 9 and 10) to influence his behavior.

The proposition that a perpetrator must be more blameworthy than an accessory – who knowingly assists the perpetrator – might be taken as either an analytical truth or an empirical probability. In the second case, this would mean a regularity apparent from the consistent evidence of historical experience, but nonetheless contingent on circumstance and so possibly inapplicable in a given case. It would then be perfectly possible to describe Argentina's military juntas, for instance, as complicit in the crimes of their subordinates.

If analytically true, by contrast, the proposition that perpetrators are more blameworthy than accessories would mean that head honchos, in virtue of their greater wrongs, simply could not – by definition – be characterized as complicit in such crimes. Alas, legal history offers no ready basis for selecting between these two views of complicity, because the need to choose has never before been squarely confronted.

These several perplexities explain why it is that international prosecutors have preferred to steer clear of complicity when seeking ways to link the upper echelons to the lowers' actions in mass atrocity prosecutions. Such prosecutors have thus been concerned not only with winning convictions

---

[80] *Prosecutor v. Brdanin and Talić*, Case No. IT-99-36-A, ICTY Appeals Chamber (April 3 2007), ¶¶ 410–413. There is scant support in precedent from customary international law for the court's position in this regard, as scholarly critics have observed.

[81] Id. at ¶¶ 413–415.

[82] I owe this observation to Professor Elies van Sliedregt, Professor of International Criminal Law, Free University of Amsterdam, correspondence with author, Nov. 2008.

but also in doing so in ways that accurately mirror the nature and extent of a defendant's relative contribution to the larger wrong. The evidence adduced by social science and historiography in this regard hence proves germane to their task.

Prosecutors have good reason to believe, as the Argentine experience described in the next section suggests, that it is not enough simply to convict those on trial – consistently with what the law permits – but that a conviction should strive to tell a larger story defensible to pertinent publics and that doctrinal choices may affect the success of such efforts.

THE UNINTENDED CONSEQUENCES OF COMPLICITY: AN ARGENTINE EXAMPLE

Conceptual niceties of the sort discussed here may initially strike the reader as no more than a professorial shell game. But they can have lethal consequences. In the late 1980s, certain justices on Argentina's Supreme Court sought to reverse an appellate court's characterization of the country's former military juntas as perpetrators,[83] reclassifying them instead as instigators, and hence, merely accessories. Junior officers were outraged at the implication that *they* were the true perpetrators. Soon indicted on that basis, these junior officers staged a series of barracks uprisings, gravely threatening the democratic transition then in progress.[84]

The justices' approach offended junior officers because it appeared to minimize the facts that the latter had acted pursuant to superiors' orders, issued through a formal chain of command, enforced by a hierarchical organization with considerable disciplinary powers. None of these undoubted circumstances found any recognition in a legal theory of complicity, which conceived the juntas as mere accessories to wrongs perpetrated by inferiors at lower ranks. Such a legal account of events was hence entirely unacceptable to them. When complicity takes the form of incitement, moreover, there are always objections that freedom of speech will be unduly encroached. This is true even when the speech in question has apparently incited atrocity and been accompanied by more material forms of support.[85]

---

[83] Corte Suprema de Justicia, 30/12/1986, "*Causa Originariamente Instruída por el Consejo Supremo de las Fuerzas Armadas en Cumplimiento del Decreto 158/83 del Poder Ejecutivo Nacional/recurso extraordinario*," Fallos (1986–309–5, 10–12, 23, 29–30) (Arg.).

[84] Carlos Nino, *Radical Evil on Trial* 116 (1999) (describing how the prospect of more trials produced a backlash in moderate military opinion, favoring their curtailment).

[85] See, e.g., C. Edwin Baker, *Genocide, Press Freedom, and the Case of Hassan Ngeze* 20–2 (Univ. of Pennsylvania Law Sch. Pub. Law and Legal Theory Research Paper Series, Paper No. 46, 2003).

Argentina's experience notwithstanding, it may usually be wrong to suppose that this or that way of classifying the relations among parties to mass atrocity much affects the response such trials elicit. Perhaps the elaborate effort to inculcate a favored interpretation of recent history is simply too clever by half. Maybe all that matters to public opinion is the fact of conviction or acquittal. In this view, criminal law may be too blunt an instrument to engage self-consciously in complex efforts to influence collective memory by the more particular story it tells. That is what neoclassical economics would predict, at any rate, in its assumption "that choices are invariant to the manner in which a problem is framed."[86]

But prosecutors and their executive sponsors often clearly *believe* that the new "official story" must be told in a manner that will most contribute to shoring up a precarious new democracy in a country just emerging from oppressive rule or civil strife. To this end, they eschew accessorial liability in prosecuting prior rulers wherever law permits otherwise. The new round of pending prosecutions against chiefs of state and top military officers – in Chile, Argentina, Peru (Fujimori, in particular), and elsewhere – thus rely heavily on the law of superior responsibility and perpetration by means of an organizational apparatus (discussed in the next chapter).

These concerns about signaling and storytelling do not exhaust the problems with trying former rulers as accessories. A more basic obstacle is finding admissible evidence of their instigations. The surreptitious character of most such communication presents a very serious problem here. The Rwandan genocide was quite almost unique in this regard. The state-sponsored radio campaign called directly for attack on the nonruling ethnic group and was followed, almost immediately, by such attacks.[87] More typical is the former Yugoslavia, where the link between rulers' speech and ensuing violence was weaker. Radio broadcasts from Belgrade called only for the formation of self-defense groups to protect against anticipated violence by non-Serb neighbors.[88] Neither superior responsibility nor enterprise participation requires any such direct evidence of communication from the defendant to criminal compatriots.

---

[86] Christine Jolls, Cass Sunstein, & Richard Thaler, "The Behavioral Approach to Law and Economics," in *Behavioral Law and Economics* 50 (Cass Sunstein, ed., 2000) (noting that traditional "economic theory assumes . . . that the language of a media account or advertisement has no effect on behavior, holding the information content constant").

[87] Gregory S. Gordon, "A War of Media, Words, Newspapers, and Radio Stations: The ICTR Media Trial Verdict and a New Chapter in the International Law of Hate Speech," 45 Va. J. Int'l L. 139, 150–2 (2004).

[88] *Prosecutor v. Guran Jelisić*, Case No. IT-95-10-A (Jul. 5, 2001).

It is possible to construe enterprise participation as a form of complicity, although the ICTY has not done so. This approach would be much more demanding of prosecutors than enterprise participation or common law conspiracy. Through aiding and abetting, prosecutors can hold each participant in the enterprise liable for the criminal acts of every other, but only if they can show how each individual "contributed substantially" to the criminal acts or results of every other. Finding substantiality can only be done case by case and so would require the prosecutor to demonstrate, separately and seriatim, the link between each participant and every other. This would entail conceptualizing the enterprise as simply a series of dyadic relationships, no more and no less.[89] For instance, to hold A liable for D's acts, if they were connected only via B and then C, would require meticulous demonstration by prosecutors that A contributed significantly to B's wrongs, who contributed significantly to C's, who in turn contributed significantly to D's.

This would be impossible, as a practical matter, if the enterprise was defined to encompass more than a handful of people. Conspiracy does not require any such painstaking analysis of the relation between particularized individuals, as monads. But that is its danger, no less than its attraction. Nowhere in the tribunal's judgments, moreover, will one find any acknowledgment that Anglo-American conspiracy doctrine has positively influenced its thinking, much less RICO. Perhaps this is not entirely surprising, since all the well-known objections to conspiracy and RICO charges reemerge with the tribunal's woolly doctrine of enterprise participation.[90]

The reason why complicity fails – the practical impossibility of establishing a substantial contribution by every participant to every other's – seems to lay bare the inherent limits of methodological individualism in our response to mass atrocity, some may say. Insofar as criminal law remains wedded to such an individualism, it too seems to stand condemned. A turn to complicity would also obscure the genuinely collective nature of the wrong, the way the whole appears greater than – or at least different from – the sum

---

[89] This way of characterizing an organization, as a series of bilateral contracts, is central to an influential school of economic thought. See, e.g., *The Firm as a Nexus of Treaties passim* (Masahiko Aoki et al., eds., 1990). Sociologists of organization rightly reject its dismissal of horizontal and other interactional processes among triads not linked to one another through formal agreements. Harrison White, "Agency as Control in Formal Networks," in *Networks and Organizations* 92, 96 (Nitin Nohria & Robert G. Eccles, eds., 1992) (arguing that it is "a retreat from institutional reality" to view organizations as simply "an aggregation . . . or field of pair ties").

[90] For such criticisms, see Susan Brenner, "RICO, CCE, and Other Complex Crimes," 2 Wm. & Mary Bill Rts. J. 239, 303 (1993).

of the parts. We simply cannot do without the concept of an "enterprise," after all, despite all the problems with its current uses, dissected above.

The preceding observations explain the reluctance of ICTY prosecutors and judges to rely on accessorial liability, though authorized by the court's statute, when alternatives counting the accused as perpetrators can credibly be advanced. Still, defining the criminal enterprise in the more modest way suggested by the law of complicity might not entirely be a bad idea, insofar as it reduces the serious danger of the prosecutorial overreach here discussed.

5

The Bureaucracy of Murder

The key challenges that criminal justice confronts in coping with mass atrocity, as we have seen, trace to a central dilemma: law and evidence permit liability far beyond the few individuals who can practically be prosecuted, but even these few can be convicted only through theories of liability that blame them for wrongs beyond their complete control or contemplation.

This may first appear largely a practical concern about scarce resources: only a few of the big fish can be prosecuted (internationally, at least) for only a small fraction of the misconduct by a limited number of the small fry. Yet this practical problem quickly raises a vexing normative question about how to assess relative degrees of responsibility among an atrocity's myriad participants. Answering that question in turn requires determining what misconduct by which subordinates can be ascribed fairly to specific superiors and their peers. There often will be many such people arrayed along a chain of command, within a general staff, or among the members of an interbranch, policymaking committee. Differing answers to the preceding queries yield distinct choices about whom to prosecute, for which offenses. The scarcity of prosecutorial resources makes these challenges still more fraught with controversy.

Prosecutors at the national and international levels have responded differently to these concerns. At the ICTY, prosecutors turn to enterprise participation because the doctrine readily reaches beyond army bureaucracies to informal power networks, enabling them to maximize convictions – even of lower echelons – and thereby further empowering their emergent professional field of international criminal law. The national prosecutor in a newly democratic state, by contrast, prefers approaches like superior responsibility that narrow the scope of blameworthy parties, because this narrowing placates executives wishing to limit prosecutions to small numbers of now-powerless individuals. New rulers publicly justify limiting trials in the interests of social reconciliation and regime consolidation. But the intention also is to ensure that trials serve the political objectives of their masters, consolidating their power, which is often still precarious.

Where such power has shifted to new elites, this means prosecuting high-ranking past leadership, as in Argentina. Where elite power has not changed hands often, it means perfunctorily trying a handful of the rank and file for exceeding orders, as in Indonesia. Only where entire ruling groups have been displaced from state power does it mean large numbers of trials for both leaders and led. Rwanda stands alone in this regard.

The upshot is that national and international courts are treating similarly situated offenders differently. Clear differences in how *many* people are tried find more subtle expression in differences over the legal rules *by which* they are tried. This study examines the second of these disparities. This inconsistency can be at least partly overcome if superior responsibility and enterprise participation are better understood and applied. Were superior responsibility's high risk of acquittal reduced, so would be the incentives to rely excessively on enterprise participation, with its imprecise and dangerously illiberal tendencies.

This chapter endorses a broadened theory of superior responsibility, drawing on some recent European jurisprudence, that conceives of the superior as controlling not the particular subordinates who commit criminal wrongs, but the larger organizational apparatus within which they labor. Chapters 9 and 10 then argue that an enterprise participation doctrine might be employed primarily to impose collective monetary sanctions on the officer corps because a military elite can readily monitor prospective wrongdoers *ex ante* and redistribute costs *ex post* to individual members who are actually culpable, thus averting punishment of the innocent.

Despite the considerable problems with enterprise participation identified by this study, the doctrine is not without value and even may be indispensable. That value would be enhanced if it were used to impart civil rather than criminal sanctions. The doctrine's illiberal dangers largely disappear when it is employed, in particular, to levy collective sanctions against members of an officer corps.

EASING SUPERIOR RESPONSIBILITY: A NEW CONCEPTION
OF EFFECTIVE CONTROL

"Civil law" has traditionally lacked the concept of conspiracy, and civil lawyers have been correspondingly sceptical about the new law of enterprise participation. Deprived of such broad-gauged, shotgun approaches – implying "agreement" from seemingly coordinated actions, however far afield – civil lawyers have long been compelled to give greater thought than common law lawyers to the types of association that should make one person criminally liable for another's acts.

Civil lawyers often employ the notions of co-perpetration and indirect perpetration by "acting through another" to make sense of mass criminality. These approaches apply even when the criminal associates do not know the others involved, and when membership in the group shifts over time without the express approval of all.[1] Such civil law thinking offers some helpful resources for international criminal law, which has drawn in this area almost exclusively from the most controversial aspects of the common law.

Especially useful here is Roxin's influential analysis of Adolf Eichmann's trial.[2] Argentine judges adopted this analysis when convicting the country's military juntas of large-scale human rights abuses.[3] German courts later used it to convict high-ranking superiors of the border guards who shot East Germans scaling the Berlin Wall.[4] Peruvian prosecutors are currently employing it against former President Alberto Fujimori. One ICTY Trial Chamber also briefly sought to employ this approach to mass atrocity in the former Yugoslavia.[5] Most importantly, the ICC Rome Statute authorizes

---

[1] Enrique García Vitor, "La Tesis del 'Dominio del Hecho a Través de los Aparatos Organizados de Poder,'" in *Nuevas Formulaciones en las Ciencias* 327, 344–8 (Carlos Julio Lascano, ed., 2001).

[2] Claus Roxin, "Straftaten im Rahmen Organisatorischer Machtapparate," in *Goltdammer's Archiv für Strafrecht* (1993). Roxin's analysis has been highly influential in Germany and beyond. Carlos Julio Lascano, "Teoría de los Aparatos Organizados de Poder y Delitos Empresariales," in *Nuevas Formulaciones en las Ciencias*, op. cit., at 353 (noting Roxin's many adherents).

[3] Juicio de los Excomandantes, Sentencia de la Cámara Nacional de Apelaciones en lo Criminal e Correccional de la Capital, 9/12/1985 at 1601. Two members of the Argentine Supreme Court, however, insisted on recharacterizing the junta's contribution in terms of "essential accessories." These judges concluded that Roxin's views had not been sufficiently endorsed by Argentine law. Corte Suprema de Justicia, 30/12/1986, "Causa Originariamente Instruída por el Consejo Supremo de las Fuerzas Armadas en Cumplimiento del Decreto 158/83 del Poder Ejecutivo Nacional/recurso extraordinario," Fallos (1986–309–5, 10–12, 23, 29–30) (Arg.). For analysis, see Kai Ambos & Christoph Grammer, "Dominio del hecho por organización: La responsabilidad de la conducción militar argentina por la muerte de Elisabeth Käsemann," 12 Revista Penal 27 (2003); Kai Ambos, *Dominio del Hecho por Dominio de Voluntad en Virtud de Aparatos Organizados de Poder* (Manuel Cancio Melia, trans., 1998).

[4] Bundesgerichtshof, July 26, 1994, 40 Entscheidungen des Bundesgerichtshofes in Strafsachen, 218 (F.R.G.). The superiors were members of the German Democratic Republic's National Defense Counsel. This is the state body that issued orders to shoot citizens scaling the Berlin Wall. See generally Brad Roth, "Retroactive Justice or Retroactive Standards? Human Rights as a Sword in the East German Leaders Case," 50 Wayne L. Rev. 37 (2004).

[5] The Chamber expressly characterized the defendant's role, in Roxin's terminology, as the "perpetrator behind the direct perpetrator." The court also relied on Roxin's

it,[6] and the Court's Pretrial Chamber has already employed it in two of its first cases, *Katanga* and *Bemba Gombo*.[7] The Office of the Prosecutor invokes it as well in its request for an arrest warrant against Sudanese President Omar al-Bashir.[8]

Roxin argues that "what happens in such events [as the Holocaust] is, to speak graphically, that a person behind the scenes at the controls of the organized structure presses a button" that results in an order that he or she can count on to be implemented, without needing to know who will actually do so or in what fashion.[9] A particular subordinate who does not comply with the order will be immediately substituted by another, so that the plan's execution will not be compromised. As the ICC prosecutor alleges in a Darfur case, "Individuals who refuse to commit crimes are dismissed and replaced. . . ."[10] The decisive factor is the fungibility of those who execute the commands.[11]

notion of co-perpetration through "joint control over the act" (i.e., the crime's *actus reus*. *Prosecutor v. Milomir Stakić*, Case No. IT-97-24-T, Trial Judgment (July 31, 2003). The Appeals Chamber, however, held that customary international law does not recognize these now-familiar "civil law" doctrines and recategorized the defendant's mode of participation in terms of joint criminal enterprise. *Prosecutor v. Milomir Stakić*, Case No. IT-97-24-A, Appeals Judgment (March 22, 2006).

[6] The Rome Statute, unlike that for the ICTY or ICTR, contains language specifically creating liability where the accused "commits . . . a crime . . . through another person, regardless of whether that other person is criminally responsible." Rome Statute of the International Criminal Court, Art. 25(3)(a). Roxin's proposal is couched as an addition to the existing list of ways in which a person may commit a crime "through another."

[7] *Prosecutor v. Germain Katanga and Mathieu Ngudjolo Chui*, ICC-01/04-01/07, Pre-Trial Chamber I, Decision on the Confirmation of Charges, ¶¶ 477–518 (September 30, 2008), at http://www.icc-cpi.int/library/cases/ICC-01-04-01-07-717-ENG.pdf; *Prosecutor v. Jean-Pierre Bemba Gombo*, ICC-01/05-01/08-14-tENG ¶ 78. The Court did not employ this approach, however, in *Lubanga*. *Prosecutor v. Thomas Lubanga Dyilo*, ICC-01/04-01/06, Pre-Trial Chamber I, Decision on the Confirmation of Charges, ¶¶ 327–67 (January 29, 2007), at http://www.icc-cpi.int/library/cases/ICC-01-04-01-06-803-tEN_English.pdf.

[8] The Office of the Prosecutor, Summary of the Case, Prosecutor's Application for Warrant of Arrest under 58 Against Omar Hassan Ahmad Al Bashir, July 14, 2008, available at http://www.icc-cpi.int/library/organs/otp/ICC-OTP-Summary-20081704-ENG.pdf; Public Redacted Version of Prosecutor's Application under Art. 58 filed on July 14, 2008, *Situation in Darfur, Sudan* (ICC-02/05-157), 12 September 2008, sec. 39. For commentary, see Florian Jessberger & Julia Geneuss, "On the Application of a Theory of Indirect Perpetration in Al Bashir," 6 J. of Int'l Crim. Justice 853, 856–64 (2008).

[9] Claus Roxin, *Autoría y Dominio del Hecho en Derecho Penal* § 24, at 270 (Joaquín Cuello Contreras & José Luis Serrano González de Murillo trans., 1998).

[10] Luis Moreno-Ocampo, "Prosecutor's Statement on the Prosecutor's Application for a Warrant of Arrest under Article 58 Against Omar Hassan Al Bashir," Office of the Prosecutor, ICC, The Hague, July 14, 2008.

[11] Edgardo Alberto Donna, "El Concepto de Autoría y la Teoría de los Aparatos de Poder de Roxin," in *Nuevas Formulaciones*, op. cit., at 295, 309.

The superior's control over an "organizational apparatus of hierarchical power," as Roxin calls it,[12] enables that superior to use the subordinate "as a mere gear in a giant machine"[13] to produce the criminal result on its own, as it were. Such an apparatus "develops a life that is independent of the changing composition of its members, and functions without depending on the individual identity of the executant, as if it were 'automatic.'"[14] The inferior's compliance with illegal orders, however, flows neither from coercion nor deception, whether by mistake of fact or law, and so the subordinate remains responsible for his or her actions. This culpability – characteristic of most foot soldiers to mass atrocity – leaves the inferior susceptible to prosecution.

Loose talk about such inferiors as gears always seemed to imply that the law must treat them as "the blameless instrument of an alien will."[15] It is likely, in fact, that Roxin drew the metaphors of men as cogs from Arendt's earlier book on the Eichmann trial, which Roxin – as a fellow German then writing on the same subject – would likely have read. Arendt, too, described the defendant as a cog in a bureaucratic machine.[16] Roxin's work might hence be seen as an effort to translate Arendt's sociopolitical analysis of Eichmann's "banality" into a legal idiom potentially acceptable to courts.

The appeal of Roxin's approach is that it does not follow from this characterization that the inferior is innocent. The ICC Statute provides that a person who commits an international crime "jointly with another or through another person" is liable "regardless of whether that other person is criminally responsible."[17] In fact, the interchangeability of subordinates implicitly envisions their compliance as knowing and voluntary; those disinclined to obey would have been replaced by more willing peers. Roxin's key insight, then, is that the more powerful parties behind the scenes may, through the organizational resources at their disposal (including the culpable inferior), be said to commit the offense. This tack may be viewed as a creative effort to give juridical acknowledgment to the bureaucratic nature of mass atrocity, without going so far as to ground liability on mere organizational membership. Its appeal lies precisely in how it performs both tasks at once.

---

[12] Claus Roxin, "Problemas de Autoría y Participación en la Criminalidad Organizada," in *Delincuencia Organizada: Aspectos Penales, Procesales y Criminológicos* 196 (Juan Carlos Ferré Olivé & Enrique Anarte Borrallo, eds., 1999).
[13] Donna, op. cit., at 309; Roxin, "Problemas," op. cit., at 194.
[14] Roxin, "Straftaten," op. cit. at 200.
[15] John Lachs, *Responsibility and the Individual in Modern Society* 12–13, 58 (1981).
[16] Hannah Arendt, *Eichmann in Jerusalem* 57, 289 (1962).
[17] Rome Statute, Art. 25(3)(a).

In Roxin's view, the superior is not a mere instigator because the latter is distinguished "by his initiative in seeking out a potential perpetrator, contacting him, convincing him to participate in the criminal activity, and overcoming his initial resistance through persuasive efforts."[18] This tells part of the superior's story, to be sure. The military superior's *ex ante* promises of impunity often are essential in overcoming inferiors' initial reluctance. These promises are credible only because the superior controls the police and military agencies that would otherwise investigate the wrongs. His or her failure to punish the subordinate *post facto* – central to the law of superior responsibility – is simply the corollary of this power to bestow impunity.

This power exceeds that of a mere instigator, however. Ordering atrocity bears a superficial resemblance to "suggesting" or recommending it, insofar as both entail speech acts. Yet the two are profoundly different in social meaning, even were their wording identical. To effectively order another person to do one's murderous bidding requires an organizational machinery that stands behind the speaker; otherwise, the statement is just instigation, a form of complicity, with punishment diminished accordingly. It is no accident that, in the ICC Statute, the word "orders" is paired in the same clause with "solicits" and "induces," verbs associated with liability as a mere accessory.[19] The ICC prosecutor, hence, prefers to avoid invoking this mode of participation, even when there is ample indication, as in *Katanga*,[20] of a defendant's having ordered people about. In the circumstances at issue, it is only the material support afforded by the hierarchical organization to the speaker's words that makes them so effective, enabling him to know that his speech will have the harmful effect he intends. Apart from this peculiar context, the word "ordering" might plausibly be taken to refer only to a speaker's emotional register and tone of voice, which is insufficient to render him a perpetrator.

For Roxin, what defines the legal circumstance of a ranking bureaucrat like Eichmann is that he needs only to issue an order – within the framework of an organizational structure of hierarchical power – to know, to a high probability, that the order will be obeyed, however clearly unlawful.[21] The superior in a military bureaucracy, moreover, provides subordinates with tangible resources like weapons, ammunition, and financing necessary to commit their offenses. But this assistance goes beyond mere aiding and abetting, since the superior does not merely know but also intends that the

---

[18] Donna, op. cit., at 355.

[19] Rome Statute, Art. 25(3)(b).

[20] *Katanga*, op. cit., ¶¶ 544–545, 555(i)(a), 560, 563, 569.

[21] Roxin, "Problemas," op. cit., at 196; Jerusalem Dist. Ct. (Dec. 12, 1961) 36 ILR 236–37, ¶ 197.

organization's resources be put to criminal ends, ones he shares and may even formulate.

DIFFICULTIES WITH ROXIN'S APPROACH:
A POST-WEBERIAN UPDATE

Roxin's preoccupation with the formal apparatus of state bureaucracy will immediately strike a chord with those whom the Holocaust has convinced of mass atrocity's distinctively modern features.[22] Modern rationality is epitomized in bureaucracy, according to Max Weber,[23] and the Third Reich was long viewed as the quintessential "bureaucracy of murder."[24] "The 'Final Solution' *was generated by bureaucracy true to its form and purpose*," charged one influential study.[25] Another proclaimed that the German "bureaucratic apparatus showed concern for correct bureaucratic procedure, for the niceties of precise definition, for the minutiae of bureaucratic regulation, and for compliance with the law."[26]

Weber viewed bureaucracy as the most effective method of organizational control, and it is easy to see why. The bureaucrat, by hypothesis, is subject to a unified chain of command imposing strict subordination upon him even as it bestows similar supervisory powers and duties over others. The regulations governing his activities are impersonal, consistent, and complete. The rights and duties associated with particular positions are specified in advance, clarifying the scope of everyone's authority. Directives are conveyed in writing, virtually eliminating miscommunication between leaders and led. Officials are trained in the precise skills required for their positions, which they may not appropriate. Employees own none of the resources

---

[22] There are many expressions of this view, beginning with the influential work of Max Horkheimer & Theodor W. Adorno, *Dialectic of Enlightenment* 201–2 (John Cumming trans., 1991) (1944); see also Zygmunt Bauman, *Modernity and the Holocaust* 12–18 (1989); Omer Bartov, "Seeking the Roots of Modern Genocide: On the Macro- and Micro-history of Mass Murder," in *The Specter of Genocide: Mass Murder in Historical Perspective* 75, 80 (Robert Gellately & Ben Kiernan, eds., 2003); Marie Fleming, "Genocide and the Body Politic in the Time of Modernity," in *The Specter of Genocide*, op. cit., at 97, 112–13; Eric D. Weitz, "The Modernity of Genocide: War, Race, and Revolution in the Twentieth Century," in *The Specter of Genocide*, op. cit., at 53, 54–5.

[23] Max Weber, *From Max Weber: Essays in Sociology* 196–244 (H.H. Gerth & C. Wright Mills, eds., trans., 1946).

[24] Albert Breton & Ronald Wintrobe, "The Bureaucracy of Murder Revisited," 94 J. Pol. Econ. 905, 906 (1986); see also Christopher R. Browning, "The German Bureaucracy and the Holocaust," in *Genocide* 145, 148 (Alex Grobman & Daniel Landes, eds., 1983) ("The Nazis' mass murder of the European Jews was not only the technological achievement of an industrial society, but also the organizational achievement of a bureaucratic society.").

[25] Bauman, op. cit., at 17 (emphasis in original).

[26] Leo Kuper, *Genocide: Its Political Use in the Twentieth Century* 121 (1981).

required for their tasks; private income therefore remains entirely separate from the organizational fisc. Every such feature of bureaucracy contributes to maximizing the superior's control over subordinates, minimizing their freedom to pursue goals of their own.

In the 1950s and 1960s, in particular, atrocity's more modest minions were seen as "organization men," motivated by nothing more than a desire to fit in with those around them.[27] Hannah Arendt, who most influentially applied this notion to mass atrocity, seemingly revelled in the shock value of accentuating the normality of genocidal offenders, the way in which they were just like the rest of us.[28] Later genocides have often been seen in a similar light. Western foreign policymakers initially viewed even the Rwandan and Bosnian genocides in this way.[29] In Cambodia and Ethiopia, scholars stressed "the rigorous documentation of 'life histories' and 'confessions' that the party's bureaucrats compiled."[30]

A legal approach that accentuates bureaucracy's contribution to such conflagrations helps overcome the common tendency to dismiss them as recrudescent primitivism, certain to diminish over time under modernity's beneficent influence. Nuremberg's prosecutors themselves invoked primitivist tropes.[31] Today, many rightly decry this as Enlightenment hubris.[32] But it is also true that this earlier generation of theorists was generally less interested in carefully examining the empirical complexities of mass atrocity than in heralding the "destructive potential of the civilizing process."[33]

The Holocaust could have happened anywhere in the capitalist West, they implied, in its "striving to produce corpses with the same methods employed to produce goods."[34] It could happen, in fact, wherever bourgeois conformity prevailed. Such writers sought, above all, to repudiate the modernist

---

[27] This then-fashionable term was drawn from the bestseller, William H. Whyte, Jr, *The Organization Man* 3 (1956). This view found later support in the experimental social psychology of the period, such as Stanley Milgram, *Obedience to Authority* (1974).

[28] Arendt, op. cit., at 31–41.

[29] Benjamin Valentino, *Final Solutions: Mass Killing and Genocide in the Twentieth Century* 236 (2004); see also Robert D. Kaplan, *Balkan Ghosts* 22, 39–40 (1993).

[30] Edward Kissi, "Genocide in Cambodia and Ethiopia," in *The Specter of Genocide*, op. cit., at 307, 315.

[31] Lawrence Douglas, "The Shrunken Head of Buchenwald: Icons of Atrocity at Nuremberg," *Representations*, at 39, 40–3 (Summer 1998) (showing how Nuremberg prosecutors artfully depicted perpetrators' motivations as regressively but reassuringly antimodern).

[32] Michel Feher, "Terms of Reconciliation," in *Human Rights in Political Transitions*, 325, 336–7 (Robert Post & Carla Hesse, eds., 1999) (rejecting the view that modern genocide is "primarily the expression of a primitive mentality that needs to be overcome").

[33] Bauman, op. cit. at 13.

[34] Omer Bartov, *Germany's War and the Holocaust* 135 (2003). Bartov is here describing others' views.

view that "the lesson of mass murder is that the prevention of similar hic-
cups of barbarism evidently requires still more civilizing efforts."[35] The
proposition that international humanitarian law, originating in the modern West, might successfully embody moral truths of genuinely universal
validity would likely have left them incredulous.

Yet certain key features of bureaucracy are conspicuously absent from
the forms of social organizations through which many mass atrocities are
conducted. This is so even when the organization at issue is the state rather,
rather than paramilitaries or insurgent groups. We thus face the question
of whether bureaucracy – i.e., something approximating its ideal-type –
is necessary for superiors to be able to exercise the kind and measure of
control that the law may require prosecutors to prove. In other words, how
far may the facts at issue depart from this ideal-type for prosecutors to be
able to employ the law on co-perpetration through an hierarchical organization in holding superiors atop a large organization criminally responsible
for the acts of its lowest inferiors? Weber's picture may accurately reflect
Chaplin's fantasy of "modern times," but bears little relation to the human
experience of combat. More than the law on perpetration through a top-
down organization, the law of superior responsibility, as indicated, readily
accommodates the fact that *de facto* power often deviates from the *de jure*
authority established by an hierarchical chain of command.

Episodes of mass atrocity often notably depart from the rational order-
liness, sanitized precision, and efficiency suggested by the "organization
man" account. Scholars now stress instead the spontaneous initiative at
lower echelons, informal character, and face-to-face nature of much Nazi
killing,[36] to say nothing of the Rwandan (and other) experiences. Milošević,
for that matter, was in no organizational position to order the Bosnian Serb
leaders to do or stop doing anything at Srebrenica.

These newly noticed features of mass atrocity resonate with both premodern and postmodern themes: premodern, in the perpetrators' motivations – ethno-nationalist and religious fundamentalist – and postmodern in
their use of the sophisticated interfirm networking championed by *au cur-
rant* organization theory.[37] That such bizarre motivational-organizational

---

[35] Id. at 28.

[36] Richard Breitman, *The Architect of Genocide* 105–15 (1991); Christopher Browning, *The Path to Genocide* 86–92 (1992).

[37] Manuel Castells, *The Rise of the Network Society* 172–87 (1996) (celebrating informal networks as the emergent form of social organization, more efficient than bureaucracy for
economic production and other activities). On the network-like structure of Al Qaeda and
its relation to affiliates, see Peter L. Bergen, *Holy War, Inc.: Inside the Secret World of Osama
bin Laden* 195–220 (2001).

hybrids might little resemble bureaucratic conformism and yield far-reaching harm beyond anybody's effective control should no less disturb our modern self-confidence than the suggestion – so bemusing to Eisenhower-era intellectuals – that genocidal mass murders were really just bourgeois family men like the rest of us.

The more informal, unsystematic, and decentralized dimensions of mass atrocity, with the renewed importance they give to individual initiative and enthusiasm below the top ranks, also reinforce the impulse – now ascendant in international criminal law – to prioritize individual accountability over legal judgment against states. Judging states appeared to blame, by implication, the nations they represent within the world community, rather than those who led them into catastrophe. (Whether this movement may have gone too far, however, is examined in Chapters 9 and 10.)

In few countries do military superiors lightly presume the "strict subordination" that, Weber insisted, defines the ideal-typical bureaucracy.[38] In particular, they do not assume that their orders – criminal or otherwise – will invariably be obeyed, given the serious risks they may pose for inferiors implementing them. Moreover, subordinates in all large organizations, including armed forces,[39] routinely subvert the goals of their superiors when inconsistent with their own.[40]

Roxin's analysis assumes the existence of a rigidly formal bureaucracy of the sort contemplated by Weber's famous ideal-type, developed from his understanding of the authoritarian Prussian army, in which the organizational chart perfectly mirrors the behavior of the people occupying positions within it.[41] In this model, all power flows from top to bottom.[42] Managers need never struggle to maintain control in the face of significant resistance; organizational goals are set from on high and accepted by all below.[43]

For the last century, however, organization theory has greatly qualified this model, documenting and seeking to understand the many departures from it. Little of Weber's ideal-type remains generally applicable to most large organizations today. It was once widely criticized as reflecting merely the manager's normative ideal, rather than any empirical reality

[38] Weber, *Essays*, op. cit., at 214–15.
[39] Mark Osiel, *Obeying Orders: Atrocity, Military Discipline, & the Law of War* 173–85 (1999) (discussing disparities between the goals of superiors and subordinates).
[40] Charles Perrow, *Complex Organizations* 158–63 (1972).
[41] Weber, *Essays*, op. cit., at 196–244.
[42] Id. at 197, 221–4.
[43] Id. at 228–30.

demonstrable by social science.[44] But today even managers, at least in leading business schools are no longer taught this model of organizational
behavior as either descriptively accurate or, for that matter, generally desirable. "Scholars recognize that managers prefer the personal, verbal channels
of the informal system to the documents and orders of the formal. Indeed
managers spend as much time working outside the chain of command as
they do working through it."[45]

If Roxin's approach to managerial control were inextricably wedded to
an outdated model, it would offer little of value in refocusing the law of
superior responsibility. If we were to read it into the law, it could easily have
devastating consequences for prosecutions of mass atrocity. It would be easy
enough for defense counsel to show, in most cases, that their client lacked the
degree of control over inferiors posited in an ideal Weberian bureaucracy.
To ensure acquittal, defense counsel would need merely demonstrate that
their client lacked the power to readily replace sullen juniors with more
enthusiastic drones. The reinterpretation of effective control proposed here
would then prove insufficient. It would fail to increase the utility of superior
responsibility to international prosecutors or thus to restore its viability
within international law.

Replacing reluctant inferiors, moreover, may be possible in theory, but
it can often be difficult in practice to show that subordinates were actually fungible, an evidentiary burden the prosecution would bear. Especially
in a small organization, there may be few if any competent replacements
for a particular member, in which case the theory collapses, as the ICC
Pre-Trial Chamber acknowledges.[46] Even when some of his subordinates
are not readily replaceable, the superior in many organizations nonetheless
knows that his orders will almost certainly be obeyed simply because others would have no strong objection or might simply have no employment
alternatives immediately at hand. It is the superior's knowledge of probable
consequences that is at issue to his culpability here. The law thus should not
heavily rely on the dated metaphor of man the machine; that fiction is often
misplaced because it is not especially well-attuned (and certainly unnecessary) to establishing the pertinent species of linkage between superior and

---

[44] This rejection, which began in the work of Chester Barnard, was developed by the human
relations school of management and continues into the information economics of organizations, championed by Herbert Simon.

[45] Walter W. Powell & Laurel Smith-Doerr, "Networks and Economic Life," in *The Handbook
of Economic Sociology* 368, 380 (Neil J. Smelser & Richard Swedberg, eds., 1994).

[46] *Katanga*, op. cit., ¶ 512, 516. The Peruvian court that convicted Fromer President Alberto
Fujmori in April 2009 saw fit to dispense with the fungibility requirement entirely.

subordinate within most organizations engaged in mass atrocity. In assessing the superior's misconduct, the capacity to switch subordinates between positions may not be the most relevant type of control, for that matter. And the power to assign persons to positions within an organization need not be accompanied by a high degree of control over their subsequent conduct.

Roxin's approach does not take account of the latitude inferiors sometimes enjoy in determining the fate of their victims, as the moral relevance of this control type is obvious. Lack of such control by superiors is especially relevant if it is wrested from them, rather than granted spontaneously. In Argentina's Dirty War, during which officers murdered at least fifteen thousand people, junior officers were eminently interchangeable by their superiors; almost all participated in some fashion.[47] Superiors controlled the general process by which victims were chosen for abduction, in light of the campaign's objectives. But junior officers at the lowest echelons exercised great discretion over what to do with their captives after interrogation. Captives might be prosecuted by military tribunals, turned over to police for trial by civilian courts, freed from any custody, or simply killed. Neither the juntas nor high-level intermediate ranks played much role in these decisions: The power of junior officers to determine the life or death of their captives became a principal theme in their interactions with these unfortunate souls.[48]

If a junior officer who murdered a specific detainee could just as readily have freed him or her without fear of rebuke from above, then surely a fact-finder could conclude that the junta members lacked the relevant control necessary for liability. It is possible that superiors could have interceded more actively, establishing rules to govern how such choices were made. Proving that they could have done so is another matter; the subordinates' freedom to "play God" was a significant source of their compensation. Such factual complexities impede any simple application of Roxin's method and, in fact, helped persuade two Supreme Court justices to reject it when convicting the juntas, instead, as essential accessories.[49] The ICC Pre-Trial

---

[47] Mark Osiel, *Mass Atrocity, Ordinary Evil, and Hannah Arendt* 86–7 (2001).

[48] Mark Osiel, "Constructing Subversion in Argentina's Dirty War," 75 Representations 119, 141 (Summer 2001).

[49] Lascano, op. cit., at 370. Though junior officers did not enjoy quite so much autonomy during military rule in Chile, more senior officers exercised a great deal, over fundamental operational matters, as is often generally the case. Though he is hardly the most reliable source on the question, Chilean Ex-President Augusto Pinochet thus described the division of labor: "The Chief of the Army [i.e., Pinochet himself] always asks, 'What are you going to do? The question of How, how am I going to do it? is a question for the chief of intelligence,

Chamber similarly understands the method to permit classifying the "intellectual author" or "mastermind" behind the physical perpetrators as a true principal only if he is the person who "essentially decides whether and how the offense will be committed."[50] In the Argentine circumstances just described, however, questions of "how" were delegated almost entirely to subordinates, often very junior ones at that. The same will likely prove to be true, if sometimes to lesser extent, in other episodes of mass atrocity.

Roxin's analogy of human interaction within a complex organization to interchangeable parts of a machine, producing criminal acts from subordinates "almost automatically,"[51] has been expressly endorsed by the ICC.[52] Yet it is merely a metaphor and not always an especially fruitful one. It offers an indicator of only one type of control exercised over an organization's members. The ICC itself acknowledges this possibility, going so far as to suggest that:

> Attributes of the organisation – other than the replaceability of subordinates – may also enable automatic compliance with the senior authority's orders. An alternative means by which a leader secures automatic compliance via his control of the apparatus may be through intensive, strict, and violent training regimens. For example, abducting minors and subjecting them to punishing training regimens in which they are taught to shoot, pillage, rape, and kill, may be an effective means for ensuring automatic compliance with leaders' orders to commit such acts.[53]

These were precisely the acts charged to the defendants in the case before the Court. The judges here rightly retain the requirement of "effective control" by the superior. But they allow that such control might be exercised through an institution lacking the measure of formal hierarchy that Eichmann enjoyed when dispatching Hungarian Jews to their deaths far away in Auschwitz.

Formal organization on the Western bureaucratic model is sometimes unnecessary to coordinate an effective fighting force whose members are already united by years of the intimate interaction. This may involve growing

---

rather than the Chief of the Army. This is what civilians . . . don't understand." Interview, Pinochet Fact File, Daily Telegraph, July 19, 1999.

[50] *Katanga*, op. cit., at ¶¶ 515, 485. The three ICC cases mentioned here are only at preliminary stages. It is impossible to know in what direction the Court will ultimately develop Roxin's theory, once presented at full trial with further evidence and more detailed legal argument.

[51] Id. at ¶¶ 534, 539, 547.

[52] Id. at ¶¶ 515–516.

[53] Id. at ¶ 518.

up together in a single village or nearby villages of common tribal affilia-
tion. The high measure of trust among these fighters permits lines of *de facto*
authority to shift quickly in reaction to immediate contingencies without
prejudicing operational capacity. Detailed orders from superiors become
dispensable in combat because organization in combat arises instead from
this intense camaraderie and other, equally intangible elements of "social
capital." The group's members coordinate spontaneously in response to
their comrades' immediate cues, which are often unobservable (much less
intelligible) to outsiders. Such men behave at work in ways no less decentralized than they do at play, where – as observes one contemporary legal
expert – "they make football passes blindly because they always know where
the other players will be."[54]

It may come as no surprise that Western military law on superior responsibility, upon which international criminal law now builds, has been at rather
a loss to make sense of this species of social organization. Leading experts in
military law continue to describe the sources of its stunning efficacy, in con-
tests with Western armies, as "mystical" and "spiritual."[55] The proverbial
playing fields of Eton (and the easy intra-elite communication they purportedly facilitated) are apparently no match in generating so much "unit
cohesion," as we Westerners more clumsily call this phenomenon. It threatens to upset the applecart of conventional legal categories through which
we assign responsibility to individuals. We therefore find it perplexing, even
perturbing.

International courts may someday conclude that the commander of such
a force is nonetheless "acting through" or "by means of" those who perform
the criminal acts, and so perpetrates their wrongs. But the law of command
responsibility will offer little help in holding him accountable. As generally
interpreted, such law requires prosecutors to show "a functioning chain
of command, a sufficiently developed planning and orders process, and a
strong disciplinary system" to punish rule-infractions.[56] So concludes the
Special Tribunal for Sierra Leone, for instance.

In contrast, the law of perpetration by means of another, as recently
elaborated in a number of west European and Latin American countries, is

---

[54] Michael Newton & Casey Kuhlman, "Why Warlords Evade the Law (of Command Responsibility): A Plea for a More Appropriate Conception of Effective Control," unpublished
manuscript, 2009. The authors therefore conclude, in connection to a few recent, unsuc-
cessful ICTY prosecutions based on superior responsibility, "In none of these situations is
there a dearth of control, it is only implemented in different ways."

[55] Id. at 8.

[56] *Prosecutor v. Alex Tamba Brima, et al.*, Case No. SCSL-04-16-T, ¶ 557 (June 20, 2007).

more accommodating. It imagines, if you will, a village watchmaker who constructs a little clock, then winds it up and walks away, without looking back. In the present cases he has also attached that clock to a bomb, of course, which detonates well after he has left the scene.

This is a simplified version of the story that the Argentine courts sought to tell in convicting that country's military juntas in 1987. On this account, the juntas had constructed an elaborate administrative system, described in great detail by the court, for the political repression of perceived "subversives." The institutional components of this system were assembled at the very outset of military rule. Beyond that point, there was no longer any need for individual junta members to intercede directly in its quotidian functioning in order to produce thousands of ensuing crimes. Some of these occurred years later, in the country's furthest hinterlands.

The Argentine courts inferred that junta members must have intended these crimes, knew they would occur, or at least consciously adverted to a serious risk of this possibility. This is also essentially the portrait that Roxin paints of Adolf Eichmann: first as an empirical account drawn from the Jerusalem trial transcript, then as a broader theory of liability, grounded in and elaborating on that account. Roxin's theory in turn offered the Argentine judges an alluring conceptual solution in the junta case.

A striking advantage to this approach, from a prosecutor's perspective, is that the temporal focus of analysis shifts subtly away from the time and place where the harm occurs to when and where the metaphorical "watch" was assembled and wound up. Provided that no one intervenes (with the demonstrable intent of disrupting a process already set in motion) between the initial and the later points, the watchmaker is clearly responsible for the explosion and the harms it causes, though he may know neither who the particular victims will be nor the details of how they each will be harmed.[57]

---

[57] The reader may observe that the metaphor of the watchmaker, in constructing and winding up his bomb, is no less mechanical than that of Roxin's gears and cogs in a factory assembly line. In both cases, the trope (even cliché) of automatism is confessedly appealing because it finesses the fact that, in cases of mass atrocity at least, other people's deliberate actions – following the defendants' own in time – contribute to the ensuing harm. Criminal law normally considers such "intervening voluntary acts" to break the causal chain. H.L.A. Hart & Tony Honoré, *Causation in The Law* 389–94 (1959). This causal break would in turn usually require the defendant to be characterized as making only a "contribution," hence, to be merely an accessory, rather than a principal/perpetrator. Yet the law often employs "fictions" and other such metaphors when they are agreed to serve the interests of justice, because the analogy they draw is generally considered morally fitting, and the positive law itself has not yet caught up to these settled moral judgments and sociological understandings. Lon Fuller, *Legal Fictions* 6–7, 49–92 (1931). As the *Palsgraf* dissent famously argued for U.S. law, ascribing causation always involves not only counterfactual speculation

An ICC Pre-Trial Chamber has endorsed this view of the doctrine, without qualification:

> Although some authors have linked the essential character of a task – and hence, the ability to exercise joint control over the crime – to its performance at the execution stage, the Statute does not encompass any such restriction. Designing the attack, supplying weapons and ammunitions, exercising the power to move previously recruited and trained troops to the fields; and/or coordinating and monitoring the activities of those troops, may constitute contributions that must be considered essential regardless of when they are exercised (before or during the execution stage of the crime).[58]

Such an approach extends the scope of co-perpetration, however, to active contributions always historically understood as accessorial, particularly as instigation or aiding and abetting (in the common law's idiom). This characterization is one the ICC prosecutor decidedly dreads, given its implications for a reduced sentence. The Court's view of essential co-perpetration, just quoted, is well-suited to situations where prosecutors lack proof beyond a reasonable doubt of a commander's thorough domination over his subordinates at the specific instant and location where they commit atrocious acts. The unavailability of such evidence has led to notable acquittals in a number of superior responsibility cases before the ICTY, most recently in the Appeal of *Prosecutor v. Orić.*[59]

---

about what would have happened "but for" the defendant's misconduct, but also a policy judgment about how broadly to extend his "downstream" liability (i.e., beyond the most immediate impact of his actions). *Palsgraf v. Long Island Railway* 162 N.E. 99, 104–05 (1928) (Andrews, J., dissenting); see generally Hart & Honoré, op.cit., 96–102.

Considerations of public policy traditionally enter discussion of "proximate" or "legal" cause, hence only after cause "in fact" – that is, "but for" causation – has been established. In mass atrocity cases, however, prosecutors often find it difficult to cross even this preliminary threshold. To convict the defendant as a perpetrator, they must prove that his contribution was "essential" or "necessary," as the relevant civil law terms are usually rendered into English, in producing the subordinates' criminal acts or the prohibited consequences. Thus, the defendant must have been indispensable – if not his person as such, then the nature of his contribution, more abstractly considered – even as he must also have been fungible, i.e., in order to hold his superior responsible for having acted "through" him. This is paradoxical, perhaps. It is nevertheless logically inescapable if the law of co-perpetration is to be interpreted in a manner consistent with Roxin's understanding of how hierarchical organizations function. If the prosecution cannot satisfy the requirement of "but for" causation – so easy in most other types of criminal trials – then judicial analysis of the defendant's culpability could not reach the point at which considerations of public policy would enter the picture.

[58] *Katanga*, op. cit., at ¶ 526.
[59] *Prosecutor v. Nasar Orić*, IT-03-68-A, ¶¶ 33, 47–8, 60 (July 3, 2008).

Prosecution of mass atrocity in national courts, by contrast, has often required only the variety of evidence to which the ICC Chamber alludes above. It has been sufficient to establish liability – through organizational perpetration – by showing that the superior created or assumed effective control of an institution whose junior members later committed the criminal acts at issue in the regular course of their duties. The superior must also be deemed to have intended, known, or – for certain offenses – adverted to the high risk that these criminal acts would occur, among other requirements.[60]

In this way, the evidentiary burden may even shift toward the defendant, requiring him to show that he could no longer control his forces, rather than requiring the prosecutor to show that the accused continued to control them right up until the very moment when, and in the very situs where, they performed their deeds. It is common for criminal law in liberal democracies to treat such matters as elements of an available defense, which defendant's counsel must therefore establish, rather than of the prosecutor's case in chief.[61] The fate of "liberalism" – on prevailing understandings of the term, at least – does not hang in the balance here.

Those of libertarian sensibility may complain, to be sure, that this doctrinal move jettisons the presumption of innocence, if the presumption is generously construed. But the present question is precisely whether this presumption should indeed be interpreted so broadly (i.e., regarding an issue always understood to lie at its outer margins, if not beyond).[62] As a general matter, in fact, the law of evidence in many places, on many issues,

[60] To convict a defendant as perpetrator by means of an organization, prosecutors must prove, according to the ICC Pre-Trial Chamber in *Katanga*: 1) "control over the organization," 2) "an organizational and hierarchical apparatus of power," 3) "execution of the crimes secured by almost automatic compliance with the orders," 4) "existence of an agreement or common plan between two or more persons," 5) "coordinated essential contribution by each co-perpetrator resulting in the realisation of the objective elements of the crime," 6) "the subjective elements of the crimes," i.e., intent and/or knowledge, 7) "the suspects must be mutually aware and mutually accept that implementing their common plan will result in the realization of the objective elements of the crimes," and 8) "the suspects must be aware of the factual circumstances enabling them to control the crimes jointly." *Katanga*, op. cit., ¶¶ 500–538.
[61] Meredith Blake & Andrew Ashworth, "The Presumption of Innocence in English Criminal Law," Crim. L. Rev. 306, 306 (1996) (showing empirically "the frequency with which offences triable in the Crown Court . . . place a legal burden of proof on the defendant," generally with respect to a standard element of a cognizable defense).
[62] The scope to be accorded that presumption, with respect to particular offenses, might at least partly be determined in light of the avowed purpose of the international community in creating the ICC in the first instance. As specified in its Statute, that purpose is "to put an end to impunity for the perpetrators of these crimes and thus to contribute to the prevention of such crimes." Rome Statute, Preamble.

frequently allocates burdens of evidentiary production on the simple basis
of whether claimant or respondent would be more likely to possess and
readily retrieve the pertinent data. When the question is whether a commander has lost control over his forces, the defendant is surely more likely
to have such information than the prosecutor. The evidentiary burden may
be allocated accordingly.

The developing doctrine of perpetration by organization facilitates the
prosecutor's task not only concerning the crime's "objective" elements, but
also its *mens rea*. The ICC Statute understands "intent" for a crime defined
"in relation to a consequence" – such as disproportionate incidental killing
of civilians during combat, for instance – to refer to a defendant who
"means to cause that consequence or is aware that it will occur, in the
ordinary course of events."[63] The latter wording is tailor-made for our
watchmaker scenario and its organizational equivalents. For the watchmaker
knows that, in the ordinary course of events, his device will explode, unless
someone else goes "out of his way," beyond the call of duty, to prevent this
catastrophe.

OBSTACLES TO CONVICTION

When the ICC Pre-Trial Chamber chooses to focus instead on the horizontal
dimensions of mass atrocity, as it does in *Lubanga* with the doctrine of co-
perpetration, other roadblocks to successful prosecution arise. In particular,
the superior's contribution must have been objectively "essential" to the
criminal results; these harms would not have accrued had he withdrawn his
support (or acquiescence) and interceded to stop their occurrence.[64] This
can be devilishly hard to demonstrate, as it invites fact-finders to speculate
counter-factually, with little, firm legal basis for telling them when to stop.
As one careful commentator observes, for instance,

> Upon closer examination, none of Lubanga's single contributions as listed
> [by the ICC Pre-Trial Chambers] could fairly be regarded as "essential"
> to the operation of enlisting child soldiers – even without his visits to
> military camps, without his employing youngsters as personal bodyguards,
> without his general encouragement of local ethnicities to provide soldiers
> to the FPLC [*Force Patriotique pour La Liberation du Congo*], the common

---

[63] Id. Art. 30(2)(b).
[64] In the *Lubanga* Confirmation of Charges, the ICC Pre-Trial Chamber thus held that the
prosecutor must establish that the accused "could frustrate the commission of the crime
by not carrying out his or her task." *Lubanga*, op. cit., ¶¶ 342, 347.

plan – essentially carried out by others – would most likely not have failed. His "key overall co-ordinating role" was related to his general leadership of the FPLC at the time, and Lubanga may well have been indispensable as an overall commander of that military group. But does that make him a "necessary" co-perpetrator of the specific crime of enlisting child soldiers? His "essential" role may simply have consisted in *not* intervening when he learned about the recruitment of child soldiers. . . . The Pre-Trial Chamber seems to imply . . . this sort of "control through potential prevention." Yet such a concept is not easy to reconcile with the essentially active image one associates with a (necessary) co-perpetrator.[65]

The ICC Chamber itself evokes an image of near-feverish activity, in describing the doctrine's requirements:

> The leader must use his control over the apparatus to execute crimes, which means that the leader, as the perpetrator behind the perpetration, mobilises his authority and power within the organization to secure compliance with his orders.[66]

On this view, even the "desk murderer" must show transparent initiative – as Eichmann himself certainly did – to become liable as perpetrator by organization. Unlike the burglar whose very stealth betrays his guilty mind, however, the desk murderer more closely resembles the embezzler who, as he pushes "innocuous" paper, does not betray the criminality of his conduct. Its wrongful nature is not immediately "manifest" to all others around him, in other words.[67] As with the village clockmaker, people passing by his shopwindow – observing his seemingly perfunctory labors – would hardly imagine that he is up to no good. Yet his earnest energies, at least, must be apparent if they are to evidence his dedicated commitment to the criminal purpose he shares with co-perpetrators including those with whom he may never directly interact.

Whether ICC prosecutors will succeed in meeting such evidentiary challenges remains to be seen. The law of joint criminal enterprise, as Chapter 3 showed, imposes no such requirement on them to demonstrate the essential

---

[65] Thomas Weigend, "Intent, Mistake of Law, and Co-Perpetration in the *Lubanga* Decision on Confirmation of Charges," 6 J. of Int'l Crim. Justice 471, 486–87 (2008).

[66] *Katanga*, op. cit., ¶ 514.

[67] Until the twentieth century, Western law tended to assume that a defendant's culpable intention would be unproblematically "manifest" to any observers of his conduct. Criminal offenses were, therefore, defined with much less attention than today to ascertaining the defendant's exact mental state. George Fletcher, *Rethinking Criminal Law* 88–90, 115–18 (1978).

nature of the defendant's contribution to the common plan. That contribution need not even have been substantial, according to the ICTY.[68]

Neither does the law of superior responsibility, for that matter, always require that the superior's inaction caused or significantly contributed to ensuing harm. The rule is sometimes applied, after all, against a commander who assumes control *after* subordinates have already committed the criminal conduct at issue, and simply declines to seek their prosecution.[69] He cannot very well have caused or even contributed *ex post* to the commission of their crimes *ex ante*,[70] certainly not as a perpetrator, probably not even as an accessory.[71]

It may at first appear an insurmountable obstacle to any wide-ranging application of Roxin's novel approach that he devised it with only the Third Reich immediately in mind. After all, his account sought to conceptualize and justify punishment of conduct by civil servants within a legal and political system completely subordinated to a unitary, totalitarian executive. In such a public administration, an official superior can reasonably expect his directives to be carried out "in the ordinary course of events." For he knows this system to be highly centralized, effective, and implacably committed to disregarding any trifling obstacles that might be thrown up by international law. German courts after the 1990 reunification ascribed similar knowledge to former leaders of the Democratic Republic who had

---

[68] *Prosecutor v. Vasiljević*, Judgment, Appeals Chamber, Case No. IT-98-32-A, ¶ 102 (February 25, 2004), *Prosecutor v. Kvočka*, Judgment, Appeals Chamber, Case No. IT-98-30/1-A, ¶¶ 97, 187 (February 28, 2005).

[69] For a defendant in such circumstances, some judges and commentators have understandably preferred to interpret the law of superior responsibility as creating a separate offense of official dereliction, rather than a mode of liability for committing the subordinate's underlying criminal acts themselves. See, e.g., *Prosecutor v. Krnojelac*, Judgment, Appeals Chamber, Case No. IT-97-25-A, ¶ 171 (September 17, 2003); *Prosecutor v. Aleksovski*, Trial Chamber, Case No. IT-95-14/1-T, ¶ 72 (June 25, 1999), ("superior responsibility . . . must not be seen as responsibility for the act of another person."); for commentary supporting this interpretation, see Guénaël Mettraux, *International Crimes and the ad hoc Tribunals* 297, 306–10 (2005); C.T. Fox, "Closing a Loophole in Accountability for War Crimes: Successor Commanders' Duty to Punish Known Past Offenses," 55 Case West. Res. L. Rev. 443, 444 (2004). Views to the contrary include Christopher Greenwood, "Command Responsibility and the *Hadžihasanovic* Decision," 2 J. of Int'l Crim. Justice 598, 608 (2004); Daryl Robinson, "The Identity Crisis of International Criminal Law," 21 Leiden J. Int'l L. 925, 949–52, 959–60 (2008).

[70] Mirjan Damaška, "The Shadow Side of Command Responsibility," 49 Amer. J. Comp. L. 455, 468–69 (2001).

[71] The ICC Statute does not provide for liability of accessories after the fact. This position is congruent with the general direction of domestic criminal law throughout much of the Western world. Id. at 469.

issued standing "shoot to kill" orders to eastern border guards. On these facts, Roxin's theory again made good sense.

By contrast, where the state is not so all-powerful, where it has in fact collapsed almost altogether, these same legal presumptions are no longer so eminently sensible – surely not in the same manner. This conclusion, seemingly inescapable, has not prevented international prosecutors from finding Roxin's theory highly congenial for conceptualizing mass atrocities occurring in "failed states" of central Africa. It might first appear that *ipso facto* there could not exist any "ordinary course of events" in conditions approximating anarchy. From one day to the next, no one may know which "big man" may next become top dog, however fleetingly, among an array of contending warlords, for instance. In fact, often one would be unable confidently to predict the consequences of one's own efforts whenever these required the cooperation of others, such as the compliance of *de jure* subordinates.

Although the state may have failed, however, the rebel groups opposing it often assuredly have not. In fact, the leader of such an armed group likely exercises greater power over the impressionable children in his junior ranks than did Eichmann in relation to the camp guards who would murder those he ordered sent to Auschwitz.[72] It is those children who generally commit the worst atrocities, due to their still-incomplete moral and intellectual development as autonomous persons. The African rebel leader here hypothesized can come to enjoy such overwhelming power precisely because the official state apparatus has lost its monopoly of force over portions of the country's *de jure* territory. It is thus not preposterous that a single legal theory might legitimately encompass mass atrocities conducted both by totalitarian states and by insurgent groups within failed states. This theory and that comparison will likely soon receive the ICC's close scrutiny in several pending cases.

Even where a state retains great control over government officials involved in mass atrocity, it does not follow that responsibility for these crimes may always convincingly be traced to the head of state. Luis Moreno-Ocampo, the ICC prosecutor, extravagantly describes Sudanese President Omar al-Bashir as "a man exercising total control," employing it to "provide[] a guarantee of impunity to those who follow his orders, critical to ensure the continuation of the genocide."[73]

---

[72] Eichmann possessed neither *de jure* nor *de facto* authority over such camp guards, for that matter.

[73] "Prosecutor's Statement on the Prosecutor's Application for a Warrant of Arrest under Article 58 Against Omar Hassan Al Bashir," op. cit.

Demonstrating all this would indeed be necessary to establish Bashir's liability as a superior or commander. The available evidence may not support such a conclusion, however. In fact, Alex De Waal, a leading scholar of Darfur, soberly concludes, "It is clear that President Bashir does not and did not possess such individual power."[74] To hold Bashir responsible for all atrocities by his inferiors and militia allies, in virtue simply of the responsibilities inherent in command, prosecutors must "prove the case that Bashir is in total control of the state," DeWall continues. "It is not enough to compile a list of cases in which he had the last word – it is necessary to show that he had the last word each and every time," i.e., on each occasion in which atrocities ensued, if he is to be held criminally responsible for them all. This conclusion follows from DeWaal's assumption that ICC prosecutors would allege only superior responsibility against Bashir.

They will also assert his perpetration by organization, however, the requirements of which are somewhat different, as indicated. Yet another possibility: if President Bashir merely shares control of the state apparatus with other leaders, then these others must also have "agreed that the Government of Sudan counter-insurgency campaign would . . . aim at the destruction . . . of the Fur, Masalit and Zaghawa groups,"[75] as the ICC Pre-Trial Chamber contemplates in its arrest warrant. And if power is genuinely shared with peers, this means that the withdrawal of other leaders from the common plan could obstruct its realization. Their continuing agreement to that ongoing policy is causally "essential," in law's language on co-perpetration. Prosecutors must then demonstrate that there was such a persisting agreement among all who shared the power to block this criminal plan. That task could prove difficult and is not required by the law of superior responsibility, with its assumption of a single, unproblematic chain of bureaucratic command. In short, each of these legal theories presents serious obstacles to conviction.

When rebel leaders recruit and train children to be soldiers, these leaders may be prosecuted for such international crimes.[76] Even so, the current interpretation of superior responsibility by international tribunals does not hold such leaders liable for these children's every wrong thereafter, once no longer under his "effective control." Their atrocities may well have been reasonably foreseeable to him when he recruited and trained them as he

---

[74] Alex de Waal, "The ICC vs. Bashir: Debating Genocidal Intent," Making Sense of Darfur, at http://www.ssrc.org/blogs/darfur/2009/02/10/the-icc-vs-bashir-debating-genocidal-intent/.

[75] *Decision on the Prosecution's Application for a Warrant of Arrest against Omar Hassan Ahmad Al Bashir*, ¶ 150 (March 4, 2009); see also ¶¶ 216–8, 233.

[76] Rome Statute, op. cit., Art. 8(2)(e)(vii).

did. Criminal law has virtually never, however, considered even gross negligence blameworthy enough to support liability for such grievous offenses
as here involved.[77]

COURTING CATASTROPHE

A commander who intentionally trains his troops to misbehave in certain
ways adverts to the risk that they will do so. He appreciates that they may
commit atrocities even at times – perhaps especially when – they are no
longer under his control. He knows that they will often enjoy considerable
autonomy from him during field operations.[78] He also is aware that they
will then find more proximate guidance in his local commanders, who will
sometimes have moral standards less demanding than his own.[79]

For a rebel leader to field such a force under these conditions may well
fall within the law's understanding of recklessness. And recklessness is precisely the mental state required by the ICC Statute for civilian liability by
way of superior responsibility.[80] This mental state has become ever easier
for prosecutors to prove, moreover, with now-abundant evidence of communications from foreign embassies and human rights NGOs, warning the
leader – nearly in real time – of the perilous situation developing beyond

[77] As discussed in Chapter 3, a criticism of the third form of "joint criminal enterprise"
has been that, in holding defendants liable for harm merely "foreseeable" to them, the
doctrine effectively reduces the mental state that prosecutors must prove to simple negligence. The Rome Statute defines the offenses in question, however, to require a showing
of "intent" and/or "knowledge" on the defendant's part. This problem arises regardless of
which doctrine of commission a court employs for linking big fish to small fry. Employing
a theory of co-perpetration, for instance, the ICC Pre-Trial Chamber in *Lubanga* found it
necessary to construe "intent" to encompass *dolus eventualis*, which the Court translates
as "reconciling oneself" to the possibility that a harmful consequence may occur or circumstance may exist. In applying any of the possible doctrines of commission, there is a
strong temptation – given the limits of admissible evidence about the inner workings of
the defendant's mind – to dilute the statutory *mens rea* in such ways. The *Katanga* Pre-Trial
Chamber, in contrast, declined to rely on *dolus eventualis*. *Katanga*, op. cit., at ¶ 531. The
defense had there argued that the Rome Statute does not incorporate this understanding of
intent.
[78] On the frequent value of such operational autonomy in the field, as well as the problems it
creates in ascribing responsibility to superiors, see Osiel, *Obeying Orders*, op. cit., at 173–99
(examining situations in which commanders sometimes deliberately create the impression
of having "unintentionally" lost control of their troops, in order to evade responsibility
for the latter's misconduct).
[79] Jeremy Weinstein, *Inside Rebellion: The Politics of Insurgent Violence* 350 (2007).
[80] We must here enter the qualification that superior responsibility is permissible as a mode of
liability only with respect to international crimes defined in a way making them capable of
being committed "recklessly" (i.e, offenses which include recklessness among the possible
mens rea specified by statute). To prove genocide, however, prosecutors must show much
more: the superior's specific intent to destroy.

his immediate vista. These communications often are sent precisely for the purpose of facilitating later efforts to establish his *mens rea* at trial. Such evidence has indeed served international prosecutors very well in several key cases.[81]

Roxin assumes that superiors – at some point in the chain of command – have expressly ordered atrocities, even if no direct evidence is introduced at trial to this effect. There was no such evidence, for instance, before the Argentine courts that convicted that country's juntas, under Roxin's theory, for murder, kidnapping, and other major crimes. The law of superior responsibility, unlike that of perpetration by organization, does not assume that anyone issued criminal orders (or authorizations). This is because superior responsibility involves commission by omission – not by such actions as giving orders, but through one's very inactions.

Joint criminal enterprise requires even less in this respect. It does not anticipate an organizational structure of any determinate sort, much less the highly formal and hierarchical variety that Roxin presumed necessary to accomplish mass atrocity in a large, modern society like Germany. Joint enterprise doctrine also dispenses with any requirement that criminal orders have ever been transmitted at some point.[82]

In short, perpetration "through another" offers a promising alternative to these more familiar theories of liability. If it is to deliver on that promise and become a convincing way to hold mass atrocity's intellectual architects responsible to the world, we must properly interpret this body of law. It should be understood to allow the possibility that sufficient control over immediate, physical perpetrators may arise by means *other than* a highly formal, rigidly hierarchical organization. Evidence of such an organization at the precise time and place atrocities occur will often be weak or altogether lacking, even where such organization may actually have existed. The ICTY, at least, has come to demand precisely this degree of temporal and

---

[81] The first use of such evidence apparently occurred during the 1985 Argentine juntas case, in which a former U.S. Assistant Secretary of State for Human Rights testified concerning her conversations with junta members regarding early reports of disappearances in that country. She had communicated this information to Argentine President Jorge Videla, in particular, soon after credible accounts began to emerge, shortly following the military's 1976 *coup d'etat*.

[82] Not surprisingly, this feature of the doctrine has offered a considerable attraction to international prosecutors. It warrants mention here that the ICC Pre-Trial Chambers displayed early reluctance to employ the joint enterprise approach, especially its third and most controversial variant, for several of the reasons examined here in Chapters 3 and 4. *Lubanga*, Confirmation of Charges, op. cit., ¶ 318; for analysis, see Jessberger & Geneuss, op. cit., at 858; Kevin Jon Heller, "The Rome Statute in Comparative Perspective," Legal Studies Res. Paper, No. 370, Melbourne Law School, 2009.

spatial specificity for liability to be based on the responsibilities inherent in accepting and exercising a position of command.

As we have seen, however, ideal-typical bureaucracies are not the only institutional means by which leaders may exercise enormous influence over followers during episodes of mass atrocity. Informal networks, although based at times on rather "weak ties," regularly prove quite strong enough to generate much collective violence. The present challenge is thus for the law to take satisfactory cognizance of such effective institutional forms, understanding them as a mere subset of the multiple social arrangements by which people may assemble themselves to commit large-scale atrocities. Alas, human perversity in this domain displays almost infinite permutations – far too many for *ex ante* enumeration by statute, at any rate.

It must be said, in sum, that the useful first start Roxin himself offers to the notion of perpetration by means of culpable others nonetheless leaves much to be resolved. Still, it has considerable value. The "control" requirement of superior responsibility might be read to incorporate, where facts so warrant, Roxin's theory of perpetration by means of an organizational apparatus. Leaders may sometimes effectively control followers in other ways, however. Some of these will lie beyond the doctrinal reach of superior responsibility. Such mechanisms of power are nonetheless often susceptible to convincing classification as indirect perpetration, we have seen. Significantly, in its relevant language the Rome Statute makes no reference to hierarchical organizations as such, only to committing a crime "jointly with another or through another person . . ."[83]

Finally, the relevant point for establishing such control – by whatever method attained – need not always be perfectly coterminous with the particular moment and locale where the immediate violence occurs. Nothing in the ICC Statute itself nor its drafting history suggests any legislative intention to define the morally relevant place and period so narrowly. This was wise because, through decentralization of its operational processes, mass atrocity can be – and increasingly is – organized with a conscious view precisely to ensuring that such evidence of proximate control from the top will be unavailable.

In conclusion, Roxin's approach, as here amended, suggests some of the ways that legal responses to mass atrocity may be improved by attending more closely to its social dynamics, and specifically to the extent such events do or do not approximate the model of bureaucratic murder assumed by

---

[83] Rome Statute, op. cit., Art. 25(3)(a). Alas, the disjunctive wording here – "or" – impedes current efforts legally to conceptualize at once the vertical and horizontal dimensions of mass atrocity.

Arendt and her many epigones. Other models of how mass atrocity occurs, truer to other factual configurations – more common, but also more complex – will surely require quite different legal concepts and approaches.[84]

To this end, we have broached the phenomenon of mass atrocities by network, with all its organizational informality. There is also the "franchise" relation sometimes said to exist between Osama bin Laden and those who receive funding from his organization – kindred radical, Islamist groups who plan and commit mass atrocity.[85] Additionally, there exists the scenario of mass atrocity by professional community. We turn to this final possibility in the Chapters 9 and 10.

It bears emphasis, in light of this book's general argument, that the several variations on Roxin's theory here entertained remain consistent with criminal law's underlying "liberalism." Liberals understand organizations, after all, as associations of responsible individuals capable of exercising moral autonomy. If any such individual deeply dissents from the organization's objectives, he is either free to resign, request reassignment, or – if these options are unavailable – may act under a state of duress.[86] These three options are all standard moves within the repertoire of liberal moral and legal thought. The law's requirement of personal culpability as a condition of criminal liability has not been compromised.

To make our growing knowledge of how mass atrocity happens more useful to the law, it may be necessary as well to interpret such law afresh to some extent, in ways compatible with non-legal understandings of the sort offered by great journalists, historians, and social scientists. International criminal courts have not always done this, even where the authoritative sources permit. For instance, such decisions of the ICTY Appeals Chamber

---

[84] Criminologists are becoming increasingly useful to international prosecutors in helping prove requisite elements for crimes of mass atrocity. Extant efforts to this end, however, have not always been entirely careful to appreciate and respect the various points at which differences arise between legal and social scientific uses of the same terms – notably, "genocide." For instance, John Hagan & Wenona Rymond-Richmond, in their *Darfur and the Crime of Genocide* (2008), sometimes conflate the two, even while offering data undoubtedly relevant to prosecution of Sudan's leaders.

[85] Mark Osiel, *The End of Reciprocity: Terror, Torture & The Law of War* 60 (2009) (referencing scholars who employ the legal concept of a franchise – often as metaphor, sometimes more literally – in characterizing bin Laden's selective and conditional sponsorship of certain radical Islamist groups).

[86] In the latter case, his murderous misconduct is either exculpated by excuse or much mitigated at punishment, depending on whether he resides in a civil or common law country. This disagreement between the two legal cultures, both of European origin, concerns liberalism's proper meaning and requirements. Neither view ventures beyond the borders – admittedly indistinct, at times – of that philosophical orientation.

as *Prosecutor v. Goran Jelisić* have found that the crime of genocide can be committed without evidence that the small-scale harm wrought by the individual defendant was part and parcel of a larger policy aimed at group destruction.[87] Legal scholars have been rightly critical of this position.[88]

The common, lay meaning of genocide, after all, involves a plan to destroy large numbers of a protected group, even if that plan is never fully realized. In this respect, genocide resembles crimes against humanity, which are legally defined as necessarily part of a "widespread or systematic" campaign. The prevailing, popular understanding of genocide does not, moreover, require that all those involved in the process (and deserving punishment for their participation) "specifically intend" group destruction "as such." They may simply have been indifferent to it, while aware that others sought it, or merely know that it was likely to ensue from the more limited aims to which they agreed.

Current legal thought here too aims to make "genocide" less arcane a legal term of art, less thoroughly estranged from how others understand it. Such thinking refines the legal meaning of the offense so that courts will assess the individual defendant's conduct in light of the broader political context within which he operates. The challenge here, however, is to do so without allowing that context to swallow him in its vortex, either by rendering him irrelevant to larger processes or, conversely, imputing to him wrongs to which he is not meaningfully connected. Still, there is considerable value in these recent, learned efforts to shift the legal meaning of genocide back into closer alignment with what others, more knowledgeable about the real workings of such conflagrations, can teach us lawyers.

---

[87] *Prosecutor v. Goran Jelisić*, Case No. IT-95-10-A, Judgment, ¶¶ 45–48 (July 5, 2001).

[88] William Schabas, "State Policy as an Element of International Crimes," 98 J. of Crim. L. & Criminology 953 (2008); Claus Kress, "The Darfur Report and Genocidal Intent," J. of Int'l Crim. Justice 562, 566–67 (July 2005); Alicia Gil Gil, *Derecho Penal Internacional: Especial Consideración del Delito de Genocidio* 259–65 (1999); Hans Vest, *Genozid Durch Organisatorische Machtapparate* 104–25 (2002); Kevin Jon Heller, "The Majority's Problematic Interpretation of Genocide's Contextual Element," Opinio Juris, at http://opiniojuris.org/2009/03/06/the-majoritys-problematic-interpretation-of-genocides-contextual-element/.

6

Culpability, Character, and Context in Mass Atrocity

Some have lambasted as profoundly "illiberal" the conceptual innovations recently employed by international courts, described in Chapters 2 through 5. The critics acknowledge that, without these doctrinal ingenuities, criminal law might never fully reach mass atrocity's masterminds.[1] Yet, if liberal legality achieves this laudable goal only by compromising its first principles, then in the process it has surely lost its moral bearings, even sacrificed its soul. That is clearly too high a price to pay even for so seemingly unimpeachable a goal as ending impunity for genocide.

Such views, offered recently by Héctor Olásolo, Daryl Robinson[2] and Yale Law professor Mirjan Damaška,[3] may initially seem in striking contrast

---

[1] As indicated earlier, the *ad hoc* international criminal tribunals have followed the "civil law" practice of sentencing accessories to incarceration for periods significantly shorter than perpetrators. By contrast, in the United States – admittedly the most punitive of Western penal systems – accessories often receive very severe sentences when factual circumstances appear to warrant.

[2] Héctor Olásolo, "A Note on the Evolution of the Legality Principle in International Criminal Law," 18 Crim. L. Forum 301 (2007); Daryl Robinson, "The Identity Crisis of International Criminal Law," 21 Leiden J. Int'l L. 925, 925, 927, 930, 931, 958, 959, 961 (2008). Although at all these points Robinson attacks the *ad hoc* international criminal tribunals for their illiberalism, in other places he acknowledges – without apparent recognition of the inconsistency – that these legal developments might actually indicate "two incompatible liberalisms," reflecting "contradictions" within liberalism itself, as he understands the term, at least. Id. at 932, 946. The first of these strands of liberalism concentrates on protecting human rights against states that implement policies of mass murder. The 'second' liberalism, according to Robinson, focuses on due process in prosecuting those accused of these very wrongs. Yet because due process is also a human right against the state, as reflected in the International Covenant on Civil and Political Rights, the two are not so readily distinguishable.

[3] Damaška shares Robinson's concerns, insisting "on punctilious adherence to the culpability principle" and "on conventional *mens rea* requirements." Mirjan Damaška, "What is the Point of International Criminal Justice?" 83 Chi.-Kent L. Rev. 329, 354 (2008). Although

to Drumbl's, which condemns international criminal law for being *too* liberal, rather than insufficiently so. Drumbl's concern, the reader will recall, is that such law has been too individualistic in method and underlying moral theory to be fair to the lowest-echelon perpetrators of mass atrocity, considering the intense pressures for obedience to which they are often made subject by their sociopolitical context.[4] Still, both sets of critics are clearly vexed by the same underlying question: can international criminal law hope to make much real sense of mass atrocity while remaining tethered to its philosophical basis in "liberalism," as they understand it?

Their views are compatible, strictly speaking. Robinson condemns the illiberal character of legal doctrines deployed against the big fish, their alleged violation of the principle of individual culpability. Drumbl instead identifies perceived injustices to the small fry that follow from the law's liberal assumptions about the inherent capacity of every individual for moral autonomy from constraints imposed by his general sociopolitical environment. Short of true "duress," we are presumed responsible for our conduct and may be held criminally accountable for it, whatever type of society or polity we may inhabit. Duress is defined quite narrowly, moreover, to follow the common law in providing no excuse for murder as a war crime or other crimes against humanity.[5]

Robinson's criticism, a focus of this chapter, makes several missteps and ultimately proves unfounded. First it rests on an unduly libertarian understanding of liberalism,[6] equating the latter with the exclusive aim of "constraining the state's coercive power against individuals."[7] Yet other variants

---

it is "regrettable," he writes, "that genocidal mass murderers may escape punishment, it is more regrettable still to craft liability doctrines that make facts needed for the proper assessment of personal culpability immaterial, and to do so for the purpose of avoiding proof difficulties that would arise in proving these facts. If criminal law principles fall under pressure of heinous crime, they are like a sprinkler system that turns itself off when the fire gets hot. It would indeed be a disheartening irony if a justice system, designed to contribute to the protections of human rights, could properly function only by disregarding humanistic values rooted, *inter alia*, in the presumption of innocence." Id., at 355–56. Damaška is careful not to characterize the problem as a failure to adhere to liberalism, presumably recognizing the problems with invoking such an amorphous, protean term. It may warrant mention here that Damaška, who lived much of his life in Croatia, serves as counsel to a Croatian defendant, Rahim Ademi, prosecuted at the ICTY under theories discussed here.

[4] Mark Drumbl, *Atrocity, Punishment and International Law* 5, 35–41, 123–28 (2007).

[5] *Prosecutor v. Drazen Erdemovic*, Case No. IT-96-22-A, ¶ 19 (Oct. 7, 1997).

[6] Influential works in the libertarian tradition include Robert Nozick, *Anarchy, State, and Utopia* (1974) and Friedrich Hayek, *The Road to Serfdom* (1944).

[7] Robinson, op. cit., at 930.

of liberalism, concerned also with promoting due consideration for others' rights and personal autonomy as a virtue of character[8] (plus good judgment in its exercise), are entirely consistent with the doctrinal developments here at issue, we will see.

If the recent, widespread charge of illiberalism against international criminal law lacked any plausibility, it will not have required a significant part of this book to refute. Above all, that charge appeals to the sensible, defensible demand that law provide those subject to its sanctions with fair, advance warning of what conduct is prohibited. Closely related, the critics contend, law must also be fair in how it labels such misconduct. To do so, it must specify the type and precise contours of the offense that given behavior will constitute.

This measure of exactitude extends as well to law's enumeration of its modes of participation in liability, including the means by which responsibility in crime may be shared among many (e.g., conspiracy, co-perpetration, command responsibility, joint enterprise, etc.). Such specification in labeling must attain a high degree of verbal precision – again, in advance of the conduct to be sanctioned in a given case – if the moral demands of due process are to be met. Otherwise, the law will surely end up punishing people who are not culpable, that is, who are "guilty" only by virtue of their association – sometimes unwitting, even unwilling – with those truly so.[9]

This argument, however, infers too much from the legitimate expectation of fair warning. It deduces an implicit corollary: that the law must therefore clarify *ex ante*, with consummate linguistic rigor, all details of every legal rule that may later be applied against any defendant. This posture begs the central questions, however, of exactly *how much* advance warning does fairness truly require of the law, and *what kind* of process is truly "due" in a given circumstance.[10] The critics' stance also implicitly assumes that the

[8] On the relation of libertarianism to liberalism, See, e.g., Joseph Raz, *The Morality of Freedom* 18, 110, 124, 196–97, 396, 401, 404 (1986).

[9] *Prosecutor v. Dario Kordić and Mario Ćerkez*, Case No. IT-95-14/2-T, Trial Judgment, ¶ 219 (Feb. 26, 2001) ("Stretching notions of individual *mens rea* too thin may lead to the imposition of criminal liability on individuals for what is actually guilt by association, a result which is at odds with the driving principles behind the creation of this International Tribunal."). For discussion of this continuing danger, see Shane Darcy, "An Effective Measure of Bringing Justice? The Joint Criminal Enterprise Doctrine of the ICTY," 20 Amer. U. Int'l L. Rev. 153 (2005).

[10] Robinson begs yet another major question: He believes it self-evidently important "that ICL may develop as a distinct and coherent discipline." Op. cit., at 925. Again, however,

answer to these questions must be identical for all species of penal wrong. Otherwise, the presumption of innocence,[11] perhaps even "the rule of law" itself,[12] will have been deeply compromised.

The assumed need for such uniformity across all categories of penal wrong in turn relies on a misguided view of criminal law's so-called "general part," the statutory provisions that establish rules relevant to all offenses (codified in the "special part"). These provisions include, for instance, the rules on defenses – such as mistake of law – and on modes of participation, the legal focus of this book.

There is nothing in liberalism as a moral or political philosophy, however, that proscribes any variation on such matters across very different types of wrongdoing – individual versus collective, petty theft versus genocide. Indeed, for most of their histories the penal codes of longstanding, avowedly liberal societies – including Britain and the United States – demanded nothing of the sort.[13] Until recently, in most of the common law world there scarcely existed any general part, and that part played a very modest role.[14]

There was certainly no single answer in the eighteenth and nineteenth centuries to such assertedly "general" questions; and that was a time when

the proper question is that of just how distinct a "discipline" international criminal law really ought or needs to be, given the overlap between its concerns and those of closely related bodies of law, with which it might best be read *in pari materia*. Robinson's interest in erecting boundaries around his own "distinct . . . discipline" also emits the distinct and unfortunate whiff of clubbish turf-building.

[11] Damaška, op.cit., at 355–56. But see Meredith Blake, & Andrew Ashworth, "The Presumption of Innocence in English Criminal Law," Crim. L. Rev. 306, 306 (1996) (showing "the frequency with which offences triable in the Crown Court . . . place a legal burden of proof on the defendant," generally with respect to an element of an available defense). This finding leads Lacey to conclude that "the presumption that all or at least the vast majority of serious offences require proof of full subjective responsibility" by the prosecution is factually mistaken. Nicola Lacey, "In Search of the Responsible Subject: History, Philosophy and Social Sciences in Criminal Law Theory," 64 Mod. L. Rev. 350, 355 (2001).

[12] Dan Kahan, "Lenity and Federal Common Law Crimes," Sup. Ct. L. Rev. 345, 419 (1994) (noting the common "claim that lenity is essential to the rule of law . . . ").

[13] For instance, in his *Commentaries on the Laws of England*, William Blackstone – the leading English legal thinker of the late eighteenth century – did not conceive of criminal law as having any such "general part." For analysis, see Lacey, op. cit., at 359–60 (observing that Blackstone "is spectacularly uninterested in the question, 'what makes it fair to hold an individual responsible for a crime'."). A century later, James Fitzjames Stephen's *Digest of Criminal Law* (vol. 2, 1883) devoted scarcely any more attention to the question.

[14] The "civil law" world admittedly committed itself to this idea considerably earlier than did the common law.

criminal law largely confined itself to protecting private property against the indigent.[15] It follows *a fortiori* that it is still less likely that uniform answers to such questions as the meaning of individual responsibility (and the *mens rea* suitable for establishing it) would prove satisfactory once criminal law came to encompass a much broader range of wrongdoing. This wider field of concern is increasingly collective in nature, encompassing organized crime, corporate crime, and finally, mass atrocity. Yet, even as the criminalization of wrongdoing greatly expanded and diversified over time, legal opinion in the United States and Britain moved in the direction of ever more general, invariant rules, applicable to all offenses.[16] One of these rules requires that liability for any serious offense to rest on the defendant's actual knowledge or intent,[17] despite the complete absence in nearly all cases of any direct evidence on his state of mind when he committed the wrong.[18]

The most grievous wrongs have today come to be thought of as requiring the most egregious of *mens rea*. A distinguishing feature of collective criminality, however, is precisely the fact that co-participants often vary among themselves in their intentions, with the mental states of some – generally those at the bottom of the organization – falling to the level of mere indifference to, and casual acquiescence in, the aims of their superiors and the resulting harms, however colossal these may become. This is the essence of what it presumably means for one's self-consciousness to approximate that of a "cog," in Arendt's and Roxin's terms.[19]

Thus, if all participants must uphold the same "specific intent to destroy" for there to exist a "common plan" of genocide, for instance, then they

---

[15] Alan Norrie, *Crime, Reason and History*, 20–31, 42–45, 87–89, 105–07, 130–32 (1993).

[16] Especially important in this shift was the work of Glanville Williams, *Criminal Law: The General Part* (1953); see, generally, Lacey, op. cit., at 360 (contending that "only by the 1950s has the question of individual, let alone subjective, responsibility as a question of agency and of individual fairness become the primary focus for criminal law commentaries.").

[17] There is one exception: the domestic offense of manslaughter can still be committed negligently, although the sanction may extend to life imprisonment in many countries.

[18] Despite the general absence of such direct evidence, most legal scholars have always assumed that jurors – when ascertaining a defendant's mental state at the time of the criminal act – can rely on their "common sense" to engage in "mindreading." Yet recent scholarship in cognitive psychology strongly suggests that this is not so. When jurors must project a particular state – intent, recklessness, etc. – into another's mind, they do so on the basis of whether they view that person as resembling them or different from them, in key respects. Sadly, many of these respects reduce to matters of demography. Kevin Jon Heller, "The Cognitive Psychology of *Mens Rea*," 4–5, at http://papers.ssrn.com/sol3/papers.cfm?abstract_id=1155304.

[19] Corresponding to this subjective aspect is the objective element of fungibility, examined in Chapter 7. Both aspects are implied in the colloquial comparison of such people to cogs.

will virtually never count as co-perpetrators of that offense. Yet, if such a participant may reasonably anticipate anything, it is surely that his criminal compatriots will not always share his exact understanding of their mission, jot for jot, and the specific range of acts it may turn out to require or permit. This is the most fundamental insight of post-Weberian organization theory, as indicated in the preceding chapter.[20]

For this reason, in mass atrocity a participant's "intent" might defensibly extend, in the words of the ICC Statute, to "a consequence" which he "is aware . . . will occur in the ordinary course of events,"[21] although he may not necessarily also "mean to cause[] that consequence."[22] And the key wording here – "will occur in the ordinary course of events" – proves susceptible to broader and narrower interpretations. The Pre-Trial Chamber in *Lubanga* adopted a very broad (and unconvincing) reading indeed.[23] That the definition of this single word, "intent," might be construed in either a capacious or constricted manner, depending on the nature and circumstances of the particular wrong, is anathema to those claiming to defend the systematic integrity of the general part against us from the common law world, in all our slovenly, atheoretical torpor.[24] Lawyers from the "civil law" tradition are typically skeptical of this case-by-case approach, in great part because they do not formally acknowledge that judges

---

[20] As indicated in Chapters 2 through 5, the *ad hoc* international criminal tribunals and ICC quickly developed conceptual means of accommodating this insight. Hence, those immediately committing the prohibited acts (or producing the forbidden consequences) need not have been members of the joint criminal enterprise itself. And only one member of that enterprise need have had any direct connection to such physical perpetrators.

[21] Rome Statute of the International Criminal Court, Art. 30(2)(b).

[22] Id. Lawyers from the "civil law" world – perhaps too crude a category in this particular context, admittedly – often describe this understanding of "intent" in terms of *dolus eventualis*. It is recognized as such in the penal codes of several "civil law" countries, as sufficient *mens rea* for many serious offenses.

[23] The Chamber interpreted the statutory wording of "will occur" to encompass situations where the harm "may result" from the defendant's misconduct. *Decision on Confirmation of Charges, Lubanga*, PTC I, 29 Jan. 2007 (ICC 01/04–01/06-803-tEN), ¶ 352(ii).

[24] Robinson asserts that his "project is not only to discover how liberal criminal theory may illuminate international criminal law, but how international criminal law may illuminate liberal criminal theory." Op. cit., at 963. His article makes no gesture in the latter direction, however. That second aspect of his stated, worthy aspiration would require that one begin from the bottom-up, with the recent jurisprudence of the international tribunals and the facts before the judges that led them – sometimes quite reluctantly – to the doctrinal "innovations" Robinson decries. From this "data," one would then inquire into whether there might exist some broader basis – call it theory, if you like – that could justify the discrete rule interpretations that these judges reached in so many specific cases, one after another. The present chapter is intended to initiate such an inquiry.

ever "make" law,[25] a proposition wholly uncontroversial among the rest
of us.[26]

TOLERANCE FOR AMBIGUITY IN CUSTOMARY
INTERNATIONAL LAW

International law is especially congenial to common law methods in that
custom has always been accepted as a major basis for creating legal duty.[27]
Like the common law itself (particularly standards of "due care" in negligence), custom evolves over time, from one situation to the next, permitting
the scope of a rule to be defined in the course of its application to differing circumstances, in light of their moral nuances. Although a statute or
treaty may be ambiguous in some respects, there at least exists some enacted
wording to which all have agreed.

With customary law, ambiguity extends far further; hence, at any given
moment the border between what custom permits and prohibits is often
quite cloudy. The ICTY has "postulated, therefore, that the principles of

[25] John Henry Merryman, *The Civil Law Tradition* 36 (2007); Olásolo, op. cit., at 302, contending that the *nulla poena sine lege* requirement, properly understood, 'includes an
additional formal safeguard whereby the prohibited acts and the penalties must be pre-
established by norms that can be considered "laws" in formal terms and that can be issued
only by a legislative power." He concludes, "Therefore, the possibility of criminalizing
certain behaviour or establishing penalties on the basis of non-written sources of law –
such as custom or the general principles of law – which offer lesser safeguards from the
perspective of specificity and forseeability, is excluded." Id. This is, with a vengeance, what
H.L.A. Hart condemned as "mechanical jurisprudence." *The Concept of Law* 128–29 (2nd
ed. 1994) (criticizing methods of interpretation aimed at "freezing the meaning of the rule
so that its general terms must have the same meaning in every case where its application
is in question"). For a sympathetic recent response from an international criminal law
specialist in the "civil law" world, see Harmen van der Wilt, "Equal Standards? On the
Dialectics Between National Jurisdictions and the International Criminal Court," 8 Int'l
Crim. L. Rev. 229, 268–69 (2008) (expressing doubts, in light of Hart's account of law's
inherently "open-texture," about "whether international law crimes and their concomi-
tant concepts of responsibility are relatively 'context-neutral' and therefore exempt from
casuistry.").

[26] One might wish to distinguish here between saying (1) that the meaning of a particular
mens rea term can change over time as an incremental result of many judicial decisions
and (2) that any particular judge is free to apply different definitions of a *mens rea* term
depending on what the facts of the case before her (including facts in evidence concerning
the defendant's character). Yet the problem with this distinction is that, by common
law methods, it is impossible for a series of judicial decisions to change the meaning
of particular *mens rea* terms over time without, at each point along the way, a series of
individual judges determining on a case by case basis – albeit by marginal steps – that the
facts of the case before her required altering the existing meaning of the pertinent term to
some extent.

[27] Statute of the International Court of Justice, Art. 38(1)(b).

legality in international criminal law are different from their related national legal systems. . . . "[28] *Nulla poena sine lege* is perhaps the foremost "principle of legality," all agree. If this principle permits judicial recourse to customary law, then there is little reason to be troubled by the fact that, as one scholar notes of recent jurisprudence, "common law international crimes have been crucial to building the infrastructure of a truly international criminal justice system."[29]

The still 'loftier' criticism that liberalism *per se* requires a single, baseline standard on all issues of purportedly "general" relevance, regardless of peculiar features of the offense in question and the setting of its commission, proves no more sustainable than the other charges just mentioned. Lacey mockingly "caricatures" this view as "metaphysical" and "transcendental." It holds, she writes – here parodying the clipped idiom of analytic philosophy – that:

> [t]he conceptual structure of criminal responsibility consists in [certain] volitional and cognitive capacities . . . ; any departure from this conceptual structure entails logical or moral confusion: it mistakes the concept of responsibility for something else, and in doing so it makes a moral mistake in purporting to justify the attribution of responsibility to those who are not "truly" responsible.[30]

---

[28] *Prosecutor v. Delalic, Mucic, Delic & Landzo*, Case No. IT-96-21-T, Judgment, ¶ 405 (Nov. 16, 1998); See also Beth van Schaack, "*Crimen Sine Lege*: Judicial Lawmaking at the Intersection of Law and Morals," 97 Georgetown L. J. 119 (2008); Machteld Boot, *Nullum Crimen Sine Lege and the Subject Matter Jurisdiction of the International Criminal Court* (2002).

[29] van Schaack, op. cit., at 120. Schaack adds that, because international criminal law remains in relative infancy – lacking a truly comprehensive code – the ICTY and ICTR necessarily relied heavily on customary law (as they understood it), a practice that their Statutes clearly authorized.

[30] Lacey, op. cit., at 356. She cites Fletcher as a leading U.S. proponent of such an acontextual view of individual responsibility. It is true that, despite the considerable comparative materials on which he admittedly draws, these never lead him to conclude that individual responsibility itself – as reflected in differences of law – might genuinely mean something quite different in these many places, in light of their historical, cultural, or sociopolitical contexts. George Fletcher, *Rethinking Criminal Law* 394–96, 455–56, 491–97 (1978). See also Michael Moore, *Causation and Responsibility* 249–53 (2009) (seeking a metaphysical basis for culpability judgments); Still, Lacey is not actually asking the same question as the legal philosophers who inquire into the nature of individual responsibility *per se*. Such theorists do not deny that the range of activities and accompanying mental states for which people are held responsible by their societies varies widely over time and place, including the circumstances in which one person is held responsible for another's acts. Whether evidence of a person's character is deemed relevant in establishing his responsibility for certain harms is another such variable; it need not affect our answer to the abiding analytic question of what it means to hold a person responsible for something, such theorists reply. Victor Tadros, *Criminal Responsibility* 5–6 (2005).

Lacey retorts – on the basis of considerable evidence from English and comparative legal history – that we must instead "entertain the possibility that particular conceptions of responsibility might have distinctive conditions of existence – intellectual, cultural, economic, social, political, or

> It is virtually axiomatic among social scientists, as an empirical proposition, that ascriptions of responsibility to individuals – including legal ascriptions – are greatly influenced by cultural context. Such context determines, for instance, whether only the immediate, physical wrongdoer may be held accountable for his actions or also members of his work-team, family, clan, ethno-religious group, nation-state, and – more recently – his corporate or governmental employer. Today, one must add "the international community" as a potential locus of shared accountability, a development reflected in the emergent international law on the world's "responsibility to protect."
>
> Cross-cutting cleavages, as social scientists call them, are the feature of social context likely most conducive to the individualization. A person becomes morally individuated, on this view, through her simultaneous membership in a large number of societal subgroups, each imposing differing expectations. The particular combination of such groups becomes virtually distinctive to each human being as society becomes more differentiated and its subsectors multiply. Georg Simmel, "Group Expansion and the Development of Individuality," in *Georg Simmel on Individuality and Social Form* 251–93 (Donald Levine, ed., 1971). Paradoxically perhaps, we become ever more individuated by learning to appreciate how (increasingly diverse varieties of) other people view and judge us. In this sense, the capacity for exercising individuality is itself largely the creation of society and its changing structure, rather than a feature of us in some pre-social "state of nature." Charles Horton Cooley, *Human Nature and the Social Order* 179–85 (1902); George Herbert Mead, *Mind, Self & Society* 186–225 (1934).
>
> In modern society we learn to accommodate competing claims upon us by our multiple affiliations – ascriptive and achieved – struggling to reconcile the several aspects of our selves to which each such affiliation corresponds and appeals. In this fashion, our mental process becomes individuated and fine-grained, Simmel contends, including the process by which we make moral judgments of ourselves and others. The incipient international community now provides yet another collective affiliation, with attendant demands upon those at least passingly inclined to feel some sense of membership in it. These demands sometimes sit uneasily with those of one's nation-state, requiring still further mental effort and adjustment by each of us at critical assessment of their competing claims.
>
> Moral judgments of this sort and the deliberation they require are often made central, in turn, to legal judgments. Hence the criminal law on *mens rea* – with its multiplicity of imaginable mental states – has grown more differentiated over time in conjunction with these same social changes. Such changes have had ramifications, in other words, for the law's appreciation of cognitive complexity, both in how we ourselves deliberate ethically before acting and in how we evaluate the deliberation of others when the law calls their conduct into question. Thus, even as criminal law's "general part" is now more uniformly applied to many types of criminal offense, that part of the code has become more internally intricate, placing greater practical import on subtle distinctions concerning a particular defendant's state of mind at the moment of his wrongful acts. The enormous scholarly attention lavished on such distinctions for the last half-century in both the civil and common law world suggests their perceived significance to modern notions of individual accountability and, by implication, to individualism itself – even as individuals came increasingly to work (and commit crime) within and by means of large organizations.

otherwise."[31] The "conditions of existence" for ascertaining someone's partial responsibility for genocide – a responsibility shared in uncertain ways with others possibly far-afield – hence, might turn out on closer examination to be somewhat different from those involved in assessing his responsibility for an isolated act of murder, much less for shoplifting or littering.

John Gardner, a leading analytic legal theorist, reaches a similar conclusion. There is "no reason to hope [for any] general theory of *mens rea*," he contends.[32] Legal philosophers have been "too ready to diagnose theoretical problems where only ordinary moral and legal problems exist."[33] The question of which *mens rea* to require when legislating a given offense is "hostage to all the normal conflicts of value which surround the moral . . . justification of such rules," he rightly observes.[34] This is because "*mens rea* generally makes a difference to what wrong one is doing, be it morally or legally, not to one's moral or legal responsibility for doing that wrong."[35] Gardner describes the varieties of *mens rea* as "normative rules" rather than "ascriptive" ones, the latter governing such matters as whether the defendant's conduct was truly voluntary. In comparison to normative rules, ascriptive ones "pale into utter insignificance . . . are hard to spell out, or often have to be restricted in their application because of urgent normative pressures. . . ."[36]

The approach favored here, in suggesting reduced *mens rea* (at times through broad readings of "intention," where statutory ambiguity permits) and reconceived "effective control" requirements for trials of mass atrocity, has been accused of "seeking to overcompensate for material weakness through normative harshness."[37] To this charge, the author pleads guilty, unabashedly. For it is normative questions that are largely indeed at stake here, not metaphysical ones, notwithstanding the urgings of the legal scholar-critics (and the philosophers on whom they rely).[38]

As a normative matter, it is perfectly reasonable to hold to higher standards those who choose to assume control over large groups of armed young

---

[31] Lacey, op. cit., at 356. Alan Norrie, op. cit., reaches much the same conclusion.

[32] John Gardner, "Criminal Law and the Uses of Theory: A Reply to Laing," 14 Oxford J. of Leg. Studies 217, 221 (1994).

[33] Id. at 228.

[34] Id. at 221.

[35] Id.

[36] Id.

[37] Robinson, op. cit., at 944.

[38] To be fair, every normative position is either explicitly grounded in, or implicitly assumes, a certain metaphysical view or views. The normative stance defended here, however, is logically compatible with a broad range of such views, which may partly inform normative analysis without determining it.

men – without seriously training them to avoid causing pointless suffering –
when assessing their possible malfeasance than those accused of isolated,
individual wrongdoing on a much smaller scale. Fielding a substantial force
for the purpose of deploying organized violence in this manner might almost
be classed an "inherently dangerous activity." It is much like operating a
firecracker factory, in this respect.

This is not to say that the law need go so far as to hold the military
leader "strictly liable," that is, despite his diligent efforts to avoid criminal
harm by his minions. It *is* to suggest, however, that – as the *Palsgraf* dissent famously argued[39] – what is at stake is an issue of public policy over
how society, through its law, should distribute the risks of various kinds of
harm; this distribution cannot be made simply on the basis of philosophical "principle"[40] or metaphysics.[41] That said, military officers themselves
often profess to understand their duties in terms approximating strict liability, considering one another responsible for whatever wrongful damage a
subordinate commits on their "watch," as the wrongdoer's superior.[42] This
prevalent self-understanding suggests that pertinent professional norms
may be more stringent than legal ones. The law might therefore raise its
own standards without running afoul of those already endorsed by the
people whose conduct it here seeks to govern.[43]

The higher standards here at issue pertain to the mental state on which
leaders may be held responsible for mass atrocity committed by their forces.
These standards should also lower the bar on the pertinent type of "control"
over such troops, and shift the point in time at which such control must be
evidenced, questions examined in Chapters 2 and 5.

If acquittals of prominent state leaders – most recently, the ex-president
of Serbia at the ICTY[44] – have indeed revealed the "material weakness"

---

[39] *Palsgraf v. Long Island Railway*, 162 N.E. 99, 104–05 (1928).

[40] Ronald Dworkin, *A Matter of Principle* 33–71, 267–92 (1985) (offering a since-influential
distinction between moral principle and public policy).

[41] For a recent effort to ground the law of causation in an analytic approach to metaphysics,
see Moore, op. cit.

[42] Author's interviews, U.S. Army War College and Air War College. This common expression,
of obvious military provenance, suggests an acceptance of something approximating strict
liability, if only for purposes of moral judgment among fellow professionals in the armed
services.

[43] To be sure, people often are prepared to apply higher standards when making moral
judgments of others (and themselves) than when selecting a standard by which the criminal
law should judge the same conduct.

[44] *Prosecutor v. Milan Milutinović, Nikola Šainović, Dragoljub Pavković, Vladimir Lazarević,
and Sreten Lukić*, IT-05-87-T, Judgment, ¶ 283 (Feb. 26, 2009), at http://www.icty.org/
x/cases/milutinovic/tjug/en/jud090226-e3of4.pdf. The prosecution's failure to establish

of prosecutors' efforts to punish genocide, then it is proper to raise the question of how difficult the law should make their task – and conversely, how much "normative harshness" is fair to impose on potential perpetrators. Because these are normative questions, they must be debated and resolved in just such terms, rather than by reference to the timeless and essential nature of responsibility as such, still less a highly controversial definition of "liberalism." This is because criminalizing and prosecuting genocide, for instance, is simply not an act of philosophical autopsy in which the defendant's cadaver or conduct may be carved up at its *a priori* ontological joints.[45]

It is true that the criminal law may not step beyond the line of individual culpability. Yet the law itself is largely charged with the task of locating and fixing that very line in the first place (i.e., subject to the procedural side constraint of providing adequate warning about its location to future wrongdoers). This is not to say that individual responsibility has no reality independent of social and legal ascriptions of it, only that such ascriptions come to have some impact back on this reality, on how we behave. To this end, some measure of "normative harshness," perhaps considerable harshness, is no vice if in service of international law's belated but heartening experiments with overcoming impunity for such colossal wrongs.[46] It need scarcely be said, despite defense counsels' occasional insinuations to the contrary, that this is not the illiberal variety of harshness involved, for instance, in Stalinist legal theories designating whole swathes of the Russian social structure as "objective" class enemies of "the people."[47] No one is suggesting that anyone be punished *only* on grounds of a lousy character, regardless of what he has or has not done.

A preoccupation with general human capacities, equally present in all circumstances, is especially questionable in its apparent corollary that, as Lacey

Milutinović's effective control over others in the Yugoslav Army proved fatal to hopes for conviction on these grounds, as in several earlier cases before the ICTY.

[45] More precisely, although such "philosophical" inquiries are frequently helpful in developing a satisfactory answer to law's central question here, they are decidedly insufficient to that task, often largely unnecessary, in fact.

[46] This is, of course, a playfully loose paraphrase of: "Extremism in the defense of liberty is no vice." U.S. Senator Barry Goldwater, Nomination Acceptance Speech, Republican National Convention, 1964.

[47] Arkadii Vaksberg, *Stalin's Prosecutor: the Life of Andrei Vyshinsky* (1991). It is true, however, that the judicial authority to extend the definition of criminal offenses "by analogy" has been a recurrent feature of totalitarian and some highly authoritarian regimes. Until legislative revision in 1979, criminal court judges in the People's Republic of China, for instance, were expressly authorized to exercise just such authority.

laments, when ascribing individual responsibility, "only arguments which
can be subsumed within a general schema of principles are good, rational
arguments.[48] A contrasting approach would seek to take legal cognizance
of how the public policies behind the prohibition, for instance, of crimes
against humanity – and our understandings of the organizational and other
social dynamics such wrongs entail – differ from those outlawing, say, loiter-
ing or jaywalking. Such an approach would undoubtedly be more sensitive
to both empirical and normative nuance. From a more pristinely theoretical viewpoint, however, it necessarily appears unsystematic, even irrational.
That it may also be illiberal becomes yet a further abomination.[49]

Those who conceive of individual responsibility as based entirely on our
inherent volitional and cognitive capacities as rational agents have nonetheless always shared space in Western moral and legal thought – from Spinoza
and Hume through contemporary liberals like Raz and Galston[50] – with
a rather different conception. This alternative view, ancient as Aristotle,
instead grounds ascriptions of responsibility in assessments of a defendant's moral character. Because character varies greatly from one person
to another, there is nothing inherent or invariant about it, that is, other

---

[48] Lacey, op. cit., at 358.

[49] The relation of the metaphysical claim to liberalism as a moral and political doctrine is
highly uncertain at best, however, and often disputed. It would be more defensible to
say that the claim about the invariant nature of individual responsibility often coincides
with, and surely reflects one version of, the commitment to methodological individualism. This concept was first developed by Max Weber, in his *Economy and Society*, and
consists in the claim "that social phenomena must be explained by showing how they
result from individual actions, which in turn must be explained through reference to
the intentional states that motivate the individual actors." *Stanford Encyclopedia of Philosophy*, at http://plato.stanford.edu/entries/methodological-individualism/. See also Karl
Popper, *The Open Society and its Enemies* 91–98, 323 (1945); Lars Udehn, *Methodological
Individualism: Background, History and Meaning* (2001); Geoffrey Hodgson, "Meanings of
Methodological Individualism," 14 J. of Econ. Methodology 211 (2007). Some believe that
this doctrine, concerned exclusively with how to understand and explain social behavior, is nonetheless "closely related" to, even "inextricably intertwined" with – expressions
conspicuous in their conceptual sloppiness – liberalism in the sense of a political philosophy. Yet there are many methodological individualists whose political views would
not widely be described as liberal, i.e., in U.S. terms (many, perhaps most economists fall
into this category), and there are many such "progressive" political liberals who are not
methodological individualists.

[50] Raz, op. cit., 196–97 (contending that a liberal state must foster the virtue of personal
autonomy among its citizens if they are to make effective use of the freedom it affords
them). For contemporary defenses of virtue ethics, in various forms, among avowedly
liberal theorists, see, e.g., William Galston, *Liberal Purposes: Goods, Virtues, and Diversity
in the Liberal State* 213–40 (1991); Stephen Macedo, *Liberal Virtues: Citizenship, Virtue, and
Community in Liberal Constitutionalism* 254–86 (1990). On the important place of virtue
and virtue ethics within several leading liberal thinkers, even Kant and Mill, see Peter
Berkowitz, *Virtue and the Making of Modern Liberalism* (1999).

than the enduring continuum of character types that human nature itself establishes, a spectrum along which we are all arrayed. Also, we partly shape our character through our decisions over a lifetime.

It is true that the particular virtues and vices felt to be at stake in the law's evaluations of character have changed to some extent over Western history.[51] Yet the essential features of this enduring viewpoint continue to find vigorous defenders in contemporary debate, including that among legal scholars.[52] The salience of their stance in that discussion at the very least indicates, Lacey continues, "that the subjective, capacity conception is only one among several possible interpretations of individual responsibility in post-Enlightenment traditions."[53] Although drifting closer in recent decades toward this "capacity conception" of individual responsibility, the criminal law has not – through some always-upward, Whiggish progression – freed itself from contrary understandings of the concept, and so "worked itself pure."

THE ROLE OF CHARACTER IN ASSESSING CRIMINAL CULPABILITY

The gist of the character conception of individual culpability is that, as Yale Law Professor Dan Kahan begins unassumingly

[m]ost individuals know how to live law-abiding lives without ever consulting their community's criminal code. This is so because they assume
that the criminal law tracks certain basic moral norms, with which the law-
abiders and law-breakers alike are thoroughly familiar. . . . [54] The purpose
of these "interior" [*mala in se*] offenses is not so much to inform citizens

[51] For instance, the common law excuse of provocation today relies on a very different understanding of good moral character than it did historically. This doctrine long took it to be no particularly negative reflection on a person's character – for which he might be held responsible – that, upon discovering his spouse *in flagrante delicto* with another, he allowed his aroused emotions to provoke him into killing them both at once. The emotional state that led him to such lethal violence would today, however, viewed as manifesting the bad values he holds (i.e., caring too little about others' lives) and reflecting a character defect. Because his character is within his control (in relevant respect), he may be punished for conduct suggesting that he had allowed his character to become gravely deficient.

[52] Dan Kahan, "Ignorance of the Law is an Excuse – But Only for the Virtuous," 96 Mich. L. Rev. 127 (1997); Kahan, "Lenity," op. cit.; Kahan & Martha Nussbaum, "Two Conceptions of Emotion in Criminal Law," 96 Colum. L. Rev. 269, 345–46, 357–72 (1996); Karen Huigens, Virtue and Inculpation," 108 Harv. L. Rev. 1423 (1995); Peter Arenella, "Character, Choice and Moral Agency: The Relevance of Character to Our Moral Culpability Judgments," 2 Social Philosophy & Policy 59–83 (1990); see also Michael Bayles, "Character, Purposes, and Criminal Responsibility," 1 Law and Philosophy 5 (1982).

[53] Lacey, op. cit., at 357.

[54] Kahan, "Ignorance," op. cit., at 130, 140; see also Kahan, "Lenity," op. cit., at 400–01.

of what conduct is prohibited as it is to create or increase penalties for conduct that is already understood to be absolutely forbidden by independent
laws or social mores. This is why individuals . . . do not need to consult
these statutes to be put "on notice" that their conduct is unlawful.[55]

From these unobjectionable observations, Kahan proceeds to infer that

a person is rightly condemned as a criminal wrongdoer not only for
knowingly choosing to violate the law, but also for exhibiting the kind
of character failing associated with insufficient commitment to the moral
norms embodied in the community's criminal law. . . . When we condemn
someone for being inattentive to moral obligations, we are saying that she
lacks the values that would have motivated a good person to perceive the
real value of things.[56]

Or more simply, because her conduct is reprehensible, she displays a defect
of character. Kahan speaks here of "values" reflected in "the community's"
law. That leaves the question of which community he has in mind. Often
with international crimes, after all, the values of the national community
(or larger portions thereof) turn out to differ in key respects from those of
international community and its law.[57]

Leaders of states that perpetrate mass atrocity often are disconcertingly
successful for key periods in transforming community values or "common
morality" – sometimes also the positive law – in support of their homicidal
policies. At that point, the domestic community's "social mores," in Kahan's
terms, offer most citizens little warning as to the possibility of later prosecution by international courts. National leaders, however, are today put on
clear notice of this prospect by the very legal developments described in this
book[58]; they also receive fair warning – almost in real time – of what they
may be held accountable for through direct reporting to them from human

---

[55] Kahan, "Lenity," op. cit., at 401.

[56] Id. at 130, 144.

[57] The disparity between the moral judgment of the international and national (or, more
often, subnational, ethno-religious) community implies that each may also maintain
diverging understandings of personal virtue and vice. Yet those at the pinnacle of power
in nondemocratic states often operate with considerable autonomy, to put it mildly, from
the expectations of common morality – however its demands may be understood – even
within their national societies.

[58] More controversially, van Schaack, op. cit., at 120, argues, "Today's defendants were on
sufficient notice of the foreseeability of ICL jurisprudential innovations in light of extant
domestic penal law, universal moral values expressed in international human rights law,
developments in international humanitarian law and the circumstances in which it has
been invoked, and other dramatic changes to the international order . . . brought about in
the postwar period."

rights NGOs monitoring events on the ground. If leaders are reckless in their response to such warning, they reveal grave weakness of character – often much else.[59]

At this point, Kahan's argument takes a bold, even startling step: he draws from the preceding conclusions – about the relation among character, community mores, and due process – the further implication that the criminal law may "tell [those subject to it] that if they suspect that some species of immoral conduct may evade the reach of the law, the only sure way to avoid punishment is to do what they know is right, not what they think is legal."[60] There is no virtue in seeking to learn the exact nature of one's legal duties if one's purpose in so doing is not "an earnest and laudable attempt to obey," but rather to discover and exploit "fortuitous gaps in the law."[61]

In handling these "gaps," the criminal law accords a prominent, if often unacknowledged, place to the moral character of defendants, both actual and prospective. The gaps or ambiguities arise at three key points. First, they appear in the legislative process of drafting the desired wording for statutes and treaties, when determining how precise the pertinent terms should be, in order to provide fair warning, at very least, to those later governed by these

---

[59] Admittedly, Kahan's observations would be highly questionable if taken to imply that during episodes of mass atrocity "common morality" of the sort he has in mind closely tracks for most people international criminal law or even the law "on the books" of the particular authoritarian or totalitarian state. He clearly does not have such states in mind, of course.

But they are precisely the ones whose leaders generally perpetrate mass atrocity. It is such states that most readily afford them the power to do so, after all. On the uncertain relationship at such times between common morality and positive law, both national and international, see Mark Osiel, *Mass Atrocity, Ordinary Evil, and Hannah Arendt: Criminal Consciousness in Argentina's Dirty War* 88–103 (2001); Drumbl, op. cit., at 3–6, 29–35. A closely related feature of mass atrocity, still more problematic for the character theory of culpability, is that participants at all levels in a chain of command generally fail to display the indicia of moral viciousness on which courts and others conventionally rely in part when assessing an individual's culpability. Osiel, id. at 43–49 (describing the absence of such evidence of unethical character, before or after their criminal acts, in either Adolf Eichmann or Argentine "dirty warrior" Alfredo Astiz); see also Seth Mydans, "Trials in Cambodia Expose the Cogs in a Killing Machine," N.Y. Times, March 10, 2009, at A6 describing Him Huy, head of the guard detail at a Khmer Rouge killing field, who took part in thousands of executions. "A farmer and the father of nine, he is optimistic, hardworking, and quick to smile, seemingly comfortable to be who he is and at ease with his memories. Neighbors seem to like him. 'Even the young people, when they have a party they always invite him,' said his wife, Put Pen Aun. Asked to describe himself, Mr. Him Huy said . . . 'I'm a good man. I never argue with anyone. I never fight with anyone. I have good intentions as a human being.'"

[60] Kahan, "Ignorance," op. cit., at 141.

[61] Id.

rules. Certain ambiguities will almost inevitably remain in the wording of a ratified provision. A second set of uncertainties emerges when the provision must be interpreted; in resolving an ambiguity, should the court adopt a broad or narrow reading, for instance, of the scope of prohibited conduct? Third, ambiguity sometimes comes to the fore in ascertaining the facts to which such legal rules, once clarified, must be applied.

All three assessments implicate the moral character of defendants. Regarding the last of these, when fact-finders must determine whether the prosecution has satisfied its evidentiary burdens, in many legal systems they may employ evidence about the defendant's overall moral character. They may use such evidence to resolve whether any doubt they may harbor concerning his guilt is "reasonable," requiring his acquittal. In parts of the "civil law" world, even the record of a defendant's prior criminal convictions is often admissible in assessing his character for this purpose.[62]

The first variety of ambiguity mentioned briefly above concerns a different type of legal actor: legislators and treaty drafters may choose to leave certain terms vague in order to delegate interstitial law-making to courts and regulatory agencies. This is often the case, for very good reasons.[63] "Delegating power to an agency to close such gaps as quickly as they are discovered is one device for responding to the law's persistent incompleteness,"[64] Kahan

---

[62] Philip L. Reichel, "Civil Law Legal Traditions," in 1 *Encyclopedia of Crime and Punishment* 235 (David Levinson, ed., 2002). "In civil law countries there are few limits on evidence presented during trial since anything that might shed light on a person's guilt or innocence is expected to be considered. Germany offers a good example. Character evidence, including prior convictions, can be introduced.... [i]n practice the defendant's criminal record is usually read into the court record just before the closing arguments of the trial."

[63] Kahan discusses several such reasons for legislative delegation of this sort, in "Lenity," op. cit., at 398–428. This is not to deny that such delegation may sometimes become excessive – in fact, constitutionally infirm. Nicolas Szabo, "Origins of the Non-Delegation Doctrine," at http://papers.ssrn.com/sol3/papers.cfm?abstract_id=1156482. It would be wrong to imply, moreover, that such delegation through statutory vagueness necessarily seeks to encourage expansive interpretation of criminal offenses. It rather aims, more precisely, to foster the exercise of practical judgment in light of the particular facts (and their moral nuances) before the tribunal or jury. Such case-specific circumstances sometimes warrant mercy, display of which is impeded by precise, stringent wording in the definition of an offense. William Stuntz, "Unequal Justice," 121 Harv. L. Rev. 1969, 2036–39 (2008) (criticizing how "the mechanical nature of contemporary drug law" unduly limits jurors's discretion to show lenience, when warranted). Stuntz observes, "Vague liability rules once were, and might be again, part of a well-functioning system of checks and balances," whereby fine-grained situational assessment by fact-finders counterbalances the broad discretion of prosecutors. Id. at 2039. Excessive verbal exactitude can as readily lead to overinclusiveness vis-à-vis a prohibition's underlying purposes, after all, as to underinclusiveness.

[64] Kahan, "Ignorance," op. cit. at 139.

observes. The resulting ambiguities in an enacted prohibition are then no mere oversights, but at least sometimes the result of considerable artistry in couching its verbal instantiation.

Where the statutory or treaty provision strives for excessive precision, these gaps often appear very quickly. This is because, with many species of misconduct, wrongdoers can be expected to "loophole" and "lawyer" their way around legislative exactitude. They will predictably devise novel means to subvert the clear ends of a prohibition. A good way to circumvent such circuitousness is through "prudent obfuscation of the law's outer periphery," as Kahan puts it.[65] Legislative intent must hence be deliberately elusive, in key places. Through such obscurantism, the authors of a statute or treaty veritably invite courts to determine whether some ingeniously novel conduct at the nether reaches of a legal prohibition falls within its terms.

The aim of such willful ambiguity in legislative drafting is to deter not so much "the strategically heedless," Kahan continues, but rather "the impudently inquisitive."[66] For '[i]t is not that person's deliberate ignorance of, but rather her exacting attention to, the law's fine points that we must regard as a "false and diversionary stratagem[]," a form of "game playing and evasion," that we should construe the law to discourage.... '[67]

There is surely much truth and appeal to this legislative technique, even if Kahan's clever formulation of it likely exaggerates the extent of self-conscious calculation generally involved. He offers several examples of intentional statutory indefinition, including the concept of "criminal enterprise" within U.S. racketeering legislation[68] – one of the very sources of the "joint criminal enterprise" rule in recent international criminal jurisprudence.

Finally, in response to deliberate delegation by law-makers, courts must decide how to interpret the hazy wording along a continuum of possibilities from quite broadly to very narrowly. Here too, the defendant's character proves pertinent. The accused is often punished more harshly despite – indeed, in part because of – his punctilious *ex ante* efforts to ascertain his duty, if he has clearly undertaken these with a view to testing the limits of

---

[65] Id. at 129.

[66] Id. at 137.

[67] Id. Kahan's quotations are from a judicial opinion in which the court rejected a "mistake of law" defense/excuse. *People v. Marrero*, 507 N.E.2d 1068, 1071 (N.Y., 1987).

[68] Racketeer Influenced and Corrupt Organizations Act, 18 U.S.C. § 1961–1968. This statute has been effectively employed against the Ku Klux Klan, as well as many other organizations engaged in criminal activity.

what he might "get away with." Such concerted inquiries often betray not a commendably conscientious character, but a vicious and villainous one.

This fact leads some to question the merits of the lenity rule, notwithstanding its "near-constitutional status" in the minds of others.[69] After all, "When a potential offender believes that an ambiguous statute is likely to be construed narrowly, she is more likely to engage in conduct that in fact violates the statute than she would if she believed the statute were likely to be construed broadly."[70] In fact, "The class of persons who would benefit from systematically narrow constructions is pervaded by those who intend to injure other, innocent individuals."[71] By contrast, many people make concerted efforts to avoid such injury to others. This virtue of character is not uniquely liberal, of course. Yet insofar as the potential injury would also often violate others' rights (as liberalism understands these), it is a virtue to which liberals, among many others perhaps, may lay solid claim.

To summarize what we have said thus far, the moral character of a person accused of crime is central to virtually every step in how the prohibition invoked against him is drafted, interpreted, and applied to the facts of his case. The preceding analysis of how the character of the accused influences judgments of his individual culpability in criminal law has major implications, in turn, for how to assess the doctrinal inventiveness by international courts examined in this book. In their accusation of illiberalism, critics of such innovation claim that these doctrinal approaches "assume[] that judges are able to determine that persons are 'responsible' independently of the terms of the" applicable law.[72]

Exactly right. This is entirely appropriate where the terms of such law are themselves enigmatic (whether intentionally or otherwise), inviting more fine-grained judicial analysis of normatively relevant facts about the

---

[69] Kahan, "Lenity," op. cit., at 345, 346; Brad Roth, "Coming to Terms with Ruthlessness: Sovereign Equality, Global Pluralism, and the Limits of International Criminal Justice," manuscript, 2009 ("Violations of *nullum crimen sin lege* are quintessential abuses of legality because they so frontally defy the concern for predictability and accountability in the exercise of power.").

[70] Kahan, "Lenity," op. cit., at 404. To believe that high-level perpetrators of mass atrocity will seek to exploit such legal ambiguities *ex ante*, we must admittedly assume that they are rational actors. The fact that they order such atrocities in the first place, despite the existence of an ICC to prosecute such offenses, is no indication of their irrationality. For the Court's ability to acquire custody over defendants remains weak as long as such people remain in power or in close alliance with their successors.

[71] Id. at 417.

[72] Robinson, op. cit, at 943.

accused – facts bearing on his character and hence potentially on his culpability as well. In its methods for resolving doubts about individual responsibility, the character approach to criminal law authorizes – even embraces – the very assumption that Robinson dismisses as self-evidently silly (since apparently unworthy of refutation): that aspects of culpability relevant to both liability and sanction may accurately and fairly be determined in part by reference to character evidence "beyond the text" of the law itself. This is particularly appropriate where the suspect has sought legal knowledge precisely in order to evade the clear purpose of a *mala in se* prohibition. This is the case, for instance, of the Sudanese leaders who recently sought legal counsel on how to engage in ethnic cleansing while ensuring they do not display the *mens rea* for genocide.[73]

WHEN LAW DISCOURAGES "CUTTING IT CLOSE"

It is worth pausing here for a moment to observe that there are two, very different situations that involve "conduct that sits on the boundary line between socially desirable and socially undesirable. . . ."[74] In one case, the law permits, even encourages people governed by it to come very close to the line. This is fitting where the distance between socially valuable conduct and harmful conduct may be very slight.

For instance, many who find themselves prosecuted for fraud in the sale of corporate securities are primarily engaged in a perfectly legitimate, socially valued activity: facilitating the sale of stocks and bonds by companies needing to raise capital to satisfy consumer demand for their products. But such people will sometimes mistakenly stray off an ever-shifting path of permissibility, often difficult to discern, as by excluding a piece of information from Securities and Exchange Commission filing that new, more aggressive agency regulators later determine to have been "material," in light of how its nondisclosure contributed to exaggerating stock value. Many people can be seriously harmed by such mistakes, no doubt. Still, the securities laws – in their infinite intricacy and the superficial indistinguishability (to all but cognoscenti) between what they permit and prohibit – represent perhaps the archetype of offenses that, though by no means inconsequential, are nonetheless *mala prohibita*.

---

[73] Author's confidential interviews, The Hague, December 2008. Forcible deportation may constitute a crime against humanity if knowingly conducted as part of a widespread or systematic attack on a civilian population.

[74] Kahan, "Lenity," op. cit., at 400.

One easy way to encourage people to draw up close to the edge is to offer them the excuse of mistake if they don't actually know their conduct to be illegal. In some areas of the law, such as the U.S. Tax Code, even unreasonable mistakes of law obstruct conviction, provided the taxpayer can convince the fact-finders that he held a genuine, good faith belief that the Code allowed the treatment he afforded the disputed income or deduction.[75] For better or worse, Americans clearly do not consider it sinful to pay the government no more than it is actually owed, even where this may require considerable research into discovering the permissible methods of such mitigation.

In the second situation, by contrast, the law discourages us from getting anywhere near the boundary between legal and illegal. This is proper when the prohibited conduct bears no close relation to any socially valued activity that the law encourages. Here, it is fair to punish those who decide to take the risks of toeing the line; in the prior situation, it is not. There, as Kahan observes, "because these [*mala prohibita*] laws are understood to invite individuals to come right up to the line between what is a crime and what is not, obscurity as to where that line is drawn is indeed grossly unfair."[76]

The distinction between these two types of legal prohibition and the variant circumstances they contemplate has major implications for how to write the law, resolve uncertainties in its application, and handle a "mistake of law" excuse. Specifically, it provides a compelling basis, as writes Brad Roth, for "distinguishing when *nullum crimen*-related rules are a technicality from when they are a matter of moral principle."[77] When ambiguities arise during the trial of atrocity cases, in particular, the question may often be one of whether the defendants were engaged in genocide or "merely" in the crimes against humanity of extermination or violently forcing thousands of people from their homes and villages at gunpoint. However one wishes to characterize such conduct, it clearly lies nowhere near the core of any species of conduct that the law allows, much less encourages.

---

[75] *Cheek v. U.S.*, 498 U.S. 192 (1991). It is therefore troubling, as several scholars have observed, that the ICC Statute affords such a basis for acquittal by including knowledge of illegality within (parts of) the definitions of its offenses. See, e.g., Kevin Jon Heller, "Mistake of Legal Element, the Common Law, and Article 32 of the Rome Statute: A Critical Analysis," 6 J. of Int'l Crim. Justice 419, 419 (2008) (contending that "Art. 32 potentially recognizes a wide variety of exculpatory mistakes of legal element."); Kai Ambos, "Remarks on the General Part of International Criminal Law," 4 J. of Int'l Crim. Justice 660, 668 (2006) ("if the soldier is not aware of the unlawfulness of the order and the order was not manifestly unlawful, such a mistake will be considered relevant [as negating his or her *mens rea*].").

[76] Kahan, "Lenity," op. cit., at 400.

[77] Brad Roth, correspondence with author, March 2009.

A person of good character instinctively steers well away from the edge of a prohibition that clearly tracks the core of "common morality," the basis of all *mala in se* crimes. Anyone who finds himself in a no man's land between genocide and crimes against humanity is highly unlikely – in Kahan's delicate phrasing – to have displayed sufficient sensitivity to the community's moral values as enshrined in its law. For the international community (no less than the national), this common morality is most convincingly embodied in its criminal code. That code wholly and equally forbids both species of atrocity. There is no variety of internationally valued activity that either of these forms of massive violence closely approximate in nature. Hence there is no danger of overdeterring legitimate social activity through broad drafting and construction of their criminalization. To be sure, this observation is truer of genocide and crimes against humanity than of war crimes. After all, when war is waged in legitimate self-defense, lethal violence serves – by hypothesis – the publicly prized end of collective self-preservation (more socially-valued anywhere, for that matter, than selling securities). Also, the line between proportionate and objectively excessive uses of force is sometimes thin. So is the line between anticipatory self-defense and criminal acts of aggression. Subjectively, lawful acts of warfare often differ from criminal ones only in regard to the actor's momentary mental state. Whether his conduct proves permitted or prohibited then turns on refined conceptual distinctions (among categories of *mens rea*), as applied to a factual question on which no direct evidence will exist. Vicissitudes of this sort make a stronger case for judicial lenience toward such conduct. They also ruefully lead one influential ICTY judicial officer to acknowledge in private, "In war, there will be war crimes." The same cannot be said, however, of sexual slavery or ethno-religious persecution.

Moreover, in a genuine national emergency, national leaders seeking to restore public order may reluctantly find it necessary to employ methods that would otherwise be indefensible – including methods abrogating non-derogable international human rights.[78] Yet in principle, at least, this latitude no longer extends, as the House of Lords held in the Pinochet case, to such grave international crimes as torture.[79] It is true that no genuine revolutionary situation, such as that across much of Europe in 1848 or

[78] Int'l Covenant on Civil and Political Rights, Art. 4(2).
[79] These crimes are sometimes deemed subject to international prosecution because they cannot, by definition, be conducted in one's "official capacity." Alternatively, it is possible to contend that even if one does not relinquish such official capacity through such acts, the public servant nonetheless remains subject to international prosecution. In denying Chilean Dictator Augusto Pinochet immunity from prosecution, the British Law Lords

following the First World War,[80] has ever been put down in a manner consistent with the rule of law. But even if state leaders reasonably come to conclude that forbidden methods are essential to staving off revolution, as Pinochet and many compatriots no doubt believed (with some reason)[81] in 1973, they must nonetheless risk international criminal liability in resorting to such methods today.

When all is said and done, the mastermind of mass atrocity may actually be more like a burglar than an embezzler, after all. His very conduct – say, the documented order leading to forcible deportation of an ethno-religious group from his country – overtly "manifests" his vicious character. So does his decision to involve himself in an "enterprise" (or hierarchical organization) whose other members – he has every reason to understand – may have still worse in mind for the unfortunate souls placed at their mercies. It may be impossible to determine, beyond reasonable doubt at least, the precise nature of the desk murderer's mental state at the moment of his own wrongful acts or omissions, as when translating and transmitting a command from his superior into an order to his subordinates. It can hardly be said, however, that his behavior reflects stunningly on a sterling character.

International law may currently display a certain haziness about which conceptual cubbyhole his misconduct would more accurately occupy. But this fact does not vitiate the legal value of the unfavorable inferences a court may draw from such misconduct about his character, hence also about how to resolve doubts about his culpability. In any event, that haziness likely will soon be largely dispelled, as international and national courts continue to develop their jurisprudence on the question, case by case.

The central point here is simply that when a person who, presented with clear options of white and black, chooses to enter so ominous a grey zone between the two, the law rightly deems him to act at his peril: he has ample warning that ambiguities in the norms governing his conduct may be read against him and that such ambiguities may indeed have been planted there precisely to dissuade him from entering that dubious zone in the first

---

differed over which of these arguments, among others, provide the most defensible ratio-nale for this conclusion. See, e.g., *Regina v. Bow Street Metropolitan Stipendiary Magistrate*, 1 AC 147, 204–05 (1999) (lead opinion of Lord Browne-Wilkinson).

[80] Charles Maier, *Recasting Bourgeois Europe: Stabilization in France, Germany, and Italy in the Decade After World War* I 41, 138–40, 150–51, 443–50, 474–75 (1975).

[81] Harvey Waterman, "Political Mobilization and the Case of Chile," 13 Comp. Studies in Int'l Development 60 (2007); Henry Landsberger & Tim McDaniel, "Hypermobiliza-tion in Chile, 1970–73," 28 World Politics 502 (1976). Such social scientists have some-times described Chile's political circumstances in 1973 as approximating a revolutionary situation.

place. It is no accident that in war, most "no man's lands" are littered with landmines.

There is nothing unfair to prospective perpetrators, then, in being self-consciously cryptic at law's borderlines when legislating the language of the most *mala in se* offenses (and modes of perpetrating them). For this is conduct that no virtuous person would ever by chance or mistake just happen to wander anywhere near committing. Without a doubt, fair warning is necessary to respecting individual autonomy, indeed a central goal of liberalism. Yet as Kahan observes, "Respect for 'individual autonomy' does not justify narrow construction to accommodate this [*mala in se*] behavior, for such conduct is, by hypothesis, aimed at infringing the moral and legal rights of other parties."[82] Lawmakers should have no qualms about being nimble in their nebulousness. They rightly seek "to remove offenders' temptation to look for loopholes *ex ante* by giving courts the flexibility to adapt the law to innovative forms of crime *ex post*."[83]

For this legislative strategy to work, however, courts must be willing to take up its challenge. As worded, the criminal law that legislators enact is, in any event, never perfectly in sync with even the clearest exhortations of common morality. Hence, behavior that might be deemed "marginally lawful . . . – whether the distribution of an uncontrolled designer drug or the possession of an unregulated but dangerous firearm – is still likely to be immoral and thus worth deterring,"[84] Kahan convincingly concludes. It is too much, and certainly inefficient,[85] to expect the world community to reconvene, via the ICC Assembly of State Parties, to amend the Rome Statute every time someone finds a clever new way to conduct atrocity on a large scale.

The entire approach just entertained offers valuable guidance for resolving whether those accused of masterminding mass atrocity have received due warning of possible punishment when international criminal law has not clearly specified in advance the (exact contours of the) particular mode of participation in liability by which courts may later link them to the violent misconduct of their followers. In particular, international law – like national courts in many countries – may construe the requirement of "effective control" (both in the law of superior responsibility and of co-perpetration through another) to mean any number of things, discussed in prior chapters,

[82] Kahan, "Lenity," op. cit., at 401.
[83] Kahan, "Ignorance," op. cit., at 139.
[84] Id. at 142.
[85] On such efficiency considerations, see Kahan, "Lenity," op. cit., at 406–18.

some of these rather less demanding on the prosecution than what the ICTY eventually came to understand this term as entailing.

To conclude, a defendant reveals a morally deficient character whenever – with respect to the gravest of *mala in se* offenses – he deliberately toes the chalk line of what law allows. If he behaves in this way, then the criminal law should not excuse him for mistakenly thinking his conduct was lawful (i.e., if the court concludes that it was not).[86] In the process of clarifying the applicable rule, the court should resolve against such a defendant any legal ambiguities on which he knowingly sought to rely.

In the heat of diplomatic bargaining (with its inevitable compromises), the ICC drafters alas rejected this final conclusion.[87] But what they offered defendants with one hand, they effectively took away – in significant respects – with the other. Thus, despite facially professing – in Article 22(2) – to adopt a stringent (i.e., "pro-defendant") approach to lenity, the ICC Statute nonetheless proceeds to define several key offenses very imprecisely, and not by accident. For instance, it expressly incorporates terms that "rely heavily on value judgments," as Kai Ambos observes.[88] Certain war crimes thus are defined by reference to such inherently imprecise and normative standards as "clearly excessive" incidental harm.[89]

Other Statutory terms expressly seek recourse in extra-legal cognitive standards. Hence, the proportionality of collateral damage must be assessed "in relation to concrete and direct overall military advantage. . . . "[90] Introducing the word "overall" here necessarily enlarges the court's factual inquiry so as to ensure that reasonable experts will often differ over whether a particular exercise of force was excessive, depending on how they weigh several contradictory aspects of the overall operational environment. The term "anticipated" is then added to this formulation, so that the full statutory wording reads "overall military advantage anticipated." This

---

[86] Although others differ, Heller argues that achieving this goal at the ICC may eventually require amending its Statute. "Mistake of Legal Element," op. cit., at 443–45.

[87] Rome Statute of the International Criminal Court, Art. 22(2). The provision's wording was suggested by the U.S. delegation to the drafting convention. The Clinton administration favored this strong formulation because it effectively precludes the ICC from "discovering" new crimes without express authorization from the Assembly of State Parties. Understandings of fair warning among many drafters prompted other states to accept the U.S. wording without debate. *The Rome Statute of the International Criminal Court: A Commentary*, 752–56 (Antonio Cassese, et al., eds., 2002).

[88] Ambos, op. cit., at 670.

[89] Rome Statute Art. 8(2)(b)(iv).

[90] Id.

move embraces ambiguity with still further abandon. For now, the legal assessment demands that judges project themselves into the boots of the commander as he assesses a range of prospective battlefield events, most of which will never have materialized. It may be difficult to fathom exactly what "strict construction" of such a rule would even mean.

In addition, the Statute maintains so-called blanket norms that make susceptibility to punishment turn on evolving international rules external to the treaty itself. Thus, the crime of "persecution" is delineated in a way allowing the Court to extend the variety of protected groups beyond those enumerated in the Statute. Persecution may thus become a crime when directed against members of groups defined on the basis of "other grounds that are universally recognized as impermissible under international laws"[91] (i.e., at some future date).

Finally, the ICC Statute invites judicial extension of crimes against humanity to "other inhuman acts of a similar character,"[92] embracing of criminalization by analogy. This sits uneasily with the lenity principle, and most readings of *nulla poena sine lege*, to put it mildly. In light of all this, it is difficult to know how seriously to take, and how strictly in practice to apply, the Statute's avowed rule of lenity in resolving legal ambiguities.

No such restrictive rules of interpretation may be found, in any event, within the Statutes of the Special Court for Sierra Leone, the Special Court for Lebanon, or the Extraordinary Chambers of the Courts of Cambodia. Consistently with their own Statutes,[93] the ICTY and ICTR themselves rightly interpreted international criminal law to treat atrocity's architects differently from those who keep well clear of the line between conduct that is criminal – extravagantly immoral, in fact – and behavior just arguably a millimeter short of criminal. Their jurisprudence here should set the example for such other international and hybrid courts.

Lawyers from the civil law tradition may pride themselves on their more punctilious precision in legislative drafting and greater modesty in judicial interpretation. But the increasingly "activist" record of Western European courts over the last half-century, especially the European Court of Human

---

[91] Id. Art. 7(1)(h).

[92] Id. Art. 7(1)(k).

[93] The Statutes of these Tribunals differ from the ICC's in that they lack any general provision on *mens rea*, any comprehensive list of elements of crimes, and any language aiming to diminish the relative weight of international custom vis-à-vis the rest of the Statute. It warrants mention as well that there is no "void for vagueness" rule within general international law.

Rights, far surpasses the ambition of most common law judges, suggesting a major disparity between word and deed. The true, *sub rosa* attitude of many Continental lawyers today toward the common law's greater tolerance for ambiguity calls to mind the famous University of Chicago maxim: Yes, very good in practice, but it just doesn't work in theory – that is, our theory of the proper place of judging within a democracy.

PART II

THE POLITICAL CONTEXT OF
LEGAL CHOICE

7

Must National Prosecutions Serve Global Concerns?

LEGAL STRATEGIES FOR TRANSITIONAL JUSTICE IN POSTCONFLICT SOCIETIES

Trials of kingpins for mass atrocity seek more than retribution for past wrongs and deterrence of future ones. Properly conducted, national prosecution can enable states to reestablish themselves as moral authorities that legitimately represent an entire society, including groups that were recently repressed. Trials also seek to influence the collective memory of the catastrophic events they publicly recount and officially evaluate. Revising public understandings of the country's recent past by dispelling impressions propagated by authoritarian predecessors often becomes a central objective.

New rulers regularly employ atrocity trials in an effort to bring the nation together and establish a new conception of the past. Though they may publicly disavow such a lofty aspiration, they often seek to become intellectual architects of a revised national identity. Through prosecution, they aim to separate the evil past from a brighter future; between these points stands the trial, as the symbolic "act of unequivocal demarcation."[1]

How sharp a break with the past is really necessary or desirable, to be sure, often becomes more controversial than new rulers would like. Some insist the past regime was not really so bad; others that it was execrable and rupture with it is not yet sufficient. Some contend that even large-scale criminal prosecutions do not break sufficiently with the past.

In South Africa, for instance, trials of apartheid's rulers and police torturers would necessarily have left untouched its many thousands of white

---

[1] Marcia B. Hartwell, "The Role of Forgiveness in Reconstructing Society after Conflict," J. Humanitarian Assistance, June 3, 2000.

beneficiaries, few of whom played any direct role in perpetrating its crimes.[2] The dichotomous schema of victims and victimizers, derived from criminal law's contrast of accuser and accused, utterly ignores this third category. Focusing on benefited bystanders may be crucial to understanding the extent of apartheid's societal support and longstanding survival. But this approach – with its insistence on greater moral nuance than a binary opposition permits – places many more highly contentious issues on the table than public policy can readily accommodate without imperiling a precarious transition.[3]

Surrounded by such controversies, national courts are almost inexorably "drawn into historical debates which shake the mythical foundations of the nation: the suffering of all Jews [in the Eichmann trial], the guilt of all Germans [in the 1960s prosecutions of concentration camp guards], or the meek collaboration of all Frenchmen [such as Papon]."[4] Prosecutors

---

[2] Mahmood Mamdani, "Reconciliation without Justice," S. Afr. Rev. Books, Nov.–Dec. 1996, at 3, 5. Mamdani thus argues that what is most needed during such transitions is not criminal justice, but social justice for South Africa's poor blacks. If justice is to be sacrificed for reconciliation, he adds, it may be no less important to seek that between victims and beneficiaries than between victims and perpetrators.

[3] For instance, Mamdani's attention to beneficiaries, although potentially fruitful, may define the category too narrowly, focusing as he does on white-owned companies. This focus ignores the extent to which many blacks themselves were among apartheid's "beneficiaries," not only those employed directly by the state but also by the many foreign corporations that would never have invested so heavily there – generating much employment and wealth for later redistribution – but for the political stability afforded by the apartheid state. Average income levels for South African blacks working in manufacturing have been significantly above total per capita income levels in the vast majority of sub-Saharan countries. In 1997, for instance, there were 598,492 African/Black manufacturing employees in South Africa with a total income of R15,076,292,000. Statistics S. Afr., South African Statistics 2000 7.12 (2000). On average, these employees earned R25,190, or US$5,464, given a 1997 Rand-to-dollar exchange rate of 4.61:1. Lawrence H. Officer, "Exchange Rate between the United States Dollar and Forty Other Countries," 1913–99 (2002), at http://eh.net/hmit/exchangerates/. In contrast, the per capita income in thirty-six of the forty-one other sub-Saharan African countries was less than $850 in 1997. UN Statistics Division, National Accounts Main Aggregates Database.
    Once the concept of beneficiary is thus enlarged, however, it becomes very unclear what sort of remedy – if any – might follow from introducing this third category into political and legal analysis. In any event, it is questionable whether the country's high rates of investment and economic growth were attributable to apartheid per se. Although that law surely facilitated subordination of black laborers in ways from which many white companies profited, it is difficult to disentangle apartheid's causal effect on wealth creation from the fact that, from a comparative perspective, South Africa's courts offered so much more legal protection to property and contract rights than did other African states.

[4] Richard A. Wilson, "How Do International Criminal Tribunals Write Histories of Mass Human Rights Violations?" 14 (2003) (unpublished manuscript), at www.ucl.ac.uk/spp/hr/download/paper_RichardWilson.doc.

choose defendants and construct their legal arguments accordingly, with a self-conscious view toward conveying a certain message about how the country came to suffer such an apocalypse.

The principal lesson national prosecutors seek to impart is that responsibility for mass atrocity is not widely shared, but is confined to a few notorious individuals.[5] On this view, large groups and institutions, particularly those with enduring political power, cannot be blamed collectively for what the country has suffered. Hence, for instance, the recurrent efforts in Germany, Japan, and Russia to distinguish the contribution to mass atrocity by special forces, other elite units, and party militants from that of the regular conscript army, whose role official mythmakers invariably minimize.[6]

Legal responsibility for criminal policies resides with those who made them, on this view.[7] The old regime they created thereby suffers severe discredit, facilitating transition to the new. Even high-ranking subordinates who implemented such policies are in turn categorized as "followers," despite often exercising great responsibility in concretizing their terms. The majesty of the law at such tumultuous times consists not in vainly maintaining a façade of apolitical neutrality, but in openly serving a decent, worthy politics. The law will provide a range of options from which prosecutors must choose; they will make these choices on bases not fully governed by law.[8]

But by what then? Because such trials are always "conceptualized as part of a political program,"[9] as David Cohen observes, public debate should focus on the legitimacy of that program, not the fact that it is political.[10] In the heady first days of democratic transition, there are always loud voices demanding a more ambitious program of retribution, often formulated

---

[5] This does not mean that national courts are more lenient than international ones, however, regarding conditions of imprisonment or length of sentences.

[6] Martin Shaw, *War and Genocide* 150 (2003). In fact, however, regular army units in all three states regularly participated in mass killings of civilians. Id.; see also, e.g., Omer Bartov, *Hitler's Army* 69 (1992).

[7] Lutz Niethammer, *Die Mitläuferfabrik: Die Entnazifizierung am Beispiel Bayerns* 21–4, 536–652 (1982) (describing how de-nazification proceedings adopted strict evidentiary rules to classify all but the highest echelons as followers, thereby facilitating their reintegration into German society).

[8] Mark Osiel, *Mass Atrocity, Collective Memory, and the Law* 247–8 (1997).

[9] David Cohen, "Transitional Justice in Divided Germany after 1945," at 41 (unpublished manuscript).

[10] Judith Shklar, *Legalism: Law, Morals, and Political Trials* 145–7, 155–6 (2d ed. 1986).

in avowedly collective terms.[11] On assuming office, Iraq's Coalitional Provisional Authority and Governing Council, for example, first wished to prosecute more than six thousand Sunni military and bureaucratic elites.

Cooler heads almost always prevail, however, in such situations. The Governing Council quickly reassessed, deciding to indict barely a dozen of Saddam's highest ranking associates. For similar reasons, ambitious postwar Allied programs for trying several thousand mid-echelon Nazis – and still broader plans for de-nazification of German and collaborationist elites – were soon abandoned.[12]

Prosecution of such numbers necessarily takes many years, if done with any semblance of due process. The delay enables perpetrators to outlast the political cycle that discredited them and permitted their indictment. By the time of trial, they may even be more popular than those who placed them in the dock. When extradited to The Hague, for instance, Milošević was very unpopular at home because he was viewed as responsible, through diplomatic miscalculations, for the NATO bombing that caused Serbians much discomfort. By the time he began his legal case in defense, however, polls showed him again to be the most popular political figure in Serbia.[13]

Long delay also gravely weakens the message of legal accountability that new rulers wish to send when announcing such trials. National prosecutors are far more attentive to temporal considerations than their international counterparts. Those in The Hague are not immune to extralegal constraints of course, but are subject to different political cycles, based on shifting sentiment in the UN Security Council concerning the efficacy and costs of their endeavors. By 2003, this sentiment had shifted subtly but significantly against them.

A quiet consensus emerged, among most who closely follow the legal response to mass atrocity,[14] that prosecution – whether in national,

---

[11] Insofar as such demands reflect mere spitefulness, they are inexplicable to neoclassical economics. Colin Camerer & Richard H. Thaler, "Anomalies: Ultimatums, Dictators, and Manners," 9 J. Econ. Persp. 209, 214–6 (1995) (discussing bargainers' tendency to punish other players excessively for prior behavior as problematic for economic theory).

[12] Cohen, "Transitional Justice," op. cit., at 17.

[13] Daniel Simpson, "Milosevic Trial Leaves Most Serbs Cynical," N.Y. Times, Aug. 9, 2002, at A8 ("Milosevic's popularity rocketed during the early weeks of the trial."). In fact, he had just been reelected to Parliament, from his jail cell in The Hague. The Serbian Prime Minister (Zoran Djindjic), who extradited him, had since been assassinated, in likely retaliation for the extradition.

[14] The reference here is to legal scholars, political scientists, diplomats, and some human rights advocates, albeit not to activists committed *a priori* to prosecuting all major rights abusers, regardless of national context. See, e.g., M. Cherif Bassiouni, "Prosecuting Saddam

international, or hybrid courts – should focus almost exclusively on top leaders, for simple charges, easily evidenced, and susceptible to completion within a couple of years.[15] Doing so is the only way to harmonize the legal process with predictable political cycles, which cannot be ignored without gravely risking the law's legitimacy.

Fallen dictators will never be as despised as when first dislodged, when the country's woes seem wholly attributable to them. Electoral support for Communist parties in Russia and eastern Europe, for example, began rising markedly just a few years after the demise of the Soviet Union.[16] Likewise, democratic successors will almost never be as popular as when first elected.

This explains the prosecutorial strategy adopted toward Saddam Hussein: a quick, first trial based on a small subset of his wrongs for which solid documentary and witness evidence readily existed, rather than a broader indictment, telling a larger story about the extent of his oppressive rule throughout the country.[17] The ICC's Chief Prosecutor adopted the same

Hussein," Foreign Pol'y, July 2005 (endorsing the Iraqi leadership's decision "to start the trial based on a few specific and well-documented instances of abuse," with a view that a "narrower focus might help prevent Saddam from turning the trial into a political stage"); Ruth Wedgwood, "Where Should Saddam Hussein Be Tried?," Legal Aff. Debate Club, July 5, 2005 ("The initial decision of the Iraqi tribunal to use selected and exemplary instances of Saddam's ruthlessness is a wise one.").

[15] The Special Court for Sierra Leone uses this strategy. It "was established for the sole purpose of prosecuting persons who bear the greatest responsibility for serious violations of international humanitarian law." *Prosecutor v. Kallon & Kamara*, Case Nos. SCSL-2004–15-AR72(E), SCSL-2004–16-AR72(E), Decision on Challenge to Jurisdiction: Lomé Accord Amnesty, ¶ 13 (Mar. 13, 2004). David Cohen attributes its successes to its insistence on "limiting time and resources, and . . . going after . . . fewer but bigger names." Press Release, Noel Gallagher, Media Relations, Univ. Cal. Berkeley War Crimes Studies Ctr., "War Crimes Center Issues Report on Sierra Leone Court" (May 5, 2005). The current view that trials should be completed within a year or two after political transition returns discussion to an early argument of Samuel P. Huntington, *The Third Wave: Democratization in the Late Twentieth Century* 231 (1991).

[16] Jerry F. Hough et al., *The 1996 Russian Presidential Election* 53–4 (1996). A December 1999 survey found that "more than seven-tenths of Russian voters said they believed that the Soviet Union should not have been dissolved, while a paltry twelve percent expressed satisfaction with the way Russian democracy was developing." Michael McFaul, "Ten Years after the Soviet Breakup: A Mixed Record, An Uncertain Future," J. Democracy, Oct. 2001, at 87.

[17] Christopher Drew & Tresha Mabile, "Desert Graves Yield Evidence to Try Hussein," N.Y. Times, June 7, 2005, at A1 (describing the Kurdish capture and the delivery to prosecutors of "documents that help carry responsibility for the killings up the chain of command" and show Saddam's awareness of murderous orders issued by his recently appointed deputy for Kurdistan).

approach to Sudanese leaders responsible for crimes against humanity in Darfur.[18] To be sure, bringing up cases slowly has the virtue of encouraging a given defendant to view his or her interests as distinct from those who may follow. This separation discourages cooperation in a single strategy of legal defense and reduces the possibility of organized societal opposition to such prosecutions and the new regime conducting them.[19]

This technique becomes unnecessary, however, once the new government sends clear signals that only the head honchos will face trial. This approach might be a scapegoating of sorts, insofar as the scope of criminality actually extended much further, but such are the costs of reconciliation and relegitimation. These costs are admittedly considerable wherever participation in serious wrongdoing has been pervasive. But this exercise of prosecutorial discretion is defensible insofar as selection criteria reflect the defendants' degree of wrongdoing, as opposed to more invidious considerations.

Ethnic considerations have been prominent in many domestic prosecutions of mass atrocity in the successor states of the former Yugoslavia and in Rwanda, where many among ruling elites bear responsibility comparable to those they prosecute.[20] In particular, close observers of the Rwandan proceedings contend that their objective appears not to be achieving true social reconciliation or transcending interethnic conflict by particularizing responsibility, but to continue such conflict by other means, with threat of prosecution as the now-favored method of intimidating unruly rivals for power.[21]

The power shift – from Hutu to Tutsi rule – was so sudden and so complete that domestic political constraints on the numbers of perpetrators subject to prosecution all but vanished overnight. This was even more the case than in Argentina after the military junta's sudden collapse because of its failure in the Malvinas/Falklands War, thereby permitting prosecutions. There, the

---

[18] Marlise Simons, "Two Face Trials at The Hague over Darfur Atrocities," N.Y. Times, Feb. 28, 2007, at A3 ("Court officials said the prosecutor favored a strategy of focusing on specific events to which he can link individuals, rather than pursuing broad, ambitious indictments.")

[19] For a game-theoretic formulation of this tactic of "stringing things out," see Avinash K. Dixit & Barry J. Nalebuff, *Thinking Strategically* 19–21 (1991).

[20] See, e.g., Nigel Eltringham, *Accounting for Horror: Post-Genocide Debates in Rwanda* 27–33 (2004).

[21] Alison Des Forges & Timothy Longman, "Legal Responses to Genocide in Rwanda," in *My Neighbor, My Enemy: Justice and Community in the Aftermath of Mass Atrocity* 49, 58–62 (Eric Stover & Harvey M. Weinstein, eds., 2004); Filip Reyntjens & Stef Vandeginste, "Rwanda: An Atypical Transition," in *Roads to Reconciliation* 101, 115–16 (Elin Skaar et al., eds., 2005); Filip Reyntjens, "Rwanda, Ten Years On: From Genocide to Dictatorship," 103 Afr. Aff. 177 (2004).

officer corps retained sufficient power to ensure that President Raul Alfonsín sought to limit trials to very small numbers.

But selectivity of some sort is nonetheless normally essential to transitional goals because, as a practical matter, if the number of prosecutions reaches into the hundreds or thousands, then trying individuals for their discrete wrongs ceases to be any different from blaming whole groups for collective harms. This is particularly true if individual prosecutions are aimed exclusively at members of one social group, when those of another committed comparable wrongs. Ethnically selective prosecution of this sort has been prominent in the courts of successor states of the former Yugoslavia.[22] Collective attributions of blame are thereby reinforced, not overcome.[23]

Reconciliation cannot occur, to be sure, if the questionable basis of prosecutorial selectivity itself calls the legitimacy of pending trials into wide doubt.[24] Victim groups and indicted perpetrators, for different motives, share an interest in drawing public attention to the fact of prosecutorial selectivity. To victims, concerns with democratic institution-building as a rationale for prosecutorial restraint will often seem no less repressive of urgent moral imperatives and emotional needs than earlier preoccupations with nation-building and the authoritarian policies it often rationalized.[25] Prosecution can only individualize public attributions of responsibility in a convincing and defensible fashion if its ascriptions of responsibility are consistent with the actual culpability of those it pursues. Otherwise, the resulting illegitimacy quickly compromises the larger political objective by indicating that the real blame lies elsewhere than where courts have placed it.

[22] Ulrich Garms & Katharina Peschke, "War Crimes Prosecutions in Bosnia and Herzegovina (1992–2002)," 4 J. Int'l Crim. Justice 258 (2006).

[23] Timothy Longman et al., "Connecting Justice to Human Experience, Attitudes toward Accountability and Reconciliation in Rwanda," in *My Neighbor*, op. cit., at 206, 223–4; Timothy Longman & Théonèste Rutagengwa, "Memory Identity, and Community in Rwanda," in *My Neighbor*, op. cit., at 162, 172–5. As for the former Yugoslavia, opinion surveys find that even the putatively individualizing ICTY prosecutions have had this collectivization effect. Miklos Biro et al., "Attitudes toward Justice and Social Reconstruction in Bosnia and Herzegovina and Croatia," in *My Neighbor*, op. cit., at 183, 192–6; see also Dinka Corkalo et al., "Neighbors Again? Intercommunity Relations after Ethnic Cleansing," in *My Neighbor*, op. cit., at 143, 148.

[24] Mark A. Drumbl, "Collective Violence and Individual Punishment: The Criminality of Mass Atrocity," 99 Nw. U. L. Rev. 539, 549–50 (2005) ("Choices of which atrocity to judicialize and which individuals to prosecute are so deeply politicized that it is problematic to pretend that they are in any way neutral or impartial, two characteristics often attributed to and propounded by law.").

[25] Arturo Escobar, *Encountering Development: The Making and Unmaking of the Third World* 10–14, 52–3, 86–9 (1995).

The greater the power transfer from old to new rulers, the greater the political space for serious prosecutions, space that national prosecutors may then exploit. Selective prosecution is surely most defensible when concentrated on former rulers than on their lowliest minions. The more problematic situations occur when regime change has not occurred or has been merely formal, evincing no real transfer of power from rights abusers to rights-respecting successors. In contemporary Indonesia, for example, prosecutors seriously pursued only enlisted personnel.[26] There, as in national courts of the former Yugoslavia, indicting small numbers of rank-and-file soldiers has enabled elites to frame war crimes as aberrational excesses, unconnected to official policy.

Selective prosecution is still less defensible when controlled by parties responsible for wrongs identical to those charged against defendants, as in Rwanda. There, a state run by Tutsis sought aggressively to prosecute even the most minor Hutu *genocidaires* while taking little action against Tutsi Armed Forces officers responsible for war crimes of greater gravity.[27] In transitional societies in which a greater transfer of power has occurred, prosecutors strive to strip former chieftains, who may only recently have enjoyed mass support, of any vestigial legitimacy, especially when such rulers or their allies seek return to high office.[28]

If criminal trials were to demonstrate how a large segment of society had endorsed or even participated in mass atrocities, then victims and the public at large would no longer be content to vent their rage on a small handful of now-powerless individuals. They would instead blame a much larger number – perhaps all who served in the officer corps or occupied responsible positions in the civil service, or even an entire ethnic-based political party like the Sunni Baathists in Iraq. Once mass trials

---

[26] David Cohen, *Intended to Fail: The Trials before the Ad Hoc Human Rights Court in Jakarta* at vi–ix, Int'l Ctr. for Transitional Justice, ed., 2003 (adding that "prosecution cases . . . and judgments . . . typically do not go beyond the narrowest facts . . . or provide a broader . . . account of the widespread, systematic, and organized nature of the crimes . . . [thereby obscuring] participation by Indonesian military, police, or security units").

[27] Correspondence from Lars Waldorf, Dir., Human Rights Watch, Kigali, Rwanda Field Office, to author (June 10, 2005); see also Int'l Criminal Tribunal for Rwanda, ICTR Detainees: Status on 16 August 2005.

[28] Most legal scholars considering this problem assume that maximum independence for prosecutors and courts from elected executives is an unqualified good at such times. But see Philip B. Heymann, "Should Prosecutors Be Independent of the Executive in Prosecuting Government Abuses?" in *Transition to Democracy in Latin America: The Role of the Judiciary* 203, 211–13 (Irwin P. Stotzky, ed., 1993) (identifying situations in which a prosecutor viewed as a "loyal supporter and an informed insider" may be more effective in pursuing reform).

appear aimed at such large groups rather than at individual members, they threaten to unleash potentially interminable cycles of intergroup violence.[29] If the public comes to distinguish victims from victimizers in this way, then judicial condemnation of defendants for their individual actions becomes unconvincing and irrelevant to events, which may then take a violent turn.

Killing to avenge the honor of slain kin often engenders cycles of recipro-cal violence that, as Bourdieu notes, "obey the same logic as gift exchange."[30] Each side's fears and paranoia feed the other's. Crime by members of one ethnic group, for instance, will strengthen solidarity within the other vic-timized group, whose members hence become more inclined to act as a group, both in self-defense and in more aggressive countermeasures. This perverse dynamic can be exploited by militants on either side. The Kosovo Liberation Army knowingly provoked reprisals from Serbian forces against Albanian civilians, for instance, to solidify Albanian support.[31]

Focusing national attention on specific acts of individual wrongdoing consciously aims to dampen such collectivizing temptations. "Absolving nations of collective guilt through the attribution of individual responsi-bility," intoned Chief ICTY Prosecutor Richard Goldstone, "is an essential means of countering the misinformation and indoctrination which breeds ethnic and religious hatred."[32] A noble sentiment, assuredly. But when indi-vidual responsibility for grievous wrongs is very widely shared, this effort requires considerable sleight of hand; it may aspire to create a new found-ing myth for the nation, but threatens to degenerate quickly into simply a not-so-noble lie.

HOW THE CHOICE OF LEGAL DOCTRINE AFFECTS DEMOCRATIC TRANSITION

Social constructionists stress that law can tell many stories about the same episode of mass atrocity, framing it in alternative ways, each with differing implications for understanding what went wrong.[33] Economists will rightly

---

[29] Mahmood Mamdani, *When Victims Become Killers: Colonialism, Nativism, and Genocide in Rwanda* 233 (2001) ("The perpetrators of the genocide saw themselves as the true victims of an ongoing political drama, victims of yesterday who may yet be victims again.")

[30] Pierre Bourdieu, *Pascalian Meditations* 193 (Richard Nice trans., 2000).

[31] Rogers Brubaker, "Ethnicity without Groups," in *Remaking Modernity* 470, 478 (Julia Adams et al., eds., 2005).

[32] Ruti Teitel, "Bringing the Messiah through the Law," in *Human Rights in Political Transi-tions: Gettysburg to Bosnia* 177, 183 (Carla Hesse & Robert Post, eds., 1999).

[33] Osiel, *Collective Memory*, op. cit., at 59–78.

respond that, among several ways of recounting the past, prosecutors will surely choose that most consistent with their interests in pleasing executive masters, who seek democratic transition on particular terms. In this respect, prosecutors may be seen as "agents" of executive "principals." Displays of prosecutorial independence, in prosecuting former rulers, virtually never occur in new and unstable democracies.[34]

The confessedly simplistic nature of the historical analysis we lawyers can offer at such times becomes its very virtue, in advancing the higher goal of political transition through social reconciliation.[35] Prosecutors thus aim to construct their cases with a view to sending reassuring signals that mass atrocity trials are not really so different from those of the garden variety in which the innocent many arise in accusation of the guilty few. On this view, judges and prosecutors should do everything within their powers – consistent with standards of technical competence and professional ethics – to discourage the impression that transitional trials are novel and disturbing, requiring exercises in difficult and perhaps arbitrary line drawing between those few who will stand trial and the much larger numbers of culpable parties who will not.

The law of superior responsibility has proven to best serve national purposes of reconciliation after civil war and democratic transition. Although American lawyers invariably invoke *Yamashita* as the single fount of all jurisprudence on the subject,[36] it was in fact the military courts of many nations that were instrumental in developing this doctrine. Judges from Australia, France, Britain, China, and Italy, for instance, all applied it extensively to war criminals in the regions their countries briefly occupied after World War II.[37] The doctrine, thereby, became the common currency of mass atrocity prosecutions in many parts of the world during this period, firmly establishing itself as integral to the national experience of transitional justice.

International legal debate gives much less attention, and accords less weight, to transitional constraints at the national level than to long-term aspirations for international criminal law, the arena in which participants in this debate can expect to exercise most influence. This is part of the larger democratic deficit in international legal institutions, insofar as international

---

[34] For a rare and courageous exception, see Human Rights Watch, "Peru: Special Prosecutor Faces Dismissal," *Human Rights News*, May 5, 2005.

[35] Osiel, *Collective Memory*, op. cit., at 30–9, 146–61.

[36] *Yamashita v. United States*, 327 U.S. 1 (1946).

[37] See, generally, David Cohen, "The Legacy of Nuremberg: Models of Command Responsibility" 6–9 (2003) (unpublished manuscript).

prosecutors are not democratically accountable to members of a transitional society.[38] The *ad hoc* international tribunals, in particular, define the field's central purposes almost exclusively in terms of retribution and deterrence, not reconciliation or restoration of shattered social bonds in war-torn countries; their statutes and judgments are explicit in this regard.[39] Only when such tribunals begin to accord greater weight to how their punishment practices might affect the reconciliatory objectives of postconflict societies will such objectives be realized.

The severe constraints on prosecution by national courts in most locations of mass atrocity bolster the view that international courts should continue to take the initiative in developing new law,[40] the ICC's "complementarity" doctrine notwithstanding. International tribunals even do a more thorough job of documenting what transpired, "delving deeper into social context and historical interpretation" than national truth commissions, because "they are less susceptible to pressures from high-ranking perpetrators of the *ancièn regime*, on the one hand, and the nation building imperatives of newly installed post-authoritarian officials on the other."[41]

The inclusion of such broader context, however, quickly presents the danger of attributing too much of that context to the defendant – the problem here called the culpability constraint. This danger has long existed in domestic prosecutions of organized crime: western European prosecutors of individual mafia members, for instance, "often charge 'organized crime' as aggravated forms of ordinary offenses, thus permitting a more complex portrait of the organization to emerge at trial," including events beyond the defendant's contemplation or control.[42]

---

[38] Madeline Morris, "The Disturbing Democratic Defect of the International Criminal Court," 12 Finnish Y.B. Int'l L. 109, 112–13 (2001).

[39] See, e.g., *Prosecutor v. Serushago*, Case No. ICTR 98–39-S, Sentence, ¶ 20 (Feb. 5, 1999); *Prosecutor v. Furundžija*, Case No. IT-95–17/1-T, Judgment, ¶ 290 (Dec. 10, 1998). Ralph Henham, "The Philosophical Foundations of International Sentencing," 1 J. Int'l Crim. Just. 64, 68–9, 81 (2003).

[40] Mireille Delmas-Marty, "Global Crime Calls for Global Justice," 10 Eur. J. Crime, Crim. L., & Crim. Just. 286 *passim* (2002) (arguing that global crimes must be tried before international rather than national tribunals in order to maintain legitimacy and efficacy); Jane E. Stromseth, "Introduction: Goals and Challenges in the Pursuit of Accountability," in *Accountability for Atrocities: National and International Responses* 1, 4 (Jane E. Stromseth, ed., 2003) ("In states where such egregious behavior has occurred, domestic judicial systems are often in shambles and national leaders may be the ones perpetrating or tolerating the atrocities; [even officials of good will are] frequently constrained by a lack of resources.").

[41] Wilson, "How Do International Tribunals Write History . . . ," op. cit., at 12.

[42] Jacqueline E. Ross, "Dilemmas of Undercover Policing in Germany: The Troubled Quest for Legitimacy," 50 (Mar. 11, 2005) (unpublished manuscript).

The preoccupation of international prosecutors with building new law at the global plane does not make them completely indifferent to the legitimacy of their efforts in the countries from whose horrors their cases derive, to be sure.[43] Selecting defendants in international tribunals, in particular, is influenced by these concerns just as in municipal courts. Yet the decision rule is almost the opposite. Rather than limiting liability to a few top chieftains of the repressive ruling group, defendant selection in international courts has consistently sought to broaden liability to kingpins of all culpable groups, irrespective of how small a group's contribution to the total horrors.[44] International prosecutors worry about preserving their legitimacy in the eyes of communities whose members committed the most atrocities.

To this end, they have sought to indict offenders from other communities, whose leadership is generally responsible for a far smaller share of overall wrongs. This explains the decision by Chief Prosecutor Carla del Ponte, for instance, to indict Croats and Bosnian Muslims at the ICTY and her expressed desire to prosecute bosses of the Tutsi Armed Forces (RPF) at the ICTR.[45] As a result, the Tutsi-controlled Rwandan government ceased all

---

[43] Other UN agencies, in fact, were long instrumental in promoting national reconciliation through amnesties of major rights abusers. Carsten Stahn, "United Nations Peace-Building, Amnesties and Alternative Forms of Justice: A Change in Practice?," 84 Int'l Rev. Red Cross 191, 191–202 (2002). In recent years, the UN Secretary-General, at least, has entirely reversed course, formally rejecting amnesty for war crimes, genocide, and crimes against humanity. Report of the Secretary-General, *The Rule of Law and Transitional Justice in Conflict and Post-Conflict Societies*, UN Security Council (Aug. 23, 2004). Diplomats negotiating peace accords are invariably attentive, nonetheless, to obstacles presented by possible international prosecution of such wrongs. See, e.g., Richard Holbrooke, *To End a War* 106–8 (1998).

[44] A qualification to this generalization must be entered regarding the decisions of ICC Chief Prosecutor Luis Moreno-Ocampo to seek indictment of those he considered the world's most serious international offenders, wherever they may be found. In so doing, he spurned the counsel of some, including influential voices at Amnesty International, that ICC indictments should reflect the geographical fact that crimes within the Court's jurisdiction occur in many regions other than sub-Saharan Africa. His policy and its resulting decisions on case selection proved no less controversial, however, than del Ponte's opposing emphasis on ethnic and geographical "diversity." African leaders, including those of the continent's most constitutional democracies, soon came to condemn the Court as an instrument of neocolonial power in the region, the new avatar of the white man's "civilizing mission." See generally, Rebekah Heacock "African Bloggers React to ICC Charges against Sudanese President al-Bashir," at http://globalvoicesonline.org/2008/07/16/african-bloggers-reactions-to-charges-against-al-bashir.

[45] Victor Avigdor Peskin, "Virtual Trials: International War Crimes Tribunals and the Politics of State Cooperation in the Former Yugoslavia and Rwanda" 269–70, 480 (2005) (PhD dissertation, Univ. of Calif., Berkeley); Carla del Ponte, with Chuck Sudectic, *Madame Prosecutor: Confrontations with Humanity's Worst Criminals and the Culture of Impunity* (2009).

cooperation with the ICTR, preventing witnesses from traveling to Arusha, until the Chief Prosecutor relented and abandoned her investigations of Tutsi war criminals.[46]

This allocation of prosecutorial resources displays a seeming symmetry, designed to signal impartiality, that is, to groups (especially in Serbia) actually responsible for the vast majority of crimes. Hence, the private suggestion by certain ICC judges to the court's Chief Prosecutor that he pursue war crimes charges against the Congolese government, after accepting its referral of a case against antigovernment rebels.[47] The approach may initially appear unimpeachable, until one realizes that the second set of defendants – Croats, Bosniaks, or Tutsis – will almost invariably have perpetrated far fewer and less grave offenses than many readily indictable among the more culpable community – Serbs or Hutus.[48]

Such a prosecutorial strategy largely failed to legitimate the international tribunal among the most virulently genocidal groups while simply ensuring its equal illegitimacy among all others, minor and major wrongdoers alike. This was the frequent effect within the successor states of the former Yugoslavia and in Rwanda,[49] although some recent evidence is less disheartening.[50] But at least this sort of selectivity, in search of seeming

---

[46] Id. at 497–506, 512–13. The UN Security Council subsequently declined to renew del Ponte's ICTR appointment. The *ad hoc* tribunals themselves have sought to impose only the most limited restrictions on prosecutorial discretion in the selection of defendants from among those apparently responsible for similar wrongs. Hassan B. Jallow, "Prosecutorial Discretion and International Criminal Justice," 3 J. Int'l Crim. Justice 145, 154–8 (2005) (describing the ICTR's requirement that defense counsel establish a "discriminatory motive" on the prosecutor's part).

[47] Interview with ICC Legal Counsel, in The Hague, Neth. (Aug. 2005). Sitting officials fall within the court's jurisdiction, since its Statute eliminates all official immunity from prosecution. ICTY Statute, Art. 7(2).

[48] John R.W.D. Jones, "The Gamekeeper-Turned-Poacher's Tale," 2 J. Int'l Crim. Just. 486, 493 (2004). Jones criticizes the Prosecutor's approach here as "the strategy of a politician ... [which] has no place in a court of law. Justice does not consist of indicting all 'sides,' irrespective of the comparative seriousness of the crimes charged. The survivors of the Warsaw Ghetto Uprising were not prosecuted for fighting for their survival, even if the odd act of misappropriating foodstuffs might be considered ... 'plunder.'" Jones, a British barrister, served as defense counsel to a Bosnian (Muslim) defendant. Id. at 486.

[49] Dina Temple-Raston, *Justice on the Grass* 124 (2005) (describing the presence of several thousand protestors when Chief Prosecutor Carla del Ponte sought to discuss prosecution of RPF war criminals with Rwandan president Paul Kagame in June 2002); Jack Snyder & Leslie Vinjamuri, "Trials and Errors: Principle and Pragmatism in Strategies of International Justice," Int'l Security, Winter 2003/04, at 5, 21–2, 27–8 ("Survey results suggest that there has been a public relations backlash against the ICTY in Serbian areas.").

[50] See, e.g., Diane Orentlicher, *Shrinking the Space for Denial: The Impact of the ICTY in Serbia*, Open Society Institute (2008); Lara Nettelfield, *Courting Democracy in a Post-Conflict State: The Hague Tribunal's Impact in Bosnia & Herzegovina*, chap. 4, forthcoming.

moral symmetry, does not induce prosecutors to choose legal rules at odds with those preferred by national peers, on similar facts. In other words, it does not affect international prosecutors' preferred approach to conceptualizing association in crime.

The question of symmetry is especially acute in a society making the transition to peace from a civil armed conflict in which both sides committed war crimes of comparable gravity. Both international prosecutors and foresighted political leaders at the national level aspire to impartiality at such times, but understand its requirements very differently. The preferred response at the international level is now to prosecute all culpable parties, both winners and losers alike, as exemplified in del Ponte's strategy.

The still-favored approach in the national locale – across the political spectrum – is often to prosecute none at all. This is true even where – indeed, especially where – violations have been pervasive. This posture is defended not simply in pragmatic terms, moreover, but as morally apposite to the uniquely tragic nature of civil war and its aftermath.[51] The notion of reciprocal pardon remains widely appealing in such societies – even to those long identified with human rights causes and movements[52] – as a suitable legal method to reconcile former belligerents and their respective sympathizers to mutual coexistence.

International humanitarian law, in demanding prosecution for major rights abuse, is not genuinely universal in its moral understanding, insofar as it arose in response to a specific situation – unilateral, state-sponsored atrocities, especially the Holocaust – fundamentally distinct from the civil wars of countries like El Salvador and Colombia, in which antagonists display moral equivalence in their "symmetrical barbarism."[53] The entire project of international humanitarian law was thus implicitly conceived on the basis of empirical assumptions – and corresponding moral intuitions – that prove irrelevant to many circumstances to which such law is today increasingly applied.

All things being equal, international prosecutors, like their national peers, report that they prefer cases against big fish to those versus small fry. Both the

---

[51] Iván Orozco Abad, *Sobre Los Límites de la Conciencia Humanitaria: Dilemas de la Paz y la Justicia en América Latina* 256, 240–6 (2005).

[52] Id. at 27–8, 171–4.

[53] Id. at 4–5, 12–15, 25–6. Orozco Abad is mistaken, however, if he believes such situations can be analyzed satisfactorily in terms of a bargain and implicit contract between rights abusers on the left and right. This approach ignores the weighty moral and material claims of the many third-party victims. Within his native Colombia, for instance, such victims include more than one hundred thousand people internally displaced in recent years by left and right during the country's civil war.

ICTY and ICTR quickly acquired custody over several upper echelon perpetrators. The ICTR, for instance, had custody over one of the genocide's key architects, Colonel Théoneste Bagosora, for nearly six years before putting him on trial. But convicting such leaders is much more difficult than convicting followers, because of the frequently major gaps in available evidence and unresolved doctrinal complexities of the sort this study examines. The ICTR's first case, against Jean-Paul Akayesu, hence concerned a decidedly minor player, the mayor of a small town. The first Sudanese officials indicted by the ICC for that government's crimes in Darfur were from the middle echelons, not among those who had planned and ordered the crimes.[54]

Many convictions, especially at the ICTR, have hence involved lower and middle-level offenders.[55] The bigger fish have been indicted, to be sure, for broad-ranging, multipartied conspiracies to commit genocide.[56] But group trials of this sort proceeded at a glacial pace, and few prosecutors who began them remained to see their completion.[57] Understandably frustrated, young prosecutors seek simultaneously to try smaller fish in shorter proceedings, as relief from their plodding longer term labors.[58] They have career incentives to show results before applying for new jobs.

Prosecutors realized, moreover, that they could make crucial advances in international criminal law with these more modest defendants, on such issues as the defenses of superiors' orders and duress, for instance.[59] Establishing rape as a means of committing genocide – and as a crime against humanity – could most easily be achieved through small fry prosecutions,[60]

---

[54] Franck-Petit, interview with Antonio Cassese, former President of the UN Commission of Inquiry on Darfur, Int'l Justice Tribune, March 5, 2007. Cassese describes the ICC's first indictments for Darfur as directed against "mid-level" offenders. He describes one such defendant as "a very good civil servant who really knew how to organize things," but adds that "the brains are higher up."

[55] As of August 16, 2005, convictions include two councilors, resembling U.S. city ward leaders, four bourgmestres, who are like town mayors, and one prefect, similar to a U.S. state governor. ICTR Detainees, op. cit. Only one military officer had been convicted, although that case has been appealed. Id. ICTR prosecutors report that their bosses, the Chief Prosecutors, have failed to communicate any clear strategy, concentrating instead on the ICTY, on which the international media has focused the public spotlight. Peskin, "Virtual Trials," op. cit., at 415–18.

[56] Waldorf correspondence; see also, e.g., *Prosecutor v. Bagosora*, Case No. ICTR-96–7-I, Amended Indictment (Aug. 12, 1999).

[57] Waldorf correspondence, op. cit.

[58] Id.

[59] The ICTY's first judgment made significant new law on the former issue. *Tadić* Appeal, ¶¶ 153–157. On Chief Prosecutor Goldstone's decision to try Tadić first, despite having custody over six others, including a Croat general, see Michael P. Scharf, *Balkan Justice* 98–100, 222–4 (1997).

[60] *Kvočka* Trial ¶ 145 ("Rape may constitute severe pain and suffering amounting to torture.").

and prosecutors considered this a particularly important goal for international criminal law, even though rape's status as a war crime – indeed, a
grave breach of the Geneva Conventions – was already clearly established.[61]
In addition, important procedural questions could be addressed as easily
through trials of minor as of major participants.

Junior officers facing stiff sanctions also have incentives to offer evidence against superiors in exchange for a lighter sentence, facilitating the
latter's conviction. Prosecutors of mass atrocity thus seek to exploit the
natural animosity of inferiors toward superiors who deny issuing criminal orders, depriving subordinates of mitigating evidence. Finally, trials of
lower echelons permit exploration of vital historical and moral issues that
big fish prosecutions cannot: They reveal how bureaucratic routine and
casual indifference enable even the humblest functionaries to cause enormous suffering, permitting barbarity to become widespread.[62] This lesson,
requiring periodic reiteration, cannot readily be imparted through the trial
of a Milošević, Pinochet, or Hussein.

The scope and solidity of the new professional field of practice increase
through all such cases. That international criminal law now constitutes
not simply a distinct body of law but also a separate field of professional
practice (and scholarly study) is apparent in many developments, such as
the publication of several scholarly journals and treatises for practitioners.[63]
The more that settled law is produced, the more that the new experts in the
field may legitimately claim the promising careers this practice increasingly
beckons. Incentives for international prosecutors to decline cases against
small fry have been therefore slight. The behavior of both *ad hoc* tribunals
has been thoroughly consistent with these facts; prosecutors proceeded with
prosecutions of lower echelons, against whom somewhat better evidence
and clearer law existed, over those of higher ranking officials also in custody.

It should not be surprising that such prosecutorial priorities have drawn
sharp criticism. One commentator laments, for instance, that Tadić's prosecutors "were willing to spend [twenty] millions of dollars, thousands of
hours, and years of judicial activity to obtain this single conviction of an

---

[61] Geneva Protocol, I, Arts. 75–6.
[62] José E. Alvarez, "Rush to Closure: Lessons of the *Tadić* Judgment," 96 Mich. L. Rev. 2031, 2092 (1998) ("Emphasis on such persons tends to produce accounts of mass atrocities that provide more satisfactory explanations of their bureaucratization.").
[63] See, e.g., John R. W. D. Jones & Steven Powles, *International Criminal Practice* (3d, ed. 2003). Scholarly journals include the *Journal of International Criminal Justice* and the *International Criminal Justice Review*, in addition to more specialized professional newsletters and loose-leaf services.

insignificant perpetrator."[64] And it is true that the perceived necessity of facilitating regime transition by limiting liability below the very top ranks was simply not a significant factor in prosecutorial decisions about resource allocation. Nothing about the professional milieu in which such international criminal lawyers circulate could realistically have made it so.[65]

National prosecutors are more tightly tethered. They do not enjoy such latitude to indulge expansionary aspirations for their professional domain. Their obeisance to executive masters rests on two unfavorable factors. First, their human capital is firm-specific[66] – not readily marketable in the private sector.[67] Second, this capital is invested in a civil service with a weak recent history of professional autonomy.[68] Such prosecutors have an elective affinity, in fact, for theories of liability predicated on the tight subordination of agents to principals. This is their own professional experience, after all: near-complete domination of politically sensitive cases by their executive superiors. Conversely, the considerable professional autonomy enjoyed by international prosecutors creates an elective affinity for liability theories

---

[64] Cohen, "Transitional Justice," op. cit., at 11.

[65] By contrast, judges in the European Court of Human Rights are demonstrably constrained by the extent to which the country designating them for appointment endorses or rejects an expansive "law-making" role for that Court. Erik Voeten, "The Politics of International Judicial Appointments: Evidence from the European Court of Human Rights," at SSRN: http://ssrn.com/abstract=1266427. This finding is a useful rejoinder to the casual and common assertion that international judges are necessarily biased toward expansive interpretations of their professional mandate. John McGinnis, "The Appropriate Hierarchy of Global Multilateralism and Customary International Law: the Example of the WTO," 44 Va. J. Int'l L. 229, 243 (2003).

[66] Human capital is firm-specific when an employee cannot readily transfer work skills from his or her current employer to another. An organization whose human capital is firm-specific has market power over its employees superior to competitors whose human capital is more generic. Ronald J. Gilson & Robert H. Mnookin, "Sharing among the Human Capitalists: An Economic Inquiry into the Corporate Law Firm and How Partners Split Profits," 37 Stan. L. Rev. 313, 354–60 (1985).

[67] It is extremely uncommon in most of the world for prosecutors or other government lawyers to move readily or regularly between public and private service over the course of a career. Mark J. Osiel, "Lawyers as Monopolists, Aristocrats, and Entrepreneurs," 103 Harv. L. Rev. 2009, 2051–3 (1990).

[68] Gretchen Helmke, *Court under Constraints: Judges, Generals, and Presidents in Argentina* 154–7 (2005) (discussing how judges strategically shift loyalty based on anticipated changes of government); see also Rebecca Chavez, *The Rule of Law in Nascent Democracies: Judicial Politics in Argentina* 30–48 (2004). In weak new democracies and even in authoritarian states, prosecutors exercise nontrivial independence when executive masters are clearly losing public support and appear likely to leave office soon. But such is not usually the case when new democratic rulers first take office, at which point their popularity is often very high. No serious empirical scholarship exists on national variations in prosecutorial independence, however.

presupposing comparable freedom of action and full information in other elites, those they prosecute.

In contemplating the exercise of universal jurisdiction, for instance, these national prosecutors and investigating magistrates face severe constraints. Even where national law otherwise permits universal jurisdiction, there is rarely any significant domestic constituency for prosecuting foreigners for harms perpetrated overseas against noncitizens. Off the charts, in this respect, are Judge Baltasar Garzón's Spanish detention orders and indictments, naming nearly one hundred officers from Argentina alone, including many of the lowest echelon.

The exceptional character of these indictments proves the rule. In Spain, however, there at least existed a constituency for prosecution among the sizable community of Argentine and Chilean refugees, many of whom (and whose murdered family members) had held dual citizenship. For all their ambitious scope in defining the criminality at issue, moreover, even Garzón's orders employed only the most standard, well-accepted doctrines on modes of commission. His orders concerning upper echelon officers, in fact, consistently emphasize the defendants' position as hierarchical superiors.[69]

International prosecutors, by contrast to most at the national level, enjoy human capital that is much less firm-specific; these lawyers enter the field only after considerable distinction within national legal systems to which they may readily return. Public service in such estimable bodies as the ICTY, moreover, enhances prosecutors' *savoir-faire* and interpersonal connections, making them readily marketable to other leading international bodies.[70] Distinguished service of this disinterested sort can, in fact, quickly catapult an international prosecutor into the firmament of an emergent transnational elite, in which one's increasing social capital opens up a world of professional opportunity. For example, following his tenure as the first ICTY Chief Prosecutor, Richard Goldstone moved on to a position on South Africa's Constitutional Court and his successor, Louise Arbour, to one on the Canadian Supreme Court. Several ICTY judges have also moved on to the new ICC.

At the very highest echelon, occupied by Chief Prosecutors and judges, international criminal law has not yet developed a discernible career track. Those reaching these positions do so after careers primarily in bench and

---

[69] See, e.g., *Auto de Procesamiento a 98 Militares Argentinos*, Sumario 19/97-l, Nov. 2, 1999; *Auto de Procesamiento y Detención del Almte Luis Eduardo Massera y nueve más*, Diligencias Previas 108/96-G, Oct. 10, 1997.

[70] See generally Michael Barnett & Martha Finnemore, *Rules for the World: International Organizations in Global Politics* 156–73 (2004).

bar of particular nation-states, to which most return. In this respect, the field is still not yet fully professionalized. Below this level, however, professionalization is advancing quickly, through the establishment of stable career trajectories by which younger lawyers move predictably from one international organization to another. American lawyers at the Nuremberg proceedings, from Justice Jackson on down, returned to domestic legal careers often little affected by their international experience. At that time, continuous civil service on the international plane was impossible; today, it is well institutionalized.

Today most young lawyers, judicial clerks, and interns at The Hague's international criminal tribunals have trained at the world's most renowned universities. Yet only fifteen years ago – when the first two *ad hoc* tribunals were getting started – prosecutors and defense counsel were recruited almost entirely from the ranks of far less prestigious law schools. The Americans, for instance, worked largely in the trenches of criminal courts in Santa Clara and Los Angeles counties, acquiring rich early experience in cross-examination, which served them well as the new tribunals came to adopt such "adversarial" courtroom procedures.

The educational and early professional background of newer recruits is now decidedly more elite, and the social milieu of elite international prosecution consequently more rarefied. No professional harm ensues from a résumé of successful prosecutions that, alas, unintentionally aggravated social tensions or upended a fragile reconciliation in the distant locale from which its paltry principals were drawn. The readiness to prosecute small fry – easy at hand, conveniently powerless, fertile fodder for assertive lawmaking on vital procedural questions – is not entirely unique to international prosecutors. Paradoxically perhaps, such readiness is often widely shared by immediate victims, who consistently report preferring punishment of the neighbor – often a local militia member – who caused them proximate harm and with whom they must daily interact. One Bosnian woman laments, for instance, "The one who raped me is not Milošević; he is the man I see passing every morning under my window. As long as nothing is done about that, there can be no peace."[71] Such sentiments suggest that confining criminal trials to head honchos will not fully placate vocal constituencies wholly uninterested in orchestrating prosecution around the aim of legitimating new rulers.

---

[71] Béatrice Pouligny, *The Forgotten Dimensions of "Justice" Programs: Cultural Meanings and Imperatives for Survivors of Violent Conflicts* 3 (2005) (quoting a young woman in Mostar).

This is not to say that transitional justice should allow itself to be held hostage to the obsessions of a small minority of victims. On the contrary, the main objective of national reconciliation at the level of intergroup relations is social peace. Pursuing this objective through public policy involves altogether different processes than reconciliation on the interpersonal plane, where psychological and emotional issues are primary and inescapable. Macro-social reconciliation frequently fails to produce interpersonal reconciliation or psychological equanimity at the micro-level, and vice versa.[72]

It is unclear whether the first should even aspire to have much influence on the second. Concepts like forgiveness, developed in reflection about interpersonal conflict, face severe difficulties when extrapolated to the macro-institutional plane, in a more than metaphorical way. Jacques Derrida thus rightly concludes that forgiveness occupies a realm of personal experience necessarily external to the rule of law, a domain into which law cannot properly or effectively intrude.[73]

Still, the impulse to pursue one's most proximate tormenters and to seek the state's assistance to this end – well expressed by the Bosnian woman earlier – successfully shaped the several thousand trials conducted by occupying powers in postwar Germany. Though many high-level Nazis were in Allied custody, prosecutions instead "relentlessly pursued" mostly "the lowliest perpetrators who participated in beating, mistreating, or executing even a single POW."[74] The pressure to do so came not from within Germany, but from the general public within Allied states, for whom abuses by the small fry appeared most palpable, their wrongfulness most intelligible.

Disagreement often exists within successor states, between new rulers and non-elite victims, on how to rank order prospective defendants. The national prosecutor's preoccupation with limiting trials to top chieftains, in other words, often turns out not to be shared by many fellow nationals. They may elect his executive bosses, but few transitional societies have become such vigorous democracies that more prudent elites cannot contain popular

---

[72] Brandon Hamber & Richard A. Wilson, "Symbolic Closure through Memory, Reparation and Revenge in Post-conflict Societies," 1 J. Hum. Rts. 35 (2002) (describing reports of trauma counselors in postconflict societies).

[73] Jacques Derrida, "To Forgive: The Unforgivable and the Imprescriptible," in *Questioning God* 21, 25–6 (John D. Caputo et al., eds., 2001).

[74] Cohen, "Transitional Justice," op. cit., at 10. Cohen blames the wrath of domestic public opinion in Allied countries for this prosecutorial decision, whereas prior scholars have mostly blamed Cold War considerations and the enduring political influence of middle-echelon Nazis for the failure of occupying powers to prosecute the latter.

preferences in this area. Retribution remains a salient goal for both elites and the general public, but is understood differently as prioritizing quite different wrongdoers.

Transition to democracy thus brings into relief the disparate preferences of voters and their elected representatives. In few countries are prosecutors elected; their incentives therefore align with executive superiors more than with victim groups among democratic voters. The two groups tend to concur only in preferring simpler, readily intelligible charges based on national law, like murder and rape, to more complex offenses drawn from international law, such as persecution of a crime against humanity: "It is impossible to rewrite the myths of a nation if you do not even address that nation in a language it understands," as Stephen Holmes observes.[75] National law generally does so more effectively than international, especially when nationalistic impulses elicit skeptical responses to the very idea of the latter, as is often the case.

Prosecutors in civil law countries – where most mass atrocities occur – are not accustomed to exercising much discretion in charging, even in cases of no political import. Control from above in this respect, therefore, does not greatly sully their professional self-image. On the other hand, civil law prosecutors – unlike their common law counterparts – traditionally have an ethical duty to prosecute every case for which sufficient admissible evidence is available.[76] This duty would seem to impede prosecutors from following executive suggestions to abandon cases that, although legally strong, appear politically explosive. Their formal duty, however, has had no observable impact on prosecutorial conduct during democratic transitions, notwithstanding the civil lawyer's much-vaunted respect for formalities. Influence by national executives over prosecutors has been noteworthy even in so-called hybrid tribunals formally under UN management, as in East Timor.[77]

In summary, in the aftermath of mass atrocity, concerns about the precarious legitimacy of new democratic and judicial institutions powerfully influence prosecutorial choice of defendants and doctrines at both national and

---

[75] Stephen Holmes, "Why International Justice Limps," 69 Soc. Res. 1055, 1071 (2002).

[76] Máximo Langer, "From Legal Transplants to Legal Translations: The Globalization of Plea Bargaining and the Americanization Thesis in Criminal Procedure," 45 Harv. Int'l L.J. 1, 37 (2004) (noting "the rule of compulsory prosecution" in many civil law countries); see also, e.g., Costituzione, Art. 112 (Italy).

[77] Christian Ranheim, *Internationalised Courts and Fair Trial Standards: The Case of East Timor* 7–9, 14–16 (2005). Hybrid tribunals are located in the state where the wrongs occurred, but combine judges of national and foreign origin, the latter being experts in international law, on which such courts partly rely, in addition to national law.

international levels.[78] The choices made on these different planes may operate in greater or lesser congruity, depending on national circumstances too context specific – thus requiring correspondingly close empirical analysis – to be readily theorized.

Theory's task here is to find recurrent patterns, through careful comparison of prior cases, that are potentially useful for guiding decision makers in future ones. This demands that we avoid imposing any single, blanket prescription, putatively applicable to all countries, while treating contextual variation as ambient noise. It also demands, however, that we not lose ourselves in the infinite uniqueness of each national species of the genus. In this endeavor, it is best to presume that "there is no opposition between fine-grained work, uncovering variousness, and general characterization, defining affinities. The trick is to get them to illuminate one another,"[79] in the interests of improving both law and scientific understanding.

This entails pursuing two aims at once: "First, a recognition that each nation's transitional experience is unique and molded by distinct social, cultural, and historical factors; and second, that there are basic moral understandings, legal principles, and logistical issues common to all democratic transitions."[80] New rulers in a transitional society would be strategically prudent to acknowledge generously the second of these facts in order to ensure that the international community affords them maximum latitude in respect to the first.

---

[78] A further form of prosecutorial selectivity likely to limit the legitimacy of international courts for many is their inability to indict offenders among the world's major powers (e.g., President Vladimir Putin) for the many war crimes of Russian armed forces in Chechnya. Antoine Garapon, "Three Challenges for International Criminal Justice," 2 J. Int'l Crim. Just. 716, 717 (2004).

[79] Clifford Geertz, *Available Light: Anthropological Reflections on Philosophical Topics* 227 (2000). The present study focuses more on the task of defining affinities than on uncovering variousness.

[80] Daniel Rothenberg, "Burma's Democratic Transition," Hum. Rts. Brief, Winter 2002, at 10, 13.

8

The Conflicting Incentives of National and International Prosecutors

Domestic courts are important for developing international law wherever countries accept it as locally enforceable, as many increasingly do.[1] This law can develop in a "coherent" manner, some contend, however, only if courts at national and international levels interpret its content consistently. This is unlikely to occur when national and international prosecutors favor disparate doctrinal options for conceptualizing the same misconduct.

Their preferences are likely to diverge when each option has opposite consequences for their careers. This is sometimes true of the choice between superior responsibility and enterprise participation. International prosecutors face incentives to favor the latter, and national prosecutors the former (and other ways to narrow the law's reach), especially when the transfer of power from old leadership is not yet complete.

INCENTIVES FOR INTERNATIONAL PROSECUTORS

Prosecutors in The Hague have their eyes on a prize rather different – much larger, in their view – from that valued by national prosecutors: the development of international criminal law, as an institutional resource to which the world may increasingly turn for punishing – and perhaps preventing – mass atrocity, when states are "unwilling or unable" to do so in national courts.[2] The growth of "criminal enterprise" law, examined in this study, is not the only evidence of their successful urgings on the tribunal in

---

[1] Anne-Marie Slaughter & William Burke-White, "The Future of International Law Is Domestic," 47 Harv. Int'l L.J. 327 (2006); *New Perspectives on the Divide between National and International Law* (Janne Nijman & Andre Nollkaemper, eds. 2007); Harmen van der Wilt, "Equal Standards? On the Dialectics between National Jurisdictions and the International Criminal Court," 8 Int'l Crim. L. Rev. 229 (2008).

[2] This is the wording employed in the ICC Rome Statute, Arts. 17, 18.

this regard. In response to prosecutorial prompting, "[a]lthough the [UN Security] Council declared that the [*ad hoc* international criminal] Tribunals would not create new law, the ICTY has substantially broadened the rules governing civil wars, and it has lowered the thresholds for the triggering of the rules on international conflicts,"[3] as one careful scholar observes.

Their goal of enhanced potency for international criminal law leads prosecutors to rank policy objectives in this order: first, retribution and deterrence, with reconciliation a distant third.[4] This set of priorities reflects a time horizon, as deterrence aims, for the long run, to cultivate a more stringent international law enforced by stronger international tribunals capable of discouraging mass atrocity before it occurs. Attendant disruptions within transitional societies, however unfortunate, are therefore viewed as short-term bumps on the long road to global justice.

Not surprisingly, then, the ICTY Prosecutor was confessedly slow to recognize the need for any direct communication about the tribunal's activities and judgments to residents of the former Yugoslavia. It took eight years before the ICTY initiated a small outreach program to explain its evidence-gathering and legal judgments to family members of victims in the former Yugoslavia, and the comparable Rwanda tribunal's efforts have been similarly sparse.[5] The delay reflected an intelligible decision to commit these tribunals' limited resources to developing the future field of international criminal law, rather than to demonstrating its immediate relevance to past victims.

The decision also corresponded with prosecutors' interests in developing a body of valued expertise and a new field of legal practice many will continue to ply. To serve its noble ends most effectively, international criminal law must acquire a cognitive core of impartial learning, over which certain lawyers must necessarily gain and display mastery. There is nothing necessarily pernicious in any of this, for as a leading sociologist writes,

The development of a specialized body of formal knowledge and skill requires a group of like-minded people who learn and practice it,

---

[3] Allison Danner, "When Courts Make Law: How the International Criminal Tribunals Recast the Laws of War," 59 Vand. L. Rev. 1, 61 (2006).

[4] Oct. 2003 Prosecutor Interview. See also *Blaškić* Appeal, ¶ 678 (first listing as sentencing objectives "deterrence," "prevention," and "retribution," with "rehabilitation" mentioned as the fifth and last objective and reconciliation excluded entirely).

[5] Victor Peskin, "Courting Rwanda: The Promises and Pitfalls of the ICTR Outreach Programme," 3 J. Int'l Crim. Just. 950, 951 (2005). Learning from their mistakes, the Chief Prosecutor of the Special Court for Sierra Leone quickly made such outreach a high priority.

identify with it, distinguish it from other disciplines, recognize each other as colleagues by virtue of their common training and experience with some common set of tasks, techniques, concepts, and working problems, and are inclined to seek out each other's company, if only to argue with each other. . . . The [resulting] boundaries create a mutually reinforcing social shelter within which a formal body of knowledge . . . can develop, be nourished, practiced, refined, and expanded.[6]

Admittedly, international criminal lawyers, both prosecutors and defense counsel, can be expected to flourish in tandem with the new law they are creating in almost every case they try and with the emergent field of legal practice they are constructing through these labors.[7] The precise contours of the incentives they confront, however, are by no means obvious. International prosecutors have incentives to win convictions, of course. But what if this can be done, in a set of related cases, only at the risk of imperilling the very legitimacy of the judicial institutions on which their future careers may depend? After all, international criminal law could soon be discredited and thus fail to become a well-institutionalized career path if the new tribunals either fail to convict big fish or do so in ways widely regarded as professionally deficient and morally objectionable.

This prestigious new field of practice could easily founder on either or both of these shoals, along with the tribunals in whose halls it breeds and the careers of the lawyers now staking their future on its efflorescence. If one desires that these courts thrive, it is tempting to see in their growth an inexorable trend, ever "emerging,"[8] always "gaining strength,"[9] "developing a momentum of their own"[10] – an "irreversibly advancing"[11] historical process toward an international rule of law. Such wishful thinking is rife within the scholarly journals, where priests of international law preach to one another. One learns, for instance, that "it is now clear that the criminal proceedings against [Pinochet in England] were the leading edge of a profound transformation, [inducing] a raft of countries to secure the

---

[6] Eliot Freidson, *Professionalism: The Third Logic* 202 (2001).

[7] For a discussion of how new fields of legal practice are created and gain socioeconomic prominence through entrepreneurial efforts by their founders, see Yves Dezalay & Bryant G. Garth, *Dealing in Virtue: International Commercial Arbitration and the Construction of a Transnational Legal Order* 18–62 (1996).

[8] Nina H.B. Jørgensen, *The Responsibility of States for International Crimes* 280 (2000).

[9] Christine Bell, *Peace Agreements and Human Rights* 264 (2001).

[10] Geoffrey Robertson, *Crimes against Humanity* 267 (1999).

[11] Francis M. Deng, "Frontiers of Sovereignty: A Framework of Protection, Assistance, and Development for the Internally Disabled," 8 Leiden J. Int'l L. 249, 272 (1995).

legal bridgehead claimed by British judges."[12] Inexorably onward, it would seem, marches humanity's army.

That the emergence of international criminal courts displays some connection to broader processes of globalization lends plausibility to this laudable hope. But entirely possible is a very different scenario: that such courts will prove the product of an evanescent mood and a passing concatenation of political forces, peculiarly conducive to their brief ascendance, and the world will then witness another half-century of dormancy in this area, as occurred after the Nuremberg trials.

Convictions that fail to meet accepted professional standards present career risks potentially as great as would a series of highly embarrassing acquittals – especially of a Milošević or Karadžić – on even a significant subset of the charges against the defendants, as could easily have occurred, insiders report. Charging defendants with enterprise participation (especially of the third type), rather than superior responsibility, helps greatly in winning convictions, but toes the line of professional acceptability.[13]

The doctrine of enterprise participation thus risks discrediting the emergent field of expertise on which everything else depends – not only petty careers, but the fate of humanity, on some accounts. Charging defendants with superior responsibility, in contrast, satisfies fellow legal professionals – as well as lay opinion makers influenced by them – but only at the great risk of losing one's cases. The upshot presents both a recurrent ethical dilemma for individual prosecutors and an economic predicament for them all, in their shared professionalization project.[14]

Which of the contending incentives just identified is more powerful? This is an empirical question. Watching the behavior of ICTY prosecutors – how they formulate their indictments and frame their closing arguments – provides the answer. Their clear preference for enterprise participation reveals that short-term risks to the field from possible acquittals far outweigh for them any longer term dangers to it from professional disapproval and political disestablishment.

---

[12] Diane Orentlicher, "Whose Justice? Reconciling Universal Jurisdiction with Democratic Principles," 92 Geo. L.J. 1057, 1132–3 (2004).

[13] For arguments to this effect, see Allison Marston Danner & Jenny S. Martinez, "Guilty Associations: Joint Criminal Enterprise, Command Responsibility, and the Development of International Criminal Law," 93 Cal. L. Rev. 75, 132–42 (2005); Steven Powles, "Joint Criminal Enterprise: Criminal Liability by Prosecutorial Ingenuity and Judicial Creativity?" 2 J. Int'l Crim. Just. 606, 614–19 (2004).

[14] Magali Sarfatti Larson, *The Rise of Professionalism* 49–52, 74, 104 (1977) (analyzing professionalization as a collective "project" by entrepreneurs within an occupational group).

INCENTIVES FOR NATIONAL PROSECUTORS

In transitional societies, incentives are quite different, but equally ambiguous, and so can cut both ways. On the one hand, because the law of superior responsibility – as the ICTY understands it – is now so hard to prove, its allegation risks acquittal of former rulers. The cost of this fiasco to new rulers could well be politically fatal. Failed prosecutions would also reopen the question of who was really responsible for the country's horrors. Publicly reexamining so controversial a question, after indictments seemed to answer it, can destabilize the already precarious transition such trials sought to advance.

To ensure that this does not happen, prosecutors have an interest in pursuing charges that are easier to prove. ICTY precedents construing enterprise participation may therefore soon become quite valuable to national prosecutors confronting this predicament, assuming that executive superiors allow them to employ it. It is significant here that national (and hybrid) courts are now increasingly likely to apply international law in such domestic proceedings, a development widely regarded as one of the most important in transnational governance.[15]

On the other hand, the interests of such new executive rulers, as we have seen, lie in restraining the public's retributive passions. Otherwise, prosecution cannot easily be limited to top former chiefs. Prosecutors thus have an interest in steering clear of legal techniques that imperil the clear demarcation between the big fish and the slightly smaller fish – much less the minnows – also clearly responsible for grievous wrong.

For national prosecutors, then, charging defendants with enterprise participation may often be politically imprudent in the extreme, because the doctrine all but invites a much wider and far-reaching enumeration of actionable wrongs and the people implicated in them – often including many still among a country's elites. The problem is especially acute when the composition of national elites, as trials begin, has yet changed little. Such was certainly the case in the successor states to the former Yugoslavia, for instance.[16] In short, the law of enterprise participation and of complicity reduces the risks of acquitting priority defendants, but increases the grounds for prosecuting many nonpriority ones. This is because criminal enterprise is often very broad indeed.

---

[15] Ryan Goodman, "Human Rights Treaties, Invalid Reservations, and State Consent," 96 Am. J. Int'l L. 531, 541 (2002).

[16] See, e.g., Human Rights Watch, *Croatia: Conviction Spotlights Justice Failings* (2004).

In contrast, superior responsibility offers a method for delimiting liability that is both professionally unimpeachable and politically palatable. It confines trial to defendants whose relative responsibility, compared with other culpable parties, is conspicuously greater. Superiors are always a much smaller group than participants in an enterprise. The law of superior responsibility is also professionally punctilious because it errs always on the conservative side: allowing criminal liability to fall short of moral culpability, but never overreaching it. Enterprise participation risks the opposite error and so poses more serious moral problems, no less than the political ones discussed.

As with their international colleagues, we should ask: which of the countervailing incentives here identified prove more powerful in influencing national prosecutors? No clear empirical pattern has yet emerged. There have not yet occurred many national war crime prosecutions of high-ranking officials since the ICTY's development of enterprise participation law. But those national prosecutions that have taken place or are pending clearly indicate a prosecutorial preference for strategies, like superior responsibility, that minimize the scope of culpable parties likely to come before the courts.[17] The prosecution of Argentina's military officers, for instance, reflected this pattern.[18]

The upshot is that chances for coherent development of an international criminal law on modes of commission are weakened, in significant extent, by the divergent incentives of prosecutors bringing such cases before national and international courts. Through its doctrine of complementarity,[19] the ICC – unlike the ICTY or ICTR – accords priority to domestic tribunals in redressing mass atrocity. Their interpretations of international law, including superior responsibility and enterprise participation, will therefore influence the development of these doctrines. The threat that conflicting prosecutorial incentives pose to international law's coherence may therefore increase as national courts begin to assume the primary enforcement responsibilities assigned them by the ICC Statute.

---

[17] For a discussion of how Peruvian prosecutors intended to use the law of superior responsibility against former President Alberto Fujimori, see Human Rights Watch, *World Report 2001: Questions and Answers regarding Peru's Criminal Prosecution of Fujimori*. On interest in the doctrine among prosecutors in certain successor states of the former Yugoslavia for redressing war crimes, see Org. for Security and Co-operation in Europe, *War Crimes Trials before the Domestic Courts of Bosnia and Herzegovina: Progress and Obstacles* 21, 45–6 (2005).

[18] Mark Osiel, *Mass Atrocity, Ordinary Evil, and Hannah Arendt* 15–24 (2001).

[19] Rome Statute, op. cit., Art. 1.

Much has been made in recent years of how international courts have begun to influence national ones through judicial dialogue.[20] In this way, cosmopolitan norms and self-understandings are increasingly injected into once-parochial, municipal adjudication. International prosecutors have begun to play a similar role, as the ICTY increasingly refers pending cases to national courts in successor states of the former Yugoslavia.[21] In the resulting dialogue with national counterparts, such prosecutors seek to propagate their favored legal theories, including enterprise participation.[22]

National counterparts will not likely be persuaded if the argument made here is correct. However distinguished and sophisticated their international interlocutors, however alluring from a professional standpoint the conceptual constructs conveyed, national prosecutors will be skeptical, at the very least. These lawyers know they operate in an entirely different political milieu that requires them to play by different rules and to an almost exclusively domestic audience.

INTERNATIONAL INFLUENCE ON DOMESTIC PROSECUTION: THE INTERNATIONAL CRIMINAL COURT

There has been some incautious academic talk of a complementarity more "proactive" or "positive" than contemplated by the ICC treaty drafters. This new species of complementarity would involve the Chief Prosecutor in gentle promptings – backed by threat of international prosecution – to induce more genuine domestic efforts at accountability in countries initially reluctant to honor their treaty commitments to the international

---

[20] Anne-Marie Slaughter, *A New World Order* 101 (2004) (lauding a global process of professional socialization through which judges come to feel "tied together not only by the awareness of foreign courts and decisions but active transjudicial dialogue on common problems ranging from privacy to the death penalty").

[21] Press Release, Security Council, "Security Council Endorses Proposed Strategy for Transfer to National Courts of Certain Cases involving Humanitarian Crimes in Former Yugoslavia," UN Doc. SC/7461 (July 23, 2002) (recognizing ICTY's broad strategy for the transfer of cases involving intermediary and lower level accused to competent national jurisdictions); see also Press Release, "Tribunal Decides to Refer the Case against Radovan Stankovic to Bosnia and Herzegovina," (May 17, 2005) (transferring this case to Bosnia to comply with the Security Council's request that the ICTY concentrate on cases involving the most senior leaders and transfer cases involving those who may not bear this level of responsibility to national jurisdictions).

[22] Human Rights Watch, *Justice at Risk: War Crimes Trials in Croatia, Bosnia and Herzegovina, and Serbia and Montenegro* 5 (2004) (noting biases of judges and prosecutors and poor case preparation by national prosecutors as problems arising when the ICTY refers cases to national courts in states of the former Yugoslavia).

community.[23] This is surely a pleasing possibility. Knowledgeable voices in leading human rights nongovernmental organizations (NGOs), however, remain very sceptical of professed results to date.[24] No one has begun to demonstrate the workings of such a causal connection in a given case (i.e., by methods minimally satisfactory to any serious social science). The prosecutor himself soon abandoned this tack in any event, acknowledging that it had been a misstep to attempt such political deals, comparing them even to Neville Chamberlain's 1938 Munich pact with Hitler, and affirming that his job was simply to follow the law and the facts wherever they led.

Several powerful states have been quite wary of the ICC, however, where it and its Statute seek to foster far-reaching liability for criminal commanders and other leading officials. Hence, it is unsurprising that, when ratifying the ICC treaty, states recently responsible for mass atrocities, such as Indonesia, have sometimes declined to incorporate its provision on enterprise participation into national law.[25] They thereby ensure that their prosecutors will not use it before national courts. To similar effect, international NGOs that educate sitting judges from certain African countries in international criminal and human rights law report that several months after returning home their most receptive students have often been stripped of judicial office, and that their other, more cautious students, to avoid that fate, have relearned to judge little differently than before their foreign training.[26]

One response to the diverging paths of domestic and international prosecutions may be that it simply reveals the dangers of allowing international criminal law to encroach too ambitiously on the legitimate preserves of national law, at least in democratic societies. Why do we need any international law of criminal participation, one might ask, if its effect is only to foreclose a variety of policy options that should remain available to elected leaders in new constitutional democracies? The problems on which this study has lavished many pages would simply disappear if international

---

[23] See, e.g., William Burke-White, "Proactive Complementarity: The International Criminal Court in the Rome System of Justice," 49 Harv. Int'l L. J. 53 (2008); Carsten Stahn, "Complementarity: A Tale of Two Notions," 19 Crim. L. Forum 87 (2008).

[24] Christopher Hall, Director, International Justice Project, Amnesty International, Nov. 2008, interview with author; In at least one place, however, such efforts have recently borne some fruit, although the "national" court in question is really a hybrid, including foreign prosecutors and judges. William Burke-White, "The Domestic Influence of International Criminal Tribunals: The International Criminal Tribunal for the Former Yugoslavia and the Creation of the State Court of Bosnia & Herzegovina," 46 Colum. J. Transnat'l L. 279 (2008) (describing interactions between the ICTY and the war crimes section of the State Court of Bosnia and Herzegovina).

[25] Rudi Rizki, judge and professor of law, Padjajaran University, in Bilbao, Spain, July 2005, interview with author.

[26] Christopher Hall, op. cit.

law would only butt out. On the other hand, the new law of joint criminal enterprise might be seen as extending domestic prosecutors' palette
of possibilities, increasing rather than restricting their range of doctrinal
choice. This broader range would be legitimate as long as they or those who
appointed them can be held politically accountable for such choices. The
methods for ensuring such accountability would remain entirely a matter
of national law.

THE PERILS OF PREMATURE "COHERENCE" BETWEEN NATIONAL AND INTERNATIONAL COURTS

To speak casually of a need for "coherence" is not necessarily to assume
that national and international courts must employ precisely the same rules
for tying the violent acts of the small fry to the intentions of the bigger
fish. That assumption is open to question and some reject it, in fact. The
question of coherence has become quite significant as the ICTY, in the
completion strategy of its later years, has referred many cases and files
on potential defendants to national courts in the successor states of the
former Yugoslavia.[27] In domestic trials, these courts will apply national
rules on sharing of responsibility – unless newer global ones, spawned in
international courts,[28] are adopted. Legal norms on these matters now vary
from state to state, depending on vicissitudes of national legal history.[29]
Lawyers recognize that such variation – seemingly slight to the uninitiated
layperson – can easily affect results, determining guilt or innocence, as well
as the length of sentences.

So we must ask: Just how uniform do such rules need to be, that is, when
the offenses themselves (genocide and such) are uniquely international in
character, arising from expectations of the world at large? Are we greatly
troubled that different results would be reached on the same facts of mass
atrocity in an international court as opposed to a national one?

---

[27] The ICTY's Rules of Procedure and Evidence provide for such referrals. Rule 11 *bis*. On the
operation of this rule in practice, see Sarah Williams, "ICTY Referrals to National Jurisdictions: A Fair Trial or a Fair Price?" 17 Crim. L. Forum 177 (2006); OSCE/ODIHR/
ICTY/UNICRI, Report of the Expert Workshop, "Supporting the Transition Process:
Lessons Learned and Best Practices," The Hague, 2008. One of the greatest successes
to date is documented in Bogdan Ivanisević, "The War Crimes Chamber in Bosnia and
Herzegovina: From Hybrid to Domestic Court," Int'l Center for Transitional Justice (2008).

[28] To be sure, in formulating such rules, international courts in recent years drew heavily on
the greater experience of national legal systems, and have sought out general principles on
modes of liability common to these systems.

[29] For evidence of some of this inter-state variation, see generally E. Ivicević, "The Implementing Criminal Law Concerning Criminal Command Responsibility," in *Responsibility
for War Crimes: Croatian Perspectives, Selected Issues* (Ivo Josipović, ed., 121, 2005).

Some commentators credibly view the ICTY's approach to shared responsibility, particularly its broad notion of criminal enterprise, as a potentially powerful source of customary international law, binding upon national courts in the same way as that tribunal's jurisprudence on more substantive questions, such as, say, the meaning of persecution as a crime against humanity. The ICTY itself has not hesitated to apply its accumulating jurisprudence on superior responsibility to noninternational armed conflicts – for which ratified treaty norms on the matter are virtually nonexistent[30] – although it is national (not international) courts that will inevitably hear the vast majority of charges arising from criminal misconduct in wars of this variety.

Others retort that uniformity between states in their implementation of international law is more important on certain matters than on others.[31] Not among these, surely, are recondite rules on collective participation in crime, for these turn on distinctions most laymen would regard as lawyerly hair-splitting.[32] States should be free to follow their own path, adhering to longstanding national legal rules when apportioning responsibility among members of a criminal group. The international community does not have nearly so strong a stake here as in, for instance, the legal definition of genocide. On this view, states are entitled to a "margin of appreciation" in their preferred approaches to honoring duties of international criminal and humanitarian law, just as they now routinely enjoy regarding their duties under international human rights law.

Even when defining genocide, to be sure, national legislation in certain states (such as Spain and much of Latin America) broadens the range of protected groups to include those defined by socioeconomic status or political ideology.[33] The Genocide Convention itself does not extend its defensive umbrella to groups of either sort. Such states simply choose to

---

[30] Kai Ambos, "Individual Criminal Responsibility, Article 25 Rome Statute," in *Commentary on the Rome Statute of the International Criminal Court* (Otto Triffterer, ed. 743, 770a–770c 2008).

[31] For a range of European and American views on this matter, see, generally, *New Perspectives on the Divide Between National and International Law* (André Nollkaemper & Janne Nijman, eds. 2007); Nollkaemper, *Domestic Courts and the Rule of International Law* (2008).

[32] Such rules do not meet any of the conditions for custom to become efficient. Eugene Kontorovich, "Inefficient Custom in International Law," 48 William & Mary L. Rev. 859 (2006) (observing that efficient customary rules emerge only when there is frequent interaction and side-switching between all pertinent parties on the particular issue).

[33] Santiago O'Donnell, "Latin America Extends the Definition of Genocide," Int'l Justice Tribune, Nov. 5, 2007, at 1 (describing legislative and judicial enlargement of the crime of genocide in Argentina, Brazil, Mexico, Bolivia, and Spain).

afford greater protection to mass atrocity's victims than international law is generally understood to require.

National legislation of this variety raises far less concern about the coherence of international law than when states fall below a uniformly accepted "floor" of protection. In other words, international law here sets no "ceiling" of protection beyond which states may not stray, i.e., as long as they continue to honor defendants' procedural rights. International human rights advocates, such as Amnesty International, generally champion the notion of uniform standards for all states, as in the legal meaning (for the ICC's complementarity rule[34]) of a state's unwillingness or inability to prosecute, a failure that activates the Court's jurisdiction.[35] On this issue, any national deviation from universal standards is repudiated as illegitimate, as a contemptible backsliding toward impunity.

The posture of such NGOs is quite different, however, when states depart from current global norms in order to expand – rather than contract – the reach of human rights guarantees. The centrifugal effect of such departure in "fragmenting" international law, however, is much the same. The point here is not to accuse human rights advocates of logical inconsistency, but rather to suggest the unimportance of such consistency in how national and international courts (or national courts in some countries versus others) apply international criminal law. Perfect doctrinal coherence between all such courts is a goal that can surely wait for a later day, if at all, especially – as with genocide's definition – on issues where countries should be encouraged to experiment in extending law's empire through ever-evolving custom.

Legal coherence will also be undesirable, or at least premature, where democratic leaders of postconflict societies choose to privilege reconciliation over retribution in their policies of transitional justice.[36] Where countries seriously risk a return to civil war or authoritarian rule, they may freely decide (as Chapter 11 contends) to prosecute only the very worst offenders, such as deposed regime leaders, rather than the hundreds or thousands of others criminally culpable for mass atrocities. Narrow rules on superior responsibility at the national level will help limit the scope of these prosecutions, compared to broader international doctrines of criminal enterprise.

Where national prosecutors fall well short of "floor" international standards of accountability, to be sure, international courts such as the ICC may

---

[34] ICC Statute, Rule 17.

[35] Christopher Hall, Director, International Justice Project, Amnesty International, Marie Curie Lecture, Grotius Centre, Leiden University, Nov. 2008.

[36] I owe several observations in this paragraph to Clifton Strickler and Andreea Ion-Baiasu.

then rightly step back into the breach, deploying to this end their novel, far-reaching rules on modes of participation. Global goals of retribution and general deterrence can thus reassert themselves at this later point, if national aims of restoring peace among still-embittered neighbors receive grossly undue weight (i.e., in the consensus judgment of the wider world). International expectations and national constraints thereby can be accommodated, albeit in a variety of *ad hoc* ways yet impossible to codify in any rule. Formulating such a legal rule – with relevant exceptions, and identifiable exceptions to those exceptions – may well prove possible at some downstream stage of legal development.

For good pragmatic reasons, then, national and international legal systems may for a time acceptably diverge. Disharmonies between them can be confronted later in the game, after legal experiments at both levels have been put forward and, in time, evaluated for their full ramifications. For now, the higher priority is surely on finding, from one national case to the next, a practicable middle ground; this will require not a bright-line rule but a flexible, context-sensitive balancing of deterrent, retributive, and reconciliatory concerns. To this end, international criminal law can become more attentive to national preoccupations without altogether abandoning enterprise liability. The main point here is simply that in matters of transitional justice, international law does not demand that "one size fit all" any more than on other issues.

FURTHER DIFFERENCES BETWEEN NATIONAL AND INTERNATIONAL PROSECUTORS: POWER DISPARITIES

One might be tempted to analogize the relation between national and international prosecutors to that between national and international business lawyers. Strong alliances have developed between attorneys in the great financial centers and their local counterparts, advising on national law, in the course of large cross-border business transactions. Local counsel must ensure that contemplated deals comply with expectations of national authorities. But local lawyers also become representatives of global capital within their own domestic legal and political systems. They are inevitably drawn into the new transnational professional elite, eventually often as near-equal partners. They have powerful incentives to bring their country into conformity with international standards, which reflect what foreign investors expect from a country's legal system before committing substantial resources there.

National prosecutors face no such incentives. Few can realistically contemplate a career like that of Luis Moreno-Ocampo, who has moved with relative ease from prosecuting mass atrocities domestically to doing so internationally. Their interests do not lie in deferring to wealthier global lawyers who represent powerful foreign interests. Like the large law firms doing international finance, international prosecutors may similarly represent the tides of globalization. But the wind at their back blows much less forcefully.[37]

The attraction of national and international prosecutors to disparate doctrines could easily have been neutralized, even reversed, had these doctrines been differently interpreted. Enterprise participation could have been read more narrowly by limiting the scope of a given enterprise's purpose and membership, much as U.S. courts have sometimes done with conspiracies and racketeering.[38] Conversely, superior responsibility could readily have received wider scope than it currently enjoys at the ICTY. It technically applies, after all, to all soldiers exercising "command," even at the lower echelons, such as noncommissioned officers. Other courts, moreover, have not demanded such stringent evidence that the defendant exercise "effective control" over both the particular subordinates and on the specific offenses they committed.[39] Alternatively, the nature of the control that prosecutors must show could be understood more narrowly, as proposed in Chapter 5.

These courts have also sometimes required no more in culpable mental state than mere negligence. The ICTR, moreover, has read the doctrine

---

[37] Efforts by legal scholars to understand human rights lawyers as part of a larger international ruling class, in the tow of multinational corporations, have been satirically suggestive, but conceptually and empirically sloppy. See, e.g., Kenneth Anderson, "Secular Eschatologies and Class Interests of the Internationalized New Class," in *Religion and Human Rights* 107, 113–15 (Carrie Gustafson et al., eds., 1999) (contending that lawyers in the international human rights community hold a worldview that is "a nearly exact mirror of the allegiances and preferences of global capital, of which it is a Siamese twin joined at the hip"). Similarities exist, to be sure, in such facts as shared attendance at a handful of the most elite universities (and appreciation of the nuances of French cheese and Belgian chocolate). But whether this common cultural capital has any real significance – economic or even sociological, much less for legal policy – is entirely unclear. But see, generally, Leslie Sklair, *The Transnational Capitalist Class* (2001) (offering an avowedly Marxist analysis of cross-border professional linkages).

[38] See, e.g., *Kotteakos v. United States*, 328 U.S. 750, 776 (1946) ("But as [the enterprise] is broadened to include more and more, in varying degrees of attachment to the confederation, the possibilities for miscarriage of justice to particular individuals become greater and greater."); see also Note, "*Elliott v. United States*: Conspiracy Law and the Judicial Pursuit of Organized Crime through RICO," 65 Va. L. Rev. 109, 127 (1979) (describing cases holding that "the activities making up a multiple criminal conspiracy must be connected"). See, generally, William LaFave, *Criminal Law* 594–602 (2003).

[39] David Cohen, "The Legacy of Nuremberg: Models of Command Responsibility" 5–11 (unpublished manuscript); see also David Cohen, "Transitional Justice in Divided Germany after 1945," 3–13 (unpublished manuscript).

more capaciously, extending it even to the former director of a private radio station that propagated hate speech shortly before the genocide.[40] His "subordinates" were simply his radio audience, his control over them evidenced by no more than their ceasing to attack UN forces after radio announcers so requested, followed by their continuing violence against Tutsis.[41] (This is a highly questionable use of the doctrine.) There is thus nothing deeply intrinsic to either doctrine – that is, independent of the present scope of its judicial understanding – that necessarily draws national or international prosecutors to it.[42]

It would be wrong to imply that national and international courts compete for the right to prosecute mass atrocity. The very opposite is closer to the truth; each almost invariably prefers the other to take jurisdiction. A troubling development in this regard is the proclivity for states to refer atrocity prosecutions to the ICC despite an apparent ability to conduct them at home. Pursued domestically, such trials stir up much political acrimony, leading some national leaders to seek to dump them at the door of international tribunals, which might then conveniently be blamed for imposing an unpopular result that municipal courts should rightly be prepared to reach on their own.

These incentives are perverse; they establish a variety of adverse selection whereby the ICC must allocate scarce resources to sifting through a substantial number of complex disputes not properly on its docket. This process, in turn, requires difficult judgments about a given state's actual – but disavowed – ability to prosecute. It also means that defendants otherwise likely to be prosecuted under superior responsibility would instead be tried as participants in a joint criminal enterprise, with predictably differing results.

In the attention it devotes to individual incentives, this study does not wish to suggest that lawyers in the fields of international human rights and humanitarian law are motivated primarily by venal concerns. To be sure, considerable venality has been apparent at the ICTR where, according

---

[40] Gregory S. Gordon, "A War of Media, Words, Newspapers, and Radio Stations: The ICTR Media Trial Verdict and a New Chapter in the International Law of Hate Speech," 45 Va. J. Int'l L. 139, 179–83 (2004) (describing the tribunal's Nahimana judgment).

[41] Gordon, id., at 180.

[42] That ICTR judges have been so much more indulgent of broad prosecutorial readings of superior responsibility likely reflects the generally lower quality of that court's judicial personnel, on all accounts. This fact suggests that a more complete account of the relevant variation would need to address judicial incentives and capabilities, in addition to the prosecutorial ones examined here.

to the closest study of it to date, "the idealistic spirit that helped spark the creation of the contemporary human rights movement is rarely evident" and "workaday concerns such as pay, benefits, and promotion often leave little room for reflection about how to reform the administration of justice."[43] It also is true that nongovernmental humanitarian organizations regularly engage in fierce and counterproductive competition among themselves and other rivals for resources.[44]

THE CONSCIENCE OF HUMANKIND, OR ARCHBISHOPS OF THE NEW CHURCH?: THE UNCERTAIN PLACE OF HUMAN RIGHTS LAWYERS

Human rights lawyers sincerely imagine themselves – ourselves – as representing the conscience of humankind, however pretentious this may sound.[45] In fact, it is their ideals – to make international law a more potent remedy to mass atrocity – that actually define and constitute their self-interests within this new field.[46] By this I mean that, although their ideals explain why these lawyers ended up within this particular field, they thereafter have an interest in advancing its scope and authority entirely apart from how doing so contributes to their normative commitments. "The propriety of 'good intentions,'" as Bourdieu observes, "does not necessarily exclude an interest in the profits associated with fighting a 'good fight.'"[47] Once

---

[43] Victor Avigdor Peskin, "Virtual Trials: International War Crimes Tribunals and the Politics of State Cooperation in the Former Yugoslavia and Rwanda" 421 (2005) (PhD dissertation, Univ. of Calif., Berkeley).

[44] Alexander Cooley & James Ron, "The NGO Scramble: Organizational Insecurity and the Political Economy of Transnational Action," 27 Int'l Security 5 *passim* (2002) (documenting how inter-NGO competition prolongs failed aid projects and unwittingly assisted criminal militias in Bosnia); W. Hays Parks, "Special Forces' Wear of Non-Standard Uniforms," 4 Chi. J. Int'l L. 493, 502–4 (2003) (attributing to rivalry over "market share" the resistance of NGOs to humanitarian aid in Afghanistan by U.S. Army Civil Affairs); see also Yves Dezalay & Bryant Garth, *The Internationalization of Palace Wars: Lawyers, Economists, and the Contest to Transform Latin American States* 131–5, 163–7 (2002) (indicating how incentives influence lawyers' behavior in international human rights practice).

[45] Until recently they would have called it the civilized conscience. On the history of this benevolent self-image among public international lawyers, highlighting its patronizing aspects, see Martti Koskenniemi, *The Gentle Civilizer of Nations* 2–13 (2001).

[46] Alexander Wendt, *Social Theory of International Politics* 113–35 (1999) (analyzing how principled ideas may define and construct interests).

[47] Pierre Bourdieu, *Masculine Domination* 113 (2001). This approach is quite different from seeking "to explain acts of altruism in terms of power," the view that "when we act kindly toward other people, we are motivated, whether we know it or not, by a desire to exercise a measure of control over their lives, for our act of kindness puts them partially in our power." Leszek Kołakowski, *Freedom, Fame, Lying, and Betrayal* 3 (1999).

one is accepted as a player in the game, one's ideals and self-interest begin to steer increasingly in the same direction, such that it becomes impossible to demonstrate which motivating force drives particular conduct. One acquires a vested interest in disinterestedness.[48]

Normative ideals often have more material groundings, after all. Most grand theories of international law since the sixteenth century, in fact, can readily be traced to the author's dependence on patronage by particular interests, according to intellectual historians.[49] And no major religion ever acquired a broad following and wide influence without the concerted efforts of a particular social stratum, different in the case of each faith, whose members first cultivated and proselytized it.[50]

International human rights bids fair to become the ruling faith of our era. "With the collapse of the certainties of Marxism, liberal progressivism and the cold war, 'universal human rights' has become the only surviving meta-narrative," observes Stanley Cohen.[51] We international lawyers naturally offer ourselves as the rightful bearers and exegetes of this ascendant faith. But just as all world religions have, in their doctrinal content, mirrored the social interests of their class carriers, so too the current cult of human rights – the concentration of global collective conscience around humanitarian ideals, a development predicted long ago by Emile Durkheim – reflects our particular professional worldview. Its dissemination also reinforces our social influence, extending it both to parts of the world and social domains of where lawyers and legal argument have hitherto enjoyed little prominence. Whether this is better for the world at large may be debated; that it is best for human rights lawyers is beyond dispute.

---

[48] This fact in turn prevents one from arguing that the observable conduct of such lawyers can be explained exclusively on the basis of their professional self-interest, rather than motivated by commitment to the field's intrinsic moral value.

[49] Richard Tuck, *The Rights of War and Peace: Political Thought and the International Order from Grotius to Kant* 141–2 (1999).

[50] Max Weber, *The Sociology of Religion* 80–94 (Ephraim Fischoff, trans. 1963) (1922).

[51] Stanley Cohen, "Crime and Politics: Spot the Difference," 47 Brit. J. Soc. 1, 13 (1996). In a similar spirit, see also Michael Ignatieff, *Human Rights as Politics and Idolatry* 87–88, 147–49 (2001).

PART III

NEW POSSIBILITIES AND SOLUTIONS

9

Collective Sanctions for Collective Wrong

Current law grapples inadequately with certain characteristic features of mass atrocity, as this study has shown. But the legal intractability of these features is not attributable to any historical novelty, for few of these features are entirely new or even unique to mass atrocity, strictly speaking. The continuing failure to find a suitable solution remains to be explained. What accounts, then, for the intractability?

A first response will likely be that criminal law rests on theoretical assumptions that simply do not fit, do not accommodate the centrally relevant facts. The criminal law assumes a world of unencumbered individuals, independently interacting.[1] A criminal conspiracy, for instance, is not conceived as a self-determining collective subject, but rather as a vehicle through which the wills of individual persons conjoin. As an assemblage of dyads, which form into wheels or chains, it is never quite a truly collective entity with dynamics of its own. Criminal law is inherently about the punishment of individuals for their culpable acts, in this view.[2] Larger processes and structures, intrinsically collective to the core,[3] must therefore be translated or reduced

---

[1] George P. Fletcher, "Collective Guilt and Collective Punishment," 5 Theoretical Inquiries L. 163 (2004); see also Meir Dan-Cohen, "Responsibility and the Boundaries of the Self," 105 Harv. L. Rev. 959, 988 (1992) ("Criminal law professes an individualistic ethic that allegedly precludes any form of collective responsibility.").

[2] This view ignores how criminal liability for corporations, often resulting in multimillion-dollar fines, aims to deter organizational misconduct, entirely apart from *post facto* retribution against culpable individuals, such as those controlling the company. It is true, however, that such organizational costs are ineffective in deterring criminal management insofar as they can often be passed along to shareholders. Daniel R. Fischel & Alan O. Sykes, "Corporate Crime," 25 J. Legal Stud. 319, 349 (1996).

[3] Emile Durkheim, *The Rules of Sociological Method* 50–9 (Steven Lukes, ed., W. D. Halls trans., 1982) (1964) (showing the *sui generis* character of large social processes, which are often imperceptible to analysis of isolated instances and evidenced only by aggregate data, such as national statistics on suicide).

to interaction between such individuals to become intelligible, susceptible to legal analysis.

This reductionism is unsatisfactory because mass atrocity, as Drumbl writes, "requires more than just an extension of the dominant discourse of ordinary criminal law, which embraces liberalism's understanding of the individual as the central unit of action and thereby deserving of blame when things go terribly wrong."[4] We need, instead, a way of "truly recognizing the riddle of collective action"[5] at the center of such events. A legal sociologist would predictably say that "international criminal law addresses the symptoms of the problem – the discrete criminal acts, de-contextualizing them and failing to address the roots of the atrocities; that is, inter-ethnic suspicion, hatred, and fear."[6] Where the organization of the social whole largely determines the character and conduct of its parts, exclusive attention to these constituent components risks missing everything of significance to moral judgment and social understanding. The intractability of the dilemma posed at the outset of this study may originate in this fact.

This obstacle may be described as ontological, because it concerns the law's capacity to recognize the reality of mass atrocity: its inherently collective features, organizational dynamics, and power relations, which operate on a conceptual plane distinct from the acts and intentions of individual persons. To function satisfactorily, the law arguably requires a different level of analysis, at which such supra-individual factors and forces are not treated as derivative of "real" ones of flesh and blood. "There seems to be an inverse relationship between the number of individuals involved," as Sanford Levinson writes, "and the efficacy of traditional legal analysis as a mode of comprehending it. Law loses its power as anything more than a formal analysis when the individuals involved pass beyond a small number."[7] Further assertions to this effect could readily be multiplied, from equally distinguished legal scholars as well as social scientists.

The problem with law's individualism, the argument continues, is not only methodological or ontological but also normative. Justice requires that

[4] Mark A. Drumbl, "Collective Violence and Individual Punishment: The Criminality of Mass Atrocity," 99 Nw. U. L. Rev. 539, 604 (2005) ("The depoliticized legalist language of 'right' and 'wrong' may not reflect the heavily political nature of mass violence or the necessarily political task of transcending it."); see also Alan Norrie, *Crime, Reason and History* 10 (2002) ("Criminal law is, at heart, a practical application of liberal political philosophy.").
[5] Mark A. Drumbl, "Pluralizing International Criminal Justice," 103 Mich. L. Rev. 1295, 1309 (2005).
[6] Iavor Rangelov, "International Law and Local Ideology in Serbia," 16 Peace Rev. 331, 335 (2004).
[7] Sanford Levinson, "Responsibility for Crimes of War," 2 Phil. & Pub. Aff. 244, 245 (1973).

criminal sanction falls only on the blameworthy. If criminality by members of a group leads to punishing the entire group, then punishment is almost certain to descend partly on the innocent. And "sanctioning groups instead of individuals is categorically immoral or unjust," because it "imposes strict liability on group members who are not wrongdoers."[8] No liberal society could defensibly do so, for the most grievous wrongs.

This conclusion is unduly pessimistic, however, as the present study shows. The notion that something loosely called "liberalism" or "liberal legality" stands in the way of confronting mass atrocity has a puzzling poignancy. After all, liberal political theory clearly directed much of its moral and intellectual firepower throughout the nineteenth and twentieth centuries against precisely such ideologies of intolerance.[9] Liberal politics certainly never faced any obstacle to acknowledging and condemning these evils.

COLLECTIVE SANCTIONS?

Another reason to doubt this diagnosis is that Western law routinely penalizes people as members of collectivities for harmful actions in which they have not engaged, when other members have done so. These penalties may be called collective sanctions. It does not at all follow from the fact that "everyone is to blame," in other words, that no one may be held responsible. The practice of holding members of a collectivity responsible for wrongful acts by a subset of its number is actually quite pervasive,[10] even in the United States – purportedly the global epicenter of individualism.

American legal rules employing collective sanctions decidedly do not make moral culpability a necessary condition of liability or of bearing the brunt of the sanctions to follow. "Liberal individualism aside, legal doctrine and jurisprudence routinely personify certain collectivities, treating them as if they were individuals for purposes of legal liability and moral responsibility," one scholar recently notes.[11] The many forms of collective sanction our law employs prove that it is simply not so uncompromisingly committed to an astringently individualist liberalism as we sometimes assume. The proliferation of such rules is inconsistent with strict adherence to any liberalism

---

[8] Daryl Levinson, "Collective Sanctions," 56 Stan. L. Rev. 345, 424 (2003) (describing "the conventional view").

[9] This preoccupation finds early expression, for instance, in Julien Benda, *The Treason of the Intellectuals* 3–29, 43–177 (Richard Aldington trans., 1969) (1928). See, generally, Yael Tamir, *Liberal Nationalism* 3–6, 140–1 (1993).

[10] Tamir, id. at 141.

[11] Levinson, "Collective Sanctions," op. cit., at 425.

by which moral responsibility may be ascribed only to individuals for their acts, not for membership in groups. George Fletcher thus defends collective sanctions on the basis of an avowedly illiberal and romantic or communitarian moral theory, rather than the economic reasoning employed here to similar result.[12]

Many of these rules are of recent vintage and so cannot be dismissed as "an unfortunate atavism of pre-liberal or primitive societies."[13] Far from a vestige of premodern law, collective sanctions are today widely and self-consciously employed in lawmaking as a regulatory strategy. For instance, recent legislative efforts to stanch terrorist financing impose penalties on financial institutions that fail to monitor use of deposited funds for criminal purposes.[14] Such legal methods are so frequently used, in fact, that it would be hard to say they are disfavored even presumptively.

Collective sanctions aim to delegate deterrence to a close-knit private group because the frequency of interaction among its members reduces the costs of monitoring and information gathering, compared to those the state or other outsiders would incur. The law of partnership has long relied on this rationale to justify joint and several liability of all partners in a law firm for malpractice by any of their number.[15] The law relies on such collective responsibility to create *ex ante* incentives for group members to police one another, so that they will not have to later suffer the costs of misconduct by their brethren.[16]

---

[12] George P. Fletcher, *Romantics at War* 37–43, 77–91, 148–78, 201–14 (2002). Fletcher stops short of defending criminal sanctions against whole nations, arguing instead that a nation's collective responsibility should simply mitigate the punishment of individual members who contributed to mass atrocity.

[13] Levinson, "Collective Sanctions," op. cit., at 348. This persistence is surprising, he notes, for "whereas from a moral perspective we should expect collective sanctions to disappear from modern societies because moral responsibility has become individuated, from a functional perspective perhaps we should expect them to disappear because the state has bloomed while groups have withered," a fact reflected in "the atomism and anonymity of modern urban (or suburban) life." Id. at 361.

[14] Mariano-Florentino Cuéllar, "The Mismatch between State Power and State Capacity in Transnational Law Enforcement," 22 Berkeley J. Int'l L. 15, 18, 54 (2004).

[15] Levinson, "Collective Sanctions," op. cit., at 375, 379; Unif. Partnership Act §§ 13–15, 16 U.L.A. 600 (2001).

[16] As Levinson writes, "Solidary groups are often in a better position than outsiders to monitor and control their members. Groups typically have better information about their members' behavior, as well as an array of cheap but effective internal sanctions that can be used to shape their members' incentives. Consequently . . . an outside sanctioner can often more efficiently deter wrongdoing by collectively sanctioning the group rather than attempting to target individual wrongdoers directly." Levinson, "Collective Sanctions," op. cit., at 394–5.

Collective sanctions are even more common in international law.[17] When the International Court of Justice (ICJ) holds a state liable for a wrong, it often orders compensation or restitution.[18] Paid from the general coffers of the offending state, such compensation effectively sanctions only its taxpayers collectively, including many who may have opposed the state's wrongful conduct. Genocide and interstate aggression are among the offenses for which collective sanctions of this sort are possible. Both are clearly crimes, even if the liability they create, when attached to states rather than individuals, goes by a distinct term of art. There is growing support for the view, in fact, that the international community's recent preoccupation with strengthening the law of individual criminal liability has unduly distracted it from enduring problems of state responsibility.[19] Renewed attention to these problems now partly concentrates on state reparations to victims of mass atrocity.[20]

Collectively sanctioning taxpayers creates incentives for citizens, who will know *ex ante* that they will later share responsibility for the state's crimes, to oppose the adoption of their leaders' criminal policies. There is also a normative argument: When state-sponsored mass atrocity enjoys the substantial support of a country's population, its citizens should share the costs of redressing it. This is especially true when the regime perpetrating the atrocities was relatively democratic and responsive to popular will, like Serbia during the Balkan wars.[21]

---

[17] Nina H. B. Jørgensen, *The Responsibility of States for International Crimes* 167 (2000) (maintaining that remedies imposed by the International Court of Justice "presuppose collective responsibility in the sense that they are directed against the wrongdoing state as such"); Hans Kelsen, *Peace through Law* 74–5 (1944) ("The statement that according to international law the State is responsible for its acts means that the subjects of the State are collectively responsible for the acts of the organs of the State.").

[18] Statute of the International Court of Justice, June 26, 1945, art. 36(2)(d), 59 Stat. 1055, 1060, T.S. No. 993, at 30.

[19] See, e.g., Mariano-Florentino Cuéllar, "Reflections on Sovereignty and Collective Security," 40 Stan. J. Int'l L. 211, 249 (2004) ("It is not obvious that we should take the advent of individual responsibility [in international law] as an opportunity to banish collective responsibility."); Stephen Holmes, "Why International Justice Limps," 69 Soc. Res. 1055, 1073 (2002) ("To individualize [criminal] responsibility is, to some extent, to exculpate a community that should, in truth, bear a considerable burden of guilt."). There has been much progress in thinking through legal issues of state responsibility – if not yet in implementing the results – including a proposal that contemplates that the notion of state criminality will become a feature of international law. U.N. Int'l Law Comm'n, Report of the International Law Commission, ¶¶ 72, 76, U.N. Doc A/56/10 (2001).

[20] *The Handbook of Reparations* (Pablo de Greif, ed., 2006).

[21] For a recent argument to this effect, see Thomas Franck, "State Responsibility in the Era of Individual Criminal Culpability," Butterworth Lecture, Univ. of London, October 10, 2005.

The argument is still stronger insofar as it becomes possible to distinguish (and discipline) citizens who supported the criminal policies from their opponents and victims, although this should not be absolutely necessary for merely monetary sanctions. Still, the ties between citizens of a nation-state and their ability to influence national leaders are significantly weaker than the ties between members of the country's officer corps and those officers' ability to influence military comrades of comparable and lesser rank. If the law already permits a measure of collective monetary liability in the former case, it should surely have no qualms about doing so in the latter.

The near-exclusive reliance of domestic criminal law on individualistic premises has always been more a matter of pragmatic efficacy in advancing normative ends than of philosophical foundations. So too was the recourse of international law until 1946 to collectivism; that is, liability for states but not natural persons. There was never any essential property of the international system per se that precluded individual criminal liability, any more than there were ever constitutive features of domestic law barring a greater appeal to collective criminality. A greater appeal of this sort began with the U.S. racketeering statute.[22] The criminal law's shifting use – domestically and internationally – of collectivism and individualism should thus be viewed not as "essentialized principles locked in a Manichaean death struggle."[23] Rather, like science, their use is always pragmatically experimental and provisional in its conclusions.

In cases of mass atrocity, does it make more sense for law to seek liability for individual persons or for states, entire countries? Our answer to this question should surely be informed by what is now known about how and why such events occur in the first place. The more extensive the public collaboration in such wrongs, the more defensible surely becomes such a wide-ranging penalty as state responsibility. But penalizing every taxpayer equally and indiscriminately is still rather rough justice, especially where one ethnic or religious group has employed the state to repress members of another such domestic group. There are other possibilities in any event, as here defended.

States may be civilly liable for genocide; Bosnia-Herzegovina, for instance, sued Serbia to this end in the ICJ. To make its case, Bosnia had to stress how genocide "was not about the intentions and acts of certain individuals, but

---

[22] In both cases, the obstacles have always been "political," not "metaphysical," in Rawls' terms. John Rawls, *Political Liberalism* 11–15, 97 (1993).

[23] Clifford Geertz, *Available Light: Anthropological Reflections on Philosophical Topics* 227 (2000).

about a state policy, its implementation."[24] Even hooligan gangs, suddenly become paramilitaries, had to be characterized as "all acting under the responsibility of Belgrade." Individual persons may also may be criminally liable for genocide in the ICC, the *ad hoc* international tribunals, and in the national courts of many states.

But there are problems with each approach, from both the perspectives of retributive justice and efficient deterrence. Liability for individual persons seems to ignore the palpable and morally pertinent fact that such people control the state apparatus – its human and material resources – deploying these to their pernicious ends, ends shared by many fellow citizens. Without such organizational means and mass support, administrative massacre on a large scale could not occur.

On the other hand, holding the state itself responsible for the actions of its ephemeral officeholders, who often act without constitutional or other legal authority, is vastly overinclusive, for it imposes nontrivial penalties on many innocent people (i.e., far beyond the scope of those responsible in any meaningful way for serious wrong). The rules on joint criminal enterprise might be seen as offering a way, however rudimentary and still unsatisfactory, to walk the line between these two extremes, corralling a potentially large group of responsible parties within law's conceptual reach without embracing entire ethnic groups or national populations, many of whose members' contributions (most Bosnian Serbs, for instance) were probably *de minimus*, at worst.

Apart from this concern with justice, it is also true that holding entire states responsible for the actions of a few officeholders may get the incentives backward and so deter no wrongdoing, insofar as the largest portion of sanction will not fall on those most responsible for causing such wrongdoing – those who, without need even for formal indemnification (if only the state is liable), may now pass this cost along readily to their countrymen.[25] The recent response to this problem, evidenced in the Pinochet case, has been to say that officeholders who commit international crimes act only in their individual, not their official, capacity. But with this move, the state and its

---

[24] Heikelina Verrijn Stuart, "Genocide on the Agenda for ICJ's 60th Anniversary," Int'l Justice Tribune, May 22, 2006 (describing statements of Phon van den Biesen, Bosnia's legal respresentative).

[25] A right of lawbreakers to indemnification for personal liability incurred on an organization's behalf may often under-deter such wrongdoing. The U.S. Model Business Corporation Act (Section 5), for instance, allows a company to indemnify managers who acted without reasonable grounds to believe their conduct was unlawful, if such conduct served the company's interests, as determined by corporate insiders.

citizen-taxpayers are entirely off the hook,[26] even where there was considerable public support for and collaboration in implementation of the ruler's repressive policies.

For the moment, we seek here only to clarify the problem, illuminate its terms, but not to solve it.[27] In seeking a solution, it is true that we must not entirely conflate the incentives of officeholders with the interests of the public institutions they temporarily govern or, for that matter, the incentives of corporate managers in the private sector.[28] But it also is true that mass atrocity often occurs in places where democratic politics are either largely absent or poorly institutionalized and where the distinction between public resources and private wealth is thus not widely respected.

In such circumstances, the conduct of political institutions can often be fairly characterized and understood as an extension of private agendas. Under personalistic dictatorships or even authoritarian kleptocracies, in particular, increasing the state's wealth, scope, and power through unlawful activity often yields direct and immediate benefits for its putative "servants." The state's interests are virtually indistinguishable from theirs.

COLLECTIVE SANCTION OF MILITARY OFFICERS: A PROPOSAL

If collective responsibility for mass atrocity exists, it does not have to entail, as many seem to believe, the acquittal of individuals who contributed, each in his or her small way, to that result. Collective responsibility should lead, instead, to collective sanctions. Collective sanctions against an entire officer corps or pertinent subdivision could effectively deter and fairly redress mass atrocities brought about by a small subset of its members. Such civil remedies would add a multiplier effect to any initial deterrent achieved by the threat of criminal prosecution. After all, many legal systems, particularly in the "civil law" world, administer both types of sanction in a single proceeding.

In its organizational structure and professional culture, a military elite is well suited both to monitor prospective wrongdoers and to redistribute

[26] Marina Spinedi, "State Responsibility v. Individual Responsibility for International Crimes," 13 Euro. J of Int'l L. 895, 898–9 (2002).
[27] The most promising way to begin seeking a solution would be by examining how the incentives of public officeholders differ from those of private parties.
[28] The differences are rightly stressed by Daryl Levinson, "Making Governments Pay: Markets, Politics, and the Allocation of Constitutional Costs," 67 U. Chi. L. Rev. 345 (2000) (noting the "fallacy of composition" entailed in inferring a public institution's desire for greater wealth and power from the material interests of its individual and ephemeral officeholders).

to culpable individual members any costs initially inflicted on the military group as a whole, thereby largely averting any true collective responsibility. The resulting revenue, diverted from officers' salaries, might also be legally earmarked for victims and their families.

Collective responsibility generally punishes the innocents along with the guilty, such as through the internment of all Japanese Americans in response to sabotage and other treasonous activities by a small few of their number. As Kolakowski remarks,

> The phrase "collective responsibility" is bound up, in our minds, with associations of the worst kind. It conjures up visions of occupying powers murdering people at random in revenge for attempts at resistance; of hostages taken and killed; of terrorist attacks in which hundreds of people, quite uninvolved in whatever it was all about, end up dead; of hatred for whole nations, peoples, or races because of the wrongs, real or imaginary, that we feel we have suffered at the hands of some of their members.[29]

The widespread subjective experience of *post facto* bystander guilt could make officers more inclined to part willingly with this money than if it simply flowed into the general coffers.[30] And victims might be more likely to accept it, overcoming their initial reluctance to translating retributive demands into restitutive ones, as Durkheim might put it.[31] Earmarking would thus facilitate the resource transfer on both ends by changing the social meaning of what is given and what is received.[32]

International law nowhere forecloses the present proposal, even if it does not expressly authorize it. Its prohibition of collective punishment of civilians during armed conflict[33] is irrelevant here. This proposal seeks to strengthen deterrence at the micro-level of interpersonal dynamics. Its success depends, however, on the efficacy of such larger institutions as courts – military and civilian, at the national and international levels – in making credible the threat of collective monetary sanctions. Such institutions do not yet exist in many places, particularly in the military justice systems of many poor countries.

[29] Leszek Kołakowski, *Freedom, Fame, Lying, and Betrayal* 53 (1999).
[30] On bystander guilt, see Jon Elster, *Closing the Books: Transitional Justice in Historical Perspective* 241–3 (2004).
[31] Emile Durkheim, *The Division of Labour in Society* 68–9 (W.D. Halls trans., 1984) (arguing that restitutive judgments encounter less social opposition because they are designed to restore the recipient to the previous condition).
[32] On this phenomenon, see Viviana A. Zelizer, *The Social Meaning of Money* 215–16 (1997).
[33] See Art. 75 of the Protocol Additional to the Geneva Conventions of 1949 (Protocol 1).

The mechanics of the present proposal require greater development, which is better pursued in more specialized venues. However, its basic idea is simply this: when a high-level officer is convicted of mass atrocity, fellow officers of the same or higher rank within his relevant unit would collectively suffer monetary sanctions. If silence by peers initially makes it impossible to distinguish culpable officers from the rest, then all corps members above a certain rank would bear collective sanctions costs *pro rata*, unless and until they broke silence and identified those to be prosecuted.

Military commanders might be viewed here as society's lowest cost providers of insurance against atrocity.[34] Because they are better placed than anyone else – including subordinates on the crime scene – to prevent such wrong, senior officers should bear the primary risks and costs of its occurrence, according to economic theory. Such officers will, therefore, more attentively scrutinize the conduct of co-equals and subordinates if they know they will all bear some costs from others' wrongdoing, perhaps as co-participants in a joint criminal enterprise (or simply as co-perpetrators, for that matter).

This line of analysis may offer the best rationale for the law of enterprise participation: the officer corps (or pertinent subdivisions thereof) can itself credibly be conceived as a joint criminal enterprise through which the crimes are perpetrated, by the acts of some members and the omissions of others. This would be a very different usage of the doctrine from that currently employed by the ICTY. No agreement in furtherance of a common criminal design and no shared criminal intent would need to be proven, because the first form of enterprise participation would simply not apply. But acquiescence among bystanding officers could fairly be characterized as making them part of an "organized system" of rights abuses, as the doctrine's second form permits. If their liability to collective sanctions is to be strict, however, then the current mental state required for this form – knowledge of the illegal system and intent to further its purposes – would have to be dropped.

The prospect that acquiescent officers will suffer some personal disutility on account of misconduct by culpable peers increases incentives to organize in ways that minimize the likelihood of grievous misconduct. If mass atrocity does occur and the group's members are then collectively sanctioned, they

---

[34] Allison Marston Danner & Jenny S. Martinez, "Guilty Associations: Joint Criminal Enterprise, Command Responsibility, and the Development of International Criminal Law," 93 Cal. L. Rev. 75, 148 (2005).

will have incentives to reorganize themselves – their institutional practices and procedures – along lines better calculated to discourage repetition.[35]

Well-positioned bystanders are prominent in social scientific accounts of mass atrocity.[36] They occupy no place in current legal analyses, however, for the criminal law has never presumed to reach them.[37] As long as this remains true, such bystanders will have little incentive to restrain more violent comrades in arms, over whom they might exercise influence through professional ties. Mass atrocity is nonetheless often best apprehended and attacked not as a single, simple failure by a junior officer, like Lieutenant William Calley,[38] to obey the law, but as a multiple, compound failure, whereby less conspicuous backup support systems – bystanders among fellow officers, in this case – fail to come to the rescue. Most disasters involving large organizations share this feature.[39] Even if the worst potential offenders cannot be directly deterred by law's threats, others around them and with influence over them may often be more susceptible to law's influence.

Bystanders may be defined, for present purposes, as people whose intelligent intercession would likely prevent, halt, or significantly reduce the scope of the wrongs. Bystanders might be said to provide "negative support," no less essential than the positive variety.[40] In the Third Reich, for instance,

---

[35] On the other hand, it is true that "avoiding collective sanctions can sometimes be better accomplished, from the group's perspective, by hiding wrongdoing rather than by preventing it from occurring." Levinson, "Collective Sanctions," op. cit., at 390. Threat of collective sanctions, under this scenario, need not enhance internal monitoring because such scrutiny would risk uncovering some misconduct otherwise invisible to outsiders, thereby subjecting the group itself to sanctions. The group might then rebel against these efforts to harness internal disciplinary mechanisms to external goals its members do not equally share. The relative strength of these alternative hypotheses, under differing factual circumstances, requires further analysis.

[36] Stanley Cohen, *States of Denial: Knowing about Atrocities and Suffering* 140–67 (2001) (describing the role of bystanders with the institutional capacity to stop mass atrocity). For further discussion of the role of bystanders in mass atrocity, see, generally, Svetlana Broz, *Good People in an Evil Time* (2004); Jane A. Piliavin et al., "Responsive Bystanders: The Process of Intervention," in *Cooperation and Helping Behavior* 279 (Valerian J. Derlega & Janusz Grzelak, eds., 1982); Ervin Staub, "Transforming the Bystanders: Altruism, Caring, and Social Responsibility," in *Genocide Watch* 162 (Helen Fein, ed., 1992); Bibb Latané & John M. Darley, "Bystander 'Apathy,'" 57 Am. Sci. 244 (1969).

[37] Drumbl, "Collective Violence," op cit., at 591.

[38] Calley was the U.S. Army lieutenant convicted of ordering his troops to fire on women and children at My Lai, South Vietnam. *Calley v. Callaway*, 519 F.2d 184, 191 (5th Cir. 1975).

[39] Charles Perrow, *Normal Accidents: Living with High-Risk Technologies* 4–5 (1984) (describing the regularity of multiple, interacting failures in most large, organizational disasters).

[40] Benjamin Valentino, *Final Solutions: Mass Killing and Genocide in the Twentieth Century* 32 (2004).

"it was not necessary for Germans to believe, nor even necessary for them to approve [of the Holocaust]. For the Nazi state to thrive, its citizens had to do no more than go along, maintaining a clear sense of their own interests and a profound indifference to the suffering of others."[41] A leading historian concurs: "The road to Auschwitz was built by hate, but paved with indifference."[42]

If bystanders to mass atrocity are guilty of anything, perhaps they display a variety of guilt that the law should not touch, cannot cognize. This intuition is what led Karl Jaspers, when analyzing the role of German passivity in Nazi crimes, to distinguish criminal guilt from other types – political, moral, and even metaphysical – no less real, he thought, but properly beyond law's reach.[43] Perhaps bystanders may rightly be blamed for one or more of these other three "guilts." In this regard, I have even heard a Croatian legislator publicly acknowledge, after a short lecture on Jaspers' ideas, that he himself felt a "political responsibility" for the atrocities committed by fellow Croatians during the Balkan Wars, a responsibility based in their shared commitment to the political goal of Croatian independence from Yugoslavia.[44]

Social scientific study of bystanders focuses on deficits in their empathy for atrocity's victims and consequent failure to come to their aid.[45] The present approach, by contrast, concentrates on their intimacy with the perpetrators and the sway over them that this relationship permits. Existing scholarship seeks ways to elicit bystanders' altruism and thereby override the risks they face in acting to prevent harm. The present approach seeks instead to harness their self-interest by increasing the costs and attendant

---

[41] James J. Sheehan, "National Socialism and German Society: Reflections on Recent Research," 13 Theory & Soc'y 851, 867 (1984).

[42] Ian Kershaw, *Popular Opinion and Political Dissent in the Third Reich: Bavaria 1933–1945*, 277 (1983).

[43] Karl Jaspers, *The Question of German Guilt* 25–6 (1948). Yet the way Jaspers cut up the categories likely strikes us as strange and ultimately unhelpful; in particular, criminal guilt should not be equated with legal guilt, because civil liability for damages or injunctive orders (requiring institutional reform) are possibilities worthy of consideration, at least in such cases. And criminal guilt surely overlaps with moral guilt, as generally understood, because it is the immorality of certain acts – like murder – that causes them to be classified as criminal, after all.

[44] Transitional Justice Conference for Balkan Legislators, UN Development Program, Igalo, Montenegro, Aug. 18, 2006.

[45] See, e.g., *Altruism, Sympathy, and Helping* (L. Wispé, ed., 1978); Leon Sheleff, *The Bystander: Behavior, Law, Ethics* 18, 21, 43–7, 191–202 (1978); Erwin Staub, *The Psychology of Good and Evil* 480–96 (2003); Michael Stohl, "Outside of a Small Circle of Friends: States, Genocide, Mass Killing and the Role of Bystanders," 24 J. Peace Res. 151, 158–9 (1987).

risks of inaction for failing to prevent harm. Prior writing largely views relevant bystanders as exogenous to the repressive apparatus, whereas this study views them as endogenous to it. With this perspective, one hopes that what is lost in optimism about human nature – and about the capacity to inculcate moral norms[46] – will be gained in humanitarian impact and unsentimental understanding. Like prior approaches, the present aims above all to overcome bystander indifference.[47]

Individual culpability imposes moral constraints on criminal law that have dissuaded it from seriously entertaining this approach. The scrupulosity of liberal jurisprudence in this regard has led us to undervalue efficiency gains to be reaped from threatening collective sanctions for mass atrocity.[48] But courts regularly impose nontrivial costs on persons whose cooperation is deemed essential to implementing judicial remedies.[49] Enterprise participation offers a conceptually congenial means to this end by focusing legal attention on the purpose and scope of the criminal collectivity.

Conventional violent offenders are unlikely to be deterred by the threat of sanction for reasons varying from perception biases to cognitive pathologies.[50] But military officers are much more rational actors, trained to think in terms of the comparative cost of alternative methods for goal attainment. Efficiency considerations are closely aligned here, moreover, with those of consequentialist morality insofar as the threat of collective sanctions would effectively deter many war crimes from occurring. The key questions thus become: Could collective sanctions be designed not only to attain such deterrence but also to work compatibly with the culpability principle? Could they be made to work, at the very least, in ways reducing incompatibility to a morally acceptable minimum?

To these ends, by what means might law help shift the burden initially borne by the collectivity as a whole to the particular members bearing most culpability? Cost shifting within a collective is easier with civil than with criminal sanctions, to be sure. The sanction of incarceration, in particular,

---

[46] Such inculcation, or so-called socialization, is the approach preferred by most sociologists, psychologists, humanists, and others who study behavior in extreme situations. Christine Horne, "The Internal Enforcement of Norms," 19 Eur. Soc. Rev. 335, 336 (2003) (describing internalization as the process whereby difference "between a social norm and a personal value, between the social interest and the self-interest" dissolves).

[47] On the nature and vicissitudes of bystander indifference during mass atrocity, see Victoria J. Barnett, *Bystanders: Conscience and Complicity during the Holocaust* 117–33 (1999).

[48] Efficiency is here employed in ways compatible with both Kaldor-Hicks and Pareto conceptions.

[49] Douglas Laycock, *Modern American Remedies* 305–7, 346–62 (2002).

[50] Paul Robinson & John Darley, *Justice, Liability and Blame* 204–05 (1995).

is obviously not one that can be as readily reallocated among members as if it were, say, a credit for toxic emissions traded among a group of corporate polluters. No one would seriously defend incarceration, however brief, of an entire officer corps, without evidence that every officer contributed in some nontrivial way to the atrocities in question.

But sanctions of a monetary nature – that is, docking of salary – deserve serious consideration here. Monetary penalties might be directed, for instance, at all superiors overseeing those who committed acts of mass atrocity. The formal chain of command will often readily permit their identification. Or sanctions might sometimes fall within a certain subdivision of the corps: a particular division, regiment, brigade, or other unit readily demarcated from the rest.

To the officers so identified, the law might apply an irrebuttable presumption of pecuniary accountability. This sanction would not require any legal showing that these officers had been negligent in a duty of oversight; hence they could not introduce evidence of faultlessness to evade penalty. Such evidence would only be relevant to refuting an allegation of personal liability. But none would have been made. It was only the individual perpetrator, acting through a joint criminal enterprise, who had criminally wronged. Other members of this enterprise must simply share in the costs of redress. Costsharing of this variety is pervasive throughout Western law and is not new to international law. As early as the seventeenth century, Grotius argued that, whereas laws of repayment allowed citizens to share responsibility for their ruler's debts, it did not permit them to share his criminal guilt.[51]

The suggestion here is to make collective sanctions on groups follow from the criminal liability of individual members. This is not a radically novel approach. Efforts to redress large-scale state-sponsored criminality almost invariably involve, even invite, such moves. They are exemplified in German reparations to Israel for the Holocaust and U.S. reparations to interned Japanese Americans.[52] These remedies impose costs not primarily on actual wrongdoers, but on private individuals in their collective capacity as taxpayers. Neither German nor American taxpayers bore any personal liability for causing these wrongs, yet all such citizens incurred the compensatory burden.

---

[51] Hugo Grotius, *De Jure Belli ac Pacis Libri Tres*, bk. II, ch. XXI, at 538 (Rev. John Morrice, ed., 1715) (1646); id. bk. III, ch. II, at 36–7. When the state's debts arise from criminal penalties, however, the distinction ceases to be very helpful.

[52] Civil Liberties Act of 1988, Pub. L. No. 100–383, 102 Stat. 903 (1990) (providing reparations to Japanese Americans). Some $1.6 billion were distributed.

The legislation by which these programs were adopted was not very controversial in either country.[53] Thus, we may infer public consent to these collective assumptions of shared responsibility. Such consent is intelligible in light of the occasional willingness of individuals to understand themselves nonindividualistically, even as participants in a collectivity whose other members committed grievous wrong in its name. Only personal identification with the culpable collectivity could explain this public readiness to incur such costs. The psychological mechanisms at work here might be put to somewhat broader use. They augur well for applying collective sanctions in other ways to different episodes of mass atrocity. The law might, in the aftermath of such conflagrations, induce members of an officer corps to adopt a similar view of themselves: as members of a culpable collectivity, ready to assume the costs of compensating its victims and monitoring comrades against prospective recurrence.

Collective sanctions are most sensible where the individuals to be treated as a group display a clear capacity for collective agency – agency both to prevent and punish the pertinent misconduct. This capacity lets the group inculcate group norms in potentially miscreant members and monitor them closely in advance of any wrongdoing, thereby helping prevent it. Collective agency can also let the group identify actual criminals thereafter, passing on to them much of the entity-wide costs it may initially bear.

In some instances, however, this capacity for collective agency may be utterly lacking. It may be, for instance, that colonels in one army division turn out to have no capacity whatsoever to identify, influence, or control likely wrongdoers among officers of similar rank in other divisions, with different duties, many miles away. Moreover, imposing a duty of *post facto* redress only on those with demonstrable capacity to prevent harm may create perverse incentives to design the organization to minimize the number of officers with such capacity, thereby freeing the rest from accountability. To prevent this from occurring, responsibility for cost sharing must be strict – not based on negligence of any kind. Only then would incentives be optimal, so that officers' self-interest would clearly lie in devising an organizational structure with internal mechanisms maximizing the capacity of its members, individually and collectively, to prevent and redress mass atrocity.

---

[53] Paul Dubinsky, "Justice for the Collective: The Limits of Human Rights Class Action," 102 Mich. L. Rev. 1152, 1184–5 (2004); Lily Gardner Feldman, "The Principle and Practice of 'Reconciliation' in German Foreign Policy: Relations with France, Israel, Poland and the Czech Republic," 75 Int'l Aff. 333 (1999). On the U.S. legislative debate, see 100th Cong. 2nd Sess., 134 Cong. Rec. S4386, April 20, 1988.

Such officers would not face any criminal liability under this approach, even for dereliction of duty, much less atrocity itself. They thus would not need to make a substantial contribution to the wrong as required by the law of complicity nor display effective control over atrocity-perpetrating peers as superior responsibility demands. Merely to compel their sharing in redressing wrongs by errant brethren does not require finding them liable for anything. The moral hurdle for imposing monetary loss is obviously much lower than for incarceration.

This approach does not encroach on the culpability principle in the slightest, since officers would knowingly consent to strict pecuniary responsibility before accepting any position to which it might attach. They understand that directing large groups of men with arms is an inherently dangerous activity. Admittedly, unless the entire corps were penalized for every mass atrocity, there could be some uncertainty about which subdivision of the officer corps might be designated the joint criminal enterprise responsible for it. Such uncertainty, however, could only enhance the officer's incentives to ensure that no subdivision to which he could plausibly be ascribed ever committed such wrongs. There is, hence, no need under this approach to cure legal uncertainty in defining the criminal enterprise. This ambiguity in the doctrine, vicious in its current and more ambitious uses, becomes a virtue in its more modest usage defended here.

If one accepts the preceding analysis, the question then becomes: What features of an officer corps – of its organizational structure and cultural system – might give members the collective internal capacity to prevent war crimes *ex ante* and punish them *ex post*? The next chapter assays this question.

10

The Collective Responsibility of Military Officers

How, then, might the law help create and cultivate within modern armies the institutional characteristics enabling them to steer clear of mass atrocity?[1] Much can be said in ready response to this question. First, militaries in many developed countries increasingly lure enlistees by promising instruction in technical skills marketable on departure.[2] Those attracted on this basis are more susceptible to environmental clues about the changing costs and benefits of military membership than conscripts or those enlisting for patriotic motives.

Still, much of an officer's investment in years of demanding training becomes costs unrecoverable on leaving the corps. Most of the human capital acquired within combat positions in particular is firm-specific. It is unique to warfare; little demand exists for it in the peacetime economy. There also is no market among states for the services of a distinguished officer. It is axiomatic that he may sell these services only to his country of citizenship; few states need – or even insist on – covenants not to compete in employment contracts with their officers. Each state thus enjoys monopsony power over such laborers,[3] whom it consequently binds with long-term contracts of adhesion. Private military contractors like Blackwater absorb only the smallest fraction of retired officers.

[1] See, generally, Mark Osiel, *Obeying Orders: Atrocity, Military Discipline & the Law of War*, 233–46 (1999) (offering several arguments to this end).
[2] The proportion of officers trained in dual-use technologies (technologies relevant to the private sector no less than to military operations) and generic managerial skills is growing. Charles C. Moskos et al., "Armed Forces after the Cold War," in *The Postmodern Military: Armed Forces after the Cold War* 1–6 (Charles C. Moskos et al., eds., 2000).
[3] David Segal & Meyer Kestnbaum, "Professional Closure in the Military Labor Market: A Critique of Pure Cohesion," in *The Future of the Army Profession*, 349 (D. M. Snider & G. L. Watkins, eds., 2002); Yagil Levy, "Soldiers as Laborers: a Theoretical Model," 36 Theory & Society 187 (2007).

In short, alternative labor markets are few and mobility opportunities correspondingly limited. The high costs to an officer of exit from the corps enhance its collective capacity to sanction his deviance – hence also to deter it *ex ante*. The corps's market power lets it control the terms and conditions of his professional and personal life to a degree unimaginable in such professions as law, medicine, engineering, or accounting, where more liquid labor markets make expertise readily transferable between organizations.

One might first suppose that the most important sanctions available to an officer corps in policing members' misconduct would be court-martial, followed by lengthy incarceration. Both require strong evidence of personal culpability for serious wrong, however.[4] More powerful in influencing members' daily calculations are sanctions, which are easier to assess against them: Such sanctions are of lower magnitude, but higher probability.[5] They especially include denial of expected promotion to higher rank, with a corresponding stasis in compensation. In many countries, moreover, non-promotion for those above a certain rank leads to compulsory retirement under up-or-out personnel policies embodied in regulation. This "sanction" is levied without any liability finding, hence without the need for superiors to demonstrate wrongdoing of any sort. More draconian measures, such as demotion to lower rank and cashiering, require more elaborate procedures, although not a verdict of criminal fault.[6]

If violating group norms risks these serious sanctions, the individual officer's incentives to adhere are strong. The efficacy of these measures derives from the fact that they both stigmatize and impose economic pressures. Other officers might be initially reluctant to impose such strong sanctions on a peer. But if a seriously unruly member really threatens high costs for other officers, strong interests in expelling him should develop on the first sign that he posed this risk, leading quickly to preventive intercession. This reflects the fact that groups will seek to limit their average costs by seeking members with low expected costs relative to other members and discharging those with high expected costs.

---

[4] Before bringing charges, unit commanders must conduct an investigation into the alleged offenses; they are generally reluctant to bring weak cases to court out of concern that "an acquitted service member [will] return to the unit and flaunt his 'victory' over the command." David A. Schlueter, *Military Criminal Justice: Practice and Procedure* § 1–7 (6th, ed., 2004).

[5] The armed forces have increasingly made use of nonpunitive and nonjudicial measures to address violations of military standards. Nonpunitive measures include transfer in assignments, administrative discharges, administrative reductions in rank, extra training, written or oral reprimands, and withdrawal of privileges and passes. Id. § 1–8(B).

[6] Id. § 1–8(B)–(C).

Intercession is especially likely in response to the risk of war crimes because officers know from historical experience that such crimes often elicit reciprocal violations from an adversary, which have been legally justified – until recently at least – under traditional rules of reprisal.[7] The belligerents' mutual self-interest in preventing a cycle of retaliatory violence largely explains the creation and relative efficacy of such *jus in bello* prohibitions.[8] What distinguishes the collective sanctions approach is its explicit recognition that, at such times, appeals to professionalism and professional ethics are, on their own, unlikely to motivate enough preventive intercession by bystanding officers. Professional ethics has repeatedly proven to offer a weak reed against the winds of contrary self-interest, although at rare moments, a more disinterested professionalism may have induced officers to rein in criminal comrades, if only because of the "*ad hoc* nature of death squads or their perceived lack of discipline."[9]

Group sanctions do not merely punish negative conduct but also reward positive behavior. Awarding honorifics, such as medals of distinction, is a form of positive sanctioning common in armed forces that is generally done to recognize heroic action in combat. Heroism can take many forms, however. It customarily involves the courageous use of force when facing the risk of violent death. But it increasingly extends to the courageous nonuse of force as well. Medals have been awarded in recent years, for instance, to U.S. officers for refraining from deadly force in combat, thereby preventing collateral civilian casualties by more cautious conduct.[10]

Mass atrocity throughout the world would surely decline if other armies followed suit, prioritizing heroic risk-taking of this sort in the award of medals and promotions. Shaming rituals were once regularly employed in the U.S. military and continue to be by armed forces elsewhere.[11] Some such rituals are designed to reintegrate the offender. Punishment and its rituals are reintegrative if they seek to restore the social relationships fractured by crime.[12] Other punitive rituals aim to signify and symbolize the offender's

[7] Frits Kalshoven, "Belligerent Reprisals," 21 Neth. Y.B. Int'l L. 43 (1990).
[8] Eric A. Posner, "A Theory of the Laws of War," 70 U. Chi. L. Rev. 297, 301–6 (2003).
[9] Bruce B. Campbell, "Death Squads: Definition, Problems, and Historical Context," in *Death Squads in Global Perspective: Murder with Deniability* 1, 21 n.20 (Bruce B. Campbell & Arthur D. Brenner, eds., 2000) (describing military restraint at the end of El Salvador's 1980s civil war).
[10] Anonymous interview at U.S. Air War College, Maxwell Air Force Base, in Montgomery, AL (Oct. 2003).
[11] On the nature of such rituals, see Harold Garfinkel, "Conditions of Successful Degradation Ceremonies," 61 Am. J. Soc. 420, 422–3 (1956).
[12] On reintegrative shaming and recent attempts to revive it within Western criminal law, see, generally, John Braithwaite, *Crime, Shame and Reintegration* (1989).

expulsion. More so than economic sanctions alone, they also properly signal and express the nature and magnitude of the moral wrong reflected in mass atrocity.[13]

The most frequent group sanction of all is the quiet social practice – often imperceptible to outsiders – of ostracism in personal interaction, as through averting eye contact when passing in the hallway and deliberately sitting at another table in the mess hall. These informal sanctions can be levied by individuals acting alone and so are costless to the group, whereas more formal sanctions entail coordinating individuals' conduct through institutions, which is more costly.

If a member cherishes the esteem of his colleagues, they may have a devastating effect on him simply by manifesting their disrespect.[14] Threat of fines or incarceration, hedged as they are with procedural preconditions, are generally less potent than the threats to reputation.[15] Such threats are particularly pertinent to military officers, because they "are attracted to and sustained in military life by pride in belonging to a valued group, concern over winning admiration and fellowship of colleagues, accumulation of honor, and largely symbolic recognitions of success."[16] Threats to reputation are particularly potent when it is difficult for the individual realistically to imagine a life outside the group. Contemplating a completely new career is often painful, but especially when one faces alternative life choices far less attractive in the long run than present ones.[17]

This is the case with military officers in countries in which professional soldiers enjoy material circumstances superior to most civilians, including those who are better educated. Informal sanctions are also especially powerful when the group in question is discrete and insular, having minimal contact – by choice or circumstance – with the external world, as is often the case of officers even in rich countries.[18] That an officer corps has informal

---

[13] On the properly expressive function of criminal punishment for severe wrongs, see Dan Kahan, "Social Meaning and the Economic Analysis of Crime," 27 J. Leg. Stud. 609 (1998).

[14] Philip Pettit, "*Virtus Normativa*: Rational Choice Perspectives," 100 Ethics 725, 745 (1990).

[15] Dan M. Kahan, "Social Influence, Social Meaning, and Deterrence," 83 Va. L. Rev. 349, 354 (1997) (summarizing empirical evidence that "the perception that one's peers will or will not disapprove exerts a much stronger influence than does the threat of a formal sanction on whether a person decides to engage in a range of common offenses").

[16] James Waller, *Becoming Evil: How Ordinary People Commit Genocide and Mass Killings* 192 (2002) (citing John Keegan, *A History of Warfare* (1994)).

[17] Eric A. Posner, "The Regulation of Groups: The Influence of Legal and Non-Legal Sanctions on Collective Action," 63 U. Chi. L. Rev. 133, 142 (1996).

[18] Cf. Charles C. Moskos, "Toward a Postmodern Military," in *The Postmodern Military* 14, 25–7 (Moskos, et al., eds. 1949) (describing growing differences between civilian and

sanctioning mechanisms at its ready disposal does not ensure, of course, that these will be employed to laudatory ends.

The point of imposing monetary sanctions on the officer corps as a whole is precisely to enhance the incentives of its innocent bystanders to deploy these powerful mechanisms more vigorously to desirable ends. The logic of the proposal here resembles the False Claims Act in creating incentives for whistle-blowing against misconduct.[19] That statute has been highly successful in uncovering large-scale fraud against the U.S. government. Under that law, dutiful government employees have incentives to disclose the fraud only after it has occurred, to be sure, but their superiors' knowledge that this will later occur effectively discourages fraud *ex ante*, in some cases.

Whenever sanctioning is delegated from the state to a societal subgroup, its leadership must usually further delegate these tasks.[20] A specialized subset of enforcers and gatekeepers thereby arises, deciding who shall be disciplined and who promoted to higher office. The disciplinary function within militaries is largely delegated not to ordinary fellow officers, but to Judge Advocate Generals (JAGs).[21] As licensed lawyers, they have had considerably more formal education than most officers, with their compensation in part determined accordingly.[22] Their years of higher civilian education generally exceed even those of higher ranking officers who seek their counsel on humanitarian law. Now integrated into operations at all levels, JAGs work closely with commanders and operators to advise them as they develop rules governing the use of force.[23]

As lawyers, JAG officers also are members of a learned profession whose civilian ranks they may soon expect to join and whose nonmilitary norms

military worldviews in the United States). On this aspect of Argentina's armed forces, see Mark Osiel, *Mass Atrocity, Ordinary Evil, and Hannah Arendt*, 105–23 (2001) (describing the influence of religion on the behavior of Argentina's military).

[19] 31 U.S.C. §§ 3729–33 (2000).

[20] Cf. Daryl Levinson, "Collective Sanctions," 56 Stan. L. Rev. 345, 419–22 (2003).

[21] Schlueter, op. cit., § 8–3(A)–(B)(1).

[22] For example, in the U.S. Air Force, 49% of officers have a BA or BS, and 51 percent have advanced or professional degrees. "Personnel Facts," Airman: Magazine of America's Air Force (Jan. 2004) at 34, 36. Even though JAG officers are paid the same amount as their equivalent officer ranks, JAG officers enter the service as first lieutenants (rather than second lieutenant, the entry level for other officers) and are normally promoted to captain six months later. The U.S. Army Judge Advocate Gen.'s Corps, Frequently Asked Questions 5 (June 2005 ed); Def. Fin. and Accounting Serv., 2005 Military Pay Rates: Complete Active Duty and Reserve Monthly Drill Pay Tables (Jan. 2005)). Because this is a faster rate of promotion than that of their non-JAG peer officers, Brig. Gen. Charles A. Dunlap, Jr, "The Role of the Lawyer in War," 4 Chi. J. Int'l L. 479, 489 (2003), in practice this means that they are more highly compensated early in their careers.

[23] Frederic L. Borch, *Judge Advocates in Combat* 322 (2001).

have considerable purchase on them.[24] Their relative independence from
even civilian superiors at high levels in the U.S. Defense Department was
recently made apparent, for instance, in the public disclosure by active
duty JAGs of their professional disagreement with civilian White House
and Defense Department lawyers about interpretation of the Convention
Against Torture in its application to Al Qaeda detainees.[25]

The capacity of an officer corps to impose its norms and sanctions on
errant members, as well as on more junior soldiers, finds further footing
in the way court martials deliberately tilt the procedural scales in favor of
prosecutors.[26] This is done in myriad ways, to an extent that would clearly
be unconstitutional and publicly unacceptable in civilian society. That this
imbalance is legally authorized in Western democracies illustrates that "a
strong, solidary group may exert control over the behavior of its members
in ways that will be normatively problematic from the perspective of society
more generally."[27]

The cost of acquiring information to identify and prosecute deviant
members of a social group is often steeper for external state officials, acting
on behalf of society at large, than for the group itself, employing internal
procedures of its own devising. Privacy norms in the wider world and in
its law may impede external inquiries. But privacy within military life is
limited to an extent "that would be considered Orwellian" almost anywhere
else in modern liberal society[28] and that is unknown in other complex
formal organizations. The absence of privacy reduces the expense an officer
corps must incur to learn the identity and activities of culpable members –
knowledge necessary to supervise and sanction them.

These several considerations suggest that officer corps almost everywhere
should form the type of collective entity capable of implementing sanctions
on its members with particular efficacy. These entities should be good, in
particular, at ensuring that any collective sanctions initially levied against the
group are successfully transferred to culpable individuals. What has been
lacking is simply the lever by which to lift these existing mechanisms of
social sanction into more effective service of atrocity prevention. To be sure,
when war criminality among an officer corps is widespread, the likelihood

---

[24] They are subject to the profession's constraints and responsibilities on joining the civilian
bar. Model Rules of Prof'l Conduct, Preamble (2003).
[25] John Barry et al., "The Roots of Torture," *Newsweek*, May 24, 2004, at 28, 32.
[26] For example, in the Army, the prosecutor is detailed by the "staff judge advocate" for the
commander convening the judicial proceedings. Schlueter, op. cit., § 8(3)(B)(2).
[27] Levinson, "Collective Sanctions," op. cit., at 386.
[28] Id.

of effective internal sanctioning is slight. It may be only when the number of miscreant members relative to the corps is few that collective sanctions work to deter war crime by officers.

If inculpable officers fail to shift the burden to culpable ones, they may thereby become culpable themselves, not in the original wrong, but in such independent offenses as dereliction of duty or obstruction of justice. As culpable parties, they then collectively bear monetary sanctions that should continue to lie where they have fallen. These penalties may defensibly be inflicted on them as a group, in other words, unless and until they employ internal sanctioning mechanisms to distinguish culpable from inculpable parties to the initial wrongs. At that point, the collective sanctions externally imposed on the collectivity and its inculpable members may be withdrawn or reduced.

The basic idea in all this is that those who can most readily help avert mass atrocity may be moved by motives no less banal than those often committing it. As Waller writes, "Just as ordinary people can commit extraordinary evil, ordinary people can also subvert extraordinary evil."[29] It may be helpful to incentivize them to do so.

DEFEASANCE FOR DISCLOSURE: UNCOVERING COVER-UP BY CREATING INCENTIVES TO SNITCH

Most discussions of legal response to mass atrocity focus exclusively on *post facto* remedies. Much of the preceding analysis, in contrast, shows how collective sanctions might help prevent war crimes from occurring in the first place. Such sanctions can also be made to serve the former objective, however – not in punishing initial wrongdoers, but in extracting information about them from others. A serious obstacle to the prosecution of war crimes in many countries has been a *post facto* cover-up among officers taking no part in the original wrongs.[30] Inducing such innocent bystanders to divulge what they know about culpable brethren has often proved impossible. This was true in Argentina, for instance, for an entire decade after the downfall of its military regime in 1983.[31] The problem is not confined to military dictatorships, however. When U.S. troops killed two dozen Iraqi civilians in the town of Haditha, no inquiry was begun until

---

[29] Waller, "Becoming Evil," op. cit., at 277.

[30] See, e.g., Seymour M. Hersh, *Cover-Up: The Army's Secret Investigation of the Massacre at My Lai* 4, at 3–8 (1972); Martha Mendoza, "No Gun Ri: A Cover-Up Exposed," 38 Stan. J. Int'l L. 153 (2002).

[31] Osiel, *Ordinary Evil*, op. cit., at 18–21.

three months later, and only after *Time* magazine informed the military of its own investigation into the events.[32]

Collectively sanctioning bystanders is often the only effective means of eliciting their cooperation. People in insular groups frequently refuse to share inculpatory data about an errant member with outsiders. This refusal occurs less frequently, to be sure, when the deviant's identity is known to many members, because then it is harder to discover who snitched. But even in that situation, among military officers a tacit oath of silence usually holds. Hoarding information is particularly common when it is clearly being sought for litigation. Group members who share such potential evidence with nonmembers risk ostracism, banishment, and sometimes far worse.[33] This solidarity in silence is quite perverse from the perspective of enforcing legal policy.

Moreover, its strength seems paradoxical and even illogical, insofar as the group's collective self-interest clearly lies in purging itself of its few bad apples. It is often just a few individuals, after all, whose misconduct has brought official scrutiny, public recrimination, and stigmatizing shame on the group, most of whose members are *ex hypothesi* innocent of initial wrongs. The capacity for a purge to reestablish the legitimacy of a public organization thus partly explains the early appeal of lustration programs in Central and Eastern Europe after the Cold War.[34] The good guys have an interest in dissociating themselves from the bad, as do even the "pretty bad" from the truly awful.

Criminal law faces a classic collective action problem in that the group's long-run interests in cleaning house and moving on diverge from the short-term interests of individual members in avoiding informal sanction for snitching. The information-forcing function of collective sanctions is well tailored to overcome the evasive ignorance endemic to the sort of organizations responsible for mass atrocity.[35] Public disclosure by a single officer may be enough, as in Argentina, to reach and pass the tipping point, unleashing a cascade of further revelation by others. For instance, in 1995 Navy

[32] Colin H. Kahl, "How We Fight," 85 Foreign Affairs, 83, 99, Nov./Dec. 2006.

[33] Ian Weinstein, "Regulating the Market for Snitches," 47 Buff. L. Rev. 563, 583–4 (1999) (explaining dangers faced by criminal defendants who cooperate with authorities).

[34] Roman David, "Lustration Laws in Action: The Motives and Evaluation of Lustration Policy in the Czech Republic and Poland (1989–2001)," 28 Law & Soc. Inquiry 387, 405–7 (2003) (describing how lustration programs sought to restore public trust in state institutions by purging most serious wrongdoers among civil servants).

[35] William H. Simon, "Wrongs of Ignorance and Ambiguity: Lawyer Responsibility for Collective Misconduct" 1 (unpublished manuscript) (explaining how legal duties of inquiry can inhibit evasive ignorance of wrongdoing among professional peers).

captain Adolfo Scilingo confessed his participation in murdering dozens of detainees by dumping their drugged bodies from a helicopter into the sea.[36] A rash of similar disclosures ensued from other officers and were prominently reported by the country's news media. These revelations ultimately compelled chief commanders for each of Argentina's armed forces to apologize repeatedly to the nation for atrocities committed during the Dirty War of the 1970s.[37]

Officers' responsiveness to collective sanctions for atrocities committed by comrades will depend on many factors, particularly whether benefits from the crimes later eliciting such costs are widely shared. When non-perpetrators derive little value from comrades' crimes – perhaps because pillaged property is hoarded – the sanctions required to elicit inculpatory information need not be as severe. Their cost–benefit calculations can be tipped more easily in favor of snitching.

In contrast, innocent officers – anticipating sanctions for the crimes of miscreant peers – may be more likely to resign their commissions than potential perpetrators. Reliance on incentives would also fail if bystanders' propensity to become rescuers was largely predetermined by prior factors like age, ethnicity, class, or gender. But those who rescued Jews in Nazi Germany and Nazi-occupied Europe, for instance, displayed no such sociological commonalities.[38]

Penalties for nondisclosure must be strong enough to hurt. Otherwise, costs to individual members of disclosure will outweigh those of continued silence and will become an accepted cost of doing business. Where loot-seeking is a central motive for atrocities, the threat of future monetary sanctions would need to be quite high to override more immediate incentives. And threats to this end by "failed states," in particular, are unlikely to be very credible, to say the least. The use of collective monetary sanctions might therefore ultimately need to be imposed by international law, at some point, not merely in the military codes of nation-states. Although the rank and file would never have reason to fear prosecution in The Hague, those superiors commanding them and authorizing their looting would then have good reason to anticipate liability, under either of the two legal doctrines this book examines.

---

[36] Horacio Verbitsky, *The Flight: Confessions of an Argentine Dirty Warrior* 7–8 (1996).
[37] Osiel, *Ordinary Evil*, op. cit., at 20–1.
[38] Nechama Tec, *Resilience and Courage: Women, Men, and the Holocaust* 83–8, 97, 223–4 (2003); Nechama Tec, *When Light Pierced the Darkness: Christian Rescue of Jews in Nazi-Occupied Poland* 150, 152 (1986). Both works conclude that rescuers sprang from all corners and sectors of society.

At the same time, caution is required – particularly when the enterprise participation doctrine extends sanctions so far afield to those whose influence may be quite limited. Because this doctrine permits disciplining so many actors, the severity of penal sanction thereby imposed must be attenuated accordingly. Monetary penalties – first collective, then individualized – permit finer-grained calibration to this end than the blunter instruments of incarceration and expulsion.

A potential problem arises because any financial burden imposed on government, including its military organizations, often can simply be passed on to taxpayers. Taxpayers are notoriously dispersed, lacking in solidarity and thus in the political clout necessary to prevent such perverse burden shifting. The deterrent effect desired here might therefore prove unreliable. The solution is to require by statute that collective sanctions take the form of salary reduction, rather than a decrease in the overall military budget.

Another objection might be raised. When "exit" from an organization is difficult, members are driven to rely more heavily on "voice" to manifest disapproval with its policies.[39] Exit from military (and paramilitary) organizations is often impossible in the short run. Voice is similarly constrained, however, by hierarchical structures and corresponding rules limiting criticism of superiors by subordinates. Without much exit or voice, then, armies thus lack the normal mechanisms by which most organizations acquire internally available information necessary to correct errors in their direction. Fortunately, these institutional features do not much impede the information-forcing function of collective sanctions. The information to be shared generally moves laterally, rather than vertically, as to military police and others charged with investigatory functions. Similarly, informal peer pressure against miscreant comrades moves horizontally among officers of comparable rank.

Economists focus on rules that reconcile self-interests because they assume that people readily respond to incentives. Responsiveness is viewed as axiomatic and uncontroversial, and therefore as a given.[40] This view is a mistake. Responsiveness to incentives is, rather, a variable that requires careful assessment of its empirical extent in particular circumstances. Sociologists have always known this.[41] Unresponsiveness to material

---

[39] Albert O. Hirschman, *Exit, Voice, and Loyalty* 30–43 (1970).

[40] More precisely, responsiveness varies only in terms of its intensity: the degree to which a party reliably appropriates the net receipts associated with its efforts.

[41] A century ago, Max Weber observed that Polish peasants reacted to higher hourly wages in German cities not by working more, but by working less, since the same lifestyle could now

incentives is common, in fact, for nonmarket behavior,[42] a domain including war and genocide. Even in markets, incentives sometimes fail to influence conduct. In labor markets, for instance, employers' increased reliance on material incentives to improve work performance has proven counterproductive where team production prevails, which hampers managers' efforts to distinguish one worker's contribution from another's.[43] Small combat groups in wartime are the epitome of team production.

Social science shows how small groups of soldiers motivate one another in combat.[44] The breaking down of such cohesion in the enemy's forces, conversely, is crucial to military success. An army at war seeks less to annihilate the individuals composing its adversary than simply to prise them apart.[45] It is not only soldiers' shared self-interest in survival that leads to combat cohesion; collective sanctions play a major role. Beginning with boot camp, drill instructors often punish an entire platoon for the failings of a single or few members.[46] The rationale for such practices is that they mirror the demands of combat itself, during which one soldier's errors may easily cause the death of comrades.

These practices create powerful incentives for soldiers to monitor one another for scrupulous compliance with group norms. So too does the collaborative work of army general staffs. Hence the need collectively to sanction the entire team – in this case, all officers in the immediate perpetrator's unit. There is some evidence, from surveys of junior officers, that their superiors are sometimes all too attentive to career incentives at the expense of their subordinates' welfare.[47]

---

be maintained by less exertion. Wolfgang J. Mommsen, *Max Weber and German Politics 1890–1920*, at 24 (Michael S. Steinberg trans., 1984) (1959).

[42] For recent empirical studies in nonmarket contexts, see generally Charles S. Carver et al., "Responsiveness to Threats and Incentives, Expectancy of Recurrence, and Distress and Disengagement: Moderator Effects in Women with Early Stage Breast Cancer," 68 J. Consulting & Clinical Psychol. 965 (2000); Kevin Milligan, "Subsidizing the Stork: New Evidence on Tax Incentives and Fertility," Nat'l Bureau of Econ. Res., Working Paper No. 8845 (2002).

[43] Armen A. Alchian & Harold Demsetz, "Production, Information Costs, and Economic Organization," 62 Am. Econ. Rev. 777, 779–80 (1972).

[44] Edward A. Shils & Morris Janowitz, "Cohesion and Disintegration in the Wehrmacht in World War II," 12 Pub. Opinion Q. 280 (1948).

[45] Gordon Tulluck, *Economics without Frontiers* 6 (2006).

[46] Steven A. Gilham, "The Marines Build Men: Resocialization in Recruit Training," in *The Sociological Outlook* 150, 159 (Reid Luhman, ed., 1999).

[47] Mark R. Lewis, "Army Transformation and the Junior Officer Exodus," 31 Armed Forces & Soc'y 63, 66 (2004).

Below the very top ranks, further evidence suggests that most perpetrators of mass atrocity are driven by material motives and situational pressures. These economic and psychological factors create distinct incentives.[48] The deeper causes of the Rwandan genocide, for instance, stem less from ethnic ideology than from a fierce competition for land and food, aggravated by rapid population growth.[49] More modestly, Martin Shaw rightly observes that "robbery has become an even more important part of genocide, as perpetrators steal the homes, consumer goods and cash of the victims."[50] In Sri Lanka, for instance, during Sinhalese mob violence against Tamils, "businesspeople burned out competitors' stores and considerable fortunes were lost and made under cover of rioting."[51] In the French Revolution, about which scholars long stressed the passions of class antagonism and attendant political ideology, "many people saw opportunities to forward their own interests and settle old scores opened up by the crisis of 1789," Charles Tilly now writes.[52] Even the Holocaust found considerable support in the material benefits gleaned by many ordinary Germans in the confiscation of Jewish property throughout occupied Europe, according to recent historiography.[53]

---

[48] Mahmood Mamdani, *When Victims Become Killers: Colonialism, Nativism, and Genocide in Rwanda* 194 (2001) (concluding of the Rwandan genocide that "the spread of massacres gave free reign [*sic*] to forces of banditry and pillage"); Jan T. Gross, *Neighbors: The Destruction of the Jewish Community of Jedwabne, Poland* 48–70 (2001) (describing how Polish neighbors murdered nearly every Jewish resident and seized their property); Michael Mann, *The Dark Side of Democracy* 312–14 (2005) (describing motives of Nazi collaborators in Southern Europe); William Reno, *Warlord Politics and African States* 79 (1998) (describing materialistic motives of young militia members in West African civil wars); Valery Tishkov, *Chechnya: Life in a War-Torn Society* 103–6 (2004) (asserting, on the basis of ethnographic observation, that "material gain was the main incentive" of most Chechen combatants); David Chandler, *Voices from S-21: Terror and History in Pol Pot's Secret Prison* 143–55 (1999) (describing motivations of torturers in Khmer Rouge prisons, disclosed in interviews); see also Benjamin Valentino, *Final Solutions: Mass Killing and Genocide in the Twentieth Century* 43–6, 56, 60 (2004).

[49] Paul Magnarella, "The Background and Causes of the Genocide in Rwanda," 3 J. Int'l Crim. Justice 801, 821 (2005).

[50] Martin Shaw, *War and Genocide* 137 (2003).

[51] Carolyn Nordstrom, *Shadows of War* 31 (2004).

[52] Charles Tilly, *Roads from Past to Future* 154 (1997).

[53] Götz Aly, *Hitler's Beneficiaries: Plunder, Racial War, and the Nazi Welfare State* 8 (2007) ("The cascade of riches and personal advantages – all derived from crimes against humanity, for which ordinary Germans were not directly responsible but from which they gladly profited – led the majority of the populace to feel that the regime had their best interests at heart."); Ad van Liempt, *Hitler's Bounty Hunters: The Betrayal of the Jews* (2005).

In light of such facts, there is reason to think that an incentive-based approach to averting mass atrocity might work, despite the few countervailing factors acknowledged earlier.[54] The question then becomes: how might the law more effectively induce such bystanders to honor their duty, in a way commensurate with the actual wrongfulness of its violation? From the present perspective, that query turns into: what combination of incentives – positive and negative, formal and informal – elicits the optimal level of collective self-discipline to this end?

Economists often distinguish between the optimal and maximal levels of a public good, because the maximal can generally be obtained only through trade-offs with other such goods. In the present case, this would mean that there might be some level of super-compliance with prohibitions against atrocity that could compromise a military's more central purpose of ensuring national security. Perhaps the line between lawful and unlawful wartime violence might, in some places, become so vague that soldiers would consequently abjure effective fighting methods that fell within law's uncertain penumbra. And it is true that many key features of international criminal offenses remain poorly defined, such as both the *actus reus* and the *mens rea* for "torture," posing some such risk of over-deterrence.

But it is entirely speculative that changes likely to decrease atrocities could compromise an army's fighting capability in nontrivial ways. Hence, divergence between optimal and maximal levels of atrocity prohibition is unlikely. This conclusion would have to be revised if it could be shown that, for instance, honoring the torture prohibition caused a country to lose a war, perhaps by preventing it from acquiring necessary information from enemy detainees.

That the collective sanctions here proposed involve a soft variant of strict liability – for financial fines – should not give great pause, since no individual's personal liability, criminal or civil, is at issue. Individual officers would become civilly liable only if they failed to pay monetary sanctions levied on them individually as members of the culpable collectivity/criminal enterprise, and then only for this failure, not the original wrongs. Anyone who disclosed inculpatory information about others would be exempt. Liability would thus be presumptive, but rebuttable, defeased by disclosure. Those who did not disclose or did so only after others had already done so would remain on the hook.

---

[54] Also possible is prosecution for dereliction of duty, a separate but much lesser offense, than the initial wrongs. 10 U.S.C. § 892(3) (2000). The mental state for this offense is identical to that of superior responsibility.

Civilians are often surprised to learn that our historically hallowed opposition to Good Samaritan duties – as morally supererogatory – is by no
means shared in many militaries, whose members have a legal duty to report
other soldiers' misconduct.[55] Given this duty to act, a failure to honor it –
before the crime is consummated, at least – will sometimes even amount to
complicity in the other's offense. Our skepticism about obligating others to
act as their brother's keeper finds little resonance among brethren in arms,
whose norms have always been considerably more communitarian.[56] In the
soldier's moral universe, after all, current lives must regularly be risked not
only to protect an injured comrade, but even on occasion to retrieve his
corpse from enemy possession. Throwing oneself on a live grenade to save
nearby comrades, moreover, has not been an uncommon practice.[57]

The communitarian cast of military morality operates wholly in harmony
here with economic analysis: Both endorse collective sanctions, albeit on
different grounds. In this respect, we find a felicitous confluence of ethical
universes often considered incompatible.[58] Collective monetary sanction of
senior officers for participation in a joint criminal enterprise employs both
logics. It is at once consistent with the corps' internal self-understanding as
a self-monitoring professional community and an efficient external device
for leveraging the solidarity of a tightly knit group to deter wrongdoing by
members. Unlike enterprise participation as used by the ICTY, moreover,
collective sanctions do not require reliance on implausible fictions, such
as that the defendant joined an "enterprise" (of whose boundaries he was
never entirely aware) and that by so doing he actually "committed" the
foreseeable offenses of all other members.

Is it possible, in this way, to make up for motivational deficiencies in
the knave while preserving the healthier ways most officers orient their
professional behavior? Or do disciplinary policies that assume egocentric
motivation necessarily tend to exacerbate the very propensities they decry,
enervating the internal motivation to do good work through preoccupation

[55] Lawyers, too, have such duties to report misconduct. For example, they are required to
report wrongdoing up the ladder in the corporate context, which has created incentives to
avoid acquiring knowledge of such wrongs. Simon, "Wrongs," op. cit., at 45–6.
[56] On this feature of military life, see Osiel, *Obeying Orders*, op. cit., at 212–15, 263–5; see also
Shannon E. French, *The Code of the Warrior: Exploring Warrior Values Past and Present*
1–18 (2003).
[57] Damien Cave, "Missing in Action: The War Heroes," N.Y. Times, Aug. 7, 2005, § 4, at 1.
[58] But see Edward L. Deci, Richard M. Ryan, et al., "A Meta-Analytic Review of Experiments
Examining the Effects of Extrinsic Rewards on Intrinsic Motivation," 125 Psychol. Bulletin
627 (1999); Bruno Frey & Reto Jegen, "Motivation Crowding Theory," 15 J. Econ. Surveys
589 (2001); Ernst Fehr & Armin Falk, "Psychological Foundations of Incentives," 46 Euro.
Econ. Rev. 687 (2002).

with extrinsic rewards and penalties? The spontaneous impulse toward public virtue, however real and sincere, in many professionals and other workers may be doused by the insinuation that one must be constantly monitored to ensure against opportunistic behavior. If treated as clock watchers, they may become so, confirming their superiors' worst suspicions and leading to a vicious cycle of ever closer supervision. A sincere "service ethic" or sense of vocation is essential to genuine professionalism in any field. And those agreeing to give their lives for their country, in particular, should surely not be encouraged to apply their minds too often to considerations of personal self-interest.

But because human motivation is mixed and complex, public policy does not really face an either/or choice here, as if any compensation of soldiers beyond the minimum wage would destroy more disinterested motivations for public service. Even those, like Dan Kahan, who contend that public policy should rely more on the trust-inspiring dynamics of reciprocity, nonetheless concede that these must "be supplemented with appropriately tailored incentives, most likely in the form of penalties aimed specifically at persistent free riders."[59] Almost no one will sacrifice self-interest if he thinks he's being made a chump.[60] When policymakers reify the typologies of social science, public life faces false dichotomies. These should be resisted; it is thus well to recall that Adam Smith first conceived his account of the market's invisible hand in a book on the philosophy of moral sentiments.

The challenge for institutional design is to find ways to foreground and cultivate the sense of social responsibility within individuals, including military officers, while preserving punishment options, kept well in the background, for those who lack more public-spirited impulses. Leading scholars in political theory and the economic analysis of law have given considerable thought to this challenge.[61] To this end, regulators today routinely employ "enforcement pyramids" of increasingly stringent sanctions, for instance, in several policy domains. Their creative application to military professionals points the way for future analysis.

---

[59] Dan Kahan, "The Logic of Reciprocity: Trust, Collective Action, and the Law," 102 Mich. L. Rev. 71, 79 (2003).

[60] Ernst Fehr & Simon Gachter, "Reciprocity and Economics: The Economic Implications of *Homo Reciprocans*," 42 Eur. Econ. Rev. 845 (1998).

[61] Ian Ayres & John Braithwaite, *Responsive Regulation* 19–53 (1992); Geoffrey Brennan & Philip Pettit, *The Economy of Esteem* 260–6 (2004); Philip Petit, "Institutional Design and Rational Choice," in *The Theory of Institutional Design* 67–85 (Robert Goodin, ed., 1996).

11

Being Economical with Amnesty

Amnesties from criminal prosecution for departing dictators and war criminals pose vexing moral dilemmas for transitional societies. These questions normally define the central terms of discussion and debate. Rightly so. But let us briefly consider, as an excursus to this book's central argument, whether the decision to grant such amnesties also might be susceptible to economic analysis.

Trading justice for peace would first appear a congenial object of such analysis, for it resembles the process of plea bargaining that legal economists have long examined. An amnesty from prosecution resembles such bargains in that the departing dictator gives up something of value (i.e., political power, sometimes also the "truth" about his or her crimes) in exchange for freedom from criminal trial. Amnesties are executory contracts. The political faction granting the amnesty (i.e., the new constitutionally empowered leadership) derives the benefit of the bargain immediately – in the fact of the dictator's departure – whereas the value to the dictator himself and his henchmen accrues over time. But given this disparity in the parties' time horizons, the question arises whether any stable state of equilibrium is possible.

Let us begin by considering a modest thought experiment, perhaps proposed by an economist who was politically tone deaf, immune to shifting breezes of moral opinion. This economist might go so far as to propose that some country should offer itself as a permanent place of refuge for departing dictators and their henchmen. The world would thereby rid itself of its worst oppressors, quite efficiently; they would, when the chips are down, welcome the chance to escape justice in their homeland or in The Hague. The designated country of refuge would, in essence, sell the international community a sort of public good, one that others would gladly pay for.

Buyers would include peaceful neighboring countries and rich democracies, perhaps even the departing dictators themselves (i.e., those fearing
overthrow). The freedom-loving people governed by the dictator might
even pool the necessary funds themselves to purchase this service. After
initial qualms perhaps, all such parties would quickly recognize that the
benefits of such a scheme could vastly exceed its costs. If it could get the
incentives right, this approach would significantly facilitate transitions to
democracy throughout the world.

This suggestion is by no means entirely hypothetical. For a time, in fact,
as *The New York Times* observes, "Some countries, like Panama," for the
Western hemisphere, at least, "even specialized in welcoming the autocrats
into their midst. That explains why Raoul Cédras of Haiti and Jorge Serrano
Elías of Guatemala, both of whom have successfully fended off extradition
requests so far, find themselves living comfortably in Panama. So does
Abdalá Bucaram of Ecuador. . . ."[1] France long served a similar function for
much of francophone Africa, and to this day regularly resists extradition of
accused war criminals and *genocidaires* for prosecution in such courts as the
ICTR.[2]

From a utilitarian perspective, the solution of a tolerated haven from
international criminal justice might well be eminently appealing: many
people would be made better off by a nonviolent transition to a new regime,
whereas the few who would be left worse off (i.e., oppression's surviving
victims who desire trials for their tormenters) could readily be compensated
through inexpensive side payments, public monuments to their suffering,
flattering treatment in public school history texts, tax credits for their children's education, other reparations, and similarly creative remedies. The
claims of the dead – that is, the dictator's murdered victims – would not
count in this calculus, of course, because they occupy a realm beyond pain or
pleasure. The defrocked dictators – still very much alive, their utility function thus relevant to the analysis – might even enjoy one another's company,
sharing as they likely do certain temperaments and tastes in luxury goods.

It is worth reflecting for a moment on the fact that this approach would
now strike almost everyone as morally unacceptable, even appalling. It surely
reveals, if nothing else, the extent to which the moral sensibility underlying

---

[1] Simon Romero, "Living in Exile Isn't What it Used to Be," N.Y. Times, Oct. 7, 2007 at 16.
[2] Some suggest that China is now competing aggressively with France for the role of propping
up tottering African dictators (in exchange for privileged access to petroleum resources),
and that the French Foreign Ministry has taken particular umbrage at this incursion
on its longstanding sphere of influence. See http://www.eursoc.com/news/fullstory.php/
aid/1694/The_End_Of_FranceAfrique_.html.

international opinion has shifted on such matters. The shift seems well set-tled, albeit really quite recent. A quiet retreat on the French Riviera (or some equally agreeable locale and clime) was the realistic aspiration of many a doddering despot for decades, after all. That even economists could now propose such a solution only in hushed tones, disclaiming attribution, sug-gests their recognition – or at least their recognition of others' recognition – of utilitarianism's limits in this domain as a defensible guide to action.

That said, a broadly economic approach nonetheless may yield some insight toward understanding the dynamics at play in the policy choice between amnesty and prosecution, a decision faced during all transitions from dictatorship to democracy and often, as well, in war's aftermath.

AMNESTY AS AN INCENTIVE TO ABDICATE

Persuading dictators and their minions to part with power is almost never easy. Their repressive policies are often self-sustaining. Having resorted for so long to sticks, these tools become sunk costs, in an experienced cadre of secret police, for instance. Continued reliance on sticks thereby becomes cheaper than switching to carrots. Even if carrots would have been more efficient earlier on, buying back a modicum of public support, which has been depleted long ago, can be very costly. Victims too may have sunk costs in a traumatic past (i.e., psychic costs they similarly mistake as recoverable through persistence in political resistance to even a liberalizing regime).

This is path dependence at its most perverse. As political resistance to their rule increases, the temptation for autocrats to stay with methods tried and true, ratcheting up repression, is strong.[3] South Africa took this per-ilous path in the early 1980s, for instance. Undeterred by threat of later prosecution, repressive rulers may gamble they will win outright, with no need for compromise – or die gloriously while trying, in a blaze of bullets. The statistics bear them out. In Africa, of those who assumed political office at the national level in recent decades, nearly 60 percent ended up exiled, imprisoned nationally, or murdered.[4] From this fact, some reasonably con-clude that the prospect of international prosecution could add little to deter those bent on mass atrocity, given the risks they have already embraced.[5]

---

[3] On the economic "logic" of such repression, see Gordon Tullock, *Autocracy* 63–5 (1987); Ronald Wintrobe, *The Political Economy of Dictatorship* 127–44 (1998); Adam Przeworski & Jennifer Gandhi, "Cooperation, Cooptation, and Rebellion under Dictatorship," 18 Econ. Theory 1 (2006).

[4] John Wiseman, "Leadership and Personal Danger in African Politics," 31 J. Mod. African Stud. 657 (1993).

[5] Julian Ku & Jide Nzelibe, "Do International Criminal Tribunals Deter or Exacerbate Humanitarian Atrocities?" SSRN Paper Collection (July 2007).

The appetite for risk among nondemocratic leaders is one any theory of regime transition must acknowledge and confront, even if few prudent academicians could begin to fathom it. "Unfortunately, humility and a healthy sense of mortal vulnerability are not common characteristics of despots," as Gray writes. "To feel the force of any deterrent threat they must imagine that their power is limited and that their reign will end – and soon."[6]

The descent into deeper repression has nonetheless sometimes been averted by promises of amnesty from prosecution. An amnesty – whether explicit and legislative, or implicit, through prosecutorial discretion – can facilitate democratic transition and help end civil wars. As a strategy for legitimating a new regime, criminal trials display declining returns, in any event; once those below the top echelons have been granted amnesty, marginal costs to legitimacy from further amnesties to more modest underlings drop quickly.

A careful study of the process in Guatemala shows how symmetrical amnesties enabled "elites to compromise on their most basic disputes and establish informal networks that secured each other's vital interests, thus laying the basis for political stability and a consolidating of democratic governance."[7] Amnesty best achieves its objectives when the carrot it extends, in exchange for confession of vital information (about the location of victims' bodies, for instance), is accompanied by the stick of possible prosecution or the credible threat of material consequences if its beneficiary fails to deliver the *quid pro quo*. Only South Africa has seriously attempted such an approach. This is amnesty without illusions, at its least sentimental, stripped of all appeal to normative ideals of reconciliation, which often harbor woolly theological and other illiberal notions.

Amnesties are not of a piece, cut from the same cloth.[8] The best ones are narrowly tailored to political constraints and seek maximal possible accountability.[9] They form part of a larger set of reforms, enacted (or at least executively decreed) after public debate, designed to alter military and police training in ways that integrate human rights standards. High-ranking

[6] David Gray, "An Excuse-Centered Approach to Transitional Justice," 74 Fordham L. Rev. 2621, 2676 (2006).

[7] Rachel M. McCleary, *Dictating Democracy: Guatemala and the End of Violent Revolution* 3 (1999).

[8] William Burke-White, "Reframing Impunity: Applying Liberal International Law Theory to an Analysis of Amnesty Legislation," 42 Harv. Int'l L.J. 467, 518–33 (2001).

[9] On how amnesties may be tailored to this end, see Ronald C. Slye, "The Legitimacy of Amnesties under International Law and General Principles of Anglo-American Law: Is a Legitimate Amnesty Possible?" 43 Va. J. Int'l L. 173 (2002).

military leaders linked to rights abuse must be discharged, as in South Africa, if they cannot be prosecuted.

Continued amnesty is conditioned on the effective implementation of such reforms. Otherwise, it legally may be revoked. The Colombian Congress made such revocability a prominent feature of its legislation aimed at inducing paramilitary and leftist guerrilla leaders to lay down their arms and disgorge the drug-trafficking profits.[10] When such leaders refused to honor these conditions, they were extradited to the United States for prosecution. Such conditionality is essential in getting the incentives right, in holding still-powerful criminals to the terms of their bargain. When the Colombian right-wing paramilitary leaders refused to honor statutory terms requiring them to disgorge unlawful profits and cease drug trafficking, they were indeed extradited to the United States for prosecution.[11]

A possible problem with making amnesty revocable, on condition of implementing promised reforms, is that those initially benefiting from the deal are generally not the same people who are later in a position to honor reform promises. Such promises may be made lightly by those who know they will not be around to pay the price of implementing them. The new rulers who replace departing dictators, moreover, may not necessarily feel any obligation to honor their predecessors' commitments in this regard, even when they have hitherto been close allies. The decision to grant amnesty is a "time-inconsistent commitment," in game theory terms: it is a perfectly rational decision to make at the time, but not to keep long thereafter.

Departing rulers have sometimes, as in Poland,[12] had the prescience to take along copies of files inculpating (as collaborators) those about to take power. This tactic effectively holds the new rulers hostage, enhancing the credibility of their promises not to prosecute predecessors. But this tactic is often impossible. Promises of impunity nonetheless gain credibility if the old regime's judiciary and prosecutorial staff, implicated in its abuses, are not entirely dislodged in the regime transition. Usually, they are not. Also important in discouraging immediate and broad prosecution, especially in central and eastern Europe after Communism's demise, has been the secret complicity of prominent dissidents during the *ancièn regime*. The implicit

---

[10] The statute as ultimately enacted, however, accorded much less weight to conditioning benefits on demonstrated performance. Human Rights Watch, *Smoke and Mirrors: Colombia's Demobilization of Paramilitary Groups* 1, 27 (2005) (criticizing this feature of the legislation).

[11] Juan Forero, "Colombia Sends 13 Paramilitary Leaders to U.S.," Wash. Post, May 14, 2008, at A11.

[12] Jon Elster, *Closing the Books: Transitional Justice in Historical Perspective* 195 (2004).

threat to disclose the records of such complicity sometimes enables departing criminal leaders – the only people who know the extent of dissident
collaboration – to resist prosecution for a considerable time after leaving
power.[13]

These domestic machinations make it hard to strike an amnesty pact that
is morally acceptable to outsiders, and hence likely to be fully respected by
international or foreign courts. But again, the risks may well be ones that
departing power holders are prepared to take, when more appealing options
are lacking. If an amnesty deal can be struck on such terms, then a later
"failure" to enforce its reform requirements would not present an entirely
negative scenario from the perspective of human rights and criminal law.
Failure to reform would, after all, effectively invalidate the prior amnesty,
revoking its immunities and permitting prior rulers to be prosecuted.

Legal scholarship purporting to show that amnesties fail to advance peace
and reconciliation tend to practice the most flagrant selection bias.[14] Countries whose relevant experience of transition does not support the author's
favored position on this question (such as Spain, El Salvador, and several
others) are simply ignored, like inconvenient cases that an opposing advocate can be expected to call to the court's attention. Such methods should
be no more acceptable in serious legal scholarship than in social science, in
which the main point is precisely to compel our confrontation with "inconvenient facts."[15] Limiting examples to the Americas, for instance, one may
observe that in Haiti and Venezuela the human rights situation deterio-
rated significantly after and despite criminal trials, whereas Brazil saw the
region's deepest drop in human rights abuse in these years, despite failing
to prosecute any rights abuse from military rule.

That amnesty is often necessary for successful transition is not to say that
it is sufficient, by any means. Angola, for instance, has seen six amnesties
granted as part of the continuing peace process there. None had any discernible effect in ending the civil war. "Each has served as little more than

---

[13] Monica Nalepa, "Skeletons in the Closet: A Dynamic Model of Regime Transitions,"
working paper, 2008.
[14] Leila N. Sadat, "Exile, Amnesty, and International Law," 81 Notre Dame L. Rev. 955, 966
(2006) (invoking only three countries – Haiti, Sierra Leone, and the former Yugoslavia –
and no social scientific data for the proposition that "longitudinal studies . . . suggest that
amnesty deals typically foster a culture of impunity in which violence becomes the norm,
rather than the exception").
[15] Max Weber, "Science as a Vocation," in *From Max Weber*, 129, 147 (H. H. Gerth & C. Wright
Mills, eds.) ("The primary task of a useful teacher is to teach his students to recognize
'inconvenient' facts – I mean facts that are inconvenient for their party opinions.").

an invitation to further bloodshed and atrocities," claims one expert.[16] In Sierra Leone, the attempt to neutralize warlord Foday Sankoh by granting amnesty and incorporating him into state rule not only failed but also endowed him with renewed resources that facilitated his re-initiation of the war.[17]

Amnesty often fails when not accompanied by a power transfer to new leaders who are genuinely committed to human rights. It is not always easy to assess their *bona fides* in this regard *ex ante*, as the case of Haiti reveals.[18] New democratic rulers may quickly prove no less corrupt or criminally inclined than their undemocratic predecessors. Although amnesties eliminate or defer the possibility of mass prosecution, other noncriminal remedies, such as truth commissions, civil compensation, and more informal mechanisms of restorative justice (such as apology and forgiveness as means of interpersonal reconciliation) among neighbors, often suffice for most purposes, at least in the short term.[19]

Monetary settlements are particularly appealing in allowing a degree of compromise through "splitting the difference," which criminal liability for serious wrong does not. Civil claims also appear to "depoliticize" the wrongs – as allegations of genocide, for instance, obviously do not – in ways that can help reestablish social equilibria. But in the aftermath of mass atrocity, few countries can afford such generous compensation schemes as those by the Republic of South Africa. To a degree little recognized, amnesty from criminal prosecution remains controversial because monetary compensation through civil recovery (for wrongful death, battery, infliction of distress, etc.) is virtually unavailable in most countries in which mass atrocity occurs. If civil litigation were to make such remedies practically accessible, the domestic pressures that may exist for prosecution would much diminish, because victims would often be content with (even prefer)

---

[16] Mary Margaret Penrose, "It's Good to Be the King!: Prosecuting Heads of State and Former Heads of State under International Law," 39 Colum. J. Transnat'l L. 193, 204–6 (2000).

[17] Bronwyn Leebaw, "Transitional Justice, Conflict, and Democratic Change: International Interventions and Domestic Reconciliation," 12 (unpublished paper), September 2005.

[18] David Gonzalez, "Aristide of Haiti: Pragmatist or Demagogue?," N.Y. Times, Dec. 31, 2002, at A3; Human Rights Watch, "Aristide Should Uphold the Law," Human Rights News, Feb. 14, 2004. On the failure of amnesty to end human rights abuse in Haiti, see Sadat, op. cit., at 991–2.

[19] Concerning the last of these alternatives (or supplements) to prosecution, the considerable literature (at the domestic level) includes Andrew Rigby, *Justice and Reconciliation* (2001); Heather Strang, *Repair or Revenge: Victims and Restorative Justice* (2002); and Declan Roche, *Accountability in Restorative Justice* (2003).

financial redress.[20] Philosophers of a deontological stripe may regard the relevant goods as "incommensurable," but that has not deterred many victims from accepting the swap. Their relative contentment should make it more difficult in turn for international human rights organizations (and foreign or international courts) to obstruct such mutually beneficial bargains between victims and victimizers at the national level. The moral intuition here is simply that those not in immediate privity with the contract's parties should not intermeddle, interfering with its execution. This remains the case even if privity of contract does exist between the state conferring amnesty and the international community whose treaties often preclude it.

Even so, to reform a country's civil justice system, in order to afford better financial compensation, is much more difficult than initiating a few criminal prosecutions. Only in wealthier countries, such as South Africa and Argentina, is civil compensation playing a major role in redressing the legacies of mass atrocity and other state-sponsored violence. South Africa has distributed more than $100 million, through its Truth and Reconciliation Commission, to twenty-thousand of apartheid's immediate victims.[21]

Such compensation does not eliminate the objections raised from the perspective of international criminal and human rights law, however. The Inter-American Human Rights Commission, for instance, has repeatedly ruled that such compensation programs do not meet the duty of member states, under the American Convention, to investigate and prosecute abuses of basic human rights.[22] International human rights advocates often speak – publicly, at least – as if tough trade-offs were never necessary. But experience

---

[20] Klauss Boers & Klaus Sessar, "Do People Really Want Punishment?" in *Developments in Crime and Crime Control Research* 126, 130 (K. Sessar & H. J. Kerner, eds., 1991) (concluding that for more than half of the types of crimes considered, victims were willing to accept private settlement, and only in the case of rape did more than half of respondents demand punishment, regardless of restitution); cf. Metin Başoğlu et al., "Psychiatric and Cognitive Effects of War in Former Yugoslavia," 294 J. Amer. Med. Ass. 580, 580 (2005) (finding the incidence of depression and posttraumatic stress syndrome to be "independent of their sense of injustice arising from perceived lack of redress from [war-related] trauma").
  On the other hand, virtually all legal systems concur that the most grievous wrongs are not fully susceptible to redress by monetary compensation. It is noteworthy that the most extensive system of compensation for mass atrocity, that of West Germany to the State of Israel and to individual Jewish claimants, was expressly justified as a supplement to the criminal prosecution of top Nazi leaders, not as a substitute.
[21] Truth and Reconciliation Commission of South Africa, *Truth and Reconciliation Commission of South Africa Report* (2003), at http://www.info.gov.za.
[22] Richard J. Wilson & Jan Perlin, "The Inter-American Human Rights System: Activities from Late 2000 through October 2002," 18 Am. U. Int'l L. Rev. 651 (2003) (summarizing compensation cases in Peru, Uruguay, Honduras, Argentina, El Salvador, and Chile).

suggests that, as criminal indictments threaten to reach further into society, inclinations to defend oneself (and one's allies) by justifying past conduct come naturally to the fore, undermining more conciliatory impulses that are taking root.

As long as new rulers are democratic, their decisions about whom to prosecute and not prosecute soon will be tested against public opinion in the electoral marketplace. A democratic public may reasonably conclude – in the aftermath of bloody civil strife, often with atrocities by both sides – that preserving new constitutional institutions and public order is more important in the short term than prosecuting all such criminals to the limits of the law. Several democratic transitions have taken this path.

This legal resolution of the predicament is particularly compelling when it is easy for many youthful contemporaries to comprehend, at least in retrospect, how so many people of good will could once have come to sign on to either side in the conflict, imagining the country's undoubted troubles to be soluble only through – fill in the blank – revolution or counter-revolution.[23]

BASES OF PUBLIC SUPPORT FOR AMNESTY

No democratic society in human history has yet successfully resisted a violent revolutionary movement, enjoying nontrivial social support, by means wholly consistent with the rule of law. Such resistance may have been possible, to be sure, in ways that simply were not apparent to historical parties, even those acting in good conscience, in the past. But the possibility remains an open question, empirically speaking.[24] Even the well-established democracies of western Europe, notably Germany and Spain, departed notably from due process and other human rights norms when fighting well-armed terrorist groups in recent decades.[25] Public opinion there did not later demand criminal prosecution of the state officials who authorized such

---

[23] Author's interviews with human rights lawyers, social scientists, legal scholars, and journalists in Bogota in November 2004 suggest that this is probably the case in contemporary Colombia.

[24] Serious methodological problems arise, to be sure, in explaining why an anticipated event or activity did not transpire, despite historical conditions suggesting a high probability that it would occur. James Mahoney & Gary Goertz, "The Possibility Principle: Choosing Negative Cases in Comparative Research," 98 Am. Pol. Sci. Rev. 653, 666–8 (2004).

[25] Craig Whitney, "Death Squad Killings of Basques: Was Spain's Government the Mastermind?" N.Y. Times, Feb. 12, 1997, at A10; Paddy Wordsworth, *Dirty War, Clean Hands: ETA, the GAL and Spanish Democracy* 407–18 (2001); Antonio Vercher, *Terrorism in Europe: An International Comparative Legal Analysis* 231–3, 245–6, 389–90 (1992).

departures. Impunity for serious state criminality is thus not uncommon even in the most impeccably democratic societies.

The disinclination to punish should scarcely be surprising, especially in countries in which the rule of law is less thoroughly established. Many people in weak democracies, facing armed revolutionary insurgencies, have clearly been willing to indulge extralegal methods to combat what they perceive as genuine threats to public order, to the security of their lives and property, and to their understanding of a decent society. It bears emphasis here that such threat perception is no mere figment of the reactionary imagination. The situation in Allende's Chile immediately preceding the military coup, for instance, was one of extreme instability and social disorder. It was celebrated as such at the time by the international left as a "revolutionary situation," foreshadowing more radical change.[26]

The willingness to see public order restored by unlawful means is similarly reflected in the enthusiasm with which military coups against democratic rulers – when those rulers are widely perceived as corrupt or incompetent – are often greeted throughout the world. In Pakistan, Gen. Perez Musharraf's coup, according to *The New York Times*, "was overwhelmingly popular in a nation weary of corrupt and incompetent politicians . . . even among the most outspoken liberals." One such newspaper editor in Islamabad observed, "What happens in these situations is that when the bad guys get thrown out, whoever throws them out looks like good guys."[27] Repressive regimes can be popular even in their repressiveness and at their most aggressive. Recent research on the Third Reich concludes, for instance, that "the persecution of social outsiders between 1933 and 1939 won more support for Hitler's regime than it lost, and that the early successes of the Second World War turned Hitler into Germany's most popular leader of all time."[28]

Public indulgence is still stronger where political repression proves to be mild or simply confined to the regime's active foes[29] and where new economic policies are successful, improving the material condition of most

---

[26] See, generally, Henry Landsberger & Timothy McDaniel, "Hypermobilization in Chile, 1970–1973," 28 World Pol. 502 (1983); Mark Ensalaco, *Chile under Pinochet* 1, 8–17 (2000); Tomas Moulin, *Chile Actual: Autonomía de un Mito* 97 (1997) (celebrating "the headlong rush that arose from plebeian protagonism, the behavior of the masses who took seriously their role as historical actors and who . . . acted with autonomy," creating for Allende "the difficulty of containing the movement once it had set itself loose").

[27] Tim Weiner & Steve LeVine, "Pakistan's Ruler Pledges to Curb Corruption," N.Y. Times, Oct. 16, 1999, at A1.

[28] Robert Gellately & Ben Kiernan, "The Study of Mass Murder and Genocide," in *The Spector of Genocide* 3, 11 (Gellately & Ben Kiernan, eds., 2003).

[29] Scott Mainwaring et al., *Issues in Democratic Consolidation* 26, 32 (1992).

citizens.[30] Chile under Pinochet is the clearest recent case.[31] Despite directing a regime that murdered more than three-thousand political opponents and tortured some twenty-eight thousand more, Pinochet enjoyed sufficient popularity that an opinion poll, conducted two months after his return from London in 2000, revealed that more than 40 percent of Chileans did not endorse the view that he was "guilty of human rights violations."[32] In late 2005, polls indicated that only a small minority of Chileans believed bringing him to trial should be a public priority.[33]

Even truly totalitarian regimes like Stalin's Russia and Hitler's Reich have enjoyed vast networks of sympathetic collaborators, numbering in the tens of thousands, people with much to fear from later opening of public files.[34] Insofar as its data may be trusted, the Soviet bloc – even at its most repressive – generated consistently higher growth rates than most capitalist societies, on average, from 1929 to the mid-1970s. It may be no coincidence that there was no mass demand for prosecution of Soviet-era crimes against humanity after Communism's collapse there.

Those disfavoring criminal trials are not confined, moreover, to the "landed oligarchy" or "big business," and they often comprise a very substantial portion of public opinion. "Polls show that today many Latin Americans would back a heavy-handed government if it proved able to resolve their countries' problems," writes one specialist in the region.[35] During an ensuing democratic transition, these people either continue to endorse what dictators did, regardless of its admitted illegality, or recognize their own complicity in now-acknowledged wrongs. If the latter, then to absolve and forgive prior criminal rulers is to absolve and forgive oneself – always tempting and hardly limited to transitional polities. Either way, for either reason, such people support amnesty.[36]

Their views find no expression in respectable scholarly journals of the developed world, of course. But in countries like Argentina, for instance,

---

[30] Gur Ofer, "Soviet Economic Growth, 1928–1985," 25 J. Econ. Lit. 1767, 1781 (1987).

[31] On the relative success of Pinochet's economic policies, especially relative to those of comparable South American countries in this period, see Juan Gabriel Valdés, *Pinochet's Economists: The Chicago School in Chile* 267 (1995).

[32] Naomi Roht-Arriaza, *The Pinochet Effect* 79 (2005).

[33] BBC News, "General Pinochet's Dance with Justice" (Dec. 2005); see also Edmundo Fuenzalida Faivovich, "Law and Culture in Chile, 1974–1999," in *Legal Culture in the Age of Globalization* 130 (Lawrence Friedman & Rogelio Perez-Perdomo, eds., 2003) (observing "the nationalistic reaction of many Chileans who saw in these actions of both Spanish and British judges a violation of Chilean national sovereignty").

[34] Richard Overy, *The Dictators: Hitler's Germany, Stalin's Russia* 304–48 (2004).

[35] Frances Hagopian, "What Makes Democracies Collapse?" 15 J. Democracy 166, 168 (2004).

[36] *Id.*

convicted torturers have no compunction about publishing well-selling books defending their crimes, and such views continue to generate considerable support in the public debate that ensues.[37] As one observer notes of both Argentina and Chile, "The contention that threats of chaos and communism had justified the suspension of democratic institutions remained a defensible position within the new public discourse – in other words, repudiating such a position was not considered a necessary condition for seeking to reconcile with the people holding the opposite position, namely that a coup against a democratic regime is never justified."[38]

Public opinion is assuredly fickle. Many will forget their own prior acquiescence in state criminality, as in Argentina, where opinion surveys during military rule suggested that middle-class informants endorsed unlawful methods in resisting leftist guerrilla groups.[39] Even so, when public sentiment shifts, voters may conclude that their first, unseasoned representatives employed amnesty to purchase short-term stability for their country at too high a price in retributive justice. They may punish such officials by voting into office others who will accord such justice higher priority and pursue it with greater gusto.

The choice between justice and stability may not be one, however, to which abstract thinking about regime transition can convincingly lay any claim to speak. "In a given transition," write two major theorists, "the specific functions of punishment and amnesty must be compared; the relative priority between the two cannot be theoretically established."[40] Still, it is wrong to imply that every case is irreducibly *sui generis*. On closer examination, as national experiences of transitional justice begin to accumulate, patterns begin to emerge, suggesting what does and does not work, under this or that circumstance.

REVOKING AMNESTY

Its aims attained, an amnesty may later be overturned by national courts as unconstitutional or by regional ones as inconsistent with the country's treaty obligations. Several Latin American states have followed this path in recent years, allowing additional prosecutions decades after the wrongs,

[37] Miguel O. Etchecolatz, *La Otra Campana del "Nunca Mas"* (2003).

[38] Michael Feher, "Terms of Reconciliation," in *Human Rights in Political Transitions* 325, 333–4 (Carla Hesse & Robert Post, eds., 1999).

[39] Guillermo O'Donnell, *Y a Mí, Que Me Importa: Notas Sobre Sociabilidad y Política en Argentina y Brasil* 23 (1984).

[40] Carla Hesse & Robert Post, "Introduction," in *Human Rights in Political Transitions*, op. cit., at 13, 18.

when political circumstances eventually permitted. The Inter-American Commission and Court of Human Rights have repeatedly held that national legislation precluding judicial investigation into the identity of offenders or the location of victims' bodies violates the Inter-American Convention on Human Rights.[41] The most recent Supreme Court to overturn such an amnesty, on these grounds, is Argentina's.[42]

A revocable amnesty works like the familiar rules on statutes of limitations, only in reverse.[43] A standard statute of limitations allows prosecution in the present, but cuts off the possibility after a period of some years. Conversely, a revocable amnesty bars prosecution in the present, but authorizes it potentially in the future, if the conditions of amnesty's concession are dishonored by its beneficiaries (or in the event of other contingencies).

If ordinary statutes of limitations permit, a tacit amnesty – not enacted by legislation or executive decree – may be overturned simply by a later decision to prosecute. This occurred, for instance, in Poland and Germany during the early 1990s, as well as in Greece in 1975. Passage of time is no obstacle to much-delayed prosecution for genocide and crimes against humanity, which carry no temporal prescription in international law.

To be sure, the salubrious effect of amnesty on regime transition will likely decline insofar as potential defendants may anticipate that promises of impunity will not be honored. The dictator's incentive to jump ship will thereby be undermined. An economic model of "trading justice for peace" works only as long as some state of relative equilibrium may be obtained through such an exchange, even if the terms of the deal may gradually obsolesce over time.

The doctrine of universal jurisdiction, permitting foreign prosecution for the most grievous international crimes, much increases the number of states that may choose to disregard national amnesty legislation. This fact may greatly reduce the bargaining value of such legislation to new constitutional rulers. But because universal jurisdiction has been exercised only quite sporadically and many amnesty recipients may have no better options on offer, the deal may still prove appealing, notwithstanding the indeterminacy of its temporal scope.[44] Gains in short-term protection often may outweigh

---

[41] Wilson & Perlin, op. cit., at 651.

[42] Corte Suprema de Justicia, 5/5/2005, causa no. 17.768, "Julió Héctor Simon y otros (privación ilegítima de la libertad, etc.)"; Fannie Lafontaine, "No Amnesty or Statute of Limitation for Enforced Disappearance: The Sandoval Case before the Chilean Supreme Court," 3 J. Int'l Crim. Just. 469 (2005).

[43] Ronald Slye, "The Cambodian Amnesties: Beneficiaries and the Temporal Reach of Amnesties for Gross Violations of Human Rights," 22 Wisc. J. Int'l L. 99, 119 (2004).

[44] I owe this observation to a reviewer of the present chapter for the *Journal of Legal Studies*.

such long-term uncertainties in the immediate calculations of a transition's potential "spoilers."[45] Evidence suggests that they often gamble that retributive passions will subside over time. This bet has usually proven correct.[46]

To make this observation is not, as David Luban accuses, to "demean the legitimacy of the yearning for justice by removing it from the space of reasons,"[47] but simply to observe a salient empirical datum, one of considerable relevance to any bargaining strategy and the political practice of transitional justice. In any event, retributive passions do not always recede so neatly with the years.[48] The dictator's assumption that they will do so may also reflect a measure of "optimism bias,"[49] a cognitive distortion to which powerful people are particularly prone. (This bias may admittedly be countered by the pervasive paranoia about their personal security that dictators often inevitably display.)

That amnesty may be successfully challenged in the courts, or reversed by legislation, is a risk with high costs but low probability.[50] Pacted transitions – negotiated respectfully rather than imposed unilaterally by the regime's democratic opponents – tend to lock in institutional constraints to change on human rights accountability that require years to overcome. The declining demand for criminal justice over time might suggest that such demand is better understood as "a situated passion" than as a self-sustaining "universal ideal."[51] But such pessimism stands strikingly at odds with the recurrent "eruptions of memory" in countries like Chile and Argentina, where demand for prosecution powerfully reemerged some thirty years after the wrongs.[52]

---

[45] Jack Snyder & Leslie Vinjamuri, "Trials and Errors: Principle and Pragmatism in Strategies of International Justice," 28 Int'l Sec. 18, 33–4, 43–4 (2004) (noting the central role of such spoilers and the consequent likelihood of amnesty following most cases of mass atrocity).

[46] Elster, op. cit., at 228–9 (describing, for several transitional societies, the "spontaneous decay of emotion, and abatement of the desire for retribution once it has been satisfied for some wrongdoers"). In postwar France, for instance, sentences of Nazi collaborators became more lenient over time. See Peter Novick, *The Resistance versus Vichy: The Purge of Collaborators in Liberated France* 161–7, 187–90 (1968); Snyder & Vinjamuri, op. cit., at 33–9 (describing enduring bargains with potential spoilers in several countries that contributed to success in the peaceful settlement of lengthy civil wars).

[47] David Luban, "review of Elster, *Closing the Books*," 116 Ethics 411, 412 (2006).

[48] Alexander Wilde, "Irruptions of Memory: Expressive Politics in Chile's Transition to Democracy," in *Genocide, Collective Violence, and Popular Memory* 3 (David Lorey & William Beezley, eds., 2002).

[49] On this frequent source of misperception, see Neil Weinstein, "Unrealistic Optimism about Future Life Events," 39 J. Personality & Soc. Psychol. 806 (1980).

[50] This "risk" is technically an "uncertainty," in that statistical probabilities cannot meaningfully be attached. Frank Knight, *Risk, Uncertainty, and Profit* 19–21, 259 (1964).

[51] Stephen Holmes, "Why International Justice Limps," 69 Soc. Res. 1055, 1066 (2002).

[52] Wilde, op. cit., at, 3.

Just how credible must the promise of impunity be for it to induce spoilers to leave office? It need not be indubitably enforceable, in the long term, to accomplish its short-term purpose. If spoilers perceive a serious risk of displacement in any event, even if they do not leave willingly, then they will surely seize a promise of nonprosecution with little hesitation. In the uncertainty of a regime transition, this is often the situation faced by the rulers' immediate underlings – among senior officers and civilian administrators – who may already face prosecution. In short, better to jump than be pushed, especially if doing so means one will not have nearly so far to fall.

Such pacts between old and new rulers are made in times that are obviously transitional. It is therefore predictable that the bargains they strike may obsolesce.[53] An effective democratic transition almost necessarily reallocates power in ways likely to call the terms of the initial deal into question later on, when former rulers and their allies no longer occupy prominent positions that enable them to obstruct change. Multinational corporations have long learned to expect their bargains to obsolesce in this way. Departing dictators and their minions accept a similar risk and bargain around it as best they can.[54]

AMNESTY AND INTERNATIONAL LAW

Are amnesties consistent with international law? Treaty law sends mixed signals; there is a duty to prosecute genocide and torture, as well as war crimes in international conflicts. But there is no treaty requiring prosecution of war crimes or crimes against humanity in civil wars. And in recent decades, most wars, producing most atrocities, have taken place largely within a single state. The ICC Rome Statute does not prohibit amnesties and even seems to contemplate them, some contend.

What about customary international law? Accompanied by truth commissions of varying seriousness, amnesty is by far the single most common legal response by states to mass atrocity, numerically dwarfing the few that prosecute perpetrators criminally.[55] Because many of these amnesties have

---

[53] Raymond Vernon, *Sovereignty at Bay* 46–59 (1971) (introducing the now-influential theory of obsolescing bargains between multinational corporations and host countries, according to which contracts initially favorable to foreign companies often tend to be renegotiated as host countries take "hostage" the plant facility and other sunk costs).

[54] On how former dictators later view their departures from power, see Riccardo Orizio, *Talk of the Devil: Encounters with Seven Dictators* (2003).

[55] Countries that have accorded amnesty in recent years for abusers of human rights and humanitarian law include *inter alia* Peru, Chile, Argentina, Honduras, Guatemala,

been granted by states in Africa, one might respond that this state practice therefore makes custom only for fellow Africans. But that interpretation would effectively disenfranchise this entire continent from any influence over the making of broader customary law.

In a word, then, amnesty plus (highly varying degrees of) truth largely defines state practice – massively and pervasively, throughout the world. We prefer to lavish scholarly attention on emergent tendencies to the contrary, but cannot deny that even recent cases often confirm older, less laudatory practice, such as the short-lived Nigerian exile accorded former Liberian president Charles Taylor and the refuge given former Haitian president Jean Bertrand Aristide by the Central African Republic and, briefly, South Africa.[56] In 2003, the United States also offered Saddam Hussein permanent exile in Bahrain, in lieu of the invasion and criminal prosecution he then suffered.

States bestowing amnesties to facilitate democratic transition or end civil wars[57] clearly do not view themselves as legally obliged to adopt this policy. But they perceive themselves as permitted to do so.[58] In publicly defending their amnesties, states do not describe them as knowing violations of their international legal obligations, granted only in grudging recognition of

El Salvador, Nicaragua, Uruguay, Colombia, Sierra Leone, Mozambique, Macedonia, Namibia, Bangladesh, Ivory Coast, Liberia, Northern Ireland, Spain, Afghanistan, Brazil, Cambodia, Haiti, Iraq, and Angola. Most such amnesties have been *de jure*; a few – such as Guatemala, Namibia, and Spain – only *de facto*.

[56] The circumstances of both exiles are described in Sadat, op. cit., at 957, 1031.

[57] For four recent efforts of the latter sort, see Carlotta Gall, "Top Suspects in Afghanistan Are Included in Amnesty," N.Y. Times, May 10, 2005, at A7 ("The head of Afghanistan's peace and reconciliation commission offered an amnesty . . . for all rebels fighting American and government forces, and even extended the offer to two of the most wanted Afghan terrorism suspects: the Taliban leader Mullah Muhammad Omar and the renegade warlord Gulbuddin Hekmatyar."); Juan Forero, "New Colombia Law Grants Concessions to Paramilitaries," N.Y. Times, June 23, 2005, at A3 (describing enactment granting immunity from extradition to the United States for leaders of the country's largest paramilitary group, in exchange for public confession of drug trafficking, disarmament, and promises to dissolve their organization); Michael Ware, "Talking with the Enemy: Inside the Secret Dialogue between the U.S. and Insurgents in Iraq," *Time*, February 28, 2005, at 26 (reporting that the United States was secretly negotiating with Sunni insurgents for an agreement whereby they would abandon arms in exchange for amnesty from prosecution). *See also* "World This Week," *Economist* (U.S. edition), March 19, 2005, at 8 ("A Ugandan delegation begged the ICC not to indict the leaders of the Lord's Resistance Army, a Uganda rebel group, that often tortures children" because "Ugandans worry that the threat of prosecution would scupper efforts to end the civil war by offering amnesty to those who surrender.").

[58] This is sufficient to constitute their *opinio juris*, according to many views of customary international law. See, e.g., Robert Kolb, "Selected Problems in the Theory of Customary International Law," So Netherlands Int'l L. Rev. 119, 121–2, 138 (2003) (discussing several scholars who hold such views).

234 Making Sense of Mass Atrocity

political constraints.[59] Rather, they defend their amnesties as presenting a welcome opportunity for the country to turn a new leaf and to embrace international human rights prospectively.[60]

Still less do neighboring countries condemn such states for violating international legal duties.[61] To the contrary, they often rejoice at the reduced risk of refugee flows into their own territory presented by peace accords in the neighboring state, which is often emerging from civil war. This rejoicing too is pertinent state practice.[62] The international community, such as it is, does prefer that postconflict states embrace the goals of "transitional justice," to be sure, along with its now-settled script of legal and institutional reforms. But a rather formalistic compliance with this script at home has sufficed for renewed legitimacy abroad; hence also for foreign trade, aid, and investment. To date, international incentives for transitional justice of a more demanding sort are quite weak. In short, then, customary international law continues to authorize amnesty, when accompanied by truth, as an acceptable national response to mass atrocity, at least where this path appears necessary to end civil war or consolidate a genuine democratic transition.[63]

As John Dugard writes,

> A general duty to prosecute international crimes under international law is not supported by state practice. On the contrary modern history is replete with examples of cases in which successor regimes have granted amnesty to officials of the previous regime guilty of torture and crimes against human-ity, rather than prosecute them. In many of these cases, notably that of

---

[59] They may say this privately, to be sure. But what public officials might privately say, when contradicting their public proclamations, has never been regarded as relevant to their state's *opinio juris* under any respectable theory of customary international law.

[60] See e.g., Agreement Reached in Multi-Party Negotiations pmbl., U.K.- N. Ir.-Ir., April 10, 1998 (the "Good Friday Agreement" agreeing to resolve much of the longstanding military conflict in Northern Ireland).

[61] Thomas Franck, "Interpretation and Change in the Law of Humanitarian Intervention," in *Humanitarian Intervention* 204 (J. L. Holzgrefe & Robert O. Keohane, eds., 2003) (arguing that one state's acceptance of the legality of another's conduct may be inferred from the first's silence about or noncriticism of such conduct).

[62] Kolb, op. cit., at 139.

[63] The near-universal acceptance of South Africa's Truth and Reconciliation Commission by the international community is evidence of this consensus. The suggestion by the Special Court for Sierra Leone, in *Prosecutor v. Morris Kallon*, Case Nos. SCSL-2004–15-AR72(E), Decision on Challenge to Jurisdiction: Lomé Accord Amnesty (March 13, 2004), that cus-tomary international law now prohibits amnesty may thus fairly be described as "absurd." Prof. William Schabas, correspondence with author. The International Committee of the Red Cross has assembled the doctrinal evidence of state practice, in its volume, *Customary International Law*, vol. 1: Rules 4017–4044 (2005). The book makes no effort to analyze the assembled materials, however, much less discern patterns within them.

South Africa, the United Nations has welcomed such a solution. The decisions of national courts likewise give no support to the duty to prosecute.[64]

That this fact is almost nowhere acknowledged in the enormous legal literature on the subject of amnesty for mass atrocities simply attests to its near-complete monopolization by those favoring prosecution. In practice, however, as international relations "realists" would predict, treaty law – with its frequent duty to prosecute or extradite – has nonetheless cast only the smallest shadow over most amnesty negotiations. We ignore this palpable fact only at great peril to any understanding of international criminal law that aspires to some purchase on social reality (i.e., as an enterprise existing outside the professorial echo chamber).

The rationale of those resisting this conclusion seems to be that because Article 38 of the Statute of the International Court of Justice treats "respected jurists" as formal "sources" of international law, it follows that for us to admit that state practice flagrantly departs from treaty law *ipso facto* weakens the claim that there is a duty to prosecute. In other words, by denying the reality of state practice, we – as potentially countervailing sources of law – move the law in the desired direction. Through a virtuous circle of self-fulfilling prophecy, if we insist – often and vigorously enough – that X *is* true, then X will eventually *become* true. This is a misconstrued constructivism run amok; to describe its adherents as succumbing to a brief bout of megalomania would be charitable.

From an economic perspective, the precommitment to prosecute – grounded in treaty – is perhaps then best viewed not primarily as a normative duty as such, but as a bargaining chip in the hands of opposition leaders, who are seeking to ease autocrats from office on favorable terms. Treaty obligations become politically salient only because of what they imply about costs the country may suffer if it dishonors these commitments, thereby eliciting international disapproval. To date, however, such costs have been minor and not borne by those who incurred them on the state's behalf. Thus, the leverage that opposition leadership can bring to bear in invoking such speculative future costs, when negotiating regime transition, remains slight.

[64] John Dugard, "Possible Conflicts of Jurisdiction with Truth Commissions," in *The Rome Statue of the International Criminal Court: A Commentary* 693, 698 (Antonio Cassese et al., eds., 2002). See also Penrose, at 204–5 (concluding that "state practice for prosecution of international crimes based on torture, genocide, and other similarly heinous crimes is practically non-existent" and thus "honest scholarship requires an admission that the Pinochet precedent cuts against existing state practice").

Some African leaders already have used threat of prosecution by the ICC to lure domestic insurgents to the bargaining table, offering nonextradition in exchange for a laying down of arms and an agreement to peace accords. This approach is not among the incentive effects that the ICC's drafters had imagined, to be sure. But it might nonetheless prove salubrious for certain war-torn societies whose denizens value peace over the possibility of criminal justice abroad.

Many legal scholars tend wishfully to assume that the process of democratic transition can be unilinear: it must begin at one point and it ends at another, the latter established by international law and both known in advance.[65] Under the beneficent influence of the international community and its law, dictatorships – guilty of human rights abuse – transform themselves into democracies respecting the rule of law. Civil wars, producing war crime and genocide, end in legal agreements producing peace. Departures from these acceptable paths become "reversals."

Because amnesty deviates from the path of "accountability" increasingly mandated by treaty, it falls outside the circle of acceptable possibilities, even provisional and temporary ones, that transitional societies may legitimately employ. Legal scholarship here risks an error very similar to that made by "modernization theory" a generation before in holding that – through increased economic and political integration – Western nation-building will be replicated throughout the non-Western world.[66] One might dignify this sort of thinking by calling it teleological, but a less portentous term is wishful thinking.

The evidence from scholarship in comparative politics suggests that it is better to understand such developments not as detours off a single transitional highway, but as manifesting a wider array of empirical possibilities, conceptualized more complexly. These possibilities would reflect how countries vary considerably in both their points of departure and destination. In fact, democratic transitions sometimes lead, in the short run,

---

[65] In this respect, such legal scholarship resembles the more overtly policy-oriented writing on democratic transition, produced by professed experts selling their services as consultants to nation-states. On the perils of this phenomenon, by one of its most distinguished practitioners, see Thomas Carothers, *Critical Mission: Essays on Democracy Promotion* 168 (2004) (criticizing the tendency to reduce the complexities of democratic transition to simplistic nostrums and off-the-rack formulas).

[66] If social science in this area now teaches anything, however, it is that, as Geertz chides, "the more things come together, the more they remain apart: the uniform world is not much closer than the classless society," a society – one might add – then widely extolled by Marxist critics of modernization theory. Clifford Geertz, *Available Light: Anthropological Reflections on Philosophical Topics* 248 (2000).

to increased interethnic conflict, prompting mass atrocity, especially where electoral mobilization precedes stable legal institutions for channeling it.[67] As economist Paul Collier notes, "Half of all civil wars are post-conflict relapses."[68]

It is an article of faith among academicians in international law – apparently requiring no empirical confirmation – that amnesty is unnecessary to establish new democratic institutions, because criminal prosecution of repressive former leadership itself helps establish and legitimize these institutions.[69] The picture emerging from comparative social science suggests something quite different from, if not quite the opposite of, what international legal scholars here assume.[70] Specifically, they confuse what is necessary to later consolidation – the rule of law – with what is necessary for the initial transition – a transfer of power.

The problem is not merely the one long recognized: that trials will anger their immediate targets, whose friends often retain power, which can be used to stop the transition in its tracks. The more serious problem is subtler. It is that the very conditions making prosecution possible also threaten the political transition on which its ultimate success depends. Considerable experience now suggests that trials are more likely to occur when the transition is least regulated by negotiation between departing and emerging

[67] See, e.g., Edward Mansfield & Jack Snyder, *Electing to Fight: Why Emerging Democracies Go to War* 2 (2005); Michael Mann, *The Dark Side of Democracy* 4, 22–5, 426 (2005); Benjamin A. Valentino, *Final Solutions: Mass Killings and Genocide in the Twentieth Century* 237 (2004) (observing that at least three of the twentieth century's largest mass killings, in the Soviet Union, Germany, and Rwanda, "followed close on the heals of failed democratization efforts").

[68] Paul Collier, *The Bottom Billion: Why the Poorest Countries Are Failing and What Can Be Done about It* 34 (2007).

[69] Diane Orentlicher, "Whose Justice? Reconciling Universal Jurisdiction with Democratic Principles," 92 Geo. L.J. 1057, 1119 (2004).

[70] The same must be said of another issue in international criminal law to which social science has consistently spoken in a different key. International lawyers now pride ourselves for finally extricating the offenses of genocide and crimes against humanity from the (long-required) nexus to armed conflict. At the same time, however, social scientists studying these same wrongs increasingly conclude that they are caused by, or are otherwise inextricable from, the waging of modern war. Eric Weitz, "The Modernity of Genocides," in Gellately & Kiernan, *The Spector of Genocide*, op. cit., at 53, 56 ("Genocides . . . almost invariably develop in the context of warfare."); Martin Shaw, *War and Genocide* 5 (2003) (contending that "genocide is best understood as a distinctive form of war," because it "uses the logic of war" and "has occurred mostly in the context of war"); Mann, op. cit., at 32 (observing that "most 20th century cases of ethnic cleansing occurred during wars or during the chaotic transfer from war to peace"); Manus Midlarsky, *The Killing Trap: Genocide in the Twentieth Century* 68 (2006) ("All of the cases of genocide and politicide examined in this book were associated with wars that were lost by the genocidal states . . .").

rulers, when repression has been recently severe, and when the old regime was least successful in its economic policies and military adventures.

Hence, for instance, high levels of recent repression (often against the new leaders themselves) may combine with low levels of national welfare (owing to failed economic policies) to reduce trust between parties to the negotiation. Trust is already problematic enough during transitions, because the instability defining them weakens reliable expectations about others' behavior. This low level of trust diminishes prospects for reaching a "pact" by which power may be effectively and nonviolently transferred.[71] With less chance of harmonious compromise, stakes rise dangerously: if repressive rulers cannot be persuaded to go peacefully, they must be driven from power.

Driving repressive rulers from power occurs rarely, however, because it is difficult and costly. It often requires violence, which breeds resentment that later impedes harmonious consolidation. Perhaps the only thing to be said in favor of this scenario is that, if it plays out, trials become quite possible, even likely. But no one sensitive to the plight of a transitional society would wish on it the circumstances that normally facilitate prosecution of repressive rulers – however otherwise desirable such prosecution, considered in isolation.

Carlos Nino and Jon Elster go so far as to suggest a quasi-mathematical equation here, comprised of factors encouraging and discouraging prosecution during regime transition.[72] They would surely acknowledge, however, that numbers could be attached to the variables, which Nino presents in conceptual terms, only through the prudent exercise of political judgment, utterly exogenous to the equation itself. The ideal scenario, of course, is surely to toss out the dictator through a popular, nonviolent uprising. There have been notable such incidents in recent history, to be sure, from the overthrow of Ferdinand Marcos in 1986 to that of Uzbek President Islam Karimov in 2004. But such scenarios are quite rare.

The prospect of military backlash that prosecutions forebode becomes important on account of these situational factors. "The specter of military intervention is a permanent constraint on the political process," Adam Przeworski rightly observes, "and the eventual reaction by the military is a consideration that permeates everyday political life in such new

[71] Mainwaring, op. cit., at 26; Gretchen Casper & Michelle Taylor, *Negotiating Democracy: Transitions from Authoritarian Rule* 10 (1996).
[72] Carlos Nino, Radical Evil on Trial 127 (1996). Elster, op. cit., at 220–1.

democracies."[73] Military backlash tends to arise exactly where and when transitions are most precarious and vulnerable, not merely to momentary "setback" but to outright failure.

Conversely, the very conditions that make prosecutions unlikely often make much easier the other mechanisms of transitional justice, particularly victim reparations. A repressive state that, through prudent economic policy and property protection, proved successful in wealth creation, for instance, is clearly in a better position later to compensate its victims than one that did not. South Africa's distribution of more than 100 million dollars to victims is again noteworthy here.[74] Rwanda's victims, unlike South Africa's, will see many of their victimizers prosecuted, but would trade places with apartheid's victims in a heartbeat, one suspects. Their degree of support for the new, postgenocide regime is surely affected by such material considerations, in some measure.

In summary, to speak with much confidence about prosecution's unique contribution to democratic transition is, to say the least, lacking in scientific support. Such reliable empirical evidence as exists suggests that truth commissions, not trials, may contribute to reconciliation and democracy consolidation.[75] It would be one thing if confidence in the utility of criminal prosecution issued from careful refutation of the relevant research in comparative politics or showed its apparent lessons to be unduly pessimistic.

Rather, we legal scholars simply ignore them.[76] Their implication is surely that national prosecution, where politically possible at all, should be limited to top chieftains, so that their most active supporters and "core constituencies"[77] (often subject to prosecution as accessories) are not given incentives to continue their support, thereby obstructing transition. Amnesty for such people, threatened by the transition, seeks to reassure them that they are not at risk and so encourages them to switch sides.

[73] Adam Przeworski, "The Games of Transition," in *Issues in Democratic Consolidation* 132 (Scott Mainwaring et al., eds., 1992).

[74] Ginger Thompson, "South Africa to Pay $3,900 to Each Family of Apartheid Victims," N.Y. Times, April 15, 2003, at A7.

[75] Charles Kenney & Dean Spears, "Truth and Consequences: Do Truth Commissions Promote Democratization?" 1 (unpublished manuscript); James L. Gibson, *Overcoming Apartheid: Can Truth Reconcile a Divided Nation?* 150–68 (2005).

[76] Conversely, social scientific studies of democratic transition, especially game-theoretic models, almost universally ignore the potential effect of international forces, especially international law.

[77] This term refers to those beyond regime elites and militant shock troops and to their larger base of support within a political party, ethnic group, or mass movement, always well short of a societal majority, however. Mann, op. cit., at 20, 505–6.

Many repressive regimes must struggle to contain tensions between hardliners and moderates who favor liberalization, even a controlled transition to democracy. If the democratic opposition signals that all those responsible for major rights abuse will later be prosecuted, this will tend to drive the moderates back into alliance with the hardliners from whom they had gingerly sought to dissociate themselves. If there is any clear lesson to be learned from a generation of experience with transitional justice, it may be this. And it should require no specifically economic reasoning to see why this is so.

Conclusion

"Who done it?" is not the first question that comes to mind as one seeks to make sense of mass atrocity. So brazen are the leader-culprits in their apologetics for the harms, so wrenching the human destruction clearly wrought, meticulously documented by many credible sources. Yet in legal terms, mass atrocity remains disconcertingly elusive. The perversity of its perpetrators is polymorphic,[1] impeding criminal courts from tracing the true lines of responsibility in ways intelligible through law's pre-existing categories, designed with simpler stuff in mind.

We specialists in this emerging body of law are often left to speak loosely, like the laymen from whom we seek to distinguish ourselves, of the "big fish" and the "small fry." These comforting colloquialisms, in fact, often seem to serve us – embarrassingly – no worse than the conceptual precision for which we continue poignantly to strive, perhaps pointlessly. Still, for ascribing blame and punishment, such ingenuous generalities – if refreshing in their unpretentiousness – cannot suffice.

Mass atrocity proves insidiously evolutionary, mutating to cover its perpetrators' tracks, subtly evading prior legal developments aimed at staunching it.[2] Top *genocidaires* resemble common criminals less than they do reputable tax lawyers, structuring each new, large corporate transaction in light of the law's latest regulatory refinements in response to the last round of innovative deals. This process is illustrated by the "outsourcing" of war crime from regular armies to irregular militias or civilian contractors and by adopting an opaque lexicon for conveying criminal commands. When

---

[1] Apologies to Freud, who employed this expression in a very different connection. Sigmund Freud, "The Infantile Sexuality," in *Three Contributions to the Theory of Sex* (1916).

[2] For several examples, see Mark Osiel, *Obeying Orders: Atrocity, Military Discipline and the Law of War* 189–91 (1999).

the Chief Prosecutor for the Sierra Leone Tribunal publicly declared that he would not prosecute any "child soldiers"[3] – regarding them more as victims than victimizers – knowledgeable commentators were quick to observe the incentives his pronouncement immediately created for rebel leaders to rely still more heavily on young subordinates of just this sort. As mentioned, top Sudanese government officials even sought expert legal counsel on how to continue their policy of ethnic cleansing so as to minimize prospects of later punishment for genocide, rather than simply involuntary population transfer.[4] No area of law is entirely free of "loopholing," it would seem.

If the intellectual architects of mass atrocity are so often a step ahead of the law in such ways, then prosecutors are doomed to play a game of catch-up. This is a game they can only lose, insofar as criminal courts must apply the lenity rule. That rule, on its face,[5] is widely understood to accord defendants the benefit of any serious doubt concerning the legality of their conduct, at the time of its commission.[6] This norm is considered closely related to, if not quite a corollary of, the still-deeper principle of *nulla poena sine lege*: one may be punished only for a pre-existing crime.[7]

---

[3] David Crane, "The Scourge of Child Soldiers: Lost Generations of Children Around the World Are Victims of Warlords and Tyrants," Toronto Mail, Feb. 28, 2008, at http://www.commondreams.org/archive/2008/02/22/7230. Crane acknowledged that the Court's Statute "mandated" him "to prosecute a child who committed a war crime between ages 15 and 18 . . . " Id.

[4] Author's confidential interviews, The Hague, Dec. 2008.

[5] In practice, however, the lenity rule has experienced "historic underenforcement" within the U.S. federal courts, at least. Dan Kahan, "Lenity and Federal Common Law Crimes," 345 Sup. Ct. L. Rev. 345, 347 (1994). In U.S. federal law, the rule is understood to require courts to adopt the "harsher" of "two rational readings of a criminal statute only when Congress has spoken in clear and definite language." *McNally v. U.S.*, 483 US 350, 359–60 (1987). Kahan convincingly argues that lenity is warranted in certain situations but not others, depending on a variety of circumstances readily discernible from the differing facts of litigated cases. Hence, there should be no general or universal "rule" of lenity (i.e., across the board for all criminal defendants). As an overarching principle, he concludes, "[l]enity is completely unnecessary to assure the fair and predictable administration of criminal justice. At the same time, the allocation of law-making authority that the rule entails . . . [i.e.,] an 'ideal' conception of legislative supremacy . . . would substantially raise the cost of criminal law while reducing its effectiveness." Id. at 397–8.

[6] The Rome Statute for the International Criminal Court provides, in Art. 22(2): "The definition of a crime shall be strictly construed and shall not be extended by analogy. In case of ambiguity, the definition shall be interpreted in favour of the person being investigated, prosecuted or convicted." Even the ICTY, which was not subject to this rule and certainly did not adhere to it, nonetheless continued to insist, albeit unconvincingly, that it would only apply rules that were "beyond doubt customary international law." *Prosecutor v. Tadić*, Case No. IT-94-1, Judgment, ¶ 662 (July 15, 1999); *Prosecutor v. Blaškić*, Case No. IT-95-14-A, Judgment, ¶ 114 (July 3, 2004).

[7] *Prosecutor v. Delalić et al.* (*Čelebići*), Judgment, Case No. IT-96-21-T, Trial Chamber II, 16 November 1998, ¶ 402.

The intermixing of "many hands" in episodes of mass atrocities makes the law's central challenge one of giving coherent shape to the subtle and shifting human relationships in a way that fairly reflects the perpetrators' dependence on one another yet limits individual liability to the extent of personal blameworthiness. To this end, resort to phantasmagoric fictions – too common in the past – must be abjured. The law must devise conceptual tools permitting careful ascriptions of individual culpability that are consistent with an accurate accounting of organizational realities, the very complexities of which impede this task.

Following episodes of mass atrocity, transitional democracies should appease the pressure for prosecution by imposing collective sanction on entities harboring culpable parties. The officer corps, in particular, is a type of collectivity well suited, in its organizational structure and professional culture, to shifting costs initially levied on it as a whole to responsible members, thus avoiding punishment of the innocent. To ensure that this shift happens, professional peers who fail to disclose pertinent evidence about miscreant comrades should bear the cost of their acquiescence in their pocketbooks. Collective sanction of this sort provides both *ex ante* deterrence and *ex post* redress consistently with the culpability principle.

At the international level, superior responsibility is today used too little and enterprise participation too much. To redress this imbalance, the latter's scope must contract while the former's enlarges. If the *ad hoc* international criminal tribunals and the ICC do not curtail enterprise participation, then convictions will be purchased on the cheap, in ways that history will not judge kindly. This view is today widely shared.[8] As a leading ICTY prosecutor lamented (shortly after retirement),

---

[8] William A. Schabas, "Balancing the Rights of the Accused with the Imperatives of Accountability," in *From Sovereign Impunity to International Accountability: The Search for Justice in a World of States* 154, 164–6 (Ramesh Thakur & Peter Malcontent, eds., 2004); Allison Marston Danner & Jenny S. Martinez, "Guilty Associations: Joint Criminal Enterprise, Command Responsibility, and the Development of International Criminal Law," 93 Cal. L. Rev. 75, 143 (2005) ("Over-expansive doctrines, unbridled prosecutorial discretion, and unpersuasive judicial decision-making may still doom international criminal adjudication."); Victor Avigdor Peskin, "Virtual Trials: International War Crimes Tribunals and the Politics of State Cooperation in the Former Yugoslavia and Rwanda" 576 (Spring 2005) (PhD dissertation, Univ. of Calif., Berkeley) ("Generations later, the [ICTY] tribunal may then well be remembered not for its actual success in moving beyond victor's justice, but for imposing a new kind of victor's justice."); Harmen van der Wilt, "Joint Criminal Enterprise: Possibilities and Limitations," 5 J. Int'l Crim. J. 91, 92 (2007) ("The elusiveness of the concept of 'common purpose' [has meant that it] degenerates into a smokescreen that obscures the possible frail connection between the accused and the specific crimes for which they stand trial.").

Although our statutes compel us to focus on individual criminal responsibility, it is all too easy for us to conclude that everyone knew what was
happening, that everyone must have participated in some way, and that
everyone must be guilty. If we adopt that approach in our work, we will
destroy the law we came to save.[9]

Our Chapter 6 responded to his concerns here, in considerable measure.
But he is surely right to raise them. In the same spirit, the new ICC began
almost immediately to display greater caution in its use of the joint criminal
enterprise idea than did the ICTY or ICTR.[10] This study has argued that such
courts should seek alternatives to joint enterprise liability by reinvigorating
the law of superior responsibility, relaxing its effective control requirement.

This may best be done via Roxin's theory of criminal commission through
dominating an organizational apparatus. Roxin's approach might alternatively be employed on a free-standing basis, as the ICC Pre-Trial Chambers have done, as one acceptable interpretation of the meaning of co-
perpetration. It remains to be seen, however, whether this most recent tack
will ultimately prove any more compelling than the prior ones in resolving the problem to which the retired ICTY prosecutor above alludes – or
whether that problem will simply be reproduced in novel but equally vexing
form.

Even with this wide array of current conceptual possibilities, dangers
abound on all sides: If requirements for conviction as an enterprise participant were tightened without at once relaxing conditions for conviction as
a commander, there is a serious danger that monsters like Milošević would
be acquitted. Conversely, if conditions for superior responsibility were loos-
ened up without reining in the law of enterprise participation, the same
facts could be credibly classified under both doctrines, in even more cases
than at present.

The law of superior responsibility lets prosecutors tell the story that most
advances democratic transition in the short run, enabling them to satisfy
elected superiors. Conversely, the law of enterprise participation recounts

---

[9] William Fenrick, "Crimes in Combat: The Relationship between Crimes against Humanity
and War Crimes," Guest Lecture, ICC-Office of the Prosecutor, March 2, 2004.

[10] The ICC's Rome Statute, in Art. 25(3)(a), expressly allows for co-perpetration both "jointly
with another" and "through another person." These options made it possible for the
Pre-Trial Chamber in the *Lubanga* case, for instance, to reject a suggestion by victims'
counsel that the case proceed on the basis of joint criminal enterprise doctrine. *Decision
on Confirmation of Charges, Lubanga*, PTC I, 29 Jan. 2007 (ICC 01/04–01/06), ¶ 325.
Thomas Weigend, "Intent, Mistake of Law, and Co-perpetration in the Lubanga Decision
on Confirmation of Charges," 6 J. Int'l Crim. J. 471, 477–8 (2008).

the narrative that most empowers international law as a long-term response to mass atrocity and the careers of those practicing it. The doctrinal solutions that prosecutors favor on each plane thus reflect diverging micro-incentives, created by the differing environments in which they work.

The challenge for independent legal thinking – that is, for those not laboring under either constraint – is to find a way to satisfy the legitimate professional concerns of both groups while ensuring "big fish" convictions consistent with personal culpability. The legal reinterpretation defended here, drawing on European jurisprudence, would bring litigation strategies of international prosecutors into closer harmony with those of national counterparts. It would thereby help international criminal law overcome some of the deep inconsistency this new endeavor already displays and further forebodes. That said, there is good reason not to impose a premature uniformity upon the approaches of national and international prosecutors in confronting the puzzle of shared responsibility for mass atrocity. This will remain the case as long as postconflict societies and the international community so consistently accord differential weight to law's competing goals of retribution and reconciliation.

This book's several sections hang together around a single argument that large portions of international criminal law may be better understood, and its purposes better advanced, by aligning incentives among pertinent parties.[11] The preceding analysis also reveals that, despite their frequent denunciation, the intellectual foundations of criminal law – in the moral theory and social ontology of liberalism – do not disable it from confronting colossal conflagrations. The problem is nothing so "deep."

And liberalism itself, we have seen, it too protean a set of doctrines to foreclose its flexible adaptation to these novel challenges. It is fully capable of acknowledging the collective nature of mass atrocities and deploying collective sanctions efficiently against them. If the law has thus far failed to develop a satisfactory account of and response to these bewildering events, the reason lies more simply in our failures of professional imagination, which this study modestly begins to redress.

Response to mass atrocity at the national and international levels can be greatly improved by reassessing the law on modes of commission to better align incentives among pertinent parties – prosecutors, perpetrators, and professional military peers. This proposal differs from prevailing approaches in harnessing the parties' private interests to public ends, rather

---

[11] On the nature of and rationale for such "top-down" approaches, see Richard A. Posner, *Overcoming Law* 172–5 (1995).

than seeking to inculcate such disinterested ideals as humanitarian concern and professional ethics (of military officers and government lawyers). To contend that these diverse interests could be completely reconciled in some happy equilibrium would be preposterous. But it is not too much to suggest a few discrete devices for achieving some limited harmonization.

The law naturally seeks a classificatory grid reaching the contributions of all parties to major wrong. The doctrine of enterprise participation best achieves this result because its tentacles reach farthest. They do so by accentuating how association in crime often displays the horizontal features of a network, rather than the vertical ones of a bureaucracy. International prosecutors, with a strong stake in their field's robust growth, favor this approach. Its very amplitude, however, encourages punishing more people for more wrongdoing than courts in transitional democracies could realistically prosecute without risking serious turmoil.

The enterprise approach also distinguishes punishable from other culpable parties with a notion of participation that is vague and potentially illiberal. The precise extent of a defendant's personal blameworthiness slips from focus as he or she is airbrushed into the foreground of a larger, insidious enterprise. The enterprise "depicted by the Prosecution in its indictments," writes one close ICTY observer, "is often no more than a general description of a set of factual events that forms the background to the charges (such as a campaign of ethnic cleansing) which may not itself be a crime within the Tribunals' Statutes."[12] At such moments, law becomes a very blunt instrument, and its resulting justice arrives only in very round numbers. Big fish and small fry swim the same sea and are caught in the same net, although their primary purposes are very different.

The law of superior responsibility offers the principal alternative for describing relationships among parties to mass atrocity. It accentuates the hierarchical dimension to association in crime, sharply distinguishing top leadership from the lowest echelons. This approach helps new democratic rulers draw the inevitable line between those who will and those who will not be punished by criminal sanction.[13] It can justify limiting prosecution to bigger fish, encouraging noncriminal sanctions for small fry, with which several transitional societies have experimented.

---

[12] Guénaël Mettraux, *International Crimes and the ad hoc Tribunals* 292 (2005).

[13] For this very reason, because it helps justify nonprosecution of many serious offenders below the ranks of top rulers, the doctrine is often disfavored by victims and human rights advocates. Marcelo A. Sancinetti & Marcelo Ferrante, *El Derecho Penal en la Protección de los Derechos Humanos* 314–15 (1999).

This approach is morally credible, for it taps into the public's intuition that those who effectively control the course of major events are more blameworthy than followers, however wrongful the latter's acts from the law's perspective. But in focusing on the dyadic relation of superior to subordinate, the law of superior responsibility irons out the complexities of control within a multilayered organization, with its tiers of intermediaries. In any event, the facts of most mass atrocities simply do not fit the model of an ideal-typical Weberian bureaucracy, in which subordinates act simply as humble and obedient servants of their superiors. This is true even of many atrocities by official armed forces, within which informal, lateral influences often count for as much as more formal, hierarchical commands. Social networks based on kinship and clan are central to how many militias and insurgent groups mobilize and organize personnel to perpetrate mass atrocity.

The law of perpetration by means of an hierarchical organization offers further, promising leads that the ICC is certain to explore in several cases. Still, as this book goes to press, there remains need for fresh thinking about how to combine the several modes of liability examined here, on the facts of particular cases, to capture more accurately their moral nuances.[14] This is a central challenge with which the field of international criminal law will continue to grapple for some time.

[14] Mark Osiel, "Combining Modes of Liability for Mass Atrocity," lecture, International Criminal Court, April 22, 2009, and forthcoming manuscript.

Index

abdication by dictators, 220–222
abduction, of children, 52, 102, 103
Abu Ghraib, 18
accessories, accessorial liability (see also aiding
    and abetting, instigation), 51, 58–59, 71, 81,
    84–90, 102, 106, 110, 239
Afghanistan, 72
Africa, 111, 176, 219, 220, 233
aggression, crime of, 60, 64, 139, 191
aiding and abetting, 59, 62, 81–82, 89, 96, 106
Akayesu, Jean-Paul, 161
Albania, 155
Alfonsín, Pres. Raul, 153
Alien Tort Claims Act, 35, 37
Al Qaeda (see also bin Laden, Osama), 72, 208
altruism, 13, 198
Ambos, Kai, 142
amnesties, xiv, 11, 218–240
    distortion in legal scholarship on, 223,
        236–239
    revocation of, xiv, 222, 230–232
anarchy, 111
Angola, 223
anomie, 69
Anraat, Frans van, 83
arbitrariness of defendant selection (see also
    prosecutors, discretion of), 20, 156
Arbour, Louise, 164
Arendt, Hannah, 20, 95, 98, 115, 122
Argentina, xiii, 16, 42, 43, 52, 86–88, 92, 93, 102,
    103, 105, 114, 152, 164, 174, 209–211, 225,
    228–231
    military prosecutions in, xiii, 42, 86, 93, 105,
        114, 164, 174, 230, 232
Aristide, Jean Bertrand, 233
Aristotle, 130

Arkan (Željko Raznatović), 55
ascription/attribution of harm to accused (see
    also mass atrocity, modes of
    commission), 1, 7, 8, 16, 25, 45, 86, 91, 110,
    126, 127–130, 153, 190, 202, 241, 243,
    248
Auschwitz, 103, 111, 198
Austria, 79
authoritarian regimes, 43, 64, 100, 147, 153, 157,
    179, 194
authority (see also control; superior
    responsibility; superior-subordinate
    relations)
    charismatic, 36
    competing/overlapping, 23, 40, 45, 64–65
    de jure/de facto (formal vs. informal), 2, 36,
        37, 40, 45, 77, 99, 104, 111
    multiple lines of, 40
automatism, 69–70, 105

Baath Party, 82, 154
Bagasora, Col. Théoneste, 161
banality, 5, 86, 95, 122, 209
"bandwagon" effect, 65
Bashir, Omar Al, 94, 111–112
Belgrade, 16, 39, 55, 67, 83, 88, 193
Bemba Gombo, Jean-Pierre, 94
Berlin Wall, 93
"big fish-small fry," 2, 8–9, 14, 17, 22, 49, 54, 67,
    68, 81, 86, 91, 119, 161–162, 165, 171, 173, 241,
    245, 246, 248
binary oppositions, 38, 58, 148
bin Laden, Osama, 43, 116
Blackwater, Inc., 203
Blagojević, Vidoje, 83
blameworthiness, see culpability

249

Pakistan, 28, 227

Palsgraf v. Long Island Railway, 128

Panama, 219

paramilitaries (see also militias), 40, 54, 68, 71, 73, 99, 193, 212, 222, 247

passions (vs. interests), 10, 13, 231

perpetrators,

differing goals of joint, 53, 57

groups as, 5–6

ingenuity of, 27–28, 135–141

mental states of, 5, 27, 34, 67–68, 75, 83, 108, 113, 114, 122, 127, 128, 137, 140, 181, 196, 215

motives of, xi, xvii, 27, 34, 53, 66–68, 83–85, 86, 108, 132, 139, 153, 181, 209, 211, 214, 215

moral character of, 130–143

persecution, as crime against humanity, 5, 83, 139, 143, 167, 178, 227

Peru, 88, 93

pillage, 38, 85, 103, 211

Pinkerton, U.S. v., 52

Pinochet, Gen. Augusto, 2, 48, 139–140, 162, 171, 193, 228

Poland, 222, 230

policy, public, 11, 81, 117, 128, 130, 148, 154, 166, 170, 176

political cycles, 150–151

Posner, Eric, 82

power (see also control), xiii, 1, 2, 10, 14, 23–28, 36–37, 39, 41, 42, 46, 54, 68, 69, 77, 78, 87, 91–92, 95, 96, 97, 99, 100, 101, 102, 106, 109, 111, 112, 115, 119, 134, 149, 152–153, 156, 165, 167, 169, 176, 180, 188, 194, 203–206, 218–224, 232, 237, 238

pragmatism, 11, 160, 180, 192

Prijedor, 62

primus inter pares, 43

professionalization, of int'l crim. law, ix, xvii, 4, 91, 162, 164, 165, 170–171, 182–184, 205

proof, burdens of, 17, 37, 106–107

Prosecutors, prosecution

discretion of, viii, 78, 152–155, 211, 158, 159, 167

incentives of, 5, 24, 78, 156, 161–162, 164, 167, 171–175, 245

motivations of, xvii, 10, 156–158, 161–162, 164, 167, 184

national vs. int'l, 4, 9–10, 15, 20, 49, 88, 91, 107, 150, 156–157, 160, 166, 169–184, 245–246

political constraints on, ix, xiii, 4, 6, 10, 156, 159

resource scarcity, 6, 91, 159, 163

self-restraint/overreach by, 30, 71, 73, 90, 153

strategies of, 21, 49, 86, 101, 111, 112, 148–166, 173, 211, 244

Prussia, 100

Przeworski, Adam, 238

punishment, 8–9, 57–59, 78, 79, 110, 117, 133, 135, 141, 143, 157, 169, 187, 189, 195, 205, 213, 217, 227, 229, 241–243, 246

sentencing, 21, 57, 59, 60, 78, 79

punitive damages, 37

quasi-firms, 45

racketeering statutes, 58, 61, 84, 89, 135, 181, 192

rape, 35, 42, 65, 103, 161–162, 165, 167

Rapp, Stephen, 51

Rawls, John, 79–80

Raz, Joseph, 130

rebel movements, (see also armed groups), vii–viii, 99, 111–113, 159, 242

reciprocity, 155, 160, 205, 217

recklessness, 75, 113, 133

reconciliation, xi, 4, 11, 92, 152–157, 156–157, 165–166, 170, 179–180, 221–225, 239, 245

reductionism, 1, 188

reparations, xiv, 191, 200, 219, 239

retribution, 11, 13, 25, 147, 150, 157, 167, 170, 173, 179–180, 193, 195, 229, 231, 245

revolution, social, xv, 43, 69, 139–140, 214, 226–227

risk, appetite for/aversion toward, risk assessment, 43–44, 79–80, 100, 105, 107, 113, 128, 138, 172–173, 196, 198–199, 205, 215, 216, 220–221, 223, 231–232, 239

Robinson, Daryl, 118, 119, 137

Roth, Brad, 138

Roxin, Claus; legal theory of, 93–117, 244

Russia, 129, 149, 151, 228

Rutledge, Justice Wiley, 38

Rwanda, xii, 7, 56, 67, 69, 70, 88, 92, 98, 99, 100, 152, 154, 158, 159, 170, 214, 239

sadism, 68

Salvador, El, 35, 38, 160, 223

Sankoh, Foday, 224

scapegoating, 152

scholarship, legal, xvi, 12, 24–25, 34

Scilingo, Adolfo, 211

Made in the USA
Monee, IL
30 May 2022

97267098R00154